PREPARING FOR THE OGT
IN SOCIAL STUDIES

J. MARK STEWART

Director of Curriculum,
Dublin City Schools
Dublin, Ohio

JAMES A. NORRIS

Former Department Chair, Social Studies,
Linden McKinley High School
Columbus, Ohio

AMSCO SCHOOL PUBLICATIONS, INC.
315 Hudson Street, New York, N.Y. 10013

Dr. J. Mark Stewart is the Director of Curriculum, Dublin City Schools, Dublin, Ohio. He has been the Social Studies Supervisor, Columbus Public Schools, Columbus, Ohio. He received a doctorate from Ohio State University and taught social studies for many years.

James A. Norris is the former Department Chair, Social Studies, Linden McKinley High School, Columbus, Ohio. A graduate of Ohio State University, he taught for many years in the Ohio public schools.

Pages 252, 358: Excerpts from *Plunkitt of Tammany Hall* by William L. Riordon, copyright 1948 by Alfred A. Knopf, Inc., a division of Random House, Inc.

Page 370: "Studies Tie Urban Sprawl to Health Risk, Road Danger," by Kathleen Fackelman, from *USA Today*, a division of Gannett Co., Inc. Reprinted with Permission.

Posttest page 1: Cartoon by Mike Lukovich in the *Atlantic Journal-Constitution* reprinted by permission of Creators Syndicate.

Contributing researcher-writers
Lillian Forman
Mandy Rosenberg, Practical Strategies, Inc.

Reviewers

Patricia Clayton, Social Studies,
 Foreign Language Coordinator
Summit County Educational
 Service Center
Cuyahoga Falls, Ohio

Russell Maruna, Supervisor of
 Academic Services
Lorain County Educational
 Service Center
Elyria, Ohio

Cover and Text Design: Merrill Haber

New Maps, Charts, and Graphs: Hadel Studio

Photo Research: Tobi Zausner

Composition: Sierra Graphics, Inc.

Please visit our Web site at: **www.amscopub.com**

When ordering this book, please specify: *either* **R 016 W** *or*
PREPARING FOR THE OGT IN SOCIAL STUDIES

ISBN 978-1-56765-630-5

TO THE STUDENT

This book provides a concise review of high school social studies benchmarks and grade-level indicators to help you prepare for the Ohio Graduation Test (OGT) in Social Studies. The book contains two tests and 33 chapters. The chapters cover topics derived from the benchmarks and grade-level indicators for each of the seven social studies standards:

- History
- People in Societies
- Geography
- Economics
- Government
- Citizenship Rights and Responsibilities
- Social Studies Skills and Methods.

Each chapter addresses a benchmark, except Chapters 16 and 33, which combine the two benchmarks in the Social Studies Skills and Methods standard.

The tests in *Preparing for the OGT in Social Studies* are modeled after the OGT Practice Test for Social Studies. One is to be used as a pretest, or diagnostic test; the other is to be used as a posttest. They will help you determine areas in which you have good understanding of the content and thinking required by particular benchmarks and areas in which you need to improve and review more thoroughly.

The text presents major ideas, important content, and thinking skills related to each benchmark. Illustrations that go with the text are intended to help explain the topics or concepts. Each chapter is divided into sections, some of which are followed by questions to help you check your understanding. Activities at the end of each chapter will help you diagnose your understanding of the content as well as the thinking required by the OGT. It is important to remember that OGT questions in social studies do not test just recall of information. Rather, they require deep understanding of concepts embedded in the benchmarks. Even the multiple-choice questions ask you to be able to think about and apply content knowledge to concepts and understandings contained in benchmarks. The OGT, in other words, calls for much more than rote memorization of facts.

In addition to content knowledge found in the grade-level indicators, it is important to pay attention to the benchmarks. Questions will test the benchmarks, and grade-level indicators tell you the content or subject matter that will be used to write questions about the benchmarks. In other words, both benchmarks and grade-level indicators are important, but the questions will be about the benchmarks. For example, benchmark B in the History Standard asks you to explain the effects of industrialization. Therefore, questions on the test will be only about the effects of industrialization, not about the causes.

Both causes and effects are important, but test questions will address only effects. The grade-level indicators then provide the content or subject matter that will be used to write questions about the effects of industrialization.

Another important factor in preparing for the OGT is to pay attention to the performance verbs in each benchmark. That is, the first word of each benchmark provides a hint about the level of thinking required. In social studies, "analyze" is used in eleven of the benchmarks, "explain" is used in four, and "use, connect, identify, compare, and evaluate" are the verbs in each of the remaining five. It is important that you recognize the difference in the level of thinking these verbs call for. Identifying, for example, calls for something less than explaining or analyzing.

Performance Verbs—What They Mean

Analyze To think about the different parts of a problem or situation to figure out the traits of the whole (e.g., looking at several two-dimensional perspectives to decide a type of three-dimensional object).

Compare To look at traits or qualities to find out what is alike and what is different. "Compare" is usually stated as "compare with": you are to highlight similarities, but differences may be mentioned.

Evaluate To determine the value of something for a given purpose based on certain standards or criteria (e.g., explaining the pros, cons, and/or results of a decision).

Explain To make clear or give reason for something (e.g., explaining factors that cause a certain kind of reaction).

Use To apply, employ, utilize, or make use of something, such as data (e.g., use data to support a thesis).

Connect To join, unite, tie together, combine, link, or associate. Similar to compare (e.g., connect one thing to another).

Identify To recognize, distinguish, know, point out, select (e.g., identify characteristics or patterns of something).

A book cannot replace good classroom preparation for the OGT. Your teachers and courses in grades nine and ten are your best preparation for the OGT. However, we believe that this book will provide valuable assistance and support as you prepare for this important test.

GOOD LUCK!

Dr. J. Mark Stewart
James A. Norris

CONTENTS

Pretest

Part I
MODERN WORLD HISTORY SINCE 1750

Chapter 1 The Enlightenment *3*

Chapter 2 Industrialization *17*

Chapter 3 Imperialism *30*

Chapter 4 World War I and the Onset of World War II *43*

Chapter 5 World War II, the Cold War, and Contemporary Conflicts *62*

Chapter 6 Cultural Perspectives *86*

Chapter 7 Oppression, Discrimination, and Conflict *104*

Chapter 8 Cultural Exchanges *121*

Chapter 9 Regions Over Time *137*

Chapter 10 Geographic Change and Human Activity *147*

Chapter 11 Patterns and Processes of Movement *158*

Chapter 12 Economic Systems *170*

Chapter 13 The U.S. Government and the Economy *180*

Chapter 14 Forms of Government *189*

Chapter 15 Governmental Change *205*

Chapter 16 Using Data and Evidence *217*

Part II
UNITED STATES HISTORY SINCE 1877

Chapter 17 Industrialization *229*

Chapter 18 Imperialism *254*

Chapter 19 World War I and the Onset of World War II *269*

Chapter 20 World War II, the Cold War, and Contemporary Conflicts *288*

Chapter 21 Twentieth-Century Domestic Affairs *303*

Chapter 22 Cultural Perspectives *337*

Chapter 23 Oppression, Discrimination, and Conflict *350*

Chapter 24 Cultural Exchanges *356*

Chapter 25 Regions Over Time *364*

Chapter 26 Geographic Change and Human Activity *372*

Chapter 27 Patterns and Processes of Movement *383*

Chapter 28 Economic Systems *394*

Chapter 29 The U.S. Government and the Economy *405*

Chapter 30 The Evolution of the Constitution *417*

Chapter 31 Governmental Change *428*

Chapter 32 Individual Rights *441*

Chapter 33 Using Data and Evidence *456*

Index *469*

Credits *485*

Posttest

1. Which of the following actions or statements most clearly demonstrates the influence of Enlightenment thought and ideas?

   A. Thomas Jefferson's ideas as expressed in the Declaration of Independence
   B. King Louis XIV's statement, "I am the state."
   C. King George III's policies toward the British colonies in North America
   D. Thomas Hobbes's arguments for the need of a government headed by a monarch with absolute power

2. If voters are trying to decide between two candidates based upon their campaign literature, voters should look for the

   A. literature with the most appealing graphic design
   B. degree to which each candidate uses facts to support his or her position
   C. number of celebrity endorsements each candidate lists
   D. amount of money each candidate has to spend on the campaign.

3. Analyze two conditions that gave rise to the growth of labor organizations in the United States in the late 1800s and early 1900s and two responses from business and/or government to the growth of labor organizations. Write your answer in the **Answer Document**.   (4 points)

4. John Locke was an Enlightenment thinker. He believed that government should act to protect people's rights, but only with the consent of the people who were governed. The people, Locke wrote, can remove the government from power. People who agreed with Locke would have

   A. supported the concept of divine right of kings
   B. believed in absolutism and the authority of established religion
   C. supported the ideas in the Declaration of Independence
   D. opposed the ideas in the Declaration of Independence.

5. How did the decision of the United States not to join the League of Nations after World War I contribute to the onset of World War II?

   A. Without the participation of the world's most powerful nation, the League was ineffective in stopping conflicts that contributed to the outbreak of World War II.
   B. Without U.S. participation, the League did not have enough troops to settle international disputes that contributed to the outbreak of World War II.
   C. The refusal of the United States to join the League prompted President Wilson to campaign against the League, making it ineffective in settling international disputes that led to the outbreak of World War II.
   D. Its refusal to join the League demonstrated that the United States favored the establishment of a German state with a strong military.

6. Because of advances in communication technology, such as the Internet,

   A. the environment is cleaner
   B. political systems are more democratic

C. opportunities to exchange information have increased
D. international cooperation is less important.

7. In the 1920s, the United States had several economic problems that eventually led to the Great Depression. One of these was

A. too few consumers were buying on credit
B. farm income was down due to overproduction
C. unemployment had decreased in most industries
D. stock prices were generally undervalued.

8. In South Africa, white Afrikaners controlled the government and the economy, while black South Africans, who comprised the vast majority of the people, had virtually no rights or power. Their different cultural perspectives eventually resulted in

A. two separate nations being formed in South Africa
B. most Afrikaners moving out of South Africa
C. most black South Africans moving to other nations
D. South Africa ending the practice of apartheid.

9. The Holocaust perpetrated by Nazi Germany during World War II was intended to

A. integrate immigrants into German society
B. segregate Jewish people in a separate, independent state
C. eliminate, through genocide, the Jewish people
D. encourage German Jews to immigrate to Israel.

10. Many Americans like to drink coffee. Coffee plants do not grow in the United States, but they do grow in Colombia. What trade policy might the United

States adopt toward Colombia to ensure a supply of coffee?

A. increase the tariff on coffee from Colombia
B. increase export taxes on U.S. products sold to Colombia
C. eliminate the tariff on coffee from Colombia
D. levy high tariffs on other products from Colombia

11. During World War I, the Armenians pledged their support to the enemies of the Turks. They did so because

A. Turkish troops killed thousands of Armenians in the years before the war
B. the Turks wanted the Armenians to set up an independent nation
C. the Turks had sided with the Russians
D. the Turks had sided with the British and Americans.

12. Opportunities for citizen participation would likely be greatest in a(n)

A. theocracy
B. dictatorship
C. absolute monarchy
D. constitutional monarchy.

13. One result of immigration in the late 1800s and early 1900s was that the United States

A. became a predominantly rural society
B. privatized the educational system
C. became a predominately urban society
D. encouraged the growth of labor unions.

14. During the 20th century, there were a number of social movements and social protests that attempted to produce change. Identify and explain two such movements or protests. Write your answer in the **Answer Document**. (2 points)

15. Since the 1950s in the United States, suburban areas have increased while

A. farmlands have also increased
B. wilderness areas have decreased
C. population has shifted from the South and West to the North and East
D. technology has increased the differences between suburban and urban areas in the United States.

16. According to the table below, what do the countries with the lowest life expectancy all have in common?

A. They are among the most highly developed nations.
B. They are former members of the Soviet Union.
C. They are in located Africa.
D. Their per capita Gross Domestic Product is among the highest.

17. Which of the following was a fundamental cause of the Cold War between the Soviet Union and the United States after World War II?

A. Both nations became members of the United Nations following World War II.
B. The Soviet Union refused to accept U.S. aid under the Marshall Plan.
C. The Soviet Union established the Warsaw Pact in response to North Atlantic Treaty Organization.
D. The two nations had conflicting political and economic ideologies.

Average Life Expectancy, for Men and Women, in Selected Countries

Country	Years	Country	Years	Country	Years
Japan	81.0	Korea, South	75.6	Iran	69.7
Sweden	80.3	Mexico	74.9	Russia	66.4
France	79.4	Poland	74.2	Guatemala	65.2
Germany	78.5	Venezuela	74.1	India	64.0
United Kingdom	78.3	Hungary	72.2	Nigeria	50.5
United States	77.4	China	72.0	South Africa	44.2
Ecuador	76.0	Brazil	71.4	Zimbabwe	37.8
Czech Republic	75.8	Egypt	70.7	Angola	36.8

According to data from the National Highway Traffic Safety Administration, from 2002 to 2003, the number of people killed in accidents involving young drivers fell from 9,251 to 8,666, a 6.3 percent drop.

The executive director of the Governors Highway Safety Association said the decline in the number of young drivers killed in 2003 might be attributable to the growing attention paid to real-world skills in driver-education classes.

More people also wore seat belts last year, and that might have saved many young drivers. The government said that 72 percent of people ages 16 to 24 buckled up in 2003, compared with 65 percent in 2002.

The data also show a steady decline in alcohol as a factor in crashes involving young people.

18. Which thesis is supported by the above data?

A. Driver training is a waste of time and money.
B. Driver training has been successful in helping to reduce traffic fatalities.
C. Young people were responsible for most traffic fatalities in 2002 and 2003.
D. Seat belts are ineffective in preventing fatal auto accidents.

Based on the information in the map, answer the question that follows.

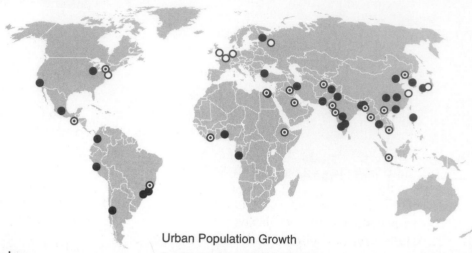

World Regions With Increasing High-Density Urban Populations, 1950–2015 (estimated)

Urban Population Growth

○ 5 million and over since 1950
● 5 million and over since 2000
◉ 5 million and over in 2015 (projected)

19. Businesses that manufacture buses for urban mass-transit systems would most likely target what area of the world in their ten-year marketing plans?

    A. North America
    B. Africa
    C. Europe
    D. East Asia

20. Compare the use of civil disobedience in the women's suffrage movement in the late 1800s with that used in the civil rights movement of the 1960s. Give an example from each movement. Write your answer in the **Answer Document**. (2 points)

21. During both World War I and World War II, many African Americans moved from the rural South to northern cities in order to

    A. enlist in the armed forces
    B. attend colleges and universities
    C. find work in wartime industries
    D. take advantage of lower housing costs.

22. In 1966, the founders of the National Organization for Women shared a cultural perspective that

    A. women should become more efficient at housework
    B. women should be paid the same salaries as men for the same work
    C. too many women were becoming involved in politics
    D. women should stop getting married and having babies.

23. What factor contributed to the migration of large numbers of people from Asia and Latin America to the United States in the late 20th century?

    A. Economic prosperity in Asia and Latin America enabled people to purchase farmland in the United States.
    B. The prospect of jobs and the opportunity to live in a democracy attracted people from Asia and Latin America to the United States.
    C. Lower real estate prices in the United States attracted retirees from Asia and Latin America.

D. Most Asians and Latin Americans came to the United States to attend college and stayed on after graduating.

24. Which of the following represents a global impact of imperialism in the late 19th and early 20th centuries?

   A. a decrease of global conflicts among imperialistic nations
   B. the modernization of technologically undeveloped countries, such as Japan
   C. a worldwide conservation movement to protect natural resources
   D. the growth of religious tolerance in imperialistic nations

25. Some level of government control exists in all economies, but the economy in which the central government plays the most direct role is the

   A. mixed
   B. command
   C. traditional
   D. market.

26. Residents living on a street that connects two busy highways want the city to install speed bumps to slow traffic and protect the safety of children who live there. Which statement could help support the position that speed bumps are needed on the street?

   A. The city will have to use tax money to install the speed bumps.
   B. Speed bumps are hard on automobile suspension systems.
   C. Three children were injured by speeders on the street in the past year.
   D. There are already speed bumps on several other streets in the city.

27. The Federal Reserve's three monetary policy tools are open-market operations, the discount rate, and reserve requirements. The most frequently used tool of monetary policy is open-market operations, which involves buying and selling U.S. government securities. If the Federal Reserve wanted to increase consumer spending, it would likely

   A. buy Treasury securities to add money to the economy
   B. sell Treasury securities to take money out of the economy
   C. raise the reserve requirement
   D. raise the discount rate.

28. A nation in which religious leaders make laws, serve as judges, and conduct foreign policy is a

   A. constitutional monarchy
   B. presidential democracy
   C. theocracy
   D. parliamentary democracy.

29. In 1918, Eugene V. Debs was arrested in Canton, Ohio, for giving a speech against the World War I military draft. He was convicted and sentenced to ten years in prison. The Supreme Court upheld Debs's conviction. This decision shows that individual rights have at times been limited in the United States in order to

   A. punish individuals who commit slander
   B. protect the right of free speech
   C. insure equal opportunity for all
   D. protect national security in times of threat.

30. The U.S. Constitution is a living document that evolves through Supreme Court decisions. Describe the decisions in *Plessy* v. *Ferguson* and *Brown* v. *Board of Education of Topeka*, and explain how they influenced the Constitution's evolution. Write your answer in the **Answer Document**. (4 points)

31. In *Regents of the University of California* v. *Bakke*, the Supreme Court struck down the university's racial quota

system for admissions, but it also ruled that race could be used as a factor in considering applicants. The Supreme Court said that race could be used as a factor in admissions because

A. the university would be guilty of libel if it did not use race as a factor in admissions decisions

B. there was a compelling government interest to have diverse student bodies at public universities

C. there was a clear and present danger if race was not used in admissions decisions

D. there was a threat to national security if race was not used in admissions decisions.

A United States World War II propaganda poster

32. The poster above may be described as a(n)

A. objective assessment of the threat to the United States during World War II

B. biased assessment of the enemy during World War II

C. biased argument in favor of isolationism during World War II

D. objective assessment of the United States' need to remain neutral.

33. The Democratic candidate and the Republican candidate for president engaged in public debates on three separate occasions during a recent presidential campaign. What would be the most credible and reliable source to use in order to determine each candidate's position on a particular issue?

A. a collection of newspaper reports on each debate

B. verbatim transcripts of each debate

C. summaries of the debates by each candidate's campaign staff

D. editorials about the debate collected from several newspapers

34. Which would be the most credible primary source about the effects of McCarthyism on individuals whom he investigated and accused of being Communists?

A. novel about the life of a McCarthy victim

B. autobiography of a McCarthy victim

C. movie about the life of a McCarthy victim

D. biography of Joseph McCarthy

35. A city is considering enacting an ordinance that would outlaw cell phone use while driving. At a public hearing on the issue, supporters and opponents of the law make the following statements:

Supporters: A study by the National Highway Traffic Safety Administration reported that cellular phone use while driving increased the risk of a crash by distracting the driver's attention from the road. Another report from the National Safety Council stated that drivers engaged in cell phone conversations take a longer time to react to traffic signals than drivers not engaged in cell phone conversations.

Opponents: The law is a bad idea because no one has been killed in a crash caused by talking on a cell phone inside the city limits. Other things also distract drivers, such as drinking coffee or tuning the radio. The city has no right passing laws that restrict people from using their cell phones.

● Which of these two statements cites reputable sources of information that support the speaker's position?

● Why does citing reputable sources of information strengthen an argument?

Write your answers in the **Answer Document.** (2 points)

36. Give two examples of Jim Crow laws and explain how they discriminated against African Americans. Write your answer in the **Answer Document.** (2 points)

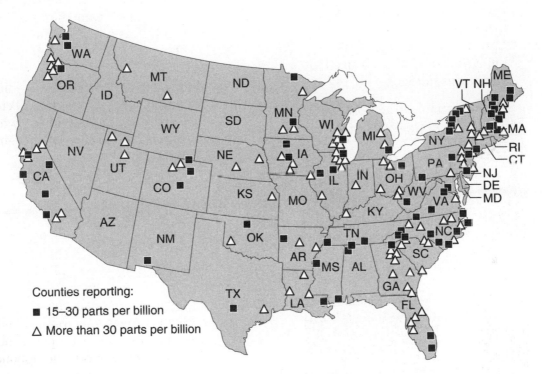

U.S. Counties With High Lead Levels in Drinking Water in 2004 (*Source*: Environmental Protection Agency data)

37. The information in the map above supports the thesis that

    A. lead levels are dangerously high in many areas of the nation
    B. lead levels are at an all-time low
    C. high lead levels are confined to one small area of the nation
    D. efforts to control lead levels are futile and a waste of money.

38. Industrialization in the 19th century had a profound and lasting effect on the United States. Which of the following resulted from the process of industrialization in 19th-century America?

    A. decreased agricultural production
    B. an overall lower standard of living
    C. growth of organized labor
    D. downsizing of most large corporations

PART I

Modern World History Since 1750

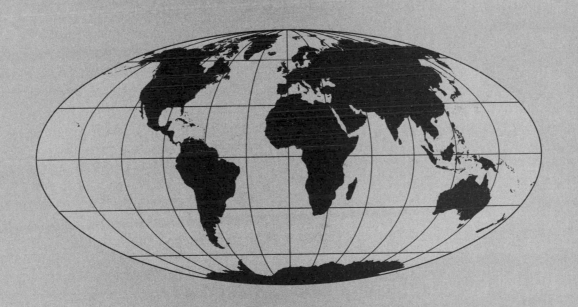

CHAPTER 1

THE ENLIGHTENMENT

BENCHMARK:

Explain connections between the ideas of the Enlightenment and changes in the relationships between citizens and their governments.

This benchmark requires you to understand the effects of Enlightenment ideas on society and government. In the late 17th and early 18th centuries, a group of European intellectuals began to question traditional concepts about both the natural world and human institutions, such as government. You need to know in some detail how the new ideas formed by these thinkers were "connected" changes in the way people thought about their place in society and their relationship to government.

This chapter explains these changes in attitude and behavior by describing the effects of the Enlightenment on governments, economics, and religious and cultural institutions. It focuses on how Enlightenment ideas challenged religious authority and the monarchy. It then shows how this challenge developed into such conflicts as the American Revolution, the French Revolution, and Latin American wars for independence.

★ ENLIGHTENMENT AS THE RESULT OF THE SCIENTIFIC METHOD ★

The Enlightenment grew out of the *scientific revolution*, an intellectual movement that emphasized studying the natural world and the heavens rather than blindly accepting old ideas about these subjects.

Scientific Method

In the 1600s, most Europeans still believed the theory of the universe as described by Ptolemy (who lived in the second century A.D.). He stated that the earth was the center of the universe. In the 1500s and 1600s, scientists began to question this commonly held belief. The first to do so was Nicolas Copernicus, who developed a theory that the sun was the center of the universe and the earth and other heavenly bodies revolved around it. In 1609, Galileo Galilei built the first telescope. Through it, he saw that the planets did indeed revolve around the sun. However, this discovery contradicted the teachings of the Roman Catholic Church, a major power in Western Europe. In 1633,

The Copernican heliocentric (sun-centered) universe, in a 1643 publication

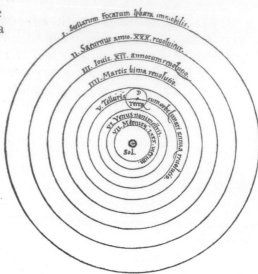

during the Inquisition (a court held by the Church to try people who did not accept its doctrines), Galileo was forced to state publicly that the earth was the center of the universe.

Development of the Scientific Method. Opposition by the church did not totally suppress Galileo's theory, however. Nor did it stop other kinds of scientific research. In the early 1600s, Francis Bacon and René Descartes began to devise new methods of explaining the natural world.

The result was the development of the *scientific method*—the study of the natural world by means of direct observation and experimentation. This method enabled the English scientist Isaac Newton to develop a theory of gravity. The principles of the scientific method were soon applied to the study of human behavior. People began to use reason rather than faith to answer questions about human nature and society. This way of thinking was so strong an influence on all kinds of intellectual activity in the 1700s that the period became known as the *Age of Reason*.

★ POLITICAL THINKERS ★

The use of reason that had characterized the scientific revolution greatly influenced political thinkers. Intellectuals, especially in England and France, began to question traditional beliefs about government and laws and to promote new theories of government based on the natural rights of human beings. Their "enlightened" ideas called into question not only the authority of the Roman Catholic Church, but the authority of monarchs as well.

English Thinkers

Thomas Hobbes and John Locke were two important English political thinkers of the 1600s.

Thomas Hobbes. In his major work, *Leviathan*, Thomas Hobbes argued that people were basically selfish. Because of their selfish nature, they needed a strong government to maintain law and order. Hobbes wrote that to achieve a strong government, people had to agree to sacrifice the right to do whatever they wished in exchange for peace and security. He called this agreement between people and their government the *social contract*. Hobbes believed the best form of government was one ruled by an *absolute monarch*. An absolute monarch is a king or queen who rules with complete and unquestioned authority.

John Locke. John Locke also wrote about the social contract. He believed that an absolute monarchy was not necessary to maintain law and order. Unlike Hobbes, he felt that people were basically good and capable of governing themselves. In his *Second Treatise of Government*, Locke stated that people were born with certain natural rights, which included the rights to life, liberty, and property. He believed that in ancient times, all humans not only enjoyed these rights, they also governed themselves. As societies became larger and more complex, they set up governments as efficient means of protecting natural rights. According to Locke, the most important part of the social contract is a government's obligation to protect the rights of the governed. This train of thought led Locke to a new and revolutionary idea—if a government did not protect the rights of its people, the people had the right to overthrow that government and create a new one.

John Locke (left), Voltaire (center), and Denis Diderot, three writer-philosophers of the Englightenment

French Thinkers

The works of Locke and Hobbes set the stage for later development. During the 1700s in France, Voltaire, Jean-Jacques Rousseau, the Baron de Montesquieu, and Denis Diderot carried the ideas of new government structures further. Although these men shared a desire to reform society, they differed in their views of what needed to be done. In France, Enlightenment thinkers were called *philosophes*, or philosophers.

Voltaire. One of the most prominent of these philosophes was François-Marie Arouet, known simply as Voltaire. Voltaire published many essays, plays, and works of fiction that reflected Enlightenment ideals. Voltaire believed in religious toleration and deism. *Deism* is the belief that God made the universe and left it to be ruled by natural law. Seeking social and political reform, Voltaire often used humor to attack the laws and customs of France. His targets were the Roman Catholic Church, the powerful aristocracy, and the monarchy. Often, Voltaire disguised his criticism in works of fiction, such as his novel *Candide*. Not surprisingly, his writings got him in trouble with the government. During the course of his career, Voltaire was imprisoned in the Bastille and exiled from his native France for many years.

Baron de Montesquieu. Charles-Louis de Secondat, Baron de Montesquieu was extremely interested in how governments worked. He studied the government of ancient Rome and closely examined the contemporary governments of France and England.

He concluded that England had the best government because it balanced the powers of competing groups in society. The English government divided power among three branches: legislative, executive, and judicial. Each branch could control the others through a system of checks and balances. Montesquieu asserted that a government with divided powers was a government of limited powers. A government of limited powers was less likely to violate the natural rights of its citizens. Montesquieu's *The Spirit of Laws* promoted this idea of separation of powers.

Denis Diderot. Another French philosophe, Denis Diderot, helped spread Enlightenment ideas throughout Europe and the American colonies with his multivolume *Encyclopedia*. The *Encyclopedia* included articles written by scholars, philosophers, and scientists. Diderot hoped this huge work would summarize all theoretical and actual knowledge.

Diderot's goal in editing the *Encyclopedia* was to change the way people thought. Many of the articles criticized the Roman Catholic Church and supported religious toleration. Other articles advanced the Enlightenment idea of social reform. The Roman Catholic Church and the French government condemned the *Encyclopedia* and tried to censor it. The church did not like challenges to its authority. The monarchy did not like radical new ideas about government and the rights of the governed. Even so, approximately 20,000 copies of the *Encyclopedia* (a very large number for that time) were printed and distributed.

★ INFLUENCE OF ENLIGHTENMENT THINKING ★

Enlightenment thinking influenced many aspects of life. These thinkers hoped that, with less government interference, middle-class people would get more benefit from their business ventures. Artists began to consider members of the middle class as well as the aristocracy as a potential audience for their work.

Economic Theory

New economic theories were first advanced by French intellectuals called *physiocrats*, who applied the theories of natural law to economics. They believed that land, or agriculture, was the source of a nation's wealth. Physiocrats also believed in *laissez-faire economy*, meaning "let it alone." In this kind of economy, the government has little or no control over businesses.

Adam Smith. Adam Smith, a Scottish economist, shared the ideas of the physiocrats. He wrote *The Wealth of Nations* (1776), which supported the theory of laissez-faire economics. Smith believed that in a free-market economy, supply and demand would determine prices and other economic decisions. He also believed that while governments should not interfere in economics, they did have a duty to protect citizens and provide public works for the betterment of society.

The Arts

During the Enlightenment, changes also occurred in the style and subject matter of the various forms of art.

Painting and Architecture. In art, the heavy, grand baroque style of the previous century was replaced by a style known as rococo. The *rococo style* was delicate and used designs based on natural forms such as shells, flowers, and animals. Rococo paintings depicted scenes from daily life, such as pastoral (rural) scenes. This subject matter contrasted with the formal religious and military themes of baroque art. The Dutch painter Rembrandt van Rijn painted many pictures of middle-class life. For the first time, the middle class became both audience for and subject matter of art and portraiture.

In architecture, in the latter part of the 1700s, the *neoclassical style* became popular. The Roman ruins at Pompeii were excavated during this period, and the discoveries there greatly influenced European styles in both art and architecture. Buildings became lighter and more elegant. In painting, neoclassical artists were interested in expressing themes such as nobility and virtue. Neoclassicists also painted heroic scenes from the French Revolution.

Literature. The influence of the Age of Reason was also evident in the prose of that period. Essays became a popular literary form in the 1700s. Their style was polished, and their arguments were logical and well-reasoned. The novel developed as a new literary form in the mid-1700s. In addition to their interest in art, the members of the new middle class became enthusiastic readers.

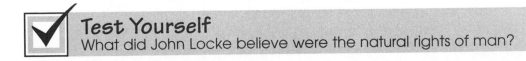

Test Yourself
What did John Locke believe were the natural rights of man?

★ ENLIGHTENMENT AND ABSOLUTE MONARCHY ★

Enlightenment writers openly questioned the authority of government at a time when most nations were dominated by absolute monarchs. These monarchs claimed that since they had been chosen by God, their authority came from God alone. An absolute monarch controlled all functions of government and exercised absolute power over all of his or her subjects.

Until the 1700s, people in general had accepted the rule of absolute monarchs. The exception was England, where, beginning in 1215 with the Magna Carta, the rights of the monarchy had been limited. But even in England, society was divided into strict social classes. Below the monarch was the *aristocracy*, which was the next level of wealth and power. The majority of people were peasant farmers. But an emerging middle class of merchants and manufacturers soon began to challenge the established social and political systems.

Enlightened Despots

Some European rulers became interested in the ideas of the Enlightenment. They understood the usefulness of these ideas and accepted them, at least to a limited degree. None of the so-called *enlightened despots* was willing to relinquish any of his or her power to the people. Their style of governing became known as enlightened absolutism.

Frederick the Great. Fredrick the Great, who ruled Prussia from 1740 to 1786, was influenced by the works of Voltaire. Frederick undertook public works projects to put more land into cultivation and to introduce new crops. These reforms made the peasant farmers more prosperous and enriched Prussia. Frederick embarked on a series of wars to enlarge Prussian territory. He introduced a civil service system into the Prussian government. By reorganizing the government according to principles of efficiency and rationality, Frederick actually strengthened his own control over the government and the nation. The main purpose of Frederick's reforms was to make himself more powerful.

Catherine the Great. Catherine the Great ruled Russia from 1762 to 1796. Like Frederick, she admired the ideas of Enlightenment thinkers. She made some attempts at reforming Russia's government. For example, she granted nobles a charter of rights that strengthened their role in government. When she first came to the throne, she had hoped to free the serfs (peasants who were legally tied to an estate for life). However, frightened by peasant uprisings early in her reign, Catherine ended by giving the owners of the estates even more power over their serfs.

Joseph II. Joseph II, who ruled Austria from 1765 to 1790, began a wide-ranging program of social, economic, and religious reforms based on Enlightenment ideas. He ended serfdom in Austria and attempted to diminish the power of nobles and the Roman Catholic Church. He seized and sold many buildings and much land belonging to the church and established a civil service to run the government. Joseph wanted to break down the old feudal system of hereditary and clerical power and privilege. Unfortunately, only a few of his reforms, including the abolition of serfdom, continued after his death. In the end, the ideals of the Enlightenment proved to be incompatible with the realities of absolute rule.

★ ENLIGHTENMENT AND POLITICAL REVOLUTIONS ★

One of the most important aspects of life that Enlightenment thinking affected was that of politics. Its influence on governments in North America, France, and Latin America has shaped the world we live in today.

The American Revolution

In 1760, George III became king of Great Britain. He was by no means an absolute monarch. The separation of powers in the English system of government was an effective limit on the powers of the monarch. In addition, the English had, over the centuries, won many guarantees of rights and freedoms that the citizens of other European nations lacked. To a large extent, male property owners in Britain's North American colonies shared the same rights and freedoms as male property owners in England. While each colony had a governor, it also had a colonial legislature that made laws for the colony.

Discord Between Great Britain and the American Colonies. Relations between Great Britain and its colonies changed drastically after 1763. That year marked the end of seven years of global warfare between Britain and France. The war was known in the North American colonies as the French and Indian War. Britain and France were fighting over land in India and Europe as well as over territory in North America. By the time the fighting ended, the British government was deeply in debt. Parliament, the British legislature, looked to the colonies as a source of much-needed funds. To increase revenue, Parliament tightened its control of colonial trade and made more effort to collect taxes that were already in place. Then, too, over the next decade, Parliament passed a series of new taxes that targeted the colonies.

New Taxes. In 1765, Parliament passed the Stamp Act, which imposed a tax on most printed documents, including newspapers. It was the first time that Parliament had levied a tax just for the purpose of raising money. All earlier taxes were for the purpose of regulating trade. The colonists were used to these taxes. They were part of the policy of *mercantilism*, which held that colonies existed as a source of raw materials and as a market for their home countries.

The colonists protested the new tax. The American colonist James Otis argued that the colonists could not be taxed by the British Parliament because they had no representatives there. The colonial rallying cry became "no taxation without representation." Their protests were met with punitive measures by the British, such as additional taxes and the quartering of British troops in the colonies. Over the next ten years, Parliament continued to tax the colonies, and the colonists continued to protest, sometimes violently.

The Revolution Begins. By 1775, fighting had broken out, and by July 4, 1776, the colonies were in revolt. Patriot leaders such as Samuel Adams and Patrick Henry had called for independence from Britain for some time. They based their arguments for independence on Enlightenment writings, especially on the work of John Locke. Patriots embraced the right to rid themselves of a government that they felt had broken the social contract.

Declaration of Independence. Virginian Thomas Jefferson was chosen by the members of the Second Continental Congress to draft a Declaration of Independence. Jefferson was well educated and familiar with the writings of Enlightenment thinkers. He borrowed many of their ideas in drafting the Declaration. Jefferson wrote that all men are born with the natural rights to life, liberty, and the pursuit of happiness. It is no accident that the words of John Locke and Thomas Jefferson are similar.

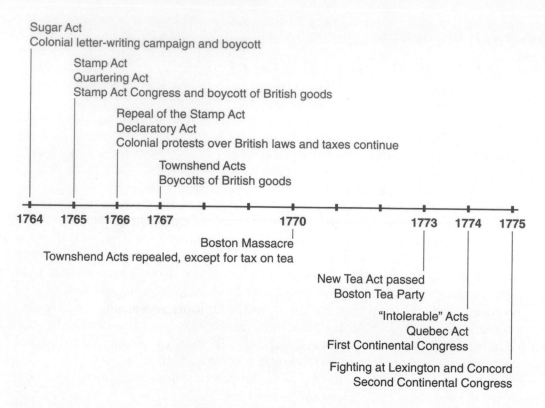

Sugar Act
Colonial letter-writing campaign and boycott

Stamp Act
Quartering Act
Stamp Act Congress and boycott of British goods

Repeal of the Stamp Act
Declaratory Act
Colonial protests over British laws and taxes continue

Townshend Acts
Boycotts of British goods

1764 1765 1766 1767 1770 1773 1774 1775

Boston Massacre
Townshend Acts repealed, except for tax on tea

New Tea Act passed
Boston Tea Party

"Intolerable" Acts
Quebec Act
First Continental Congress

Fighting at Lexington and Concord
Second Continental Congress

Events leading to the American Revolution: 1764–1775

Constitution of the United States. Enlightenment ideas also influenced the new nation's constitution. James Madison, a Virginia delegate to the 1787 Constitutional Convention, had studied and thought a great deal about what the government structure for the new nation should be. His ideas drew heavily on Enlightenment thinkers. For example, Madison used Montesquieu's ideas of the *separation of powers* and *checks and balances* to create the legislative, executive, and judicial branches of the U.S. government and to explain their functions.

 Test Yourself
Why did many American colonists in 1776 feel they had the right to declare independence from Britain?

French Revolution

The French Revolution began as a democratic movement. When it ended, however, France was ruled by the Emperor Napoleon Bonaparte.

French Social Structure. Late 18th-century France was ruled by King Louis XVI, who exercised absolute power over his subjects. French society was divided into three classes, called *estates*. The First Estate was made up of the clergy of the Roman Catholic Church. The church owned about 15 percent of the land. The higher ranks of clergy (cardinals and bishops) came from aristocratic families and were generally wealthy and powerful. However, most members of the clergy were local parish priests, and they were often poor. All clergy were exempt from paying the *taille* (a French tax). The Second Estate was composed of wealthy nobles, who also did not have to pay the *taille*. They owned approximately 20 percent of the land in France and often occupied the highest government and military positions. The first two estates combined accounted for only 2 percent of France's population. The monarchy owned about 20 percent of the land.

Ninety-eight percent of France's population belonged to the Third Estate. It included members of the wealthy middle class called the *bourgeoisie*. These were mainly merchants. The Third Estate also included workers and servants, skilled craftspeople, and peasants (the vast majority of the French population). Although this group owned about half the land in France, the land was not equally distributed. Many peasants had no land at all, and instead worked on estates owned by the nobles. The members of the Third Estate were not exempt from the *taille*. They had to pay 100 percent of the taxes that supported the monarchy, the nobles, and the Church.

The First and Second estates of pre-Revolutionary France trample the Third Estate.

Outbreak of the Revolution. Enlightenment ideas of natural rights, the social contract, and limited powers of government appealed to the people of the Third Estate, especially to the wealthy and educated members of the middle class. Some of the members of the middle class decided to assert these ideas when King Louis XVI called the Estates-General, or assembly, into session in 1789 to pass new taxes. The representatives from the First and Second Estates had more voting power than those from the Third Estate, even though the Third Estate had the largest number of representatives. The Third Estate delegates demanded that this imbalance be corrected.

National Assembly. When the members of the First and Second Estates refused to equalize the distribution of votes, the delegates of the Third Estate withdrew from the Estates-General. They formed a separate assembly, which they named the National Assembly. Some members of the clergy and nobility joined the members of the Third Estate in the National Assembly and voted with them for reforms. Violence erupted as the people of Paris stormed the Bastille, a hated prison in the city. The turmoil soon spread from Paris into the countryside and other cities. Peasants seized the homes of the nobles, and looted and burned them.

Fall of the Bastille prison in Paris, July 14, 1789

Liberty, Equality, Fraternity! In August 1789, the National Assembly issued a revolutionary document known as the *Declaration of the Rights of Man and of the Citizen*. This statement, based on Enlightenment ideas, called for universal freedom of speech, religion, and justice. "Liberty, Equality, Fraternity!" became the main slogan of the French Revolution. In 1790, the Assembly took away the privileges of the clergy. In 1791, it issued a constitution that limited the powers of the monarchy and the aristocracy. In 1792, the French Revolution entered an even more violent stage. The new legislative body, the National Convention, overthrew the French monarchy. By then, all male French citizens who paid taxes could vote.

Napoleon Bonaparte and the End of the Revolution. The French Revolution ended with the rise to power of Napoleon Bonaparte. Napoleon had won popularity with the French people by a series of military victories (1795–1799) over foreign leaders who had attacked France in support of the royal family. By 1800, he had become First Consul of France. In 1804, he was made emperor by the French Senate and votes of the French people.

While in power, Napoleon waged a number of wars with other European countries. These resulted in the French military conquest of most of the European continent. As Napoleon seized territory, he exposed the peoples of those regions to the liberal laws of the French government, such as equality before the law, freedom of religion, and the abolishment of state religions. This was one way that the ideas of the Enlightenment spread across Europe.

Revolutions Sweep Across Latin America

Latin America is so named because most of the nations south of the United States in North and South America were once colonies of the "Latin" nations of France, Spain, and Portugal. (The French, Spanish, and Portuguese languages are based on Latin, the ancient language of the Roman Empire.) By 1790, wealthy and educated people in Latin America had read the same Enlightenment writers that had inspired the American and French revolutions—Hobbes, Locke, Montesquieu, and Voltaire. These Latin Americans had also read the writings of Thomas Jefferson and other Americans. They were ready for freedom from European rule.

Haiti and Toussaint-L'Ouverture. The first Latin American nation to gain independence was Haiti, which is the western portion of the Caribbean island of Hispaniola. The French had colonized Haiti in the 1600s, bringing thousands of Africans there as slaves. In 1791, the slave population of Haiti rose up in revolt. Their leader was Toussaint-L'Ouverture, a former slave. In ten years of fighting, Toussaint-L'Ouverture conquered the island of Hispaniola. The French sent more troops and captured him. He died in a French prison in 1803. Nonetheless, within a year of his death, Haiti declared its independence.

Other Latin American Nations. Napoleon's European conquests helped the colonists in Latin America win their independence. When Napoleon captured Spain in 1808, the Spanish colonists in Latin America seized the opportunity to achieve self-government. Rebellions broke out across Mexico, Central America, and South America. In 1821, led by Father Hidalgo, Mexico won independence from Spain. In that same year, colonists in Central America declared their independence from Spain. Led by Simon Bolívar and José de San Martín, the Spanish colonies of South America gained their independence by 1824. By 1822, the Brazilian colonists had freed themselves from Portugal. Brazil became a republic in 1889.

POINTS TO REMEMBER

- The Enlightenment was an intellectual movement that resulted when 17th- and 18th-century European philosophers began to apply reason and the scientific method to all aspects of society.

- John Locke believed that government had an obligation to protect the natural rights of the governed and that people had the right to overthrow a government that did not protect their rights.

Two 19th-century revolutionaries: Haitian general and liberator Toussaint L'Ouverture (left), and Father Hidalgo, who led the Mexican revolt against Spain (right).

- Denis Diderot published his 28-volume *Encyclopedia* to change the way people thought about the world. The *Encyclopedia* helped spread Enlightenment thinking throughout Europe and the British colonies.

- Patriot leaders in colonial North America based their arguments for independence on Enlightenment writings, especially the writings of John Locke.

- The physiocrats and Adam Smith established the ideas of laissez-faire economics and a free-market economy.

- The French National Assembly based the *Declaration of the Rights of Man and of the Citizen* on Enlightenment ideals, such as freedom of speech and religion and government protection of rights.

- Educated revolutionaries in Latin America were inspired by the writings of such Enlightenment thinkers as Locke and Voltaire, as well as by the writings of such Americans as Thomas Jefferson.

EXERCISES

CHECKING WHAT YOU HAVE READ

1. What did Thomas Hobbes believe would be the best form of government?

   A. a republic
   B. a democracy
   C. an absolute monarchy
   D. a limited monarchy

2. Enlightenment thinkers in France were called the

   A. philosophes
   B. bourgeoisie
   C. First Estate
   D. Second Estate.

3. Which nation did Baron de Montesquieu believe had the best government?

   A. France
   B. Spain
   C. Russia
   D. England

4. Which French intellectuals applied the theory of natural law to economics?

   A. Third Estate
   B. physiocrats
   C. university teachers
   D. National Assembly leaders

5. Who wrote *The Wealth of Nations*?

   A. Voltaire
   B. Thomas Hobbes
   C. John Locke
   D. Adam Smith

6. Which of the following was not an enlightened despot?

   A. Fredrick the Great
   B. Catherine the Great
   C. King Louis XVI
   D. Joseph II

7. Wealthy nobles in France belonged to which estate?

   A. the First Estate
   B. the Second Estate
   C. the Third Estate
   D. the Fourth Estate

8. What was the first area in Latin America to gain independence from a European nation?

   A. Haiti
   B. Mexico
   C. Central America
   D. South America

USING WHAT YOU HAVE READ

The Enlightenment caused long-term effects on the political, economic, and social life of Europe and the world. Read each of the statements below. Determine if each statement was a cause or an effect of change. On a separate piece of paper, write C if a statement is a cause of change or E if it is the effect of change.

1. The scientific method enabled Isaac Newton to develop a theory of gravity.

2. Thomas Hobbes and John Locke wrote about the social contract.

3. The Declaration of Independence split the United States from the rule of Great Britain.

4. Joseph II ended serfdom in Austria.

5. After the American and French revolutions, colonists in Latin America pushed for independence.

6. Montesquieu wrote about the separation and balance of powers as a way to check government's power.

7. The U.S. Constitution divided power among three branches of government: the legislative, executive, and judicial branches.

8. Samuel Adams and Patrick Henry called for independence from Britain.

9. Leaders of the French Revolution stripped power not only from the monarchy, but also from the nobility and the Church.

10. Principles of the scientific method were applied to human behavior.

THINKING ABOUT WHAT YOU HAVE READ

Imagine a local government that gives all legislative, executive, and judicial powers to just one person. Write a paragraph describing how such a government might operate.

SKILLS

The Enlightenment

Read the passage below and answer the questions that follow. Immanuel Kant was a German thinker of the Enlightenment.

Have courage to use your own intelligence! That is the motto of the Enlightenment. . . .

All that is required for this Enlightenment is freedom; and particularly the least harmful of all that may be called freedom, namely, the freedom for man to make public use of his reason in all matters. But I hear people clamor on all sides: "Don't argue!" The officer says: "Don't argue, drill!" The tax collector: "Don't argue, pay!" The pastor: "Don't argue, believe!" . . . Here we have restrictions on freedom everywhere. Which restriction is hampering Enlightenment, and which does not, or even promotes it? I answer: The public use of a man's reason must be free at all times, and this alone can bring Enlightenment among men.

Immanuel Kant, "What Is Enlightenment?" 1784

1. What does Kant believe is necessary in order to spread the ideas of the Enlightenment?

2. Why does Kant mention the officer, the tax collector, and the pastor?

3. Why does Kant believe that the public use of reason is "the least harmful of all that may be called freedom"?

4. Why do you think Kant tells people to have the courage to use their own intelligence?

5. Describe how Kant's words embody the spirit of the Enlightenment.

CHAPTER 2

INDUSTRIALIZATION

BENCHMARK:

Explain the social, political, and economic effects of industrialization.

To meet the requirements of this benchmark, you must know the effects of the Industrial Revolution. To help you review this topic, the chapter discusses the scientific and technological changes that took place in the textile industry in England in the 1700s. Effects, or results, of industrialization discussed in this chapter include the relationship between industrialization and the movement of populations, including population growth, rural-to-urban migration, the growth of industrial cities, and emigration out of Europe. The chapter explains how industrialization changed the role of labor and how this change led to the development of unions. It describes changes in the living and working conditions of the early industrial working class, particularly of women and children. Finally, it discusses the growth of industrialization around the world.

★ UNDERSTANDING INDUSTRIALIZATION ★

Did you ever try to make something by hand? Maybe you have made a batch of cookies instead of buying them at the store. Or maybe you have given someone a handmade greeting card, even though it would have been easier to buy one. Think of the advantages and disadvantages of making something by hand versus buying something that is manufactured and sold in a store.

Consider an item that is carefully made by a skilled crafts worker using simple hand tools in a home workshop. The result is a one-of-a-kind product. Making something by hand can be difficult and time-consuming, however, and these two factors make the product expensive.

Goods manufactured in a factory are made quickly. They are uniform; that is, all the products are identical. Instead of making an item from start to finish, individual workers perform separate tasks in its production. This is called *specialization*. On an *assembly line*, a product moves from station to station as workers at each station perform a different task to help complete the product. The resulting manufactured goods are inexpensive to produce when compared to handmade goods. During the Industrial Revolution, goods began to be produced in factories by unskilled or semiskilled workers.

★ THE INDUSTRIAL REVOLUTION BEGINS ★

The *Industrial Revolution* was a period of technological advancement and social change that dramatically altered the way in which people lived and worked. It began in England during the mid-1700s with the introduction of new technology to the textile industry. A textile is woven material, or cloth.

Conditions That Aided the Industrial Revolution

A number of social, political, and economic factors created the ideal conditions for industrialization. In England, these factors were (1) a growing and shifting population, (2) an abundance of natural resources, (3) a stable government, and (4) a large supply of *capital* (money for investment).

Growing Population. During the 18th century, agricultural advances in Europe led to a food surplus (more than enough food). Because food was plentiful, the population grew. At the same time, advances in medicine led to a declining death rate. This also contributed to population growth. The increase in population created an increased demand for manufactured goods.

Population Shift. In addition to population growth, England experienced a population shift as more people began to move from the countryside to cities. This rise in *rural-to-urban migration* was a result of the *enclosure movement.* Enclosure took place when landed aristocrats enclosed, or fenced in, common land that peasants had formerly used for farming and livestock. This made it more difficult for peasants to make their living. Enclosure became widely used in the Netherlands during the 1600s. During the 1700s, the practice became common in England. Enclosure resulted in more organized and more productive farming, but the loss of land forced many peasants to migrate to towns and cities in search of work. These displaced farmers eventually provided a source of labor for manufacturing and mining.

Abundance of Natural Resources. An abundance of natural resources also contributed to industrialization in England. England had large supplies of coal and iron ore. Engines and factory machines were forged from iron. Coal was used to fuel steam engines, the source of power for the new factories.

Stable Government. In addition to the abundance of resources, England had a stable government. Since it had not had a revolution since 1688, people felt secure doing business there.

Large Supply of Capital. England's trade and the income it derived from its colonial empire gave it a strong economy. Many English people had enough money to invest in new factories and businesses. Since they felt financially secure, they were often willing to try new ideas.

Textile Industry: the First Example of Industrialization

England had long been the center of textile production. Traditionally, British textiles were produced through the *putting-out system*. Craftspeople in rural areas spun flax (linen) into fiber (thread) at home. The fiber was then transported by merchants to other craftspeople who wove the fiber into fabric. Because the labor was spread out in many workers' homes, the putting-out system did not produce textiles quickly enough to keep pace with rising demand.

Weavers working at home, before the Industrial Revolution

Invention of New Machines. The putting-out system came to an end with a number of inventions that changed the way textiles were manufactured. These changes led to the creation of the first textile factories.

- In the 18th century, John Kay invented the *flying shuttle*, which improved weaving looms. Traditionally, two people had been needed to work a loom, but the flying shuttle made it possible for one person to do the job. With the flying shuttle, weavers were able to weave faster than human spinners could spin thread.

- In about 1764, James Hargreaves invented the *spinning jenny*, which allowed as many as 16 threads to be spun at once. With it, spinners were able to catch up with the weavers. These new machines were placed in special buildings, or *factories*. Now spinners, weavers, and the machines were brought together in one place.

- In 1769, Sir Richard Arkwright, an English industrialist, invented the *water frame*, a large, water-powered spinning frame that created strong thread.

- The *spinning mule*, invented in 1779 by Samuel Crompton, was a combination of the spinning jenny and the water frame. The spinning mule made strong, fine fiber.

- The Scotsman James Watt's improvement of the coal-powered steam engine in 1782 contributed to the growth of the textile industry. So did Edmund Cartwright's power loom (1785), which was run by steam power.

Effects of Steam Power. Rushing streams and rivers turned the huge wheels that had provided power used by the early factories. With the steam-powered water loom, textile factories could be built anywhere, not just near sources of water. The steam engine also contributed to the growth of steam-powered railroads in the early 19th century, which allowed merchants to transport goods cheaply long distances over land. England's coal industry grew as the use of the steam engine grew. More workers were needed to mine coal and to run steam-powered machines in factories and steam engines in ships and trains.

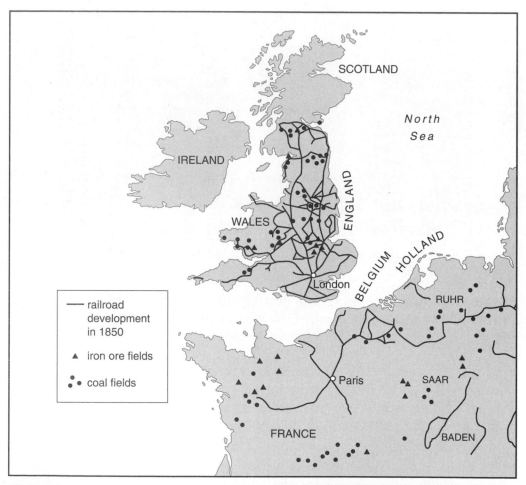

Railroads and centers of natural resources, in England and Western Europe, in the mid-19th century

Test Yourself
List three advantages England had that aided its rapid industrialization in the late 1700s.

★ INDUSTRIALIZATION AND CHANGE ★

As the Industrial Revolution grew in England (and somewhat later in other parts of Europe), it was accompanied by social and economic changes. The landscape of industrialized countries was altered as industries developed in cities and cities developed around industries. Factories needed workers, so *entrepreneurs* (people who organize, manage, and assume the risks of new businesses) built factories in cities, which had large pools of potential workers. As factories grew, more farmers moved to cities to look for work. The result was a mass migration of people from rural areas to *urban* (city) centers of manufacturing. New cities sprang up near sources of natural resources and waterways. Already established cities grew into larger, industrial centers.

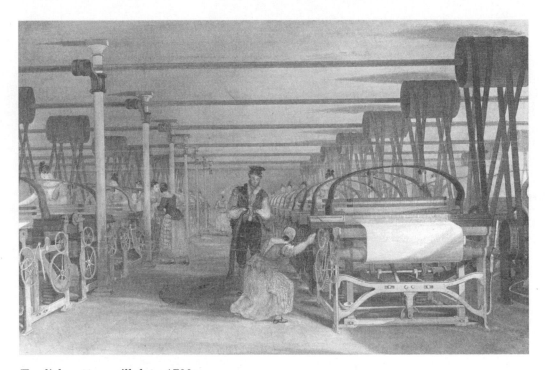

English cotton mill, late 1700s

Urban Living Conditions for the Poor

Life was hard for workers in these new industrial cities. The buildings in which they lived were called tenements. These were situated in dirty and overcrowded areas called *slums*. Entire families often lived in one-room apartments. The tenements lacked heat, proper lighting, fresh air, running water, and adequate sanitation. Alleyways and streets were narrow and dirty, and the buildings often needed repairs. The overcrowding led to increased crime and sickness. Diseases such as cholera spread rapidly because of the lack of proper sanitation. City services like police, schools, and housing were inadequate to deal with the rapid increase in city populations.

London slum street, early 19th century

Changes in the Social Structure

The social structure changed dramatically as industrialization spread. Upper-class landowners remained powerful in most industrial nations, but a growing middle class of wealthy factory owners and merchants began to compete with the upper classes for political and economic power.

New Middle Class. Middle-class families lived well. The women did not work outside the home and had servants to do the housework. Middle-class boys were sent to school, and girls received some education as well. Many members of the middle class looked down on poor people. They thought that people were poor because they did not work hard enough. This attitude grew out of *Social*

Middle-class English family, mid-19th century

Darwinism, which was loosely based on Charles Darwin's theory of the struggle for survival among animal and plant species. Social Darwinists believed that economic competition produced more advanced societies because it weeded out weak and inefficient people. They called this the *survival of the fittest.*

Status of Factory Workers. Factory workers belonged to the lowest class in the new industrial society. As farmers, they had been poor. But they had been relatively self-sufficient, had lived in more wholesome environments, and had grown at least some of their own food. As factory workers, they lived in unhealthy urban slums and worked for very low wages. Fathers, mothers, and children as young as six worked in factories six and seven days a week. Yet families still found it difficult to earn enough to buy adequate food. Besides lacking economic power, factory workers also lacked the political power to win conflicts with factory owners.

Effect of Industrialization on Emigration

During the later Industrial Revolution, many people *emigrated* (moved) from Europe to other places. They left because jobs became scarce in their native countries. By the late 1800s, machines were doing the jobs that human workers once did. These workers had to look elsewhere for work. Many came to the United States. From 1870 to 1920, more than 25 million Europeans immigrated to the United States looking for work and a better life. Some became farmers, but many stayed in the cities and took factory jobs in the Northeast and Midwest.

Changing Roles for Women

Factories changed women's roles as workers. Many factory owners hired women instead of men because they could pay women lower wages. Some factory owners believed women were easier to control and train than men. Instead of traditional farmwork and housework, poor women now worked 12 to 14 hours a day in factories. They then went home to wash clothes, clean their homes, and take care of their children. They could no longer raise food in gardens or make clothes at home. They now had to use their meager wages to buy these things.

Child Labor

One of the worst effects of the Industrial Revolution was the use of child labor. Men were still considered the primary source of income in a family, but it was not possible for a poor family to survive on the wages of only one family member. So even the children had to work. Factory owners liked to employ young children because their small fingers could easily work the machines. The owners could also get away with paying children less than they paid men.

At first, many people did not object to children working in factories. After all, farm children had always done chores. But conditions in the factories were especially dangerous for children. Many lost limbs in the machines. The cramped positions that they had to assume for their work affected their posture. Most children who worked in factories received no education. In 1833, the British Parliament passed the Factory Aid Act, which limited the number of hours that children could work. But child labor continued in most industrialized nations into the 1900s.

Test Yourself
Why did factory owners hire women and children?

★ THE RISE OF UNIONS ★

As you have read, working conditions in factories were often unclean, unsafe, and dangerous. Adults as well as children were often injured or even killed by machinery. Employers frequently fired injured workers or those who fell ill and could not perform their job. No one guaranteed workers any protection from unfair treatment. As the Industrial Revolution progressed, workers became increasingly dissatisfied with their working conditions.

Early Labor Movements

The working class had little power and few resources to achieve better pay, shorter hours, and safer working conditions. Some workers, such as the group called the Luddites in England, tried to stop the loss of jobs and poor wages that resulted from industrialization. They rioted and destroyed the new, labor-

Luddites smash a loom in an early 19th-century factory

saving machines that were taking away their jobs. The Luddites were suppressed by the British government, however, and nothing came of their revolt.

Trade Unions. Workers began to band together in *trade unions*. The unions represented workers in dealing with factory owners. Union members would strike, or stop working, to try to force factory owners to meet their demands. Trade unions spread throughout Great Britain as workers saw that strikes could be successful bargaining weapons with employers.

Nonetheless, trade unions had to fight hard to exist. At first, the governments of industrialized nations outlawed unions. Often, wealthy businesspeople and factory owners controlled these governments. Workers in Great Britain were the first to win the right to organize. In 1799, British lawmakers outlawed unions by passing the Combination Acts. The acts were repealed in 1824, but unions remained weak for several more decades. British unions became legal under the Trade Union Act of 1871, although a law that made picketing illegal was passed on the same day as the Trade Union Act.

Even when unions became legal, many factory owners found ways to oppose them. The bosses threatened workers and hired strikebreakers. Nonetheless, workers continued to unionize. By persevering, they finally won shorter workdays, higher wages, and safer working conditions.

★ PROGRESS OF INDUSTRIALIZATION ★

When other nations began to industrialize, England tried unsuccessfully to protect its lead by prohibiting the export of the inventions described earlier. The first European country to industrialize was Belgium. In 1817, an Englishman, John Cockerill, opened textile factories there. After Belgium, France and Germany began slowly modernize their manufacturing procedures.

By the 1820s, United States entrepreneurs using English technology had set up textile mills in New England. The most famous were the mills in Lowell, Massachusetts. After the Civil War, the United States experienced a surge in industrialization caused by its abundance of natural resources and raw materials. Cheap labor was supplied by the huge increase in immigrants as well as by people moving from the country to towns and cities. By the early 20th century, the United States led the world in manufacturing.

Rapid Development of Technology

Technological innovations became more advanced as industrialization spread. The period of the late 1800s, often called the Second Industrial Revolution, was characterized by greater and more rapid technological developments than the earlier industrial revolution.

Greater Use of Steel. Steel is stronger and more flexible than iron. Then, too, it does not rust. Therefore, steel replaced iron as the material from which railroad tracks, beams for skyscrapers and bridges, and machines were made.

Electricity. The use of electricity as a power source became widespread in the late 1800s. Thomas Edison produced the first lightbulb, which allowed factories to operate at night. Electric street lamps made city streets safer.

Advances in Communication and Transportation. Communication changed with Alexander Graham Bell's invention of the telephone in 1876. Edison's improvements to the telephone made it more practical for widespread use. The invention of the internal combustion engine led to the development of the automobile, which transformed transportation. The innovations that occurred during the Second Industrial Revolution helped shape the world we know today.

★ LASTING IMPACT OF INDUSTRIALIZATION ★

The Industrial Revolution had far-reaching and long-lasting effects. Aided by improved communication and transportation networks, trade and commerce spread new ideas from place to place.

Industrialization and the Balance of International Power

By the second half of the 20th century, industrialization had changed the global economy. Nations that had industrialized were rich and influential; those that had not were poor and weak. Great Britain, France, Germany, Italy, Japan, Canada, and the United States became major powers. In these countries, technological innovations were accompanied by social and political reforms.

Some nations in Europe (such as Russia, Spain, and Portugal) were and remain largely agricultural. Many nations in Africa, South Asia, and Latin America still lack the advantages of industrialization. Many receive economic aid from the industrialized nations.

Industrialization in the 21st Century

The Industrial Revolution continues in the 21st century. Many nations in Asia and Latin America that were dependent on agriculture in the 20th century are beginning to industrialize. Some of the industrialization is driven by investments from native-born entrepreneurs. Much of it, however, comes from *multinational corporations* (huge businesses that operate in more than one nation). Companies sometimes build new factories in developing countries to meet the higher global demand for goods. In some cases, however, they relocate factories to nations where they can pay workers less than those in industrialized nations. Today, consumer products purchased in the United States are more and more likely to be manufactured in other parts of the world.

 Test Yourself
How did the Industrial Revolution affect the balance of international power?

POINTS TO REMEMBER

- A growing population, a stable government, a large supply of capital, and an abundance of natural resources made England the ideal location for the development of the Industrial Revolution.
- The Industrial Revolution began in the English textile industry with the introduction of machines to replace the jobs of crafts workers.
- The population of industrial cities grew rapidly as people moved from rural to urban areas to be nearer jobs in factories.
- As machinery became more automated, fewer workers were needed, which caused emigration from Europe to the United States.
- Many early factories employed women and children because they could be paid less than men and were considered easier to control.
- Factory work was often dangerous, the hours were long, and the pay was low.
- To improve bad working conditions, industrial workers banded together to form trade unions, which initially were illegal.
- Industrialization spread unevenly around the world, reaching some areas in Africa, Asia, and Latin America only in the late 20th century.

EXERCISES

CHECKING WHAT YOU HAVE READ

1. Where did the Industrial Revolution begin?

   A. Germany
   B. England
   C. the United States
   D. France

2. Which invention improved the weaving loom?

   A. the spinning jenny
   B. the waterwheel
   C. the flying shuttle
   D. the steam engine

3. The Second Industrial Revolution was characterized by

   A. new kinds of workers
   B. industrialization in Russia
   C. a turn toward the agricultural society of the past.
   D. new technology in communications and transportation.

4. Why was life in cities different from life on farms for women factory workers?

   A. Urban women had to buy food instead of growing their own.
   B. Women on farms did not have to work.
   C. Women in cities had to help build housing for their families.
   D. Women were not allowed to work in cities, so they tried to form unions.

5. Early labor unions were

    A. appreciated by factory owners
    B. founded by women factory workers
    C. formed despite opposition by factory owners
    D. supported by governments.

USING WHAT YOU HAVE READ

The nature of work changed with the coming of the Industrial Revolution. Complete the table below to compare and contrast the making of cloth before the Industrial Revolution and after it began. Some answers have been provided to get you started.

Manufacture of Cloth

	Preindustrial Society	Industrial Society
Location of work	home	factory
Tasks performed by		
Fellow workers		
Tools of production		
Amount of time to make a product		
Cost of production		
Nature of finished product		

THINKING ABOUT WHAT YOU HAVE READ

1. During the Industrial Revolution, labor unions formed to protect workers. Today, labor unions still play a large part in many industries. Two examples of modern unions are the United Auto Workers and the Screen Actors Guild (for actors in the entertainment industry). Look on the Internet or in a library for information on unions and choose one union to study. Ask yourself the following questions: Who does this union represent? What kinds of services does the union offer? How do its members benefit from belonging to the union?

2. Pretend you are an English businessperson in the early 1800s. You want to start a business that produces cloth. Explain to your investors how you plan to set up your business. Be sure to describe the location of your business and tell the investors what you will require to make your business a success. Read about the early textile industry in Great Britain for ideas.

SKILLS

Analyzing a Primary Source

Read the following excerpt from *The Condition of the Working Class in England,* written by Friedrich Engels in 1844. Then answer the questions that follow. Base your answers on the passage and on your knowledge of the Industrial Revolution.

. . . First of all, there is the old town of Manchester, which lies between the northern boundary of the commercial district and the (River) Irk. Here, the streets, even the better ones, are narrow and winding . . . the houses dirty, old, and tumble-down, and the construction of the side streets utterly horrible. Going from the Old Church to Long Millgate, the stroller has at once a row of old-fashioned houses at the right, of which not one has kept its original level; these are the remnants of the old pre-manufacturing Manchester, whose former inhabitants have moved with their descendants into better-built districts, and have left the houses, which were not good enough for them, to a population strongly mixed with Irish blood. Here one is in an almost undisguised working-men's quarter, for even the shops and beerhouses hardly take the trouble to exhibit a trifling degree of cleanliness. But all this is nothing in comparison with the courts and lanes which lie behind, to which access can be gained only through covered passages, in which no two human beings can pass at the same time. Of the irregular cramming together of dwellings in ways which defy all rational plan, of the tangle in which they are crowded literally one upon the other, it is impossible to convey an idea. And it is not the buildings surviving from the old times of Manchester which are to blame for this; the confusion has only recently reached its height when every scrap of space left by the old way of building has been filled up and patched over until not a foot of land is left to be further occupied.
     . . . The view from this bridge . . . is characteristic for the whole district. At the bottom flows, or rather stagnates, the Irk, a narrow, coal black, foul-smelling stream, full of debris and refuse, which it deposits on the shallower right bank. In dry weather, a long string of the most disgusting, blackish-green, slime pools are left standing on this bank, from the depths of which bubbles of miasmatic gas constantly arise and give forth a stench unendurable. . . . Each house is packed close behind its neighbor and a piece of each is visible, all black, smoky, crumbling, ancient, with broken panes and window frames. . . .

1. What is the topic of this selection?

2. Why do you think Engels wrote about Manchester?

3. According to the passage, what were some characteristics of Manchester?

4. According to the passage, why did the former inhabitants of old Manchester leave their homes?

5. Do you think that articles like this helped to improve the living conditions of the working class?

CHAPTER 3

IMPERIALISM

BENCHMARK:

Analyze the reasons that countries gained control of territory through imperialism and the impact on people living in the territory that was controlled.

During the 19th and 20th centuries, European countries competed to gain control of territory in other parts of the world. This competition was called imperialism. To meet the requirements of this benchmark, you must understand the reasons that European nations engaged in imperialism. After reading this chapter, you should be acquainted with the political, economic, and social roots of imperialism. You should also understand differences in attitudes between colonizers and the colonized with regard to language and culture, natural resources, labor, political systems, and religion. In addition, you should be able to explain the impact of imperialism around the world, including the modernization of Japan, the exploitation of African resources, and political and social reform in China.

★ UNDERSTANDING IMPERIALISM ★

Probably everyone has known a bully at some point in life. Bullies use their overpowering strength or size to get their way. On a playground, the bully uses threats to get others to cooperate. If someone doesn't do what the bully wants, he or she might be attacked by the bully. The bully's victim may give in, but he or she usually remains angry at the bully for a long time.

★ DEVELOPMENT OF IMPERIALISM ★

During the late 19th century, many European nations and the United States became bullies on a large scale by engaging in *imperialism*. Imperialist nations use their power to gain political, economic, or social control over other parts of the world.

Imperialism has occurred throughout history. The Assyrians of Mesopotamia, the Romans, and the Han dynasty of China created empires in the ancient world. The Franks in Europe, the Mongols of Asia, and the Aztecs in Mesoamerica created empires in the 800s through the 1500s. From the 16th to the 18th century, England, Spain, and Portugal founded colonies in North and South America.

New Imperialism

The term New Imperialism is sometimes applied to the period in the mid- to late 19th and early 20th centuries, when European nations and the United States extended their influence over countries in Asia, Africa, and the Pacific. New Imperialism also refers to the guiding principles and ideologies that characterized imperialist nations during this period.

Roots of Imperialism

Beginning in the mid-19th century, nations such as Portugal, Great Britain, Belgium, France, the Netherlands, and Spain began to seek control of other parts of the world. In time, Russia, Japan, Germany, Italy, and the United States joined these countries in the race to colonize non-Western areas of the world. For example, by the early 1900s, European nations vied with one another in a "scramble for Africa." By 1914, only the African nations of Ethiopia and Liberia remained free of foreign domination.

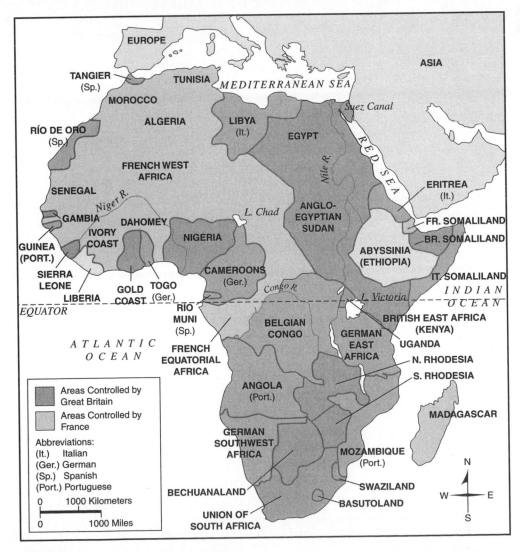

European colonies in Africa in 1914

Motivations for Imperialism

There were four main factors motivating imperialism: (1) economics, (2) nationalism, (3) a conviction that the white race was superior to all others, and (4) desire for more territory.

Economics. The economics of the Industrial Revolution played a major role in the rise of imperialism. By the late 19th century, much of Europe had become industrialized. For industrialized nations, colonies were not only a source of natural resources but also a market for manufactured goods. As manufacturing grew in importance, factory owners looked for new sources of raw materials (natural resources), such as lumber and cotton, that were needed to manufacture finished goods.

Manufacturers found what they wanted in the kingdoms and empires of Africa, Asia, and the Pacific islands. Raw materials flowed from these areas to the factories of Europe, which turned the raw materials into finished goods. Industrialized nations sent these goods back to their colonies for sale to the *indigenous* (native) peoples. The cycle of industrial nations taking raw materials from colonies and then selling the goods manufactured from them to colonies created tremendous amounts of capital for the industrial powers. These nations realized that the more they could control the sources of natural resources and new markets, the wealthier they would become.

Nationalism. *Nationalism,* which swept many European countries in the 19th century, was another strong motivating force behind imperialism. Nationalism is a feeling of intense pride in one's nation, including its language and culture. For the citizens of many European nations—and, at the end of the 19th century, the United States—colonies were not only a source of wealth, but also a source of pride. The more colonial holdings a nation had, the greater its power and the more important it was on the world stage.

Racism. Nationalist feelings were often mixed with feelings of cultural and racial superiority, as evidenced by the theory of Social Darwinism, a concept mentioned in Chapter 2. Social Darwinism is the application of Charles Darwin's theory of natural selection to humans and society. Natural selection is the theory that the species best equipped to adapt to a changing environment has the highest chance of survival. It is often referred to as the "survival of the fittest," a phrase created in the mid-1800s by the English sociologist Herbert Spencer, who applied the theory to society. Social Darwinists believed that some societies were better equipped to be successful than others, an idea closely tied to racism. Social Darwinists supported imperialism because they believed that it was natural for "stronger" societies to conquer "weaker" ones. Not surprisingly, Social Darwinists believed the white race was superior to all others. Many Westerners believed they had a duty to "civilize" the people of "inferior" races.

Politics. Imperialist nations were also driven by political considerations in their quest to acquire new territory. The race for territory was a race for political power. Nations tried to grab territory to keep rival nations from occupying it and gaining exclusive control over its resources and markets. Technology

This soap advertisement uses the racist idea of "the white man's burden": to teach others the habits of white western society.

helped Western nations to set up colonies. Advanced weapons enabled their armies to take control of territories whose people were ill-prepared to defend themselves against guns and cannons.

Test Yourself

What motives drove European nations and the United States to colonize other areas of the world?

★ THE COLONIZERS AND THE COLONIZED ★

Imperialist powers gave little thought to the rights of the people whose lands they took over. A feeling of superiority and entitlement kept these nations from even considering whether the people had a right to own and govern their own land. Imperialist nations ruled their colonies in a way that was most profitable and productive for them, not for the good of the people.

Different Perspectives

The native people's perspective on how to run their lives and societies was very different from that of the people who colonized them. This often caused conflict between the two groups. Colonizers attempted to force their political structures and cultural values, including religion and language, on the colonized. For example, when European powers established colonies in Africa, they drew boundaries that separated their colonies from those of other European colonizers. The new boundaries did not follow the people's traditional political boundaries. Not only were native groups of different cultures forced together in a single colony, they were forced to assimilate, or conform, to the culture of their European conquerors.

Languages. Western nations used a number of means to force indigenous peoples to give up their cultures. Imposing their Western languages on African people is a major example. In order to participate in the economy or deal with the colonial government, the people had to learn the language of the European power that ruled them. In government-run schools, teachers spoke the language of the colonizer, not the language of the pupils. Legal documents were written in the language of the colonizer. In some colonies, the colonizers taught that economic and social success could be achieved only by learning the new language. For instance, France believed colonized peoples should "aspire to be French," and offered its best African students the opportunity to study at universities in France. In general, the perspective of the colonizers prevailed. Today, the major languages spoken on the African continent include French, English, and Portuguese.

Natural Resources. Colonizers and the colonized had different viewpoints about natural resources as well. To the colonizers, colonies were sources of cheap raw materials. They felt justified in helping themselves. They believed that manufactured goods improved the lives of indigenous peoples, but they did not want the colonies to industrialize. They were afraid that if the colonized people acquired factories and began to manufacture goods, they would use the natural resources that the colonizers felt belonged to them. They also feared that the colonized people would compete with them on the world market. As a result, imperialist nations made sure that their colonies' raw materials were exported to the home country for use in it factories.

Although the land and resources rightfully belonged to the colonized, they received no money for them. The colonizers paid their workers as little as possible to work on farms and in mines. The profits from development and mining went to the investors and manufacturers in the colonizing nation. From the perspective of the colonized, the Western development of colonial resources was theft. In addition, lumbering and mining these resources often damaged the environment of the colony.

Labor and Economic Systems. Local economies changed dramatically under colonial rule. Before colonization, many groups had economic systems based on agriculture. People worked for themselves and farmed small plots of land or herded cattle, sheep, or goats. Once a European nation or the United States seized control, the labor force was transformed from self-employed people to hired laborers working for foreign companies. The colonizers seized local lands from farmers to create huge plantations and then forced the farmers to work on them. People who were once subsistence farmers began harvesting cash crops, such as cotton, cocoa, rubber, sugar, tea, and coffee, for foreign owners. Workers' livelihoods depended on decisions made by colonial businesses and governments. At times, workers rebelled against their colonial overseers, but they were always unsuccessful.

Political Systems. Imperial powers found a variety of political systems in the lands they conquered. Some societies had strong central governments. Others were decentralized, that is, they were local political units ruled by chiefs or leaders. Some communities were ruled by consensus—there was no specific ruler who made political decisions.

Once in power, imperialist nations imposed their own systems. They ruled colonies in one of two ways: (1) indirect rule or (2) direct rule. In indirect rule, a nation ruled a colony through established local leaders. Indirect rule was considered good because it was cost-effective (inexpensive). The colonial power did not have to hire a great number of government officials to rule a new colony. Indirect rulers had no real power, however; they were subordinate to the colonial power. This was the government system that Great Britain generally used.

Under direct rule, the colonial power ousted the indigenous leaders and installed European officials to manage the colonial government. France preferred this system. Either way, indigenous people were expected to accept the political system imposed by the colonizers. Native traditions and institutions were replaced by foreign models.

Religion. Religion was also a source of tension between colonizers and the colonized. Christian missionaries often accompanied colonial rulers. In many places, missionaries set up schools and hospitals as well as churches. Unfortunately, their attempts to help people were hindered by the belief that the people they wanted to benefit belonged to an inferior race. Missionaries believed they had a duty to "civilize" colonial peoples by converting them to Christianity. In many areas, the people's resistance to conversion led to friction and even violence.

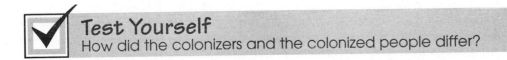

Test Yourself
How did the colonizers and the colonized people differ?

★ GLOBAL IMPACT OF IMPERIALISM ★

Western powers also radically altered countries that they never officially colonized. Two of these are Japan and China. Those countries that they did colonize are still badly damaged by the experience. In Africa today, people still feel the effects of 19th-century imperialism. Although former colonies have been freed, many inhabitants cannot shake off the sense of inferiority and anger that colonial rulers imposed on them.

Modernization of Japan

The Japanese have a reputation for adopting other cultures and turning them to advantage. If so, this may explain why contact with the West strengthened that country in some important ways.

Japan's Feudal Society. In the 1600s, Japan had cut itself off from most of the world. From about 1185 through the mid-1800s, Japan was organized into a feudal society, much like those in medieval Europe. A feudal society is one in which local lords govern their own lands, but owe loyalty and military service to a higher lord. In Japan, the highest lord was the *shogun,* or military dictator, who gave land to local lords known as *daimyo* in exchange for their loyalty. Various families controlled the shogunate over the centuries. The most famous family was the Tokugawa. Members of this family ruled Japan from about 1603 to 1868. The local lords maintained order in their lands through the services of warriors known as samurai. The emperor of Japan was a ceremonial leader having no political power. The majority of Japanese were farmers.

Western Influence. The Industrial Revolution and the resulting imperialist pressures of the 19th century ended Japan's isolation. In 1853, U.S. warships under the command of Matthew Perry sailed into Tokyo Harbor. The Japanese marveled at these steam-powered, ironclad ships armed with cannon. Perry presented the Japanese with a letter from U.S. President Franklin Pierce, requesting that Japan allow U.S. ships to trade in Japanese ports. Perry said he would return for an answer. After seeing Perry's ships, the Japanese realized that they would be unable to resist the military and industrial power of the United States. In 1854, Japan and the United States signed a treaty to open Japan to U.S. trade. Other nations soon followed the United States in establishing trade and diplomatic relations with Japan.

Shift of Power in Japan. In 1868, the *Sat-Cho* (an alliance of daimyo and samurai in Japan's southern provinces of Satsuma and Choshu) overthrew the Tokugawa shogun's government. At first, this group was opposed to opening Japan to trade. Its members soon realized, however, that Japan could not stand up to Western nations without developing its own industrial and military power. They decided to support the 15-year-old Emperor Mutsuhito. Mutsuhito called his reign Meiji, which means "enlightened rule." However, the real power lay with the Sat-Cho. They succeeded in transforming Japan from an isolated feudal society into a modern industrial power. This period is called the Meiji Restoration.

Westernization of Japan. The Meiji leaders studied the institutions of Western countries for ways to reform and modernize Japan. They organized a new centralized government with a legislative branch and a strong executive branch like Germany's. They took the United States' public education system as a model for their own. To make their military resemble the armed forces of the West, they expanded it and outfitted it with modern equipment, including new battleships. All Japanese men had to serve in the armed forces for three years. Like Western capitalists, they built factories and then sold them to investors. A national railroad system was built to carry goods and workers to the new factories. Under Meiji rule, Japan rapidly became an industrial society and important world-trading partner.

Based on observations of Western nations, Japan decided that it, too, could benefit from a colonial empire. The Japanese islands lacked petroleum and iron ore as well as other natural resources necessary for industry. The Japanese also wanted more land for an expanding population. In the late 19th and early 20th centuries, Japan fought two wars over Korea—one with China and one with Russia. Japan won both wars. The victory over Russia established Japan as a world power. Japan controlled Taiwan, Manchuria, Korea, and several islands off the coasts of China and Russia.

Test Yourself
What measures did 19th-century Japan take in order to become a modern, Westernized nation?

The End of Chinese Isolation

In the 16th century, China, like Japan, had chosen to isolate itself from the rest of the world. The Chinese economy was mainly based on agriculture. While China exported large amounts of tea, silk, and porcelain to Europe, manufacturing and trade played only a small role in its economy. The Chinese upper classes looked down on merchants.

In the late 18th century, the British brought opium, a highly addictive drug, to China. The British were spending more money on Chinese tea than the Chinese were spending on British trade goods. The British hoped that the sale of opium would increase their own profits. Millions of Chinese became dependent on this drug. Chinese officials grew concerned about the social effects of opium addiction. They outlawed it and demanded that the British end the opium trade. The British refused.

Opium War. This conflict led to the Opium War of 1839, which the British won. The subsequent Nanking Treaty created the British colony of Hong Kong and gave Great Britain special trading rights with China. Other nations began to demand similar trading rights. In time, China came under the economic control of foreign nations, including Russia, France, Germany, Portugal, and Japan. The areas that these countries controlled were known as *spheres of influence*. A sphere of influence is not a colony, but an area under foreign economic domination. Chinese resentment of foreign influence led to the Taiping Rebellion, which lasted from 1850 to 1864. As a result of the rebellion, the ruling Qing dynasty of China was fatally weakened.

Open Door Policy. The United States wanted to protect its own trading interests in China. In response to the development of European spheres of influence, it declared the Open Door Policy in 1899. This policy stated that all the nations trading in China would respect one another's trading rights. U.S. Secretary of State John Hay manipulated other countries into agreeing to the policy. The Open Door Policy promoted American interests, but it did little to protect Chinese interests.

Reforms in China. The political unrest in China led to some reforms. Chinese military and educational systems were modernized. Plans were made to create a constitutional government, although they were never carried out. In 1900 the secret society of Righteous and Harmonious Fists, known as Boxers, staged

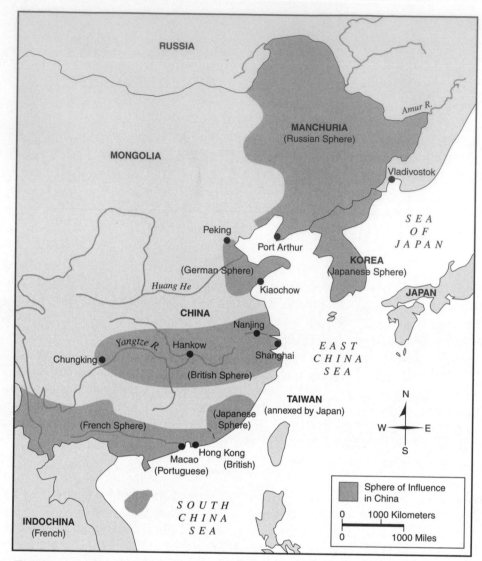

European countries had many spheres of influence in 19th-century China.

what is called the *Boxer Uprising*. The Boxers resented foreign influence and vowed to drive all foreigners out of China. Western powers helped the ruling government to crush the uprising—but at a heavy price for China. China had to give up more power to Western nations.

By the early 1900s, China was moving ahead with reforms, but unrest and conflict continued. In 1911, China's final ruling dynasty collapsed. Sun Yixian, a Chinese exile living in the United States, returned to China and established the Republic of China. It was to be built upon his Three Principles of the People: nationalism, democracy, and economic security for the people. The reforms in China were not as effective and long lasting as the reforms in Japan. The slowness of reform led to civil war in the 1930s between Sun's Nationalist forces and Communist forces in the 1930s. The civil war stopped during World War II but resumed as soon as the war ended. By 1949, the Communists had driven the Nationalists forces from mainland China. Today, a Communist government rules China.

Chinese Boxer
rebels captured by
U.S. cavalry in 1900

The Legacy of Imperialism in Africa

Most European colonies on the African continent had gained their independence by 1980. Unfortunately, the legacy of colonialism made the transition to self-government difficult for many of these newly independent nations. Because colonial powers did not want their colonies to industrialize and compete with them, they had prevented them from developing domestic industries. The economies of many African nations are still almost totally dependent on the same cash crops that they had grown as colonies. Therefore, when the prices of these crops fall on the international market, or when there is a poor harvest, these nations suffer greatly. In addition to farming, many of these nations continue to sell raw materials such as lumber, iron ore, gold, and petroleum.

Lack of industry and inadequate transportation and communication systems have made it difficult for many African nations to compete in the global economy. Some nations are extremely poor. Weak economies and tensions among ethnic groups have led to political unrest. Many countries have turned away from democracy in favor of one-party rule and dictatorships. Some countries have been torn by civil wars. The civil unrest and current struggles of many nations in Africa are a direct result of 19th- and 20th-century imperialism.

Test Yourself
Why did the new nations of Africa have little industry?

POINTS TO REMEMBER

- Imperialism is the exercise of political, economic, and social control by strong nations over weaker nations.

- Economics, nationalism, a belief in the superiority of white people, and the desire for more territory influenced Western imperialism in the late 19th and early 20th centuries.

- The Industrial Revolution contributed to a New Imperialism because the industrial powers of Europe and later the United States looked to foreign territories as sources of cheap raw materials for their factories and as markets for their finished goods.

- Social Darwinists applied Charles Darwin's theory of natural selection to humans and human society. They believed that some societies were better equipped to be successful than others.

- The colonial powers forced their cultures and political systems on their colonies.

- Japan modernized itself in reaction to the industrial and military power of Western nations. In time, it too became an imperialist power.

- Western nations carved China into spheres of influence. The Chinese rebelled in reaction to the interference of Western nations in their affairs and established a republic. A civil war between Communists and Nationalists resulted in the victory of the Communists, who in 1949 established a government on mainland China.

- The struggles of African nations after independence can be directly tied to European colonial economic, cultural, and political policies.

EXERCISES

CHECKING WHAT YOU HAVE READ

1. Colonies supplied all of the following except

   A. raw materials
   B. a market for goods
   C. new languages
   D. cheap labor.

2. In indirect rule, a nation governs a colony by

   A. installing a new government
   B. ruling through existing leaders
   C. executing existing leaders
   D. jailing existing leaders.

3. The idea that some societies are better equipped for survival than others is known as

   A. Social Darwinism
   B. emancipation
   C. direct rule
   D. manifest destiny.

4. Intense pride in one's own country is called

   A. colonialism
   B. imperialism
   C. socialism
   D. nationalism.

5. What happened when Japan opened its doors to foreign trade?

   A. Foreign powers took over Japan.
   B. Internal conflict caused the shogun to step down.
   C. Japan's economy suffered.
   D. China conquered parts of Japan.

USING WHAT YOU HAVE READ

The lasting effects of imperialism can still be seen in parts of the world, including Africa. The African continent was colonized by a number of European countries, including Great Britain, France, and Belgium. These countries ruled their colonies in different ways. Use the Internet or books from the library to research the different ways that Great Britain, France, and Belgium ruled their colonies.

1. Create a table using the headings below. List the European nation, its colonies in Africa, its method of rule, and the consequences of its governing system.

European Nation	Colonies in Africa	Method of Rule	Consequences of Governing System

2. Why do you think each country ruled its colonies so differently?

THINKING ABOUT WHAT YOU HAVE READ

Look in an almanac or use the Internet to find territories that are still under foreign rule today. Choose one of these territories to research on the Internet or at the library and answer the following questions.

1. Describe the relationship between the territory and the governing power.

2. Is the relationship similar to or different from the colonial relationships during the period of New Imperialism?

3. Analyze how you think a person born in the territory you researched feels about foreign control today.

SKILLS

Using Primary Sources

The following passage is from a letter sent by a Chinese government official, Lin Tse-hsu, to Queen Victoria of Great Britain. The letter is dated 1839. Answer the questions that follow, based on the passage and your knowledge of imperialism.

A communication: magnificently our great Emperor soothes and pacifies China and the foreign countries, regarding all with the same kindness. If there is profit, then he shares it with the peoples of the world; if there is harm, then he removes it on behalf of the world. . . .

All those people in China who sell opium or smoke opium should receive the death penalty. If we trace the crime of those barbarians who through the years have been selling opium, then the deep harm they have wrought and the great profit they have usurped should fundamentally justify their execution according to law. . . .

We find that your country is (far away). Yet, there are barbarian ships that strive to come here for trade for the purpose of making a great profit. The wealth of China is used to profit the barbarians; that is to say, the great profit made by barbarians is all taken from the rightful share of China. By what right do they then in return use the poisonous drug (opium) to injure the Chinese people? Even though the barbarians may not necessarily intend to do us harm, yet in coveting profit to an extreme, they have no regard for injuring others. Let us ask, where is your conscience? I have heard that the smoking of opium is very strictly forbidden by your country; that is because the harm caused by opium is clearly understood. Since it is not permitted to do harm to your own country, then even less should you let it be passed on to the harm of other countries—how much less to China! The foreign countries cannot get along for a single day without (tea). If China cuts off these benefits, with no sympathies for those who are to suffer, then what can the barbarians rely upon to keep themselves alive? . . . As for other foodstuffs, beginning with candy, ginger, cinnamon, and so forth, and the articles for use, beginning with silk, satin, chinaware, and so on, all the things that must be had by foreign countries are innumerable. On the other hand, articles coming from the outside to China can only be used as toys. . . .

The barbarian merchants of your country, if they wish to do business for a prolonged period, are required to obey our statutes respectfully and to cut off permanently the source of opium. . . . May you, O (Queen Victoria), check your wicked and your vicious people before they come to China, in order to show further the sincerity of your politeness and submissiveness, and to let the two countries enjoy together the blessings of peace.

1. Based on this letter, explain how you think Chinese–British trade was characteristic of the Age of Imperialism.

2. Why did Lin feel that Britain was wrong for selling opium in China?

3. According to this article, what items did China trade with Great Britain?

4. Why do you think the author used the term "barbarians" to refer to the British?

5. Do you think the author was angry with Britain? Why?

CHAPTER 4

WORLD WAR I AND THE ONSET OF WORLD WAR II

BENCHMARK:

Connect developments related to World War I with the onset of World War II.

To meet the requirements of this benchmark, you should know the consequences of World War I and how they relate to the onset of World War II. You must also be able to describe how the new technologies of the early 20th century changed the nature of warfare.

Knowledge of the Russian Revolution, worldwide depression, and the failures of the Treaty of Versailles is necessary to understand the causes of World War II. You also need to know how the military expansion of the totalitarian states of Germany, Italy, and Japan threatened world peace. Finally, you must understand how the policy of appeasement followed by democratic European leaders encouraged the aggressors and led to World War II.

★ CAUSES OF WORLD WAR I ★

World War I (or the Great War, as people of the time called it) began in 1914 when a violent act touched off a conflict that involved the entire world. Several factors helped create a climate for war. They were nationalism, imperialism, militarism, and the formation of entangling alliances.

Nationalism

Most people feel pride and affection for their countries. These natural feelings run very deep and can lead groups of people to take desperate actions when their national identity is threatened in some way.

Desire for Self-Rule. Prewar Europe was made up of several empires: the Russian, Austro-Hungarian, and the Ottoman empires. These empires were *multinational*. This means that each empire included many different nationalities and ethnic groups. The population of the Austro-Hungarian empire, for example, was made up of Germans, Hungarians, Poles, Czechs, Slovaks, Serbs, Croatians, Jews, and Gypsies. Some members of these groups resented being ruled by Austria. They felt that they had the right to rule themselves and their lands. A cultural or national group's desire for self-government is an important component of nationalism.

Rivalry Among Nations. Nationalism is fed by the pride that people take in their own culture or nation. Often, this feeling leads to competition with others. This rivalry can take healthy forms, such as international sports events. But often it can be too intense. In the early 1900s, competition among the powerful nations of Europe became deadly. Some nations began to view others not just as competitors, but as enemies.

Economic Competition. Nationalistic competition was heightened by the Industrial Revolution (discussed in Chapter 2). The economies of nations during the early part of the 20th century depended to a large extent on manufacturing goods for trade (as they do today). They needed large amounts of raw materials to make goods and to provide power for their factories. Then they needed markets in which to sell the goods. The industrialized nations of Europe competed with one another for natural resources to use as raw materials. This competition increased the tension in Europe.

Imperialism

In Chapter 3, you read about imperialism. Some nations of 19th-century Europe competed for colonies in Africa, Asia, and other parts of the world. These colonies provided raw materials needed for manufacturing and enhanced the prestige of the countries to which they belonged. The desire for colonies aggravated national rivalries in Europe. On several occasions in the early 20th century, European nations disputed over land in their colonies. These disagreements sometimes led to conflict.

Militarism

Nationalism led nations to competition over which would be the strongest military power in the world. The glorification of military power is known as *militarism*. In the early 20th century, the strongest nations of Europe began to prepare for the possibility of war. They increased the size of their armies and navies and greatly increased their stockpiles of weapons. Advancements in industrial technology allowed them to create weapons of war that were deadlier than any that had been developed before.

Alliances

War began to seem inevitable. The nations of Europe looked for friends and allies for support. Two great alliance systems were formed. Germany allied itself with Austria-Hungary and Italy. This was called the Triple Alliance. Fearing Germany, France sought an alliance with Russia. Great Britain joined them to form the Triple Entente. At the same time, the powerful nations of the two great alliance systems signed bilateral (two-nation) agreements with

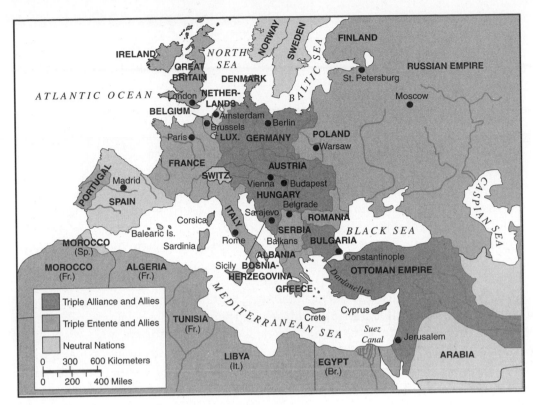

European political alliances in World War I

smaller, less powerful nations. These alliances were defensive in nature. If one member of an alliance were attacked, an ally was obligated to come to its aid. This meant that several nations might become entangled in a fight that formerly might have been limited to only two.

War Breaks Out

The stage was set. The powerful nations of Europe were ready for war. The only thing necessary was a spark to set it off. That spark came on June 28, 1914. A Serb nationalist named Gavrilo Princip shot the heir to the throne of Austria, Archduke Franz Ferdinand. Princip was a member of a group that wanted all Serbs to be united in a self-governing nation. They believed that killing the heir to the Austro-Hungarian throne would help bring this about. Instead, the assassination started a war between Serbia and Austria. Russia supported its ally, Serbia. Germany supported its ally, Austria. Soon, most of Europe was fighting. The Great War had started.

 Test Yourself
What were the major long-term causes of World War I?

★ A DIFFERENT KIND OF WAR ★

World War I differed from any other previous war. The weapons used, the style of fighting, and the global nature of the war were all horrifyingly new.

Global Conflict

The war that began in Europe soon became a global conflict. The Ottoman Empire, which stretched from southeastern Europe to western Asia, joined Germany and Austria in the war. Major battles, including the Battle of Gallipoli, were fought in the Ottoman Empire. Arab nationalists seized the opportunity to rebel against the Ottoman government. They, too, wanted self-government.

War Spreads to Colonies. Africa and the Pacific also became battlegrounds. The colonial powers of Europe attacked their enemies' colonies in these regions. Japan joined the war and seized Germany's Pacific colonies.

The British and French recruited troops throughout their vast empires. Soldiers from India, Australia, New Zealand, China, and Canada joined British troops in the European conflict. France conscripted soldiers from Vietnam and West Africa.

Involvement of the United States. The United States tried to isolate itself from the war. But its attempt to remain neutral was not successful. German submarines attacked U.S. ships. This angered Americans, who began to favor joining Britain and France in the war. In 1917, a secret message from the German government to the government of Mexico was revealed. Germany proposed a German-Mexican alliance against the United States. Angered by the German threat, the United States entered the war as an ally of Britain, France, and Russia. The Great War had truly become a global war.

New Weapons

The factories of Europe used the latest technologies to develop new weapons of war.

Submarines, Guns, and Tanks. Submarines were used on a large scale for the first time in World War I. Machine guns were developed and widely used in the fighting. Tanks were introduced by the British, and soon used by the Germans as well. Long-range cannons (big guns) were technically improved. They were now able to shoot larger shells for longer distances.

Airplanes. World War I was the first time that airplanes were used in a war. Initially, they were used for observation. Soon, however, they were converted into bombers. When machine guns were mounted on the planes, a new kind of fighting was born. So-called dogfights were battles between competing pilots who tried to shoot each other out of the sky.

An airplane "dogfight" between opposing sides in World War I

Poison Gas. Probably the most feared new weapon was poison gas. Several kinds of gas were used by both sides in the war. Some gases caused skin to blister. Others caused blindness, while still others caused suffocation or choking.

New Style of Warfare

The typical World War I soldier found himself living and fighting in a trench. Hundreds of miles of trenches, or furrows, were dug into the soil between

Soldiers in the trenches in World War I

France and Germany. Trench warefare was especially unpleasant for the soldier. The trenches were muddy and damp. Soldiers got trench foot, a condition in which the skin on the feet rotted away. Rats infested the trenches. Disease was rampant due to poor sanitation. Fresh food and medicine were in short supply. Sleep under these conditions was very difficult.

Battles began with heavy shelling that could last for hours. The attacking army then went "over the top." The soldiers climbed out of their trenches and raced across the "no-man's land" (the area between the trenches) and attacked the enemy. The casualty rate from this kind of fighting was staggering.

Total War

The Great War was different in yet another way. it was a total war—that is, it affected more than just the military personnel who fought. It also changed the lives of civilians on the home front. The fighting countries used every available resource to support the war effort. Rationing was common in all fighting countries. Americans were urged to grow their own food in "victory gardens." Factories in Europe were bombed. Homes and farms were destroyed, and many civilians lost their lives. By the end of the war, the dead (military and civilian) totaled an estimated 15 million people.

Test Yourself
In what ways was World War I different from previous wars?

★ SHORT-TERM RESULTS OF THE WAR ★

As World War I came to a close in 1918, Allied leaders tried to find ways to make a lasting peace.

Paris Peace Conference

On November 11, 1918, representatives of France and Germany signed an armistice that ended the fighting. A few months later, representatives of 27 victorious nations held the Paris Peace Conference to negotiate peace treaties, one with each of the defeated nations. The major decision-makers were David Lloyd George of Britain, Georges Clemenceau of France, Woodrow Wilson of the United States, and Vittorio Orlando of Italy. The victors did not allow Germany to take part in the negotiations.

Treaty of Versailles. The Paris Peace Conference resulted in the Treaty of Versailles, the peace treaty with Germany. Many historians see this document as fundamentally flawed and a direct cause of World War II. The *war-guilt clause* of the treaty blamed Germany for causing the war. The Germans were required to pay reparations (huge sums of money) to the victorious allies for the war's costs. Germany lost its colonies and also lost land to France and Poland. Germany's air force was eliminated, and its army and navy were reduced to small, defensive forces.

Other Consequences of the Conference. The delegates to the Paris Peace Conference changed the maps of Europe and the Middle East. The Austro-Hungarian Empire and the Ottoman Empire were broken up. Russia, which had left the war early, lost territory. After the war, new countries were formed, including Finland, Estonia, Latvia, Lithuania, Poland, Czechoslovakia, Hungary, Yugoslavia, and Turkey. Iraq, Palestine, Syria, Lebanon, and Jordan (formed from the old Ottoman Empire) became *mandates* (colonies recognized by the League of Nations) of Britain and France.

League of Nations. One seemingly positive result of the peace conference was a new international organization, the League of Nations. Its purpose was to prevent wars and keep the peace through the process of collective security. This meant that its members would defend one another against attack. As you will learn, the League did not live up to its promise.

Flaws of the Conference. The Paris Peace Conference did not solve the problems that existed before the war. In fact, it created new ones. Colonial territories did not gain their independence. Austria, Hungary, Italy, and other nations did not get all the territories that they wanted. The United States, the number-one world power, did not sign the treaty. Instead, for years the United States took an *isolationist* stand. It avoided foreign commitments. The Treaty of Versailles embittered the German people. They especially resented the war-guilt clause and the obligation to pay reparations.

The Russian Revolution

Another direct result of World War I was revolution in Russia. Two successive revolutions in 1917 transformed Russia from an absolute monarchy into a Communist dictatorship.

Russia was one of the world's industrial and military powers. During World War I, it was a Triple Entente ally of Britain and France against Germany and the Austro-Hungarian empire. Although Russia had a large army, it was unsuccessful in fighting the war.

Russia's Czarist Government. Russia had many problems. Its government, which was ruled by hereditary monarchs known as *czars*, was its biggest problem. A czar was an *autocratic* ruler. This means that he had almost unlimited powers over the people who were his subjects. For centuries, the autocratic czars had ruled Russia with force. They used secret police to put down dissent. Freedom of speech and the press were limited, and published materials were censored. They oppressed some non-Russian citizens and discouraged minority languages and customs. Laws were passed that encouraged persecution of various ethnic and religious minorities, especially Jews.

Growing Unrest. In the early 20th century, many Russians called for reforms. Factory workers wanted better working conditions and better pay. Peasants wanted a higher standard of living. The middle class wanted political power. Russia desperately needed economic, political, and social reforms. But the czarist government made only a few reforms. People seeking far-reaching changes organized to demand more.

Russia During World War I. In 1914, Czar Nicholas II led his country into war. Russia was unprepared for war and suffered many early defeats. In the first year of fighting, 4 million Russian soldiers died. The czar decided to take matters into his own hands. He left the Russian capital, Petrograd, and moved to the German front to direct the army. Nevertheless, Russia's military fortunes continued to decline. The number of defeats mounted, and many soldiers deserted. The war was a complete disaster.

Nicholas left his wife, Czarina Alexandra, in charge of the government. Alexandra believed even more fervently in absolute rule than Nicholas did. Grigory Rasputin, a mysterious, self-proclaimed holy man, encouraged her beliefs. He exercised a great deal of influence over the czarina. Rasputin seemed to have the power to help her son, who suffered from the blood disease hemophilia.

Bolsheviks. With the czar's absence and the evil influence of Rasputin, the government became more inept and corrupt. Inflation and food shortages occurred. War casualties mounted. The time was ripe for revolution.

Several revolutionary groups formed to oppose the Russian government. One of these groups, the Bolsheviks, wanted to establish a Communist government based on the ideas of Karl Marx. The leader of the Bolsheviks was Vladimir Ilych Ulyanov, who adopted the name Lenin. Lenin was well-educated, an excellent organizer, and a dynamic speaker. A true revolutionary, he was not afraid to deal harshly with those who stood in his way. During the early war years, Lenin lived in exile in neutral Switzerland. He waited for the day when he could return to Russia and lead a revolution. It was to come soon.

March Revolution. In March 1917, 200,000 workers demonstrated in the streets of Petrograd. The workers were soon joined by soldiers. This protest led to a revolution that forced the czar to abdicate (give up his throne).

The end of czarist government created a political vacuum in Russia. A provisional government set up offices in the former winter palace of the czars. A legislature, known as the Duma, became the center of the new government of Russia. It appointed a cabinet of ministers to run the country. Unfortunately, Prime Minister Alexander Kerensky was a weak and ineffective leader. The provisional government could not solve any of Russia's economic and social problems. It increased its unpopularity with the Russian people by continuing to fight the war.

Kerensky's government faced strong opposition from self-appointed local councils known as soviets. Peasants, workers, and soldiers each had their own soviets. By the fall of 1917, the soviets had become a powerful political force. The Bolsheviks dominated key soviets in Moscow and Petrograd. These called for land reform, enough food for the people, and peace.

In hopes of creating more unrest in Russia, German leaders put Lenin on a train and sent him back to Russia. This plan was hugely successful.

November Revolution. In November 1917, Bolshevik soldiers known as the Red Guards stormed government offices in Petrograd. The revolution soon

Communist leader Vladimir Lenin addressing Russian soldiers

spread to other cities, the countryside, and the army. After leaders of the provisional government were arrested, the Bolsheviks became the new rulers of Russia. They quickly outlawed most opposition parties.

Lenin and the Bolsheviks ended the war with Germany, but at a high price. In the Treaty of Brest-Litovsk (1918), Russia gave up much of its empire to Germany.

The Bolsheviks seized large rural estates and redistributed the land among the peasants. Factories were *nationalized* (taken over by the government). Czar Nicholas and his family were executed, as were leaders of opposition political parties.

Civil War (1918–1921). In 1918, Russia was still in turmoil. Lenin and the Bolsheviks had seized power but were not supported by all Russians. With aid from the United States and other Allied nations, some opponents of the Bolsheviks fought against the new government. In 1918, the White Army of the opposition began a civil war to take back control from the Bolsheviks. Three years later, the fighting ended with the victorious Bolsheviks firmly in control. They had crushed all domestic opposition groups and ousted the Allies. Almost 15 million people died in the fighting. Now Lenin and the Bolsheviks faced a new task—the job of governing the vast country.

The Soviet Union. In 1922, Russia was reorganized into the Union of Soviet Socialist Republics. The USSR, or Soviet Union, was a federation of 15 individual republics. Each was known as a soviet republic, a reference to the revolutionary councils of the Russian revolution. A Communist government was established to govern this union of republics, and Moscow became the new national capital. Lenin ruled the nation as a dictator. By the time of his death in 1924, Lenin had transformed Russia from an absolute monarchy into a Communist dictatorship.

Joseph Stalin. One of Lenin's Bolshevik followers was a man who called himself Joseph Stalin. Stalin means "man of steel." The name fit. Like Lenin,

Stalin was intelligent and calculating. But Stalin was cruder and more vicious than Lenin.

After the Russian civil war, Stalin established himself in the Soviet government. He eventually became the head of the Communist party, the only political party allowed in the Soviet Union. He put his friends in key positions of power. By 1929, Stalin had complete control of the Communist party and the government of the Soviet Union.

Stalin employed ruthless tactics to maintain his power. He used secret police to spy on citizens. Phone lines and private mail were monitored. Children were encouraged to inform school and government authorities about any disloyal actions of their parents. Schools and universities were used as propaganda tools to promote loyalty to the state. Military force was used to put down strikes and other protests. Churches were destroyed, and those who practiced their faith were persecuted.

Under Stalin, the Soviet government took total control over every aspect of public and private life. This system is called *totalitarianism*. All farms still privately owned were seized by the government and reorganized into *collective farms*. These collectives were owned and operated by the government. Formerly independent farmers became employees of the state. Those who resisted *collectivization* (the formation of collective farms out of private ones) were killed, tortured, or sent off to prison camps. To make matters worse, during the 1930s, millions died of starvation because of poor crops and the food shortages that resulted. Also in the 1930s, Stalin put thousands of people on trial for disloyalty to his government. These *purges* of the Communist party, the government, and the military resulted in the execution of many more Soviet citizens.

Test Yourself
What were the causes of the Russian Revolution?

★ LONG-TERM RESULTS OF WORLD WAR I ★

It was difficult to calculate the loss of life and property that resulted from the Great War. This devastation caused such instability throughout the world that attempts to effect a lasting peace proved totally inadequate.

World Forum. At the Paris Peace Conference, U.S. President Woodrow Wilson pushed for the creation of the League of Nations. The Treaty of Versailles contained provisions for its establishment. In theory, the League of Nations would prevent war by providing a world forum to discuss international problems. The League was also supposed to work toward disarmament. Unfortunately, members of the U.S. Senate rejected it because they felt that it would take away Congress's power to declare war. Therefore, the United States, one of the world's most important leaders, never joined. Without U.S. membership, the League, which had other weaknesses, could not enforce any of its decisions. (More failures of the League are discussed below.)

Kellogg-Briand Pact. Another attempt to prevent wars was the Kellogg-Briand Pact (1928). French Foreign Minister Aristide Briand and U.S.

Secretary of State Frank Kellogg had the idea for this agreement. Most nations of the world signed the pact, promising to "renounce war as an instrument of national policy." This idea sounded good, but like the resolutions of the League of Nations, the Kellogg-Briand Pact could not be enforced.

More Postwar Problems

Loss of life was not the only cost of World War I. The loss of property and the tremendous costs of fighting the war led to financial collapse. Most of the nations of Europe were economically devastated by the conflict. The nation that suffered the most was Germany.

During the war, Germany had simply printed more money to finance its war efforts. Terms of the Treaty of Versailles added to the debt it had incurred by this measure. The reparations Germany owed the Allies increased its economic woes. By the early 1920s, its economy had collapsed. To pay its debts, the German government printed even more paper money. This caused *inflation* (a steady rise in prices). Money became worthless. Wheelbarrows full of paper money were necessary to purchase basic necessities. American loans and investments helped somewhat to improve the German situation.

German inflation in the 1920s: burning worthless banknotes for fuel

Boom and Bust in the United States. The United States did much better financially than the rest of the world in the 1920s. American business greatly expanded. This period of economic boom brought wealth and power to the

United States and prosperity to many (but not all) Americans. U.S. investments and trade helped the struggling economies of much of the world.

Americans thought this economic boom would never end. But the U.S. economy had some serious underlying problems. First, it was actually producing too many goods. By the end of the 1920s, surpluses in agriculture and industry were lowering prices. Some factories had to shut down, and many farms had to be sold to pay debts.

A second problem was the unequal distribution of wealth. The gap between the richest 5 percent of Americans and the rest of society grew wider.

As a result of overproduction and unequal distribution of wealth, prices began to fall. Unemployment increased, leading to more farm and business failures. The stock market crash of 1929 led to the Great Depression—a time when banks closed and many people were unemployed.

Worldwide Depression. The failure of the U.S. economy had a global impact. All over the world, trade decreased, unemployment increased, and business activity slowed dramatically. This drastic slowing of the global economy, or worldwide *depression*, affected Europe, Asia, and Latin America. The global depression created social unrest in many countries. Some nations turned to socialism, while others like the United States and Great Britain made changes within the capitalist system. They gave their governments more control over their economies.

Rise of Militarist and Totalitarian States

Other countries—especially Japan, Italy, and Germany—took more drastic measures.

Japan. Like many other countries, Japan was devastated by the global depression of the 1930s. Widespread crop failures there led to famine. Many Japanese people blamed their government for the crisis. Military leaders gained popular support when they promised to restore Japan's economy. The militarists' support of the popular Emperor Hirohito also appealed to the Japanese people. Once the militarists had seized political power, their leaders began a program of territorial expansion. The rationale for this expansion into East Asia and the Pacific was that it would provide Japan with raw materials for its factories and create markets for finished industrial products.

Italy. Meanwhile, in Italy, the global depression created a political power struggle that was won by the Fascists. *Fascism* is a form of government that promotes extreme nationalism, devotion to an authoritarian leader, and one-party rule. Government becomes the ally of wealthy aristocrats, large landowners, and owners of big businesses.

The leader of the Fascist party was Benito Mussolini. Wearing a military uniform in public, he spoke at mass rallies to gather support for his government. An enthusiastic orator, Mussolini promised that Italy would return to the glory days of the Roman Empire. This goal, he claimed, would be achieved by building up Italy's industrial power and by military conquest abroad.

Mussolini took power in 1922, when 33,000 Fascists marched on Rome, the Italian capital. The Italian king, Victor Emmanuel III, was forced to declare Mussolini the legitimate leader of Italy. Mussolini took the title Il Duce, or "the Leader." The Fascists established a totalitarian state. They outlawed all other political parties, seized radio stations and newspapers, and set up a secret police force.

Germany. As you have read, Germany faced economic and political instability in the years after World War I. Like Italy, Germany turned to a Fascist government to solve its problems. The National Socialist German Workers' Party, or Nazi party, was formed in Munich in the years after the war. The Nazis were anti-Communist and strongly opposed to the Treaty of Versailles, which they saw as the source of Germany's problems. The Nazis adopted the swastika—a stylized cross—as their symbol; they dressed in brown, military-style shirts. The leader of the Nazis was an Austrian named Adolf Hitler.

Hitler was a school dropout and a failed painter. He had fought for Germany during World War I and had been highly decorated for bravery. After the war, he settled in Munich, where he became the leader of the Nazi party.

In 1923, the Nazis attempted an overthrow of the German government. Hitler was arrested and sent to prison. While there, he wrote an autobiography called *Mein Kampf (My Struggle)*. In the book, Hitler outlined his ideas and plans for Germany. He claimed that pure-blooded Germanic people were descended from an ancient race called the Aryans and were destined to be a "master race." Aryan Germans would rule over other groups, he said. He considered Jews, Gypsies, and Slavic peoples to be inferior races. Hitler's plan was for Germany to win back territories taken away by the Treaty of Versailles and to conquer new lands. The new lands would be needed, he claimed, for German expansion, or *lebensraum* (growing room).

COMPARISON OF COMMUNISM AND FASCISM

POLITICAL PHILOSOPHY	COMMUNISM	FASCISM
Leader	dictator/authoritarian	dictator/authoritarian
Political Parties	one-party rule; totalitarian	one-party rule; totalitarian
Rights of Citizens	individual rights denied; use of secret police	individual rights denied: use of secret police
Social Classes	classless society	favored upper classes
Goals	unite all workers around the world	promote national interests; extreme nationalism

By the early 1930s, the Nazis had become the largest political party in Germany. The Nazis used their political power to get Hitler appointed chancellor, the chief executive of the German government.

Once in office, Hitler established himself as dictator and outlawed all political parties but the Nazi party. Hitler ordered his personal guard, the SS, to eliminate all opposition to Nazi rule. The SS became even stronger when it joined the Gestapo, the political police force. The Nazis used schools, newspapers, radio, the arts, and even churches to gather support for Hitler and his policies. In public rallies, they burned books that questioned Nazi beliefs. They openly attacked Jews, other minorities, and Communists.

Germany began to prepare for war. The Treaty of Versailles forbade Germany to build up its armed forces, but Hitler boldly announced that he would defy the treaty. When no one tried to stop him, he was encouraged to take further actions.

★ THE COMING OF WORLD WAR II ★

The world was now ripe for an even more disastrous war than World War I. At first the democratic nations were reluctant to fight another war. Soon, however, they realized that the conflict was necessary to save Western civilization from fascism.

The Policy of Appeasement

Hitler began to look to other nations for more territory. In 1936, Germany reoccupied the Rhineland. The Rhineland was an industrial area on Germany's border with France and Belgium. The Treaty of Versailles had forced Germany to withdraw all its military forces from the Rhineland. It was to be a buffer zone between France and Germany. Hitler decided to reoccupy this area, a gamble that paid off. Fearing war, France and Britain decided not to send in troops to enforce this provision of the Versailles Treaty. Instead, they gave in to Hitler in hopes of stopping further aggression. This policy is known as appeasement.

The inaction of Britain and France increased Hitler's popularity in Germany. At the same time, it placed France in a more vulnerable position: It could more easily be attacked by the German army. Hitler felt free to carry out his plan for *lebensraum*.

In March 1938, the German army marched into Austria. Hitler announced that Austria had been annexed (added) to Germany. Austria ceased to exist as an independent country. Again, no country stepped in to oppose Hitler's act of aggression.

Hitler was not done. He announced that he also wanted to annex the Sudetenland, a part of Czechoslovakia where several million German-speaking people lived. Czechoslovakia called on its ally France for help. The Munich Conference was held on September 29, 1938, to discuss Hitler's intention. Present were the leaders of Germany, Italy, France, and Britain. Britain and France decided to allow Germany to have the Sudetenland in exchange for Hitler's promise to stop further territorial expansion. Upon returning home, British Prime Minister Neville Chamberlain triumphantly announced that the Munich agreement would bring "peace for our time." Six months later, Germany seized the rest of Czechoslovakia. Appeasement had not worked.

Axis aggression in Europe and
Africa in the 1930s

German troops occupy Prague in 1939.

Japanese Aggression

Japan, too, was looking for growing room. It looked to China's northern province of Manchuria as an area in which to expand. Japanese industrialists wanted its rich deposits of iron ore and coal. The Japanese army seized Manchuria in 1931 and established a pro-Japanese government there. Protests were made at the League of Nations, but it took no action that would stop Japan.

Relations between Japan and China were strained. A minor incident in 1937 quickly developed into open warfare. Chinese and Japanese soldiers exchanged fire at a bridge near the Chinese city of Beijing. The Japanese army used the shootings as an excuse to take over much of China. Although outnumbered, the Japanese army was well-equipped, well-trained, and efficient. Japanese soldiers swept through China, torturing and killing thousands.

Italian Expansion

Benito Mussolini sought prestige for Italy by setting up overseas colonies. Mussolini decided to begin his dream of a new Roman Empire by colonizing Africa. Ethiopia was one of the few independent nations of Africa. In 1935, Italy invaded Ethiopia and quickly conquered it. When Haile Selassie, the Emperor of Ethiopia, appealed to the League of Nations for help, the League voted only for sanctions against Italy. No one took military action against Italy. Britain's and France's policy for Mussolini was the same as their policy for Hitler: appeasement.

Alliances During World War II

Axis Powers. In 1936, Italy and Germany formed a pact to oppose communism. Then Japan and Germany created another pact against the Soviet Union. In 1937, the three powers signed an agreement of friendship and alliance. Called the *Axis powers*, they united against communism and democracy.

Allies. In 1939, German forces attacked Poland. France and Britain, allies that had guaranteed Polish independence, declared war on Germany. The next year, the German army swept across France, soon forcing the French to surrender. British forces were pushed back to the sea at Dunkirk, where they were rescued by a cooperative effort of sailors and civilians. The British now stood alone against Hitler, who tried to bomb them into submission. Britain's air defense of its skies, called the Battle of Britain, prevented Hitler from moving ahead with plans for an invasion. Germany and Italy attacked North Africa, then Yugoslavia and Greece. In 1941, Germany attacked the Soviet Union—an action that resulted in the Soviets and British becoming allies. Japanese forces bombed the U.S. base in Pearl Harbor. Soon the Allies (Britain, the Soviet Union, the United States, and 24 other nations) were all fighting against the Axis powers and their allies.

Test Yourself
How were the causes of the World War II related to the results of World War I?

POINTS TO REMEMBER

- Causes of World War I included nationalism, imperialism, militarism, and alliances.

- Important short-term results of World War I included the Russian Revolution, the breakup of the Ottoman Empire and the Austro-Hungarian Empire, the formation of the League of Nations, and German resentment of the terms set by the Treaty of Versailles.

- Long-term results of the war included: the failure of the League of Nations and other measures to keep peace; economic depression in Germany; and the rise of totalitarian states in Europe and Asia.

- Conditions in Europe after World War I set the stage for World War II. These included the worldwide economic depression and the formation of militarist and totalitarian states.

EXERCISES

CHECKING WHAT YOU HAVE READ

1. All of the following were multinational empires in 1914 except

   A. Poland
   B. Austria-Hungary
   C. Russia
   D. the Ottomans.

2. At the start of World War I, all of the following were members of the Triple Entente except

   A. Germany
   B. Great Britain
   C. France
   D. Russia.

3. When World War I began in 1914, what did the United States do at first?

   A. It tried to isolate itself from the war and did not take sides.
   B. It supported Germany and Austria.
   C. It attacked Russia.
   D. It declared war on Germany.

4. Which one of the following weapons was not first widely used during World War I?

   A. tank
   B. rifle
   C. airplane
   D. poison gas

5. The term "total war" refers to which of the following?

   A. the vast supplies of new weapons
   B. the fighting on all continents
   C. the tremendous costs in money and lives
   D. the involvement of civilians on the home front

6. World War I had all of the following consequences for Russia except

   A. early victories increased the patriotism of the Russian people
   B. the war weakened Russia socially and economically
   C. Russia experienced two revolutions
   D. the war helped make Russia a world power.

7. Which of the following events came last?

   A. the March Revolution
   B. the November Revolution
   C. the Russian Civil War
   D. beginning of World War I

8. Lenin, leader of the Bolsheviks, is best describe as a

   A. czarist
   B. militarist
   C. Communist
   D. Fascist.

9. Which of the following countries experienced an economic boom during the 1920s?

   A. Germany
   B. France
   C. Russia
   D. United States

10. The German term *lebensraum* refers to

    A. loyalty to the state
    B. growing room
    C. Jews and other non-Aryans
    D. Germany's alliance with Italy.

USING WHAT YOU HAVE READ

1. On a piece of paper, create a spider's web with the title "Causes of World War I." Start by drawing a circle; label the circle "World War I." Around the circle, write the causes of the war. From each cause, draw an arrow pointing toward your circle.

2. Pretend you are a German citizen after World War I. Create a "Wanted" poster for the Treaty of Versailles. Be sure that your poster clearly shows why the treaty was a disaster for Germany.

THINKING ABOUT WHAT YOU HAVE READ

1. Write a note comparing and contrasting communism and fascism and give it to a classmate. Be sure to include examples of each characteristic. For example, you might cite Hitler and Stalin as examples of authoritarian leaders.

2. Some historians have said that World War II was simply a continuation of World War I. Do you agree or disagree with this statement? Explain your answer.

SKILLS

Interpreting a Speech

After Italy attacked Ethiopia in 1935, Ethiopian Emperor Haile Selassie spoke to some of his troops before they marched off to war. Read the speech below and answer the questions that follow.

It is not the Emperor who wants war but the Italians who are pushing the fight. We will all die one day, either by typhus or pneumonia, but it is much better to die for our country.

The Italians will try to repulse you with machine guns. They have machine guns, but we have God on our side.

We urge you not to fight in the traditional old way of massing against the enemy. Guard against hot-headedness, because if the enemy discovers you in angry groups he will burn you as wood in a blaze. . . . If you see an airplane, leave the open spaces and hide in the forest. All soldiers with good guns should then shoot at the plane. When fighting begins you will be within range of the Italian guns. Divest yourselves of shields and spears, because they will form a brilliant target.

Do not wash your *shammas* (men's white, cotton wraparounds). Allow them to become dirty and therefore less visible. When we have defeated the invader you may again take up your shields and don clean clothes.

Comrades, I shall be with you on the battlefield to shed my blood freely with yours in defense of our common fatherland. We shall accept no such peace terms as those France proposes. I shall die with you if necessary rather than submit to such humiliation.

1. What kinds of weapons were the Italians expected to use in battle?

2. What evidence suggests that the Ethiopian fighters were not as well equipped as the Italians?

3. What other evidence suggests that the Ethiopians were not ready for a modern war with Italy?

4. How did the speaker appeal to the emotions of the Ethiopian warriors?

CHAPTER 5

WORLD WAR II, THE COLD WAR, AND CONTEMPORARY CONFLICTS

BENCHMARK:

Analyze connections between World War II, the Cold War, and contemporary conflicts.

To meet this benchmark, you must be able to relate World War II to world events that followed. You must recognize the importance of the Cold War and explain how it influenced most political events of the second half of the 20th century. You must also be able to discuss how the remnants of 19th-century imperialism have shaped political events of recent decades.

★ THE CONSEQUENCES OF WORLD WAR II ★

There were many major consequences of World War II for all countries, even those that did not participate in the war.

Nuclear Weapons

Although Japan faced defeat in the summer of 1945, it refused to surrender. On August 6, 1945, the crew of the *Enola Gay*, a B-29 bomber, dropped a deadly new weapon, the atomic bomb, over the Japanese city of Hiroshima. The explosion killed about 80,000 people almost immediately. Everything in the most immediate area of the blast (one-half mile in diameter) was vaporized. In a range of one mile in diameter all structures above ground were destroyed and 90 percent of all living creatures were killed.

Ironically, U.S. President Harry Truman had ordered the use of this new weapon to save lives. His military advisers had informed the president that their planned invasion of Japan would probably result in the deaths of 500,000 U.S. military personnel. In order to prevent these deaths, Truman ordered the dropping of the bombs. He hoped that their impact would break the resistance of the Japanese leaders. Less than a month after the bombings, Japan formally surrendered to the United States. World War II had ended.

The long-term results of developing and using atomic weapons on Japan were no less dramatic. Atomic explosions release *radiation*, which causes sickness and alters the genetic makeup of both plants and animals. It can also make the ground *sterile*, unable to support life. After the war, thousands more Japanese died as a result of the radiation.

The United States' use of the atomic bomb had another result: It stimulated the leaders of the Soviet Union to build their own weapons of mass destruction. In 1949, the Soviets tested their first atomic bomb. In 1952, the United States tested a *hydrogen bomb*, a weapon much more powerful than the atomic bomb. In 1953, the Soviet Union did the same. The nuclear arms race had begun.

The Holocaust and Jewish Immigration to Palestine

In the last months of the war in Europe, soldiers from the United States, Britain, France, and the Soviet Union swept into Central Europe. In Poland, Germany, and elsewhere these Allied forces found concentration camps that had been set up by the Germans. They used these to confine Jews, Slavs, Gypsies, Communists, homosexuals, and people afflicted with various kinds of disabilities. The Germans turned these people into forced laborers. In some camps, most of the people were murdered. Those camps whose sole purpose was to kill were called *death camps*. Up to 11 million people died, either by murder or by disease and starvation. Some 6 million of these were Jews. The deliberate policy of the German government to try to wipe out Jews, Gypsies, and other groups in Europe is called the Holocaust. (The Holocaust is discussed further in Chapter 7.)

Many Jews in Europe were able to avoid confinement in concentration camps. Thousands escaped Nazi-controlled Europe and immigrated to other countries and lands. Many went to Palestine, which had been the Jews' homeland thousands of years ago. Ever since the late 19th century, leaders of a movement called *Zionism* had been urging Jews to move to Palestine. (The consequences of the return of the Jews to Palestine are discussed in Chapter 6.)

Costs of War

War Casualties. No other war in the history of the world has been as destructive to human life as World War II. The cost in human lives can never be fully determined. Estimates place the number killed at 30 million persons.

Economic Costs. The economic costs of the war also can only be estimated. Some historians estimate the total monetary cost to be $1 trillion. The United States spent about $341 billion, including the money lent to its allies. The full extent of looting (stealing valuables and money) done by the Nazis and other combatants is unknown. Newspapers today still occasionally have stories about recent discoveries of artwork, gold, and other valuables stolen during the war. The costs of the destruction of buildings, highways, railways, and other structures are nearly impossible to determine. The economies of many European and Asian nations were destroyed. Rebuilding to prewar conditions took many years.

Refugees. The war also displaced millions of people. Those who lost their homes, possessions, and jobs faced famine, poverty, and despair. The Allies set up relief agencies to help these refugees. Some displaced people were able to emigrate from Europe to more prosperous countries such as the United States, Canada, and Australia.

The United Nations

The victorious Allies of World War II revived an old idea for keeping peace by establishing an international peacekeeping organization called the United Nations. Representatives of 50 nations met in San Francisco during the spring of 1945 to sign the UN Charter. On October 25, 1945, the United Nations was born. Since then, most independent nations have joined the organization. Today, UN membership exceeds 190 nations.

As you read in Chapter 4, U.S. President Woodrow Wilson presented a similar idea when he recommended the formation of the League of Nations at the 1919 Paris Peace Conference. During World War II, U.S. President Franklin D. Roosevelt and British Prime Minister Winston Churchill met aboard a battleship in the Atlantic. There they signed the Atlantic Charter, a list of Allied goals for fighting World War II. One of the stated goals was creating an organization called the United Nations.

Like its predecessor the League of Nations, the basic purpose of the United Nations is to preserve world peace. The UN acts as a forum for nations to settle their conflicts without resorting to war or to other acts of violence. Unlike the League of Nations, UN member nations provide military personnel to settle disputes and keep the peace. This military option, together with a stronger executive branch, has made the UN much more effective than the League of Nations.

The UN consists of hundreds of agencies that deal with potential sources of conflict. These agencies deal with such problems as human rights, disease, poverty, hunger, and environmental pollution. UN officials hope that by addressing these problems, political conflicts can be avoided.

The UN Charter describes six different bodies or parts of the organization. Each body was given a distinctive purpose. The six parts were the General Assembly, the Security Council, the Secretariat, the Economic and Social Council, the International Court of Justice, and the Trusteeship Council. The Trusteeship Council is no longer active.

General Assembly. This body consists of representatives of all member nations. The General Assembly meets annually from September through December, and at other times as needed. An elected president presides over its discussions and debates. Votes are taken on various issues. Each nation has one vote. Most issues require a simple majority, but a two-thirds majority is needed for the most important decisions. Decisions of the General Assembly are not binding. Instead, the votes serve as recommendations. The real value of voting is that it gives the UN members a chance to sway world opinion and to influence the Security Council.

Security Council. This body is the seat of power in the United Nations structure. The Security Council consists of 15 members. Ten of them are selected by the General Assembly to serve two-year terms. The five other members have permanent seats on the council: the United States, Russia, Great Britain, France, and China. Each of the five permanent members has veto power over any decision made by the Security Council.

The decisions of the Security Council are binding on all UN member nations. The council listens to grievances brought by any nation, responds to global conflicts, and tries to maintain world peace. It does this through persuasion, mediation, and (if necessary) the use of military force. UN troops have been used in Europe, Asia, and Africa.

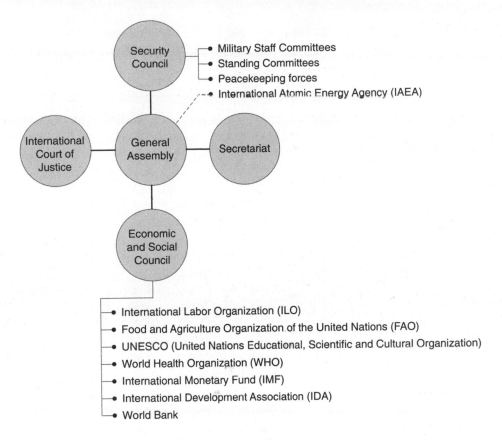

Present-day organization of the United Nations

Secretariat. The executive body of the United Nations is called the Secretariat. Consisting of administrators, bureaucrats, and technical experts, the Secretariat carries out the policies of the United Nations.

The chief executive of the Secretariat has the title of secretary general. This person oversees the day-to-day operation of all UN agencies. He or she works closely with the Security Council but also acts alone as a mediator in disputes among nations. The secretary general is chosen by the General Assembly with the recommendation of the Security Council. He or she serves for a renewable five-year term. Traditionally, the position of secretary general rotates geographically every two terms. Secretary General Kofi Annan (appointed in 1997) is from Ghana; his predecessors include Javier Pérez de Cuéllar of Peru and Boutros Boutros-Ghali of Egypt.

Economic and Social Council. This body oversees 14 specialized UN agencies and various commissions. The purpose of the Economic and Social Council (ECOSOC) is to help solve problems of poverty, hunger, and disease. It promotes higher standards of living, human rights, literacy, education, employment, economic development, and cultural exchanges. About 70 percent of the total UN budget is allocated to the agencies and commissions of ECOSOC.

International Court of Justice. This UN body is headquartered in The Hague, Netherlands. It settles legal disputes between nations and advises international organizations on legal matters. The General Assembly and the Security

Council elect the 15 court judges for terms of nine years each. Judges must be from different countries, but they are independent of any government control.

Normally, a 15-judge panel hears legal disputes. Legal proceedings include both written pleadings and oral arguments. All hearings and judgments are public. No appeals are allowed.

Cases heard by the court have included disputes over territory, maritime boundaries, diplomatic relations, the taking of hostages, rights of asylum, interference in the internal affairs of other nations, questions about nationality, and economic rights. In recent years, the court heard accusations of genocide in wartorn southeastern Europe.

Trusteeship Council. The final part of the UN structure was the Trusteeship Council. This UN body is now inactive. The purpose of the Trusteeship Council was to temporarily govern the territories that were not under the control of any nation. It also prepared those territories for independence and self-government. When Palau (a Pacific island administered by the United States) became independent in 1994, no trust territories remained under UN control. The functioning of the Trusteeship Council was suspended.

Birth of Israel

The British had controlled Palestine since the end of World War I. After World War II, Great Britain turned over control of Palestine to the United Nations. Jewish immigration to Palestine had increased dramatically before and after the war. British attempts to find a compromise between the demands of Arab Palestinians and Jewish settlers in Palestine were unsuccessful. Therefore, it was left to the United Nations to deal with the conflict. In 1947, the General Assembly decided to partition Palestine, creating independent Palestinian and Jewish states. The city of Jerusalem was to become an international city under no nation's jurisdiction.

On May 14, 1948, Israel declared itself to be an independent nation-state. Surrounding Arab nations immediately attacked Israel. Although that war was over in a few months, the conflict between Arabs and Israelis continues to this day. (This conflict is discussed further in Chapter 6.)

Test Yourself
How did the experiences of the Allies in World War II lead to the creation of the United Nations?

★ THE COLD WAR ★

The end of World War II brought about a new kind of conflict—the *Cold War*. This war was a clash of ideologies between the United States and the Soviet Union that lasted from 1945 to 1991. These countries had emerged as the two global *superpowers* (strongest powers) in the postwar years. They did not engage in a "hot war," or a war of open military conflict. It was a "cold war"

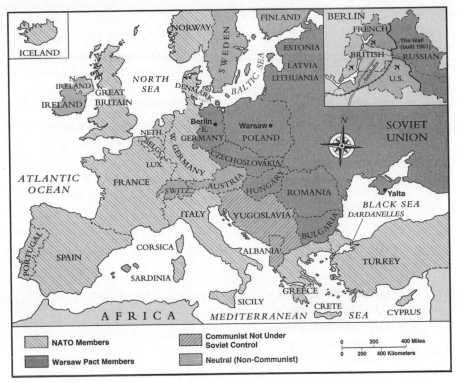

Cold War military alliances

because the two powers used words, diplomacy, propaganda, spying, and secret, hostile operations against each other. Both sides engaged in an arms race, in which they rushed to develop and build huge stockpiles of nuclear weapons.

Many of the nations of the world allied themselves with either the United States or the Soviet Union. The United States and its allies were known as the West; the Soviet Union and its allies, as the Eastern bloc. Nonaligned countries

The Cold War arms race

were sometimes referred to as the *Third World*. The term third world was also used for developing nations.

Although the two powers engaged in intense competition to gain the non-aligned countries as allies, they never fought directly with each other. Instead, each tried to induce these nonaligned countries to adopt its political and economic structure. The United States and the Soviet Union vied with one another to induce the new nations arising in Asia, Africa, Latin America, and the Middle East to adopt their respective ideologies by giving them economic aid and sending them technical assistance.

Sometimes, the Cold War heated up. The struggles over which ideology would prevail in Korea (1950–1953) and Vietnam (1965–1973) greatly increased the hostility between the United States and the Soviet Union. Both powers sent troops to those countries to help non-Communist factions fight Communist factions. But even in those instances, they never declared open war on each other.

Conflicting Goals of the Superpowers and the Division of Europe

Soon after the end of World War II, it became clear that Soviet and U.S. goals in Europe were vastly different.

Goals of the Soviet Union. Under the leadership of Joseph Stalin, the Soviet Union had the primary goal of protecting its territory from Western threats. Russia had been invaded in 1812 by Napoleonic France, and by Germany in the two world wars. At the close of World War II, Soviet troops took control of a number of East European countries: Poland, Czechoslovakia, Hungary, Romania, Bulgaria, and the eastern half of Germany. In each, Stalin set up a Communist government that would be loyal to the Soviet Union. He required these *satellite nations*, as they came to be called, to help support the Soviet economy. In case of a military threat, he expected them to act as a buffer between the Soviet Union and Western Europe. In addition, Stalin demanded that Germany be divided into two nations so that it could never again threaten the Russians.

Goals of the United States. U.S. goals for Europe were very different. The United States wanted European countries to have democratic governments so that it could count on their friendship. It also wanted them to have capitalist economies so that it could trade with them. To prevent the spread of communism in Europe, President Harry Truman began a foreign policy of *containment*. This policy aimed at containing Soviet influence and expansion. Instead of a divided Germany, the United States wanted a unified country that would be friendly to the West.

Division of Germany. As World War II was drawing to an end in Europe, Allied armies of the United States, Britain, and France marched into Germany from the west. At the same time, Soviet troops advanced into Germany from the east. The two forces joined together in the middle of Germany.

After peace was declared in Europe, Germany was divided into four zones of occupation. Each zone was to be controlled by one of the four Allied powers. The city of Berlin, which lay in the Soviet zone, was similarly divided into four areas. It soon became clear that a reunified Germany would not be possible.

The Soviets declared their zone (East Germany) to be an independent country—the German Democratic Republic. In 1949, Britain, France, and the United States joined their zones of occupation to form an independent, democratic country—the Federal Republic of Germany (West Germany). Germany and Europe were now divided between a democratic West and a Communist East. Former British Prime Minister Winston Churchill described this division as "an iron curtain" that divided the East and the West.

NATO and the Warsaw Pact

The division between East and West became more apparent with the formation of the North Atlantic Treaty Organization (NATO) in 1949. The United States created this military alliance along with 11 other Western nations: Belgium, Canada, Denmark, France, Iceland, Italy, Luxembourg, the Netherlands, Norway, Portugal, and the United Kingdom. Greece and Turkey joined the alliance in 1952; West Germany joined in 1955. NATO members pledged to go to one another's defense if attacked. These nations formed this alliance to protect one another from the Soviet Union. Members viewed the Soviet Union and its Communist satellites as threats to the peace and security of Europe.

Soviet Response. In response to NATO, the Soviet Union created its own defensive alliance, the Warsaw Pact, in 1955. Besides the Soviet Union, the Warsaw Pact nations were Albania, Bulgaria, Czechoslovakia, East Germany, Hungary, Poland, and Romania. Members of the Warsaw Pact viewed the United States and NATO as threats to their own security.

Chinese Communist Revolution

The Soviet Union was not the only Communist threat to the world. In the 1920s, Mao Zedong and his Communist followers began a revolution to take over China. During the 1930s, the Communists promised to distribute rich landowners' farmland to the peasants and improve education. This won them widespread support among the peasants. Opposing Mao in China were Jiang Jieshi (Chiang Kai-shek) and his Nationalist forces. The civil war between the Communists and the Nationalists was put on hold in 1937 when Japan invaded China. After the war with Japan ended in 1945, however, the Chinese civil war resumed.

The United States opposed the Chinese Communists and gave the Nationalists over $2 billion in aid. The Nationalists, however, were losing popular support. Meanwhile, the Communists over the period 1945–1948 gradually gained control over more and more territory. In 1949, Mao Zedong had enough of China under control to declare his government—the People's Republic of China—to be China's only legitimate one. Jiang Jieshi and the Nationalist forces fled to the island of Taiwan. With the help of the United States, Jiang set up a democratic government called Nationalist China.

Test Yourself
Why did the democratic nations oppose Mao Zedong in China after World War II?

★ INDEPENDENCE MOVEMENTS IN INDIA, INDOCHINA, AND AFRICA ★

The second half of the 20th century brought about a struggle against colonialism and imperialism. Colonial powers like Britain, France, Belgium, Portugal, and the Netherlands experienced a loss of control over their colonies. Independence movements swept through Africa, Asia, and the Pacific.

India

One of the world's largest colonies was India. British interests had controlled the Indian subcontinent for centuries. Then Mohandas Gandhi began an independence movement in 1920, which continued during World War II (1939–1945). After the war, Indian resistance grew even stronger. At the same time, some British people began to question the morality of having an empire. In 1947, the British Parliament granted independence to India. (India is discussed further in Chapter 6.)

Indochina

During the Age of Imperialism, France exerted its power over Southeast Asia. It set up a colony called Cochin China and the protectorates of Annam, Cambodia, Laos, and Tonkin. The five areas were joined in 1887 and 1893 to form French Indochina. Japanese forces overran Indochina in World War II. After the war, France decided to regain control of Indochina but at the same time to increase self-government in the area. Cambodia and Laos accepted this new status of federation with France. They were still controlled by France, but each had some authority over its affairs.

Ho Chi Minh, leader of the Vietnamese Communists

Vietnam. The people of Annam, Cochin China, and Tonkin wanted complete independence from France. Under Japanese occupation during World War II, these three areas had been allowed to join together to form the unified (but not independent) nation of Vietnam. When the war ended and the Japanese left, France wanted to regain control over Vietnam. From 1946 to 1954, there was bitter fighting between the French and the Viet Minh, a coalition party that favored Vietnamese independence. The Viet Minh was dominated by Communists. Its leader was Ho Chi Minh, who was supported by the Soviet Union and Communist China.

In May 1954, the French suffered a dramatic defeat at Dienbienphu. At the Geneva Peace Conference that followed, Vietnam was temporarily divided along the 17th parallel. North Vietnam was to be controlled by Ho Chi Minh and the Communists. A pro-French government was to be installed in South Vietnam. An election to decide on reunifying the nation was planned for 1956, but the South Vietnamese refused to participate. Since the election was never held, the country remained divided. The United States, France, and Great Britain recognized the pro-Western republic of South Vietnam. Its leader, Ngo Dinh Diem, used strong-arm tactics to put down opposition to the government. He limited freedom of the press and made mass arrests. Because of these actions, Diem was unpopular among the Vietnamese. Communist rebels (called the Viet Cong) fought against Diem in South Vietnam and soon controlled much of the countryside. In 1963, Diem was assassinated.

In 1964, the regular army of North Vietnam began to invade the South. Part of it traveled along a route known as the Ho Chi Minh Trail, which wound

The Vietnam War

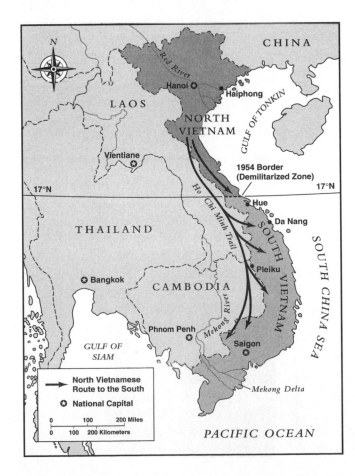

through the neighboring countries of Laos and Cambodia. Alarmed at the progress made by the Communists, the United States increased its support for South Vietnam, even though its government was unpopular and unstable. Hundreds of thousands of U.S. military personnel were sent to Vietnam to fight. In 1969, this figure reached its peak—543,000. Millions of U.S. dollars were used to prop up the failing economy of South Vietnam.

By 1968, the Vietnam War had become unpopular in the United States. Support for the war decreased as U.S. casualties increased. As a result, in 1969 the United States began a policy of *Vietnamization*. This plan included reducing the numbers of U.S. forces in Vietnam. It also involved turning the fighting over to South Vietnamese troops. Because the latter could not compete with the superior Communist forces, South Vietnam was overrun by Communist troops in 1975. North and South Vietnam were reunited under a Communist government.

Laos. France set up a protectorate over Laos in 1893. Like Vietnam, Laos was overrun by Japan during World War II. After the war, France installed a king in Laos but maintained control over the area, which was part of French Indochina.

A nationalist movement called the Pathet Lao fought against French control. It received support from the Soviet Union and North Vietnam. Meanwhile, the United States supported a pro-Western government in southern Laos. The Hmong, an ethnic minority in the mountain region of Laos, became a close ally of the United States. Many Hmong fought against the Pathet Lao.

During the Vietnam War, Laos was invaded by the North Vietnamese army and the Viet Cong. The United States bombed Communist strongholds in an attempt to stop Communist invasions of South Vietnam. In 1975, the Pathet Lao took control of Laos and set up a Communist government. It became a close ally of North Vietnam.

Today, Laos still has a Communist government, but it has a capitalist economy. Relations with the United States have greatly improved since 1975.

Cambodia. Cambodia was the home of the 6th-century A.D. Khmer Empire, a powerful political and cultural force in Southeast Asia. In 1863, France took over Cambodia and made it a protectorate. It became part of French Indochina in 1887. After World War II, Cambodia became semi-independent, remaining under French control. In 1953, Cambodia became an independent kingdom and was admitted to the United Nations two years later.

Like Laos, Cambodia became involved in the Vietnam War. Viet Cong and North Vietnamese troops used Cambodia as a supply base. The United States bombed various Communist strongholds there. At the same time, South Vietnamese troops invaded Cambodia to attack Communist bases. As warfare continued, the Cambodian Communists known as the Khmer Rouge dramatically increased their power. In 1975, the Khmer Rouge took over the country.

Under the leadership of Premier Pol Pot, Cambodia renamed itself Kampuchea. Pol Pot decided to create a rural, preindustrial society. The capital city of Phnom Penh and other urban areas were evacuated. People were forced to become agricultural workers. The government destroyed most automobiles, trucks, and industrial equipment. Businesspeople, industrialists, teachers, and other educated people were attacked. Almost 2 million people were brutally murdered in a government-sponsored program of genocide.

In 1978, Vietnam invaded Cambodia to stop the genocide. The United Nations took over Cambodia in 1992. In 1993, it held free elections for the first time. Today, Cambodia remains politically unstable.

Africa

Like the peoples of India and Indochina, those of Africa began to question colonial rule in the early 20th century. Africans who fought alongside European soldiers in World War II questioned the irony of fighting for political and social freedoms that were not granted them under colonial rule. In many African colonies, a powerful middle class emerged during the 20th century. Members of the middle class were educated and politically active. Some became the leaders of African movements for independence.

An example of one such leader is Kwame Nkrumah. He was born in the British colony of the Gold Coast, in West Africa. After attending universities in the United States and England, he returned to the Gold Coast to be a teacher in 1947. But soon he began to organize demonstrations, boycotts, and strikes against British authority. Although he was jailed many times, his efforts were ultimately successful. In 1957, the Gold Coast became the independent African nation of Ghana. It was the first sub-Saharan nation to gain independence from European colonial rule.

Nkrumah became Ghana's first prime minister. He later took the title "president for life," and became a virtual dictator (one-man government). His

Kwame Nkrumah announcing
Ghana's independence in 1957

government started many social reforms, such as building schools, providing better health care, and constructing highways. These programs, however, were expensive. Ghana's economy faltered, and Nkrumah lost popularity. In 1966, the Ghanaian military staged a *coup d'état* (overthrow of the government). Since then, the government has been overthrown several times. These frequent changes of government have kept the economy weak. In Ghana, as in many other former colonies of Africa, independence has brought about reforms and improvements. But it has also created political turmoil, social unrest, and economic instability.

Political unrest has been common throughout the continent of Africa since independence. Colonial economies were based on the exports of a few natural resources or the production of a specialized crop. For the most part, African governments have had difficulty developing industries capable of supporting an independent nation. Also, the political boundaries drawn by the European colonial powers often ignored cultural or ethnic divisions. This combination of factors made it extremely difficult for a newly independent nation to make a smooth transition to self-government. Democracy under those conditions is difficult. Often, newly independent African nations have turned away from representative government and have fallen into the hands of military dictators.

Test Yourself
What similar problems did Asian and African nations face after World War II?

★ FALL OF THE SOVIET UNION ★

Perhaps the most dramatic event since World War II has been the collapse of the Soviet Union and the end of the Cold War. For over 70 years, the Communist government of the Soviet Union maintained a totalitarian grip over its own people as well as over the people in its satellite nations. Political dissent was not tolerated, and human rights were not protected.

Causes of Soviet Collapse

The collapse of the Soviet Union had many causes. The desire of people to be prosperous and free was perhaps the most important. The arms race with the United States and weakening of the Soviet economy in the 1980s and 1990s made it possible for people to assert this desire.

Effect of the Arms Race. A chief cause of the collapse of the Soviet Union was the arms race with the United States and its effects on the Soviet economy. The United States enjoyed great economic prosperity in the second half of the 20th century. The American consumer had a wide range of choices in selecting food, clothing, housing, and entertainment. Americans enjoyed a high standard of living. The U.S. economy was able to meet consumer demands for goods and services at the same time that the government was spending large amounts of money on the military.

The Soviet consumer, by contrast, had fewer choices. In the Soviet Union, the government controlled the economy, and planners decided how many of each consumer good should be produced. Heavy spending on the military often meant a reduction in spending on consumer goods. Many basic consumer goods, such as milk, soap, meat, bread, and even toothpaste, were often in short supply. People had to stand in long lines in order to purchase these items. Housing supplies were inadequate, and there were long waiting lists for apartments. Sometimes, several families shared a single apartment.

A decision by the U.S. government in the early 1980s intensified the arms race with the Soviet Union. The United States declared it would build a new weapons system—the Strategic Defense Initiative (SDI). This system would use advanced technology to protect the United States from attack by missiles. Satellites positioned in space would detect and destroy incoming missiles. Because it would be based in space, SDI was soon nicknamed the "star wars" defense system.

Soviet leaders soon realized that they could not match the advanced technology of the United States. The cost of trying to duplicate such a military defense system was too high. Instead, Soviet citizens wanted their government to concentrate on domestic priorities. Suddenly, the government-controlled economy of the Soviet Union appeared antiquated and ineffective. There were calls for reform—both political and economic.

Gorbachev's Reforms. In 1985, Konstantin Chernenko, the powerful leader of the Soviet Union, died in Moscow. His successor was the energetic and dynamic Mikhail Gorbachev. The choice of Gorbachev as Soviet leader signaled that reforms would be forthcoming.

Gorbachev soon announced a new policy—*glasnost*, or openness. Soviet people were now free to speak openly, even to criticize the government. Previously banned books became available, and churches were allowed to open. Political prisoners were released. In a nation used to decades of totalitarianism, the policy of *glasnost* was truly revolutionary.

A second new government policy, called *perestroika*, was also revolutionary. *Perestroika* was the restructuring of the Soviet economy. For the first time, individuals were permitted to own land and factories; farmers could sell excess produce. A stock exchange was opened. Central planning of the economy was replaced with increased local and private planning.

The electoral process was also reformed. In the past, the Communist party had selected all candidates for elected offices. When people voted, they simply had given their approval to the party's slate of candidates. In a policy called *democratization*, nonparty members were allowed to run for office. As a result, a number of old-time government leaders were not reelected. New faces were seen in elected positions.

Finally, the Soviet Union began a shift in foreign policy. Gorbachev wanted to concentrate on reducing the costly arms race with the United States. In 1987, he and U.S. President Ronald Reagan met and signed a treaty that banned certain types of nuclear missiles. Gorbachev also decided to loosen the

U.S. President Ronald Reagan and Soviet Premier Gorbachev sign an agreement banning certain types of nuclear missiles.

Soviet Union's political controls over Eastern Europe. He encouraged economic and political reforms. Moreover, he made it clear that the Soviet Union would no longer intervene in these countries, even if the Communist governments there seemed about to fall.

Gorbachev's goal was to reform the Soviet system to make it stronger. Instead, his policies encouraged movements that brought about the Soviet Union's collapse.

Reform Weakens the Soviet System.   The first indication of this collapse came in Lithuania. Between 1918 and 1940, it had been an independent nation. Then it was annexed by the Soviet Union. In 1990, Lithuania declared that it was independent again. Gorbachev faced a dilemma. He wanted to force Lithuania back into the Soviet Union, but he did not want to use strong force. Force was used, however, and several Lithuanians were killed in the process. For this, Gorbachev was criticized by Boris Yeltsin, the popular ex-head of the Communist party of Moscow.

As Gorbachev's popularity faded, Yeltsin's increased. In 1991, Yeltsin was elected president of the Russian Republic. Although Gorbachev and Yeltsin were obviously political rivals, the conservative Communists, who opposed most reforms, saw both of them as threats.

In August 1991, a conservative group within the Communist party called the Emergency Committee kidnapped Mikhail Gorbachev and held him hostage at his vacation home on the Black Sea. The committee wanted to halt Gorbachev's reforms and restore the power of the Communist party.

Many people protested the attempted coup. Demonstrators in Moscow filled the streets around the Russian Parliament building. In response, the Emergency Committee ordered tanks to disperse the crowd. Then Boris Yeltsin emerged from the Parliament building and mounted one of the tanks. He declared the Emergency Committee to be illegal. When the committee ordered the tanks to attack the Parliament, soldiers manning the tanks refused. The committee was forced to back down. Gorbachev was released.

The attempted coup backfired. Instead of eliciting popular support for the Communist party, it created anger against its leaders. But public opinion did not rally around Mikhail Gorbachev either. He was viewed as weak. He saw that the real power was held by Boris Yeltsin. In one of his last acts, Gorbachev banned the Communist party in Russia. Then he resigned. All of these events were signals to various nationality groups within the Soviet Union that it was breaking up. Latvia and Estonia joined Lithuania in declaring their independence. Within months, all remaining Soviet republics declared their independence. After 70 years of power, the Soviet Union ceased to exist.

Test Yourself
Why did conservative Communists in the Soviet Union oppose many of Mikhail Gorbachev's reforms?

★ INDEPENDENCE MOVEMENTS IN FORMER SOVIET SATELLITES ★

Dramatic changes also came to the Soviet Union's satellites in Eastern Europe. Gorbachev's reforms encouraged dissent in these Communist-dominated countries.

Poland

In 1980, labor union leader Lech Walesa led a strike at the shipyards in Gdansk, Poland. He demanded government recognition of Solidarity, his national organization of workers. The government instead banned Solidarity and declared

Polish union leader Lech Walesa addresses striking shipyard workers in Gdansk.

martial law in Poland. (*Martial law* is the law of a government when it relies on the military to keep order.) In 1988, Poland was facing economic hardships. Public dissatisfaction was at an all-time high as widespread strikes crippled the nation. As a result, Polish Defense Minister General Jaruzelski agreed to legalize Solidarity and to hold free elections for the first time in almost 50 years. In the 1989 and 1990 elections, the Polish Communist party was voted out of office. Walesa was elected president of Poland.

Hungary

Other Soviet satellites also changed. The Hungarian Communist party voted to disband in October 1989. Socialists and democrats replaced Communists in the Hungarian government.

Czechoslovakia

In the same month, the government of Czechoslovakia decided to resist change by cracking down on dissent. The government arrested a group of dissidents, including popular playwright Vaclav Havel. When 10,000 people protested these arrests, the government responded by arresting hundreds of the protesters. A new protest march of 25,000 young people was met with violence from government troops. Eight days later, 500,000 people filled the streets of Prague, the capital of Czechoslovakia, to protest against the government. The Communist government was forced to resign. The following month, Havel was elected president of Czechoslovakia.

Romania

For years, Romania was ruled by Nicolae Ceausescu, a brutal Communist ruler who used secret police and torture to crack down on dissent. Nonetheless, Romanians began to protest against their government in December 1989. When a large group of protesters were killed by police in the city of Timisora, the army decided to join the protesters. Ceausescu was captured, put on trial, and executed a few days later. Free elections were held in 1990 and 1992. Communist rule had come to an end.

East Germany

Perhaps the most dramatic change came in East Germany, where Communist leader Erich Honecker refused to reform his government despite prodding by Gorbachev. In 1989, the Hungarian government decided to allow East Germans to travel though Hungary into Austria and West Germany. To prevent East Germans from escaping his regime, Honecker decided to close East Germany's borders. Demonstrations against his order broke out across East Germany, and Honecker was forced to resign.

His successor decided to open the Berlin Wall, a barrier that had separated East and West Berlin since 1961. This sparked a jubilant celebration among

Berliners tearing down the hated Berlin Wall in 1989

both East and West Berliners. Many ordinary citizens began to dismantle the wall, a symbol of Communist oppression for decades. More than any other single event, the dismantling of the Berlin Wall symbolized the failure of communism and the end of the Cold War. In a few weeks, the East German Communist party was dissolved. In the following year (1990), Germany was reunited.

 Test Yourself
Why was the dismantling of the Berlin Wall a symbol of the political events during late 1980s in Europe?

★ REGIONAL AND ETHNIC CONFLICTS AFTER THE COLD WAR ★

"Why can't we get along?" This is a question that might have been asked repeatedly in many countries around the world since the end of the Cold War.

Middle East

Conflict in the Middle East continues in the 21st century. (This conflict is also discussed in Chapter 6.) Relations between Israel and Palestinians grew worse after 2000. Both sides blame the other for increasing the violence. Several issues divide the two sides.

Jerusalem. The status of Jerusalem is one of the key issues that must be decided before peace can come. Neither side trusts the other to govern the city. Israelis gained control of the entire city during the 1967 war. They are unwilling to give up control of Jerusalem because it is the ancient capital of the Jewish people. It is also the site of the Western Wall, the most holy site in Judaism.

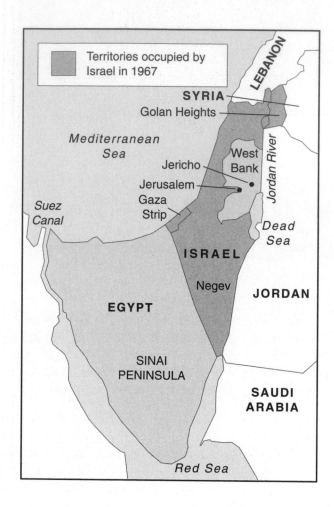

The Middle East after the 1967 Arab-Israeli war

Palestinians also have historical and religious claims to Jerusalem. They have lived in East Jerusalem (also known as the Old City) for centuries. This area is the home of many Muslim shrines, including the Dome of the Rock, the third most holy site for the world's Muslims.

Territorial Borders. The location of borders between Israel and a Palestinian state is yet another divisive issue. To 2005, Palestinian territory was broken up into segments separated by Israeli military installations and Jewish settlements. Many Palestinians wanted all borders returned to those before the 1967 war.

Refugees. A third issue in the Israeli and Palestinian dispute is the status of Palestinian refugees. During the war that followed Israeli independence in 1948, many Palestinians were forced to flee their homes. Nearly a million Palestinian refugees live in UN-sponsored camps. Palestinians claim that they have a right to live in the land of Israel.

Ethnic Strife in Africa

Ethnic conflicts in Africa threaten the peace and stability of that continent. This strife is partly caused by the political borders that were drawn by Europeans when they ruled colonies there in the 19th century.

Nigeria. Nigeria is composed of many different ethnic groups, many of which do not get along. Oil-rich Nigeria should be a wealthy country. Large foreign oil companies, however, pay low fees for extracting the oil. The oil extraction has caused pollution. The Ogoni people live in one of the areas where oil is extracted. They have protested the pollution and have called for the Nigerian government to give them a larger share of the oil wealth. Some of their protests are violent, and have led to temporary suspensions of oil extractions.

Sierra Leone. Civil war broke out in this West African nation in 1991. Since then, over 50,000 people have been killed. Over a million have been displaced.

Sudan. After gaining independence from Great Britain and Egypt in 1956, Sudan was governed for two years by a parliamentary coalition government. A military coup replaced this government with a dictatorship. When this dictatorship fell in 1964, civil disorder and the rise of other military dictatorships followed.

Strife between the Muslim Arabs in the north and the non-Muslim people in the south has kept Sudan in turmoil into the 21st century. Drought and famine have added to this country's troubles. The double disaster of civil war and famine has mainly affected the Sudanese people of the south. Hundreds of thousands of people crowd into refugee camps where they lead hopeless lives dependent on aid from the United Nations and private relief groups.

Eritrea. In 1993, Eritrea gained independence from neighboring Ethiopia after more than 30 years of warfare. The vicious fighting resulted in creating thousands of refugees. Between 1998 and 2000, Eritrea and Ethiopia fought another war, this time over a disputed border. Currently relations between the two countries are still uneasy.

Ethnic Strife in Asia

Asia too has seen its share of ethnic conflicts in recent years. One example has been the tiny island country of East Timor, a former Portuguese colony in Southeast Asia. It has rich sources of lumber and oil. Surrounding East Timor is the heavily populated nation of Indonesia, which invaded East Timor in 1975. During this invasion, one-third of East Timor's population was killed. Its economy was destroyed, and over 500,000 East Timorese became refugees. After years of struggle, East Timor was granted independence from Indonesia in 1999.

Ethnic Strife in Europe

The fall of communism in Europe led to ethnic conflicts in Yugoslavia and elsewhere in Europe.

Bosnian refugees fleeing "ethnic cleansing" in 1993

Bosnia and Kosovo. Within Yugoslavia, various groups had long resented one another. Under Communist rule, these resentments were suppressed. When communism collapsed in Yugoslavia, however, feelings of nationalism revived. Several regions declared independence from Yugoslavia, and civil wars broke out. Tens of thousands of people died in these wars. Serbian authorities, playing on the nationalistic feelings of their fellow Serbs, encouraged them to drive the Bosnian Muslims from Serbia. In 1995, for example, this *ethnic cleansing* (as they called this attack on the Muslims) resulted in the murder of some 6,000 Bosnians at Srebrenica, in Bosnia.

In 1999, the Serbian government and its allies resumed ethnic cleansing, this time in the Serbian province of Kosovo. They expelled some Muslim Kosovars from their homes and murdered an unknown number of them until massive NATO air strikes and ground troops forced the Serbs to stop.

Chechnya. This part of the Russian Republic has been devastated by ethnic strife in recent years. It was annexed by Russia in 1859, and the Chechens have long resented their Russian rulers. During World War II, Soviet leader Joseph Stalin deported a major part of the population to Kazakhstan because he believed them to be sympathetic to the Germans. These Chechens were allowed to return to their homeland only in the 1950s.

When the Soviet Union collapsed in 1991, Chechnya declared its independence from Russia. Boris Yeltsin sent 40,000 troops to fight the independence movement. But the ill-equipped Russian army suffered several defeats and by 1995 was able to regain control only of the urban areas. Russian troops withdrew in 1996, but they were sent back in again in 1999. The conflict continues to the present. To fight the Russians, Chechen rebels have used bombings and other terrorist tactics both inside and outside the borders of Chechnya.

Test Yourself
What are the main issues in the dispute between the Israelis and the Palestinians?

> ▶ POINTS TO REMEMBER

- At the end of World War II, the Soviet Union and the United States were deeply suspicious of each other's motives and policies. They engaged in a Cold War.

- Other consequences of World War II were the development of nuclear weapons systems, an increase in refugees in need of placement, the formation of the United Nations, and the creation of Israel.

- Since World War II, many former European colonies around the world have become independent.

- *Glasnost* and *perestroika* led to the opening up and eventually to the breakdown of the Soviet Union.

- The fall of the Soviet Union led to the fall of Communist regimes in the former Soviet satellites.

- The Israeli-Palestinian conflict continues.

- Civil wars and ethnic conflicts have been common in Europe, Asia, and Africa.

EXERCISES

CHECKING WHAT YOU HAVE READ

1. Which of the following countries was not a founding member of NATO?

   A. Great Britain
   B. Poland
   C. Canada
   D. Portugal

2. Which of the following countries was not a founding member of the Warsaw Pact?

   A. Romania
   B. Bulgaria
   C. Turkey
   D. Poland

3. Which one of the following statements about the Communist revolution in China is true?

   A. The fighting between Nationalist and Communist forces increased during World War II.

   B. Mao Zedong and the Communists received much support from the peasantry.
   C. Mao and the Communists retreated to the island of Taiwan.
   D. Mao refused to participate in the revolution.

4. The UN body that receives the largest share of the UN budget is the

   A. Economic and Social Council
   B. General Assembly
   C. Security Council
   D. Secretariat.

5. The first republic to declare its independence from the Soviet Union in 1991 was

   A. Georgia
   B. Poland
   C. Kazakhstan
   D. Lithuania.

6. The leader of Communist North Vietnam was

   A. Mao Zedong
   B. Ho Chi Minh
   C. Pol Pot
   D. Ngo Dinh Diem.

7. Vietnam was once under the imperial domination of what European nation?

   A. France
   B. Soviet Union
   C. Great Britain
   D. Germany

8. At the end of World War II, Germany and the city of Berlin were both divided, with the eastern sector of each being controlled by

   A. Great Britain
   B. the Soviet Union
   C. France
   D. the United States.

9. SDI are the initials of

   A. the secret police in Russia
   B. an arms agreement between the United States and the Soviet Union
   C. a defensive weapons system proposed by the United States
   D. a nuclear weapons system developed by the Soviet Union.

10. Which of the following areas is a part of Russia still in open revolt against the Russian government?

   A. Azerbaijan
   B. Chechnya
   C. Belarus
   D. Lithuania

USING WHAT YOU HAVE READ

1. Read more about the fall of the Berlin Wall in 1989. Then write a newspaper account of the events.

2. Use the Internet to research *one* of the following areas where ethnic, religious, or cultural strife has divided people. Report your findings to your classmates.

Northern Ireland	Somalia	Sudan
Congo	Liberia	Iran/Iraq
Zimbabwe	Philippines	Afghanistan
Bangladesh	Tibet	Chiapas, Mexico
Quebec	Kurdistan	Greece/Turkey
Peru	Basque regions of	
Sri Lanka	Spain and France	

THINKING ABOUT WHAT YOU HAVE READ

1. Create a Venn diagram comparing and contrasting the United States and the Soviet Union during the Cold War.

2. Work with a partner to study the issue of Palestinian statehood. Take the side of either the Israeli government or the Palestinians and make a list of position statements for that side. Prioritize your statements, listing them from the most important to the least important. Then meet with a pair of students who have taken the opposite side. Together determine if there is room for compromise between the two sides. Report your findings to the class.

SKILLS

Interpreting a Primary Source

Read the following personal recollection of the war years in Great Britain. After you have finished, write a description of how the war affected an ordinary teenager.

I am 72 now, but my memory of those war time years is for the most part fresh and sharp. My parents, two sisters and I were on (vacation) . . . the day the war began. . . . Dad left us to join his Territorial Army unit. Mother was too nervous to let us return to London, so we went to Guildford to stay with some people we had met. It was a disaster. Mother spotted bed-bugs crawling up the wall, so we left as soon as possible. At various times we had fleas, head lice, and impetigo. . . . We had so many changes in lodging and school . . . that I have no recollection of one in Worcester . . . but I do remember lying awake hearing planes droning overhead. Can you tell "theirs" from "ours" by the sound of the engine, I wondered? . . .

Eventually, my middle sister and I crossed to southern Ireland to take refuge with Uncle Frank and Aunt Lucy in Athlone. This was a gamble, as Hitler might have landed in Eire (Ireland) first. . . . We crossed the Irish Sea in February, 1941. . . . We were probably in greater danger from U-boats (German submarines) than attack from the air. We stayed in Athlone very happily until the end of the war, but Mother got restless. . . . She returned to England and stayed in lodgings near where Dad manned an anti-aircraft battery on various sites round London. . . . Towards the end of the war Dad found a tenant who rented (our) house.

Postwar Britain was an awful shock after Athlone. We could not return to our house in Milcham because our tenant was in a wheel-chair, and when the war ended the government decided tenants should have security of tenure. . . . (W)e settled in a rented house in an industrial suburb. Everything was drab, in need of repair, in short supply including food. In the bitter winter of 1947, we ran out of coal. Dad sneaked along the railway line at the back of the house picking up lumps which had fallen off the coal tenders. . . . It was stealing so we kept quiet. For Dad, a civil servant, it might have been grounds for dismissal.

With hindsight I realize we were lucky. No one in the family was killed or injured, or made a prisoner of war. Dad returned to his work at the Ministry of Health, which paid his salary throughout his army service. From 1945–1949 I worked very hard at my new high school to catch up on the education I had missed in Ireland.

CHAPTER 6

CULTURAL PERSPECTIVES

BENCHMARK:

Analyze the influence of different cultural perspectives on the actions of groups.

Every issue has at least two sides. A person's point of view about historical and contemporary events depends, in large part, on his or her own cultural heritage. This benchmark requires that you understand the different cultural perspectives of *four* historical events: the creation of Israel; the partition of India and Pakistan; the division of Germany after World War II and its reunification almost 50 years later; and the end of apartheid in South Africa.

★ CREATION OF THE STATE OF ISRAEL ★

The conflict between the Israelis and their Arab neighbors has had repercussions throughout the world. To understand why Israelis and Arabs have such intense feelings about the area that they both claim, it is necessary to know the history of both these groups.

Historical Background

Around 1200 B.C., the ancient Hebrews, ancestors of modern Jews, first settled along the eastern shore of the Mediterranean Sea in an area now known as Palestine. The Hebrews left this area during a time of famine and ended up in Egypt, where they were enslaved. The Hebrew leader Moses led them out of Egypt and back to Palestine. The Hebrews believed that Palestine was their promised land—land promised to them by God. The Hebrews established the Kingdom of Israel around 1000 B.C. and were ruled by three great kings, the last of whom was King Solomon. He made Israel powerful, and he turned Jerusalem (the capital of the kingdom) into a beautiful city.

Roman Empire. After the death of Solomon, Israel became divided and weak. A series of outsiders invaded and made Palestine part of their empires. Eventually, Palestine became part of the Roman Empire. Babylonians conquered Judah in 586 B.C. and took the people as slaves to Babylonia. They were freed in 538 B.C.

In A.D. 66, a group of Jews rebelled against the rule of Rome. As a result of the rebellion, the Romans destroyed the Jewish Temple in Jerusalem in A.D. 70. The rebellion continued for three more years and resulted in the deaths of thousands of Jews. In the next few years, Jews were forced into exile. Jews fled to Syria, Egypt, Spain, Arabia, and eventually scattered throughout Europe. This event is known as the Diaspora, a Greek word that means dispersal. Although the Jewish people were dispersed all over the world, they continued to practice their religion and maintained other aspects of their culture. Their desire to return to what they believed to be their promised land persisted.

Muslim Empire. In 638, Palestine became part of the Muslim Empire. Muslims are followers of Islam, the religion founded by the Prophet Muhammad. Even before Muhammad's death in 632, his followers in Arabia had begun a period of conquest to create an empire that spanned Southwest Asia, North Africa, and Southern Europe.

The Muslims were particularly happy at gaining Jerusalem because it contained the Temple Mount. This was believed to be the place where Muhammad rose into heaven. A shrine called the Dome of the Rock was built on the site to commemorate the event. It is one of the holiest shrines of Islam. The Dome of the Rock is adjacent to the Western Wall. This site is holy to the Jews because it is the only portion of Solomon's temple not destroyed by the Romans. Under the Muslim Empire, ethnic Arabs (the majority of people living in Palestine) converted to the religion of Islam.

Ottoman Rule. By the 15th century, the area had become part of the Ottoman Empire, a Muslim Empire ruled by the Turks in Constantinople. The Ottoman Empire, like the Muslim Empire it replaced, stretched across Europe, Asia, and Africa.

The government of this empire allowed its subjects relative freedom, as long as they paid taxes to Constantinople. Jews who lived in Palestine and elsewhere in the empire lived peacefully with their Muslim Arab neighbors. Jews who lived in Eastern Europe did not fare as well. There they were subjected to *anti-Semitism* (prejudice against Jews). In Russia, for example, the government encouraged and even endorsed violence against Jews. These violent campaigns against Russian Jews were known as *pogroms*.

Zionism. Elsewhere in Europe, Jews faced other forms of discrimination. In the late 19th century, some European Jews began a movement called Zionism. The goal of Zionism was to create a homeland for the Jewish people. The logical location for their homeland was Palestine, the promised land of the ancient Hebrews. The Zionist movement increased in strength in the early 20th century, but achievement of its goal was interrupted by the two world wars.

World Wars I and II. During World War I, the Ottoman Empire and Great Britain were on opposite sides. Great Britain was looking for allies against the Turks, the rulers of the Ottoman Empire. The Arabs, the largest Ottoman ethnic group, were eager to win their freedom from Turkish control. In what is known as the McMahon Pledge, the British allied themselves with Arab nationalists and supported Arab self-rule. In 1915, Sir Henry McMahon (a British official in Egypt) promised Hussein ibn Ali, Sharif of Mecca, that the British government would create a self-governing Arab state after the end of the war. Whether this Arab state would have included Palestine is not clear.

Arab leader Hussein ibn Ali, Sharif of Mecca

British Negotiations. In 1916, another British official, Mark Sykes, negotiated a secret agreement with a French diplomat, Georges Picot. The so-called Sykes-Picot Agreement divided up most of the post-World War I Middle East between Great Britain and France. The agreement allocated only the Hejaz, the Red Sea coast of present-day Saudi Arabia, to the Sharif of Mecca and his Hashemite followers. Many Arabs saw the Skyes-Picot Agreement as a betrayal because it contradicted earlier British statements that expressed support for the establishment of an Arab state stretching from the Mediterranean Sea to the Persian Gulf, including Palestine.

While these negotiations were taking place, the British were trying to pacify Zionists in Great Britain. One Zionist leader, Chaim Weizmann, knew several leaders of the British government, including Prime Minister David Lloyd George and Foreign Secretary Arthur James Balfour. Weizmann, a chemist, was able to help Britain produce the solvent acetone, which was vital to the war effort. In return for his help, he asked Lloyd George and Balfour to help him obtain a homeland for Jews in Palestine. In 1917, Balfour sent a letter to Zionist leader Baron Edmond de Rothschild. In the letter, Balfour said that the British government "favour[s] the establishment in Palestine of a national home for the Jewish people. . . ." This letter became known as the Balfour Declaration.

Palestine Mandate. After World War I ended, the League of Nations gave Britain control of Palestine as a mandate. The British decided to set aside parts of Palestine for separate Jewish and Arab settlements. Both groups believed that the British government had broken the promises it had made to them during the war. Nobody was happy; both Jews and Arabs wanted to control Palestine. During the 1930s, more and more European Jews began to immigrate to Palestine because of Nazi persecution.

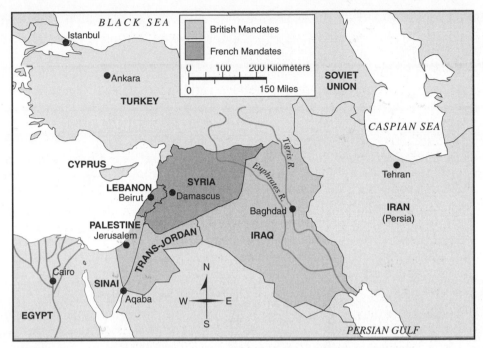

Middle East after World War I

After World War II. After World War II ended in 1945, the British were ready to withdraw from Palestine. The British turned Palestine over to the United Nations. In 1947, the UN decided to partition Palestine into Jewish and Arab sectors. The city of Jerusalem, important to Jews, Christians, and Muslims, was to be controlled by none of these groups. Instead, it would be under international control. The Arab nations were not happy with the UN decision. Palestinian Arabs were especially upset. On May 14, 1948, Jewish leader David Ben-Gurion announced the creation of Israel as an independent state. The United States and other nations quickly recognized Israel's independence.

Arab Opposition. Six of Israel's Arab neighbors (Egypt, Jordan, Iraq, Lebanon, Saudi Arabia, and Syria) invaded Israel on the day after it declared independence. With the aid of the United States, Israel won the war within a few months. As a result of the war, Israel seized much of the Palestinian Arab land. The remaining Palestinian lands—the Gaza Strip and the West Bank of the Jordan River—were taken over by Egypt and Jordan, respectively. The dream of an independent Palestinian Arab state did not come about. Instead, thousands of Palestinians fled Israel and were placed in refugee camps.

Recent Events

Over the ensuing years, Israel fought three more wars with its Arab neighbors. The 1956 Suez Crisis, the 1967 Six-Day War, and the 1973 Yom Kippur War had three things in common. They were short conflicts, Israel won each war, and each ended without a peace agreement. During the Six-Day War, Israel seized the Gaza Strip and the Sinai Peninsula from Egypt, the Golan Heights from Syria, and the West Bank and eastern Jerusalem from Jordan.

Attempts at Peace. In 1978, the first Middle East peace agreement was finally negotiated. U.S. President Jimmy Carter invited Israeli Prime Minister Menachem Begin and Egyptian President Anwar Sadat to Camp David, Maryland. The three men negotiated in private. The result was the Camp David Accords. Egypt recognized Israel's right to exist as a free, sovereign nation. Israel agreed to return the Sinai Peninsula to Egyptian control. Both countries promised to maintain peaceful relations with the other. For their efforts, Begin and Sadat were awarded the Nobel Peace Prize.

Peace negotiations between the Israelis and Palestinians have been much more difficult. Remember, many Palestinians had been forced from their homes; they have been living in refugee camps. Israel had been reluctant to give up Gaza and the West Bank for security reasons. The territories act as a buffer between Israel and its Arab neighbors. To help secure the territories, Israel began to build settlements in Gaza and the West Bank.

Palestinians did not want Jewish settlements in territories they claimed. They turned to the Palestinian Liberation Organization's military wing for help. The Palestinian Liberation Organization (PLO) was a leading group of Palestinian refugees that opposed Israel. The PLO began an armed resistance against the settlements. In retaliation, Israel began to destroy Palestinian strongholds. In 1982, Israel invaded Lebanon to attack Palestinian villages.

The Intifada. In 1987, Palestinian frustration came to a boiling point. The result was a widespread program of civil disobedience called the *intifada* (uprising). Palestinians used several tools of protest: demonstrations, boycotts, and armed attacks on Israeli targets. Many teenagers joined the *intifada* by throwing rocks at Israeli soldiers. The *intifada* was effective in creating negative publicity for Israel and, in particular, the Israeli army.

Just when all-out war seemed inevitable, compromise came. In 1993, secret meetings were held in Oslo, Norway, between Israeli and Palestinian representatives. This resulted in Prime Minister Yitzhak Rabin and PLO leader Yasir Arafat signing the Declaration of Principles. The signing took place in the United States, at the White House. Palestinians were granted self-rule in Gaza and the West Bank. The self-rule would come in stages, starting with the town of Jericho.

By 2005, however, peace in the Middle East had still not been achieved. Palestinian self-rule had not been accomplished. Violent acts had been carried out by both Israeli troops and Palestinian civilians, and animosity still existed between Israel and nearby Arab nations.

Test Yourself
Why did many Arabs oppose the UN's 1947 plan for dividing Palestine into Jewish and Arab sectors?

★ PARTITION OF INDIA AND PAKISTAN ★

If you look at a map of Asia, you will see the subcontinent of India. India is called a subcontinent because of its vast size and because it is separated from the rest of Asia by the Hindu Kush and Himalayan Mountains in the north and by the Bay of Bengal and Arabian Sea to the east and west. From ancient times to the present, the Indian subcontinent has been the home of large populations of peoples with varied religions and cultures. The historical development of these religions and cultures helps explain the differences that divide people there today.

Hinduism

Hinduism is a major religion of India today. It is an ancient religion that has developed over thousands of years. It has no known founder. Perhaps Hinduism is best described as a collection of religious beliefs. Not all Hindus practice the same rituals or beliefs. In order to seek an understanding of all things in this world and beyond, Hindus worship a variety of *deities* (gods). A perfect understanding of all things is called *moksha*. It is a goal of many Hindus because it is said to bring about a release from the pain and suffering that are a result of earthly life. *Moksha* cannot be achieved in one lifetime but only after many lifetimes. It is for this reason that many Hindus believe in *reincarnation*.

This is the belief that a person's soul is born over and over again. One's current life can help determine one's future lives. The force generated by good or bad deeds is known as *karma*. This force can help determine a person's fate in the future. A person is reborn again and again until *moksha* is achieved and the person is released from the pain and suffering of life.

Islam

Another major Indian religion is Islam. Founded in 7th-century Arabia, Islam is based on the teachings of the Prophet Muhammad. He said that he was the last in a series of prophets who received messages from Allah, the one and only God. Muhammad told his followers that they must submit to the will of Allah; they must choose good over evil. The Arabic word "Islam" means "surrender to the will of Allah." Those who practice Islam are known as Muslims.

Five Pillars. Muslims have five obligations, the Five Pillars of Islam. These five obligations demonstrate a person's submission to the will of Allah. The first pillar is faith. To become a Muslim, one must simply state, "There is no God but Allah, and Muhammad is his Prophet."

The second pillar requires Muslims to pray at five specific times of day. Prayers are recited while facing toward Mecca, the holy city of Islam. On Fridays, many Muslims pray together in a house of worship known as a *mosque*. If it is not possible to get to a mosque, a Muslim may pray wherever he or she is located.

Almsgiving, or charity, is the third pillar. *Fasting* during the holy month of Ramadan is the fourth. Each day during this holy month, devout Muslims give up eating and drinking from sunup to sundown.

The fifth and final pillar is the *hajj*. It is a pilgrimage to the holy city of Mecca that Muslims are supposed to take at least once during a lifetime. Pilgrims to Mecca wear traditional white robes and participate in various religious rituals.

Mughal Rulers Bring Islam to India. Islam was first brought to India by Turkish invaders around the year 1000. The Turks destroyed Hindu cities in an effort to gain control over Hindu India. By the 16th century, India was ruled by a group of Muslim rulers known as the Mughals. The Mughal rulers and their Hindu subjects were separated not only by religion. They had different languages and customs. The lavish lifestyle of the Mughal rulers was supported by heavy taxes on Hindu commoners. Under the Mughal leader Aurangzeb (ruled 1658–1707), Hindu temples were destroyed and Hindus were barred from government service. By the 18th century, the power of the Mughal rulers had waned. India was fragmented into small, independent states, each one governed by a local ruler called a maharajah. The lasting legacy of Mughal rule was a permanent division between two distinct Indian cultures, the Hindu and Muslim.

British Colonialism

By 1763, Britain had gained control of India. It governed through the British East India Company. The firm was in the business of trade, and the rich natural resources of India were a magnet. By taking advantage of the divisions in Indian society, the company gained tremendous political power in India and even had its own army. Agricultural goods such as cotton, tea, coffee, and indigo dye flowed into Britain. In return, the British sent manufactured goods (including textiles and clothing) to India. The British–India trade was so profitable that India was often referred to as "the jewel in the Crown" of the British Empire. The British East India Company built a network of railroads, telegraph lines, dams, schools, sanitation facilities, and other public works. These advances led to improved transportation, communication, public health, and education in India. They also led to resentment. British restrictions on native industries damaged self-sufficiency in many parts of India, causing economic hardship and even famine in some villages. By the mid-19th century, this resentment resulted in a full-fledged rebellion.

Sepoy Mutiny. The British East India Company's army was manned by many native Indian soldiers known as Sepoys. In 1857, the Sepoys became alarmed when they were issued new rifles. Rumors spread that the rifle cartridges were lubricated with pork and beef fat. (Pork is a forbidden to Muslims; Hindus consider cows to be sacred.) The Sepoys refused to accept the new rifles and began a period of fierce fighting known as the Sepoy Mutiny. The British East India Company could not control the revolt. Regular British troops stepped in to contain the fighting. As a result, the British government took over direct control of India and appointed its own official, with the title of viceroy, to govern India. As the British government increased its control over India, resentment grew among the native population.

Independence Movements

In the late 1800s and early 1900s, Indian nationalism grew and Indians began to organize. Two groups were formed to oppose British rule of India: the Indian National Congress (1885), a Hindu group, and the Muslim League (1906). These two groups shared a common goal of Indian self-rule but were divided by their religions and cultures.

During World War I, over 1 million Indians volunteered to serve in the British army. After the war, these army veterans expected increased freedom as reward for their military service. Instead, British control was increased. For example, a 1919 law allowed for the suspension of jury trial for anyone who protested against British rule in India. A few weeks after the law was passed, thousands of Indians peacefully protested in the city of Amritsar. British troops opened fire on the crowd, killing some 400 people and wounding another 1,200. The Indian government decided not to punish the army officers responsible for the killings. This incident, now known as the Amritsar Massacre, crystallized the thinking of millions of Indians: They wanted independence.

Gandhi. A dynamic leader emerged to lead the Indian National Congress—Mohandas K. Gandhi, a British-trained lawyer. Gandhi urged the people of India to adopt a policy of noncooperation with the British. To protest unfair treatment, he and his followers began openly and peacefully to disobey British

Mahatma Gandhi, with poet and politician Sarojini Naidu, leading the 1930 Salt March

laws they considered unjust. This form of protest is known as *passive resistance*. Throughout India, people began to boycott British-made goods. Many Indians refused to pay taxes or attend British-run schools. Gandhi set an example by spinning and weaving his own cloth, a practice banned by British law. Over time, these forms of passive resistance grew effective. British officials had difficulty dealing with the thousands of protesters they arrested. Sales of British manufactured goods dropped dramatically. The operation of trains, factories, and government services was interrupted. Perhaps most importantly, Gandhi and his followers were winning international approval for their actions.

In 1930, Gandhi led a protest known as the "march to the sea," or Salt March. The production and sale of salt in India was strictly regulated by the British government. Salt could be purchased only from the British, who imposed a hefty tax. Gandhi led his group of protesters on a 240-mile protest march that ended at the sea. There the protesters began to collect seawater and heat it to collect the illegal salt. As a result, Gandhi and 60,000 other protesters were arrested over the next several days.

In response to the successful tactic of passive resistance, the British government passed a new law in 1935, the Government of India Act. It allowed for local self-rule in India. Indians could elect their own local leaders in democratic elections. But the British government would continue to control India as its colony. The Government of India Act was the first step along the road to complete Indian independence. Another world war, though, would delay independence for some years.

Independence and Muslim-Hindu Conflict. When World War II came to an end in 1945, the time was ripe for Indian independence. Many British people questioned whether Britain should keep control of its colonies around the world. The British Labor party, which had taken control of the government in 1945, also favored giving India its independence. However, this opportunity for independence created a new problem. The long-repressed tensions between the majority Hindus and minority Muslims resurfaced.

The Muslim League, led by Muhammad Ali Jinnah, became an antagonist to the Congress party. Like Gandhi, Jinnah was a British-trained lawyer. Both men wanted independence from Britain, but they strongly disagreed about what an independent India would be like. Gandhi favored a unified nation under democratically elected leaders. Fearing persecution by Hindus, Jinnah rejected the idea of majority rule for an independent India. In 1940, Jinnah proposed a partition of India to secure Muslim rights. Gandhi strongly opposed this plan.

British policy encouraged the continued separation. Rather than treating all Indian colonials the same, the British government treated Hindus and Muslims differently. At the time of independence, many more Hindus than Muslims held government posts. Many Muslims feared being dominated by Hindus in a unified, independent India. At the same time, many Hindus feared the power of Muslims. During World War II, the Muslim League pledged full support to the British cause while the National Congress was boycotting participation in government.

Some Hindus pushed for the adoption of Hindi as the Indian national language, rather than Urdu, a language spoken by many Muslims. The Indian

Pakistan's first leader, Muhammad Ali Jinnah

National Congress promoted, as the Indian national anthem, a song that Muslims considered anti-Muslim. As independence drew near, it became obvious that the partition of India was inevitable.

In spite of Gandhi's efforts to achieve a peaceful solution to the question of unity or partition, violence helped decide the outcome. In 1946, thousands were killed when rioting broke out across India between Hindus and Muslims. British Viceroy Lord Louis Mountbatten decided that the partition of India was the only way to stop Hindu-Muslim fighting. On August 14 and 15, 1947, the British Parliament granted independence to two separate nations: Pakistan and India. After 350 years, British rule in India came to an end.

Partitioning of India. The partition caused tremendous upheaval throughout South Asia; the human costs of the partition were staggering. When the boundaries were drawn between India and Pakistan, many people found they were in the wrong country and were forced to leave their homes. Historians estimate that up to 12 million people became refugees; an exact number is not known. This was one of the largest migrations of people in recorded history.

Heavy fighting broke out between the two religious groups. The exact toll cannot be given, but most historians agree that between 500,000 and a million people were killed. It is estimated that tens of thousands of women were raped and/or abducted. Many of these women simply disappeared.

Since partition, India and Pakistan have gone to war three times. Political boundaries have not been settled. The result has been the loss of many more lives and political insecurity in South Asia.

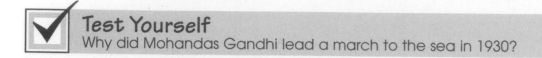

Test Yourself
Why did Mohandas Gandhi lead a march to the sea in 1930?

★ REUNIFICATION OF GERMANY ★

Eastern and Western Powers Struggle Over Germany

As World War II came to an end in the spring of 1945, the Allied armies marched into Nazi Germany and began a period of military occupation. U.S., British, and French troops invaded Germany from the west; the Soviet Union invaded from the east. In February 1945, the Allied leaders met at Yalta, a Black Sea resort town in the Soviet Union. At the Yalta Conference, Winston Churchill of Great Britain, Franklin D. Roosevelt of the United States, and Joseph Stalin decided to divide Germany into four military zones of occupation. Each sector would be under the control of one of four countries: Britain, France, the United States, and the Soviet Union. Berlin, the German capital, would be similarly divided. Western leaders hoped that this agreement would bring peace.

Conflicting Goals. At the time of the Yalta Conference, however, the goals of the United States and the Soviet Union were very different. President Roosevelt wanted to insure that Germany would have a democratic government. He insisted on free elections. Soviet leader Joseph Stalin, on the other hand, wanted to create a Soviet-controlled Communist state in Germany to buffer any attempts to invade the Soviet Union from the west. As you read in Chapter 5, a weak, divided Germany was his goal.

In 1948, Britain, France, and the United States decided to end their military occupation of Germany. The three nations hoped this action would hasten the reunification of Germany. They wanted the Soviets to hold free elections.

In response, the Soviet Union began a blockade of the city of Berlin. The Soviets cut off highways, railways, and water routes between Berlin and the West. Stalin thought these actions would make Britain, France, and the United States abandon Berlin. He also hoped the Western powers would give up their efforts to reunify Germany.

Berlin Airlift. Stalin's hopes were dashed by the Berlin Airlift. For 11 months, British and U.S. planes flew in food, medicines, and other supplies to the people of Berlin. Over 2 million tons of supplies were transported in this way. Stalin was forced to back down, and his blockade of Berlin ended in May 1949.

Divided Germany. Later that same year, Germany was formally split into two independent states. The U.S., French, and British occupation zones were united to form the Federal Republic of Germany, also known as West Germany. The Soviet zone became the German Democratic Republic, or East Germany. West Germany was organized as a democratic nation with free elections and guaranteed freedoms. East Germany had a Communist government with one-party rule and few freedoms. For the next 45 years, Germany remained divided into the Communist East and democratic West.

Surrounded by East German territory, the city of Berlin was also divided into West Berlin and East Berlin. The city of Bonn became the temporary home of West Germany's government. Because of its location and its division into East and West, the city of Berlin became a symbol of the Cold War.

Many Germans believed that their country would always remain divided. But beginning in 1989, dramatic political changes occurred throughout Eastern Europe. As discussed in Chapter 5, the Soviet Union began to lose control of its satellites. East Germany's leader, Erich Honecker, tried to keep East Germany from breaking away from the Soviet Union. However, thousands of protesting East Germans forced him to resign.

Honecker's replacement was Egon Krenz. Krenz faced the difficult task of restoring order to East Germany. He decided to defuse the social unrest by opening up the border between East and West Berlin. He hoped that the demonstrators would be satisfied and settle down. Instead, he had created the beginning of the end of East Germany. On November 9, 1989, East Germans stormed into West Berlin. Residents from both sides of Berlin began to tear down the Berlin Wall. Less than a year later, on October 3, 1990, Germany was reunited.

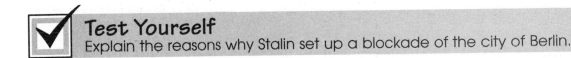

Test Yourself
Explain the reasons why Stalin set up a blockade of the city of Berlin.

★ END OF APARTHEID IN SOUTH AFRICA ★

The British and Dutch Struggle Over South Africa

In 1652, ships of the Dutch East India Company first arrived in South Africa. The company set up a settlement on the Cape of Good Hope (on the southern-most part of Africa) for the sole purpose of trade. Within five years, though, Dutch settlers known as Boers began to farm the lands around the Cape settlement. Over the next 200 years, the number of white settlers grew, and permanent settlements were created.

In 1814, Great Britain took over the Dutch settlement in exchange for a cash payment to the Netherlands. The British rulers of Cape Colony forced the native Africans off some of their lands, which were turned over to British farmers. The British government then forbade any further expansion of the Cape Colony. Neither the Africans nor the Boers were happy with the British takeover. In the 1830s, several thousand Boers decided to migrate north in search of new farmlands and to escape British rule. This northward movement of the Boers, known as the Great Trek, pitted the newcomer Boers against the native population, including the Zulus.

Boer War. The discovery of diamonds and gold in the 1860s and 1880s brought many British people to the northern parts of South Africa. The Boers did not like this influx and went to war against the British in 1899. The Boer War was fiercely fought, with both sides using terror tactics. Britain won the war and reorganized the various European settlements to form a new colony called the Union of South Africa.

South Africa Becomes Independent

In 1910, South Africa was granted self-rule, and in 1931 it became an independent nation with close ties to Great Britain. In 1948, the National party came to power. It represented the interests of the white Afrikaners, the descendants of the Boers. Although the Afrikaners were a small part of the total South African population (about 12 percent), they were able to control the government and establish policies that favored their interests.

Apartheid Instituted. The most notorious policy was the policy of *apartheid*, or complete separation of races. The people of South Africa were divided into four major groups. The most powerful group was that of the white South Africans. The other three groups were Asians (mostly people of Indian descent), Cape Coloreds (people of mixed race), and Bantus (the majority of black South Africans). Many people were displaced by the new government policy. This was particularly true for Indians and Cape Coloreds. Both groups were removed from white areas.

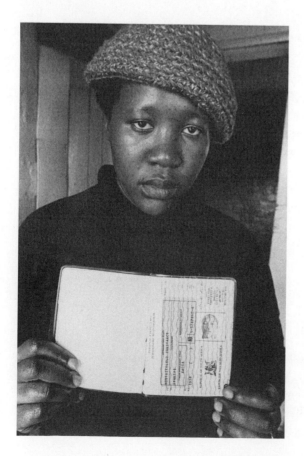

South African woman shows her "interior passbook," required by apartheid law.

Black South Africans were divided into ten so-called nations. Each nation was to be given its own homeland, called a Bantustan. These black homelands were located in rural areas, to keep them away from white settlements. Much of the land in the Bantustans was of poor quality, not suitable for farming. Opportunities for employment in the Bantustans were also poor. In theory, each of the homelands was created to be a self-governing, independent nation. In reality, no nation in the world other than South Africa recognized any of these homelands as independent nations. South Africa's land that remained under white control included major cities, choice farmlands, and mines.

Under apartheid, every nonwhite person was required to register according to his or her race. Marriage between people of different racial classifications was prohibited. Education was segregated and controlled by the white government. Police departments had tremendous powers to arrest and detain almost anyone.

Pass laws controlled movement in South Africa. Blacks in South Africa were required to carry "interior passports" to move around from place to place. Strict curfews also controlled black South Africans. Violators of the pass laws and curfews were subject to arrest and imprisonment.

Domestic Opposition to Apartheid. After apartheid was imposed in 1948, opposition to it soon followed. In the 1950s, the African National Congress (ANC), formed in 1912, issued a Freedom Charter based on the philosophy of natural rights. It stated that the South African government was not legitimate because it did not represent the will of the people. The ANC began a program of passive resistance to the Afrikaner government. Nelson Mandela was one of the leaders of the ANC.

Another organization, the Pan-African Congress (PAC), used similar tactics. In 1960, it organized opposition to the pass laws. To disrupt the system, people crowded into police stations without their passes. The police responded by traveling to Sharpeville, a black township that was the scene of large protests. They opened fire on a group of black Africans, killing 67 and wounding nearly 200. Nationwide unrest followed. During the disturbances, 11,000 people were arrested. The Sharpeville Massacre, as it came to be called by opponents of apartheid, shocked people all over the world. In its aftermath, South Africa banned the ANC and put Nelson Mandela in prison. Mandela's imprisonment actually helped the opponents of the South African government. In prison, Mandela became a symbol of apartheid's evils.

Various religious groups around the world called for an end to apartheid. These groups were joined by the United Nations, which passed resolutions condemning it.

International Boycotts. Perhaps the most effective method used against apartheid was economic boycotts of businesses that operated in South Africa by people and governments around the world. As a result of these boycotts, many foreign companies adopted a policy of *disinvestment*: They stopped operating in South Africa or investing in South African businesses. Although some argued that disinvestment would only hurt black South Africans, it proved to be an effective tool in fighting apartheid. Almost all goods became more expensive, and South African leaders found it difficult to run a self-sufficient economy.

Nelson Mandela, after his release from a South African prison in 1990

The boycott was extended to other areas as well. Some foreign governments banned travel to South Africa, and South Africa was barred from participating in the Olympics. By the 1970s, the country had become more and more isolated.

Archbishop Desmond Tutu, the black civil rights leader, called on all countries of the world to boycott trade with South Africa. Because of his stature as a religious leader, he was able to convince many around the world to support an economic boycott. This boycott continued to put political pressure on the South African government. In 1984, Tutu was awarded the Nobel Peace Prize for his efforts.

Soweto Uprising. In 1976, another event gained the world's attention. Black schoolchildren in the township of Soweto began a protest against a South African government policy in the schools. The government required all classes to be taught in the Afrikaans language or in English, but not in any native languages. When a schoolboy was killed during a demonstration, a wave of new protests swept across South Africa. The Soweto Uprising, as it was called, resulted in the deaths of about 600 students. Again, countries around the world responded with economic pressure. The United Nations called for a trade boycott of South Africa.

End of Apartheid. Change came to South Africa in 1989 with the election of F. W. de Klerk as president. He began to reform South Africa and end its political isolation form the rest of the world. First, he legalized the ANC in 1990 and released Nelson Mandela from prison. Then the South African government began to dismantle apartheid. As apartheid laws were repealed, other countries began to remove their trade barriers. In 1994, the first universal elections were held in South Africa. All South Africans, regardless of race, were permitted to vote in the election. The ANC won a majority of the votes, and Nelson Mandela was elected president of the country. Two years later, a new constitution was adopted that listed equal rights for all South Africans to enjoy. Once and for all, the policy of apartheid was ended.

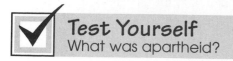

Test Yourself
What was apartheid?

> ◤ POINTS TO REMEMBER

- Both Jews and Arabs had claims to Palestine after World War II. These claims continue to be a major cause of the Middle East conflicts today.

- Because colonial India had two major, conflicting groups—Muslims and Hindus—when India gained its independence, it was partitioned to reflect regional religious differences.

- The division of Germany into two nations after World War II was the result of the different goals of the Soviet Union on one side and of the U.S. and Western European powers on the other. The two halves of Germany were reunited only after the Soviet Union broke up and Communist governments lost power in East Germany and elsewhere in Eastern Europe.

- Apartheid in South Africa was abandoned by the South African government after years of opposition by black South Africans and pressure from foreign governments, businesses, and other organizations.

EXERCISES

CHECKING WHAT YOU HAVE READ

1. What term refers to the forced exile of the Jews from Israel after the Romans had destroyed the Jewish temple in Jerusalem?

2. What British document supported the idea of a Jewish homeland?

3. How did the British win support of Arab leaders during World War I?

4. What is the Hindu belief that after death a person's soul is reborn in a new body?

5. What nation built a network of railroads, telegraph lines, dams, schools, and public works in India?

6. During his or her lifetime, a Muslim tries to complete a pilgrimage to Mecca. What is this pilgrimage called?

7. How was Germany treated by the Allies after World War I?

8. After World War II, what political act changed the German nation?

9. What act symbolized German reunification in 1989?

10. How did the white-minority South African government treat the black majority after World War II?

USING WHAT YOU HAVE READ

1. Choose *one* of the four major conflicts discussed in this chapter. Create a time line showing the major events in the history of the conflict.

2. Research the political career of *one* of the following: Chaim Weizmann, Hussein ibn Ali, Henry McMahon, Arthur James Balfour, David Ben-Gurion, Gamal Abdel Nasser, Golda Meir, Menachem Begin, Anwar Sadat, Jimmy Carter, Yasir Arafat, Yitzhak Rabin, or Shimon Peres. Create a poster that illustrates and describes the political beliefs of the person you choose.

THINKING ABOUT WHAT YOU HAVE READ

1. Imagine you are a Muslim living in India at the time of the partition. Write a letter to Gandhi expressing your thoughts about the India-Pakistan split.

2. Working with two or three other students in your class, create a peace plan aimed at settling the disputes between the Palestinians and Israelis. Include at least *five* specific points of agreement in your plan. Then present your plan to the rest of the class.

SKILLS

Opposing Viewpoints

The Soweto Uprising of 1976 has often been called the beginning of the end of apartheid in South Africa. Students were protesting a government policy that required classes to be taught in English and Afrikaans rather than the students' native language. They clashed with police, and several students died. Read the two accounts of this protest and answer the question that follows.

In 1976 I was living in the Free State town of Welkom. It was the year in which television was introduced in South Africa. . . . (Besides programs about cheerful, ordinary life,) images of children in Soweto running chaotically in clouds of dust, (of) burning buildings and buses, flashed across the screen.

Something was seriously amiss in the old Transvaal (an area of South Africa). I shudder to recall the voice . . . (that delivered) the government's spin on the 8 p.m. news. In essence, it went something like this: The cause of the "unrest" in Soweto was that black school children were ungrateful. We, the taxpayers, (had given) them schools and they simply burned them down.

(This was) confusing and disturbing. . . . I found myself at a university the following year, where I was presented with a more reliable interpretation: . . . the Soweto uprising had turned the tide of resistance to apartheid.

—Emilia Potenza

I was 10 years old when the Soweto uprising took place. I was a student at the primary school. I remember the morning of the 16th of June. . . . (W)e were told to go back to our homes, for there would be no school that day. On our way home, we could see the police troops, (water-throwing police trucks), helicopters, as well as policemen in private cars. Students were scattered all over the place, running for cover, their faces covered with cloths to avoid the teargas. There was smoke everywhere. Ambulances were (everywhere).

I was scared, as my home and my school were very far from each other. I used to travel 30 km (12 miles) from my home to school. In the end, I managed to reach my home safely. My (older) sister—who was a political activist—

explained that I should be inside the house, because children like me were being killed in the streets by the apartheid regime. The area around my house was in chaos.

Many families were helpless, shocked, and in terror when the news came that the first student—Hector Petersen—had been shot dead by the apartheid-regime police during the protest march. My sister ran away from home for the whole week because the police were after her. My parents felt helpless for they could not protect her from a police force that was regarded as "killers." . . . My sister had to wear boy's clothes to disguise herself. This helped her to escape from the police on several occasions.

—Ana Radebe

Compare and contrast the two viewpoints you have just read by explaining the similarities and the differences between the remembrances of Emilia Potenza and Ana Radebe. Write your answer on a separate sheet of paper.

CHAPTER 7

OPPRESSION, DISCRIMINATION, AND CONFLICT

BENCHMARK:

Analyze the consequences of oppression, discrimination, and conflict between cultures.

In Chapter 1 you read that, during the period of the Enlightenment, philosophers developed the idea that human beings have certain natural rights. These are life, liberty, property, and the pursuit of happiness. Today, most people who accept democratic ideas still agree that everyone has these natural, or human, rights. The benchmark for this chapter asks you to recognize and analyze violations of human rights from history and contemporary events. You need to have an understanding of the terms *discrimination*, *oppression*, and *genocide*. You should also be able to use these terms to describe actual events. Specifically, you need to know about the genocides and "ethnic cleansings" of the Holocaust, Armenia, Rwanda, Bosnia, and Iraq.

★ DEFINING TERMS ★

Oppression is the harsh or cruel treatment of people over a prolonged period of time. It includes both physical and mental mistreatment. Oppression can take many forms: political, economic, or social. For example, as the discussion of imperialism in Chapter 3 implies, the indigenous people of colonies have often been economically oppressed. The exploitation of a colony's resources by a foreign power violates the human rights of the indigenous people by denying them use of their own property. The imperialist power also oppresses them socially and politically by denying them the right to choose their own government and social structure.

Discrimination is the unfair treatment of a group based on prejudice or preconceived notions about that group. Discrimination occurs when certain people are treated differently from the rest of society because of their race, religion, gender, ethnic group, or social status. The variety of discriminatory actions can range from insulting words or behavior to physical abuse.

Genocide is a term that was coined to describe events that occurred during World War II. Historian Raphael Lemkin first used the term in his book *Axis Rule in Occupied Europe* (published in 1944). The term is based on the Greek word "genos" which means race, people, or nation, and the Latin "cide," which means killing. The term "genocide" thus refers to a deliberate and systematic effort to exterminate all members of an ethnic, religious, or national group.

★ THE UNITED NATIONS AND HUMAN RIGHTS ★

On December 10, 1948, the UN General Assembly adopted the Universal Declaration of Human Rights. This document upholds the dignity of all human beings. In part, it was a reaction to the horrendous events of the two world wars. The declaration has served as an important guideline for the actions of the United Nations. It also is a good summary of what are considered to be human rights today. The table below summarizes these rights.

Universal Declaration of Human Rights	
Article 1	All people are born free and equal in dignity and rights. They should act with brotherhood toward one another.
Article 2	Human rights apply to all, regardless of race, religion, sex, language, social origin, political opinion, or ownership of property.
Article 3	All people have the right to life, liberty, and security.
Article 4	Slavery shall be prohibited.
Article 5	Torture, cruelty, and inhuman treatment or punishments are prohibited.
Article 6	People have a right of recognition before the law.
Article 7	All are equal before the law and are entitled to equal protection.
Article 8	All people have the right to seek justice by legal means if their rights have been violated.
Article 9	Arbitrary arrest and detention are prohibited.
Article 10	All people are entitled to a fair and public trial or hearing if accused of a crime.
Article 11	All people have the right to be presumed innocent until proven guilty.
Article 12	All people have the right to privacy in their home, family, and correspondence, and their honor and reputation shall not be attacked.
Article 13	All people have the right to freedom and movement in their country.
Article 14	All people are entitled to asylum [shelter] in other countries to protect themselves from prosecution.
Article 15	All people have the right to their own nationality.
Article 16	All adults have the right to marry and have a family.
Article 17	All people have the right to own property.
Article 18	All people have the right to freedom of thought, conscience, and religion.

Article 19	All people have the right to freedom of expression [speech] and the right to freely hold opinions.
Article 20	All people have the right to freely assemble peacefully in groups. They also have the right to associate freely with others.
Article 21	The will of the people is the basis for all government authority. People have the right to participate in the government of their country.
Article 22	All people have economic, social, and cultural rights.
Article 23	Everyone has the right to work and join trade unions. All have the right to fair and equal pay for their work.
Article 24	All people have the right to rest and leisure.
Article 25	All people have the right to a standard of living that provides adequate food, clothing, shelter, and health care. Mothers and children have the right to special care and protection.
Article 26	All people have the right to education. Education should promote tolerance, friendship, and peace.
Article 27	All people have the right of access to the arts and to share in scientific advancement.
Article 28	All people of the world have a right to an international order to protect their rights and freedoms.
Article 29	All people have duties to society. The general welfare [rights and freedoms] of all will be guaranteed.
Article 30	No government, group, or individual has the right to destroy the rights and freedoms listed above.

As you can see, the Universal Declaration of Human Rights is a long list of rights and freedoms. Many of these rights and freedoms are based on the ideas of the philosophers of the 18th century (discussed in Chapter 1). Unfortunately, the protection of human rights is not always guaranteed, as the examples in this chapter show.

Test Yourself

What does Article 29 mean? "All people have duties to society. The general welfare (rights and freedoms) of all will be guaranteed."

★ THE HOLOCAUST ★

History has many instances of oppression, but the Holocaust stands out as a prime example of organized government oppression and genocide.

History of the Holocaust

Adolf Hitler and the National Socialist German Workers' party, the Nazis, came to power in Germany during the 1930s. The Nazis claimed that the German people were a superior race called Aryans. The Nazis looked down on non-Aryan people. This group included Jews, Slavic peoples, and Gypsies. They also felt that Catholics, Jehovah's Witnesses, Communists, homosexuals, and people with physical or mental disorders were inferior to them. Many of these people became victims of systematic, government-sponsored persecution and extermination. The Nazis were most relentless toward the Jews. Their murder of some 6 million Jews and 5 million other people is known as the Holocaust.

Treaty of Versailles. Germany's devastating defeat in World War I and the ensuing Treaty of Versailles created the climate for the Holocaust. The humiliating terms of the Versailles Treaty created resentment among the German people. Hitler was able to use this resentment to his advantage by blaming Jews for Germany's economic problems. In *Mein Kampf*, he refers to Jews as parasites and warns that they will hurt the Aryan race: "The mightiest counterpart to the Aryan is represented by the Jew." When Hitler took power in 1933, he had his chance to turn his racial beliefs into government policy.

Nuremberg Laws. The organized persecution of Jews in Nazi Germany began with the passage of the Nuremberg Laws in 1935. One of these laws, "The Law for the Protection of German Blood and German Honor," prohibited all marriages between Jews and German Christians. "The Reich Citizenship Law" denied German citizenship to Jews. Jews were reclassified as "nationals" and were banned from certain jobs. Access to education was blocked, and property rights were taken away. Eventually, all Jews were issued special identification cards and were required to wear a yellow star on their clothing to identify them in public. Some German cities put up signs that said, "Jews Not Welcome."

Kristallnacht. Not surprisingly, violence against Jews soon followed these measures. An incident on November 7, 1938, set off a wave of violence. A Jewish teenager living in Paris was upset that his family in Germany had been forced out of their home and deported to Poland. The teenager went to the German embassy in Paris and shot a German official. This official died two days later. Joseph Goebbels, the German minister of propaganda, used the incident as an excuse to sanction violence against German Jews.

On November 9 and 10, 1938, the violence began. German mobs roamed the streets of cities and towns, attacking Jewish-owned businesses and Jewish homes. Windows were broken. Shops were looted and property destroyed. Jewish schools and cemeteries were vandalized. Over 7,000 Jewish-owned businesses were destroyed. Hundreds of Jews were beaten, and nearly 100 died in

The day after *Kristallnacht*: the 1938 Nazi party attacks on Jews and their property in Germany

the violence. Thousands were arrested and taken off to concentration camps. The two-night campaign of violence against German Jews is now called *Kristallnacht*, which means "Night of Broken Glass." It was the beginning of ever-increasing violence against the Jewish people. Many historians consider *Kristallnacht* the beginning of the Holocaust.

The German government blamed the Jews for starting the violence of *Kristallnacht*. In retaliation, it issued a new set of restrictive laws against Jews in Germany and German-held territory. Jews were required to turn over any gold or other precious metals to the government. Jewish-owned jewelry, art, and stocks and bonds were subject to confiscation at any time. Driver's licenses were suspended. Jews were prohibited from owning weapons, carrier pigeons, or radios. A nationwide curfew for Jews was established to keep them off the streets during nighttime hours.

The Holocaust Spreads. Meanwhile, Germany was waging a war of conquest. As German troops swept through Eastern Europe, they were followed by special forces known as the *Einsatzgruppen*. These were mobile killing units. First they rounded up Jews and shot them. Then they threw the bodies into ditches and covered them over with earth. Later, mobile gas units were used to kill the victims more quickly. Although more than a million Jews were killed by the *Einsatzgruppen*, Nazi officials were not satisfied. Executions were not keeping pace with the territorial conquests of the German army.

It was decided to transport all Jews to temporary holding areas known as *ghettos* (separate, walled-off areas of cities). Troops surrounded the ghettos to control traffic in and out. Living conditions inside were miserable. Diseases spread rapidly and starvation was common. Many ghetto residents were forced to do labor in nearby fields or factories. Although uprisings occurred, the un- armed and starving ghetto residents were no match for the well-equipped and well-fed German army.

The Final Solution. By 1942, German armed forces had overrun much of Europe. Nazi plans for the extermination of European Jews were put into action. At a meeting of Nazi officials called the Wannsee Conference, a new plan took shape. Called the *Final Solution*, the plan called for the mass killing of all Jews in Europe.

A network of concentration camps were built throughout Eastern Europe. Some of these camps served as slave labor camps. Inmates worked in factories or mines. Long hours and poor nutrition resulted in many deaths.

Other camps served the same purpose as the ghettos: temporary holding areas. Jews were removed from their homes and held in these camps until they could be transported to the death camps.

Six death camps were built in early 1942. Thousands of people entered the camps each day. New arrivals were stripped of their possessions and forced into gas chambers, where they were put to death. Special ovens called crema- toriums were used to dispose of the dead bodies.

Test Yourself
Why was the Wannsee Conference significant in the history of the Holocaust?

★ ARMENIA ★

In the 1800s, many Armenian people lived in the Ottoman Empire. It was a vast, multinational empire in Southeastern Europe and Southwest Asia. The empire was ruled by Turks. Although Armenians faced some discrimination from the Turkish government, they lived peacefully with their Turkish neigh- bors. This began to change in the late 1800s, as nationalist feelings began to increase. As other minorities successfully broke away from the Ottoman Empire, the Armenians became more conscious of their nationality. They, too, wanted their own country.

Strife Between Turks and Armenians

The differences between the Turkish majority and the Armenian minority became more pronounced as the government of the Ottoman Empire grew weaker politically. Fearful that Armenian nationalism would contribute to the breakup of the Ottoman Empire, Sultan Abdul-Hamid II (ruled 1876–1909), intensified the oppression of Armenians. The oppression led to violence, which in turn led to the First Armenian Massacre.

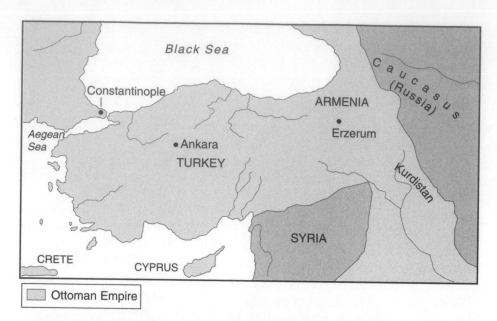

Ottoman Empire, showing Armenia in eastern Turkey

First Armenian Massacre. It is unclear whether the Turks or the Armenians were responsible for beginning the violence. Partly in protest against government oppression and partly to call international attention to their desire for an independent Armenia, Armenian rebels engaged in acts of violence against Turks. On August 26, 1896, one group of revolutionaries raided the Ottoman Bank, shot the guards, and captured about 140 bank employees. According to some accounts, Turkish mobs retaliated by killing 50,000 Armenians. Other accounts claim that Armenian activists massacred 5,000 Turks.

In 1908, the Sultan's government was overthrown by a group known as the Young Turks (officially known as the Committee for Union and Progress). Hoping for reforms, many Armenians initially supported the new government. But World War I prevented these reforms.

Second Armenian Massacre. Many Armenians living in the Ottoman Empire supported its enemy, Russia. The Ottoman government feared that these Armenians would help Russia to invade the empire. Therefore, the government began to take measures against its Armenian citizens. Some accounts state that the government merely intended to move Armenians away from the Russian border. They say that armed attacks against Armenian villagers were used only to force armed resisters to obey the evacuation orders.

Still other accounts say that the government intended to remove all Armenians from the Turkish part of the Ottoman Empire. They state that various incidents of government oppression against Armenians occurred during this period. For example, on April 24, 1915, the Committee for Union and Progress summoned a group of leading Armenian intellectuals to Istanbul and then executed them. Many other Armenians were also executed at that time in other parts of the empire. Able-bodied Armenian men were taken from their villages and towns. Many of the men believed they were being drafted into the army to fight the war. Instead, they were executed or forced into hard labor.

In the spring of 1915, after many armed clashes between government troops and Armenian villagers, the government ordered the deportation of all Armenians living in the Turkish part of the Ottoman Empire to Syria and Mesopotamia. It has been reported that the government troops forced the Armenians to travel to these areas by foot and refused them food or water. It was, in effect, a death march, and over a million died of starvation and disease. The small number of Armenians who survived this ordeal fled across the border into Russian territory—an area that is now independent Armenia.

Armenians Today. Today, there are large Armenian populations living in Egypt, other parts of the Middle East, Canada, the United States, and the independent Armenian state that was once part of Russia. Their parents and grandparents were the survivors of the Armenian genocide. Armenians around the world remember the Armenian dead and honor them on April 24, Genocide Memorial Day.

Test Yourself
Why did the Turkish government move masses of Armenians away from the Russian border during World War I?

★ RWANDA ★

Rwanda is a small Central African nation that gained independence from Belgium in 1962. Its population of over 7 million is mainly made up of two major ethnic groups: the Hutus (90 percent) and the Tutsis (less than 10 percent).

Enmity Between the Tutsis and the Hutus

During colonial rule by the Belgians, the Tutsis had enjoyed political, economic, and social power over the Hutus. The Hutus, who were the majority group in Rwanda, resented this domination. When Rwanda became independent, they began to massacre the Tutsis. The surviving Tutsis fled the country. While in exile, Tutsis formed the Rwandan Patriotic Front, a rebel army. This group invaded Rwanda in 1990, touching off a civil war.

Full-Scale Civil War. A shaky cease-fire was set up in 1993. A United Nations force was sent to Rwanda to keep the peace. It did so with some success until 1994. In April of that year, the new president of Rwanda, a Hutu, and the president of neighboring Burundi were killed as their airplane was shot down by ground-to-air missiles near the airport of Kigali, Rwanda's capital. This act of violence again plunged Rwanda into civil war.

Hutu extremists began a genocide against their Tutsi neighbors. The Rwandan army and Hutu militias set up roadblocks to prevent Tutsis from leaving the country. Death squads went from house to house killing any Tutsis

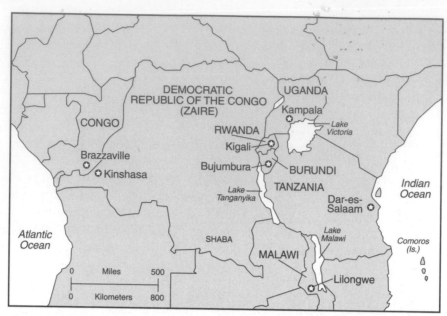

Central Africa

they could find. They also attacked and killed Hutus and Belgians who objected to the actions of the army and the militias. The United States, Belgium, and other countries evacuated their citizens. Moreover, the United Nations withdrew its peacekeeping forces.

The political vacuum allowed the Hutus to do what they wanted. Over the next four months in 1994, more than a million people were killed. The killings were especially gruesome. Men, women, children, and even babies were executed. Hutus attacked hospitals and churches to seek Tutsi victims. In some instances, average Hutu citizens were ordered to kill their Tutsi neighbors or face death themselves.

Refugees from Rwanda at a camp in neighboring Zaire (now Congo)

Uneasy Peace. In June 1994, the United Nations sent French troops to Rwanda. Meanwhile, Tutsi fighters were able to capture the city of Kigali. Tutsis, too, carried out gruesome killings. The Hutu government fled to the neighboring country of Zaire, and thousands of Hutu refugees followed. The genocide came to an end.

Test Yourself
Why did exiled Tutsis form the Rwandan Patriotic Front?

★ BOSNIA ★

Bosnia is located in southeastern Europe. The Balkan Mountains are the dominant geographical feature of this part of Europe. Various ethnic groups migrated to the Balkans during medieval times, and independent states were created then and later.

Migration to the area has continued into modern times. As a result, varied ethnic, religious, and national groups, including Serbs, Croats, Slovenians, and Bosnians, inhabit the Balkans. Collectively, these groups are known as the Southern Slavs. Although they do have similar languages and other cultural affinities, they have some major differences. The major division is one of religion. The main religions of the region are Roman Catholicism, Orthodox Christianity, and Islam. Non-Slavs, including Greeks and Albanians, also live in the Balkans.

History of Bosnia

In the 19th century, the Balkans became part of the Ottoman Empire. The Ottoman government maintained peace and order in the Balkans. Individual ethnic and religious groups were allowed some freedoms as long as they were peaceful and paid taxes to the government in Constantinople.

Decline of the Ottoman Empire. As you have read, by the end of the 19th century, the Ottoman Empire had grown weak. Because of military losses, the empire lost territory to other, more powerful countries. One area that the Ottomans lost was Bosnia, which became part of the Austrian Empire. As discussed in Chapter 4, nationalism, a desire for self-government, was sweeping throughout Europe at that time. The Serbs, the dominant ethnic group of Bosnia, were caught up in this movement. Many wanted to create a Greater Serbia to unite all Serbs who lived in Bosnia, parts of the Ottoman Empire, and elsewhere. Serbian nationalism was one of the factors that led to the outbreak of World War I.

After World War I, the Allied powers meeting at the Paris Peace Conference in 1919 redrew the map of Europe. A new nation was created to unite the Southern Slavic peoples of the Balkans. This new nation became known as Yugoslavia, meaning "kingdom of the Southern Slavs." A Serb was crowned king of Yugoslavia.

From a Serbian viewpoint, the dream of a Greater Serbia had been achieved. Other groups in Yugoslavia viewed the formation of Yugoslavia differently. They thought that unification should be the uniting of several ethnic or religious groups of equal power. They did not want to be dominated by Serbs.

During World War II (1939–1945), Yugoslavia was invaded by the Germans and Italians. Life was chaotic. Various ethnic groups took advantage of the chaos to try to consolidate power within Yugoslavia and to kill off other groups. This fighting created deep-seated hatred and suspicion among Yugoslavia's various groups.

As World War II came to a close, Communist fighters in Yugoslavia (under the leadership of Josip Broz, or Tito, as he became known) were a powerful force. They helped defeat German forces, and then set up a Communist government. Tito headed the new nation of semi-independent republics, maintaining a strong federal government under his personal control. Although he was a dictator, he set up a system to rotate government posts among the various nationalities. With measures such as this, Tito was successful in keeping the peace within Yugoslavia.

After Tito's death in 1980, his system continued for a time to maintain peace and order. In 1984, the Winter Olympics were held successfully in Sarajevo, the capital of Bosnia. But later in the 1980s, growing economic problems, widespread strikes, and a government scandal disrupted the calm. Ethnic tensions increased. At a time when other Communist governments were crumbling throughout Eastern Europe (discussed in Chapter 5), Yugoslavia's Communist party was also vulnerable. As the party's influence weakened, the various republics of Yugoslavia began to assert more independence.

Recent Events. In 1990, the Communist party of Yugoslavia was disbanded. But this did not stop the breakup of Yugoslavia. In that same year, Serbian leader Slobodan Milosevic dissolved the Kosovo government. In June 1991, Croatia and Slovenia proclaimed their independence from Yugoslavia. Soon Serbs living in Croatia rebelled against the new government and began a civil war.

Meanwhile, the majority Croats and Muslims of Bosnia voted to declare independence from Yugoslavia. Serbs there boycotted the election and began fighting against the new Bosnian government. On April 5, 1992, a rally was held in Sarajevo, the capital of newly independent Bosnia. Attending the rally were Serbs, Croats, and Muslims, all calling for peace with one another. Serbian snipers opened fired on the demonstrators, killing and wounding many unarmed people.

Beginning the next day, Sarajevo came under shelling by rebel Serbian artillery. Serbian rebels units seized roads and occupied small villages throughout Bosnia. The nation of Bosnia became a battlefield, with Croats and Muslims controlling the cities and Serbs controlling the countryside.

This was the beginning of *ethnic cleansing*. Ethnic cleansing is a program to forcibly remove an ethnic group from an area and make it available for settlement by another group. All participants in the Bosnian War practiced ethnic cleansing. But the Bosnian Serb forces, under the command of Radovan Karadzic, were the most systematic in following this procedure. Typically, the rebel Serb forces surrounded a village, told the residents to leave, and seized their property. Often, they burned their homes. Rapes and executions were

"Ethnic cleansing"

used to further intimidate the victims. It was common for civilian political leaders to be executed on the spot. Muslim men between 16 and 60 were sent to concentration camps, where many were killed and buried in mass graves. Women, children, and elderly men were often transported to a territorial border and forced to leave the country.

Milosevic's Yugoslav government supported but did not control the Bosnian rebels. International attempts to negotiate a peace settlement failed.

Family members try to identify the Bosnian victims of the Srebenica massacre.

Former Yugoslavia, after the 1995 Dayton Accords

The United Nations declared six Bosnian cities to be safe zones that were not to be attacked. Food and other supplies were sent to the refugees in these cities. UN efforts failed, however, to bring about a solution to Bosnia's fighting.

In July 1995, Serbian rebel forces overran two of the UN safe zones: Srebrenica and Zepa. About 8,000 Bosnian Muslims were massacred. Sarajevo continued to be shelled by rebel artillery. In response, the United States and its allies hit Bosnian Serb areas with air strikes. At the same time, Croatian and Muslim forces successfully attacked Serbian-controlled areas. Slobodan Milosevic did not intervene on behalf of the Bosnian Serbs. The time was ripe for peace talks.

In November 1995, representatives from Bosnia, Croatia, and Yugoslavia met near Dayton, Ohio, to negotiate a peace settlement. This agreement is now known as the Dayton Accords. Main provisions of the Dayton Accords are as follows:

1. Control of Bosnian lands was divided between the Serbs (49 percent) and Muslims and Croatians (51 percent).

2. An International Criminal Tribunal for the Former Yugoslavia was established at The Hague, Netherlands, to try war criminals. Those accused of war crimes became ineligible to run for public office.

3. The 2 million refugees were given the right to reclaim their land or to receive compensation for lost land.

4. Four military zones were established in Bosnia to maintain the peace. These zones were divided among the U.S., British, French, and joint European forces.

Test Yourself
Why did Sarajevo become a symbol of the civil war in Yugoslavia?

★ IRAQ ★

In 1979, Saddam Hussein seized power in Iraq and established a dictatorship that deprived the Iraqi people of most of their rights. By law, only one political party was permitted. About 8 percent of the population belonged to this Ba'ath Socialist party. Most citizens had no say in the government. Nor did the government guarantee people's rights.

Oppression Under Saddam

Average citizens were not permitted to leave Iraq without putting up a large amount of money to guarantee their return. Freedom of assembly was limited. Group demonstrations were permitted only if they supported the government.

Cruel punishments were administered for those who broke the law or challenged the power of the government. Such minor crimes as theft were punished by beatings, amputations, branding, and even death. Many Iraqi citizens who were accused of breaking the law simply disappeared.

Campaign Against the Kurds. The government of Saddam Hussein continued a campaign begun by previous rulers to put down a rebellious ethnic group known as the Kurds. The members of this large minority group live mainly in northern Iraq. Kurds were also a large minority in Turkey, Iran, and Syria. For years, Kurds had been agitating for an independent nation called Kurdistan, which would unit the Kurdish areas of these four countries.

In March 1988, the world was shocked to learn that Saddam's government forces had attacked the Kurdish town of Halabja, Iraq. Over a period of three days, the town was hit with artillery, bombs, and finally chemical weapons (including mustard gas and sarin). About 5,000 Kurds were killed by chemical weapons.

Halabja was only one incident in this campaign. The Iraqi army destroyed some 4,000 villages. People forced from their homes were sent to live in government-controlled towns. Perhaps as many as 300,000 Kurds were killed. The brutal attack on defenseless civilians of Halabja became a symbol of the cruelty of Saddam Hussein's government.

Intervention of Other Nations. In January and February of 1991, the United States and other nations attacked Iraq in response to Iraq's invasion of neighboring Kuwait. After just a few weeks of fighting in this Persian Gulf War, the United States and its allies defeated Saddam's armed forces. Northern Iraq came under the protection of the United States and ten other powers in a military operation known as Operation Provide Comfort. Its purpose was to establish a safe haven for the Kurds. Food and medical supplies were provided to Kurdish refugees. A "no-fly zone" was established over the Kurdish territory to prevent Iraq from bombing Kurdish targets.

In 2003, the United States again went to war with Iraq. The status of the Kurds is still an unresolved issue. While many Kurds would like to see an independent Kurdish state, the United States and many other nations are reluctant to allow the breakup of Iraq.

Test Yourself
Kurds today are a large minority in which four Southwest Asian countries?

POINTS TO REMEMBER

- Oppression is the harsh or cruel treatment of other people over a prolonged period of time.

- Discrimination is the unfair treatment of a person or group based on a variety of prejudices.

- Genocide is the systematic destruction of a large group of people.

- The Holocaust refers to the Nazi genocide that killed 6 million Jews and millions of others during World War II.

- Ethnic cleansing is a program to remove or exterminate an ethnic group from a geographical area and make it available for settlement by another ethnic group.

EXERCISES

CHECKING WHAT YOU HAVE READ

1. The Universal Declaration of Human Rights is a

   A. direct result of the Enlightenment
   B. direct result of World War II
   C. law passed by the Congress of the United States
   D. law that is followed by all members of the United Nations.

2. The Nuremberg Laws were passed to

   A. limit the right of Jews in Nazi Germany
   B. halt the spread of communism in Iraq
   C. punish Germany for war crimes committed against Jews and other minorities during World War II
   D. guarantee the rights of all Germans in Nazi Germany.

3. Organized violence against Jews in Nazi Germany began with

   A. the Final Solution
   B. the publication of *Mein Kampf*
   C. book burnings
   D. *Kristallnacht.*

4. The Kurdish people suffered at the hands of

   A. Adolf Hitler
   B. Sultan Abdul-Hamid II
   C. Saddam Hussein
   D. Radovan Karadzic.

5. The Ottoman Empire in 1900 is best described as a(n)

   A. modern Turkish state
   B. multinational empire
   C. Armenian-controlled nation
   D. powerful ally of Britain and France.

6. Bosnia is located in

   A. Western Europe
   B. Eastern Europe
   C. Southeast Europe
   D. Southwest Asia.

7. Both Bosnian Serbs and Armenians were once

   A. part of the Ottoman Empire
   B. under the rule of the Austrian Empire
   C. ruled by France
   D. allies of the United States.

8. The country of Yugoslavia was

   A. a colony of Nazi Germany
   B. created by the Allies after World War I
   C. an ally of Austria during World War I
   D. a Communist ally of Russia in the 1930s.

9. The dominant group of Africans in Rwanda before its independence were the

   A. Tutsis
   B. Burundis
   C. French
   D. Hutus.

10. Today, Kurdistan is

   A. part of the Ottoman Empire
   B. part of the Russian Empire
   C. a goal of Kurds living in Turkey, Syria, Iran, and Iraq
   D. an independent country.

USING WHAT YOU HAVE READ

1. Choose *one* of the following historical events: the Holocaust, ethnic cleansing in Bosnia, genocide in Rwanda, Iraq's

treatment of the Kurds, or the Turks treatment of the Armenians. Decide which articles of the Universal Declaration of Human Rights were violated by the event you have chosen. Explain your findings.

2. Research an example of oppression, discrimination, or conflict between cultures in the world today. Create a poster to inform your fellow students about what you have discovered.

THINKING ABOUT WHAT YOU HAVE READ

1. Create a "Wanted" poster for a group that has violated another group's human rights.

2. Either by yourself, or with a group of your fellow students, create a plan to prevent oppression, discrimination, or conflict in the world today. Share your plan with the rest of the class.

SKILLS

Interpreting Quotations

The following quotes are about discrimination and oppression. Choose one or more quotes as a basis for an essay on oppression. Be sure to give concrete examples to support your opinions.

Prejudice rarely survives experience.

—Eve Zibart

Among those who dislike oppression are many who like to oppress.

—Napoleon Bonaparte

I have always held firmly to the thought that each one of us can do a little to bring some portion of misery to an end.

—Albert Schweitzer

Tolerance implies no lack of commitment to one's own beliefs. Rather it condemns the oppression or persecution of others.

—John F. Kennedy

He who passively accepts evil is as much involved in it as he who helps to perpetuate it.

—Martin Luther King, Jr.

CHAPTER 8

CULTURAL EXCHANGES

BENCHMARK:

Analyze the way that contacts between people of different cultures result in exchanges of cultural practices.

To meet the requirements of this benchmark, you must be able to analyze cultural exchange. *Cultural diffusion* is the spread or sharing of ideas among cultures. Anytime someone comes in contact with another culture, the potential for cultural exchange exists. Since advances in communications or transportation increase contact among people of different cultures, they speed up cultural exchange.

Your daily life gives you many first-hand experiences of cultural diffusion. Mealtime is a good example of this. Think about your favorite food. Is it lasagna? Enchiladas? Stir fry? Or could it be sauerkraut with sausages? Many all-American foods, such as hotdogs, hamburgers, fries, and pizza, have been "borrowed" from foreign cuisines. You can probably think of other examples of cultural diffusion in your daily life.

You also need to understand *globalization*, a term that has been in use for about 30 years. Different people have different meanings for the term, but in general, globalization refers to the growing interdependence of the world, economically, culturally, and politically.

★ GLOBALIZATION ★

We live in a global society. What does this mean? It means that businesses and organizations are not contained within political borders. For example, a multinational business might have its headquarters in Cincinnati but own a factory in Mexico and have an office in Taiwan. A Japanese automaker might have assembly plants in Ohio. A consumer in Dayton might call to get customer assistance from an American company, but the person who handles the customer's call is in India. A Cleveland law firm might have an office in London or Rome. American fast-food restaurants can be found in Paris, Moscow, and elsewhere abroad. Business decisions made in London can affect wages and prices in Akron, Toledo, and elsewhere in this country.

A quick trip to the shopping mall gives more proof of globalization. Labels on the merchandise for sale might read "Made in China," "Mexico," or "Sri Lanka." This is true even for familiar American brands.

Globalization is increasing rapidly due to an expansion of communication and transportation systems. More and more, our links to other parts of the

Global food business: a McDonald's restaurant in Paris

Workers in a General Motors automobile plant in Shanghai, China

world are increasing each year. Political borders are becoming less important to the business world. Ease of travel allows businesspeople and tourists to travel to other parts of the globe. Improvements in telephones, computers, fax machines, and other forms of communication allow ideas to flow almost instantaneously across the surface of the globe. Electronic banking allows the flow of capital (money) from one country to another.

Cooperation and Conflict

People disagree about whether globalization is a positive or negative force in the world today. Actually, it can be both. Globalization can give the people of the world unprecedented opportunities for peace and cooperation. But, if world leaders are irresponsible or selfish, it can also lead to conflict.

Globalization as a Negative Force. Critics of globalization point out that the gap between the rich people and the poor people of the world is growing wider. People in the developing countries of Africa, Asia, and Latin America have made slow economic progress. Poverty is a major problem in the world today. Many people are barely able to obtain food, shelter, and other necessities. Meanwhile, many people living in the developed countries of Europe, North America, and elsewhere have high standards of living. Those in developed countries are usually able to meet their own basic needs and can choose among a wide array of consumer products to enhance their lifestyles.

Outsourcing. Other critics of globalization claim that the interests of workers in the United States and other developed countries are harmed by globalization. Many multinational corporations have been outsourcing jobs to other parts of the world. *Outsourcing* refers to the hiring of people in other countries to do the jobs once held by American workers. For example, manufacturing jobs have been moving from the United States to China and other Asian countries where workers' wages are low compared to those of American workers. Computer programming jobs can just as easily be done in India, where many people speak English and are well-educated, as they can be done in California or Ohio. An English-speaking Indian worker who can talk on the telephone or input text or data into a computer for an American business will probably be paid less than a person doing the same work in the United States.

Threat to National Cultures. A third major criticism of globalization is that national cultures and identities are threatened. Because of the spread of satellite TV, international media networks, and increased personal travel, U.S. and Western European fashions, music, foods, and customs are replacing local ones.

Threat to Environment. A fourth criticism of globalization concerns multinational corporations, which often disregard the environment in their drive for increased profits. They seek out countries with lax environmental laws. The smoke from their factories and other industrial wastes pollute the air, water, and land of developing countries and contribute to global warming.

Globalization As a Positive Force. Proponents of globalization agree that poverty is a problem but claim that is not as severe a problem as it has been in the past. They claim that the globalization of businesses has raised the standard of living even among the world's poorest people. They also argue that better living conditions and improved medical care have increased life expectancy in all countries of the world.

Other people point out that globalization is not the only factor to change the U.S. economy. They argue that today's economy is more dependent on the gathering and spreading of information and on service-oriented businesses than on

Computer programmers in Bangalore, India, a technology center

manufacturing. Therefore, the shortage of factory jobs in the United States would happen even without globalization. New jobs in today's economy require highly skilled workers. To meet this challenge, American workers have better access to education and training than most people around the world.

Globalization in the long term will lead to economic growth and social stability, claim its defenders. In the past, governments of developing countries often had ineffective and old-fashioned economic policies, such as relying on cash crops or exporting natural resources without leaving enough for domestic consumption. Globalization will help these governments to make better economic policy decisions.

 Test Yourself
What is the relationship between outsourcing and globalization?

★ THE ENVIRONMENT ★

In the previous section you read that globalization can damage the environment. For example, some multinational corporations build factories in countries that do not have as strict environmental laws as the United States does. The smoke and other emissions from those factories damage not only that country's ecosystem, but those of other countries as well.

Invasive Species

Another way that globalization can affect the environment is by the spread of invasive species from one country to another. These are plants, insects, and animals that crowd out or destroy native species. The emerald ash borer, a beetle that came to the United States from Asia in 2002, has been destroying trees in northwestern Ohio. The nutria, a beaverlike rodent from South America, has been infesting parkland along the Chesapeake Bay in Maryland. Native plants in the Grand Canyon are losing ground to aggressive plants that have been introduced from other parts of the world. Zebra mollusks attach themselves to ships and are carried into the Great Lakes and the Ohio and Mississippi rivers. Because these shellfish have no natural enemies in their new environments, they quickly multiply. Besides polluting the waterways and making them unsafe for other animals and plants, they choke the sewer and water systems of towns in Ohio and elsewhere.

These are a few recent examples of how the environment has been altered by "foreign invaders." Plants and animals can move across national boundaries without detection. Customs agents at major U.S. ports try to prevent this from happening, but their efforts have not always been successful.

The Case of the Powderpost Beetles. The following excerpt from a newspaper story about powderpost beetles illustrates the difficulty of controlling foreign pests.

Retirement gave Bob Miller an unexpected lesson about the connection between global trade and destructive pests. One of his colleagues' parting gifts, a mantle clock imported from China by Wal-Mart, seemed to be a dust magnet at his Reynoldsburg home. But the clock has been generating [creating] the dust, not attracting it. The culprits are tiny beetle larvae hidden inside the wooden housing that are chewing it steadily into sawdust. "When we got back from vacation last month, there was a whole pile of this powdery dust at the base of the clock," Miller said. "It was the strangest thing."

Stories of such bizarre incidents are popping up more frequently as Americans become more reliant on imported goods, which are among the leading pathways for invasive species that threaten human health, the environment, and the economy. Miller brought his clock last month to the Ohio Department of Agriculture, where experts tentatively identified the destructive insects as powderpost beetles. The clock is dotted with pinhead-size holes created by adult [insects] that emerged to find mates and lay eggs for another generation. Several species of the beetle exist in the United States, but they also are detected frequently in goods made of imported hardwoods. Second only to termites as destroyers of seasoned wood, powderpost beetles can live for months beneath the surface. Often, they don't bore their way out until after lumber has been turned into furniture or flooring. . . . Miller still can't believe that a retirement gift could have introduced destructive insects to his house. . . .

Case of the Emerald Ash Borer. One of the most destructive pests in Ohio has been the emerald ash borer. The adult beetle appears from May to July and can then travel up to one-half mile. It has a dark metallic green color and is about one-half inch in length. The insect drills into the wood of the ash, leaving distinctive serpentine tunnels under the bark and small D-shaped exit holes. The top third of the tree begins to die back, and the bark begins to split vertically. Finally, the entire tree dies.

The emerald ash borer probably came to the United States in wood-infested crates from Asia. A major infestation occurred in the Detroit area. Infested ash trees entered Ohio by means of lumber, landscape trees, and firewood. The beetles have infested native ash trees in Defiance, Franklin, Lucas, and Wood counties.

Ohioans have reason to worry: The tourism industry also benefits from the dark-red beauty of ash trees in the autumn landscape.

Battling the invasion of the emerald ash borer is not an easy task. Wooden packing crates can be fumigated, a move favored by the wood packaging industry. Or alternatives to wood packaging can be used. Increased inspection of shipping containers would be effective but costly. Ash trees themselves cannot be sprayed with effective insecticides. Once the emerald ash borer has been discovered in an ash tree, the tree must be destroyed, as well as all ash trees in a half-mile radius.

Test Yourself
How are invasive foreign plants and insects connected to globalization?

★ COLLECTIVE SECURITY ★

The collapse of communism in Europe and the rapid rate of globalization have greatly altered the way nations provide for their own security and defend themselves from attack. As you learned when you read about the Cold War in Chapter 5, the United States and the Soviet Union attempted to maintain a balance of power in the world. Neither nation became so powerful that it could dominate the other. Each country sought out defensive alliances to help safeguard its own interests. The Warsaw Pact and the North Atlantic Treaty Organization are examples of collective-defense organizations formed during the Cold War. The power of the Soviet Union and the Warsaw Pact was balanced against that of the United States and NATO; neither side was able to get the upper hand.

Since the end of the Cold War, a new world order has emerged: *collective security.* Collective security is a policy in which various governments join together to enforce mutually accepted rules for international behavior. Nations join together in organizations that promote universal interests. All aggression, whether it is aimed at one's own country or not, is considered a threat to world order. Therefore, all aggression must be opposed. World peace is the major goal of collective security. The major deterrence to aggression is retaliation by a coalition of nations that are willing to use military force or economic sanctions against the aggressor.

NATO. The role of NATO has changed from a collective-defense alliance to a collective-security organization. Formed in 1949, NATO developed a well-conceived multinational power structure. It has a permanent headquarters and an established military chain of command. It is well-suited to perform its new role of peacekeeping and security in Europe. In 1992, NATO placed economic sanctions on Yugoslavia to stop government-supported ethnic fighting. It later created a no-fly zone over Bosnia. To protect UN troops, it also employed air strikes on the Bosnian cities of Sarajevo and Gorazde. These police powers exercised by NATO proved to be successful.

Commonwealth of Independent States. A less successful attempt at collective security has been the Commonwealth of Independent States (CIS). The CIS was created in 1991–1992 by 12 former republics of the Soviet Union. Membership includes Armenia, Azerbaijan, Belarus, Georgia, Kazakhstan, Kyrgyzstan, Moldova, Russia, Tajikistan, Turkmenistan, Ukraine, and Uzbekistan. (The former Soviet Baltic republics of Latvia, Lithuania, and Estonia balked at membership.) CIS peacekeeping forces have been almost entirely Russian troops. Some authorities in Russia have been reluctant to give up their big-brother role in protecting ethnic Russians who live in other CIS nations. Until this problem can be worked out, the CIS will not have an equal, multilateral structure to promote collective security.

United Nations. Perhaps the most successful attempt at collective security has been the United Nations. The UN was formed in the aftermath of World War II. Most nations in the world are members. UN troops have been used successfully to restore order to a number of trouble spots around the globe. UN troops are currently being used to maintain peace in some countries where civil wars have broken out. The UN, however, has not been able to stop all unilateral military action (action taken by a single country for its own purposes). The goal of world peace has not been achieved.

Test Yourself
How does the United Nations illustrate the concept of collective security?

★ POPULAR CULTURE ★

Popular culture (the people's culture) often refers to those aspects of culture that are driven by the mass media. Movies, television, and publishing are examples of mass media that distribute popular culture. But popular culture also depends upon the perceptions of the people who are the consumers of the mass media. Anytime people come in contact with one another, the potential for cultural exchange or borrowing exists. Technology such as the World Wide Web helps speed up the transfer of culture.

Cultural Exchange in the Past

The sharing of ideas has been going on since ancient times. Sometimes this was intentional; sometimes it was accidental. In the ancient world, new weapons, folk stories, ideas about government, languages, food, forms of entertainment, and fashion were shared by various civilizations. When an army marched into new territories to create an empire, it carried its culture with it. When traders traveled far from home to trade for exotic goods, they took their culture along with them.

Columbian Exchange. The 16th century saw a revolutionary change in people's eating habits around the world. The *Columbian Exchange* was a result of

Christopher Columbus and other European explorers sailing to the Western Hemisphere. When they arrived here, they introduced food items that were native to Europe, Africa, and Asia. These included bananas, grapes, citrus, peaches, pears, coffee, wheat, rice, cattle, pigs, and onions. Soon, foods native to the Americas traveled back across the Atlantic Ocean to the Eastern Hemisphere. These foods included turkey, corn, tomatoes, beans, squash, potatoes, sweet potatoes, peanuts, cocoa, vanilla, avocados, and chili peppers. The effects of the Columbian Exchange were truly revolutionary. Can you imagine a restaurant in southern Italy without tomatoes, a Swiss confectioner without chocolate, or a cook in Thailand without peanuts and chili peppers? Moreover, it would be impossible to duplicate an all-American favorite—the cheeseburger—without ground beef, cheese, a wheat bun, and sliced onions.

Cultural Exchange Today

In the modern world, cultural borrowing proceeds at a more rapid pace. This is due to advanced technology, particularly in communications and transportation. The Internet, cable television, and ease of travel have facilitated the sharing of popular culture. A woman in Marion, Ohio, might use her computer to download a salsa tune recorded in Puerto Rico. A man in Youngstown might turn on his television to watch a soccer game in Italy. A couple in Shanghai, China, might go to a Western-style restaurant for dinner.

Spread of American Culture. One aspect of globalization is the rapid integration of culture. Some people fear that the culture of the United States is taking over the world. English is the language of the Internet and the language of business. American movies, music, fashions, sports, and food are dominant forces in the world. The term "McDonaldization" has been coined for the rapid spread of American culture. McDonald's restaurants (and other U.S. fast-food chains) are more and more common in major cities around the world.

Will the spread of American tastes and values cause an end to indigenous (native) cultures and the homogenization (sameness) of one world culture? Time will tell, but the answer is probably "no."

First of all, the spread of culture is two-way. American consumers are adopting British television, Latin American salsa music, Japanese animation, German automobiles, and other aspects of foreign cultures. The typical American consumer is constantly exposed to foreign ideas and products.

Second, the perception of American culture is often changed when it reaches foreign shores. The following example of simultaneous Starbucks' openings in Bloomington, Indiana, and Shanghai, China, illustrates differences in perception.

In Bloomington, Starbucks triggered mixed reactions. Some locals welcomed its arrival. Others staged nonviolent protests or smashed its windows, complaining that the chain's record on environmental and labor issues was abysmal and that Starbucks would drive local coffee shops out of business. In Shanghai, by contrast, there were no demonstrations. The chain's arrival was seen as contributing to, rather than putting a check upon, the proliferation of new, independently run coffeehouses.

Chinese couple in a Western-style restaurant in Shanghai

The local meanings of Shanghai Starbucks do not stop there. For example, when outlets open in Europe, they are typically seen, for understandable reasons, as symbols of creeping—or steam-rolling—Americanization. In Shanghai, though, guidebooks sometimes classify Starbucks as a "European-style" (as opposed to "[an Asian]-style") foreign coffeehouse. To further complicate things, the management company that operates the dozens of Shanghai Starbucks outlets is based not in Seattle but in Taiwan.

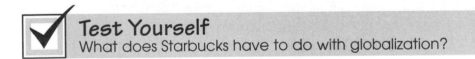

Test Yourself
What does Starbucks have to do with globalization?

★ POLITICAL SYSTEMS ★

An important aspect of globalization is the growth of political integration. Traditionally, political decisions have been made by independent nations. But economic and social globalization have resulted in the globalization of politics. Voluntary political-integration organizations, intergovernmental organizations, and nongovernmental organizations (NGOs) often make political decisions.

Voluntary Political-Integration Organizations

An obvious example of a voluntary political-integration organization is the United Nations (discussed in Chapter 5). But there are several other important organizations that engage in economic and political decision making.

European Union. The European Union (EU) is such an organization. The forerunner of the EU was developed in the 1950s by Belgium, Germany, Finland, France, Italy, Luxembourg, and the Netherlands. Between 1973 and 1995, Austria, Denmark, Greece, Ireland, Portugal, Spain, Sweden, and the United Kingdom joined, and eventually adopted the name European Union. In 2004, they were joined by ten more nations.

Initially, the EU was almost exclusively concerned with the reduction of trade barriers among its members. Today, the EU is also concerned with the issues of jobs, environmental protection, security, human rights, and regional development.

The European Union has been successful in reaching its goals. It has created a continentwide market with few barriers to trade. It has established a new monetary unit, the euro, now used in much of Europe. The standard of living has improved across the continent. Finally, the political position of Europe has been strengthened.

Association of Southeast Asian Nations. Another important regional organization is the Association of Southeast Asian Nations (ASEAN). In 1967, Indonesia, Malaysia, the Philippines, Singapore, and Thailand formed ASEAN to promote economic growth, social progress, political stability, and peace in Southeast Asia. The original five members have been joined by Brunei, Cambodia, Laos, Myanmar, and Vietnam. These countries are inhabited by 500 million people. The value of goods traded between ASEAN nations and the United States is over $700 billion a year.

African Union. The African Union (AU) was established in 1999. It grew out of an older organization, the Organization of African Unity. The AU is designed to promote the social and economic growth of Africa. It also promotes unity and solidarity among the nations and peoples of the continent. Another stated priority of the AU is to improve the status of women and youth.

Like the UN and other international organizations, the AU has a number of divisions. The Assembly, the most important part of the organization, is made up of the government leaders of the various member nations. Other parts of the AU include the Executive Council; Peace and Security Council; Court of Justice; Economic, Social, and Cultural Council (ECOSOCC); and Pan-African Parliament.

The African Union is much newer than the European Union and ASEAN. In terms of political and economic progress, it has not yet achieved the same level of success as these other two organizations. Most nations of Africa have become members of the AU, so the importance of the organization will probably grow.

Trade Organizations in the Western Hemisphere. In addition to the above organizations, three regional trade associations have emerged in the Western Hemisphere in recent years. The North American Free Trade Agreement (NAFTA) is a trade agreement among the United States, Canada, and Mexico. This 1994 agreement put an end to tariffs among the three nations. A businessperson in Columbus, Ohio, can trade with someone in Acapulco or Toronto much as he or she might trade with someone in Chicago. There are no economic barriers to stop the flow of goods or capital in these kinds of transactions. Not surprisingly, NAFTA has resulted in a tremendous increase in U.S.-Canadian and U.S.-Mexican trade. Access to more production sites and the ability to sell to more consumers have increased business activity in all three countries.

Similar to NAFTA is the proposed Central American Free Trade Agreement (CAFTA). Member nations would include Costa Rica, Guatemala, El Salvador, Honduras, Nicaragua, and possibly the Dominican Republic.

Mercosur (which means "Southern Common Market") is a free-trade agreement of four South American nations: Argentina, Brazil, Paraguay, and Uruguay. Bolivia and Chile are associate members of Mercosur. The goals of Mercosur are similar to those of NAFTA and CAFTA.

Intergovernmental Organizations

Three intergovernmental organizations with great financial and political power are the World Bank, International Monetary Fund, and World Trade Organization. Although they are not governments themselves, they influence governmental decision making through their institutional policies.

World Bank. The World Bank issues loans to governments around the world for development projects. For example, a country that wants to build a dam to generate hydroelectric power, provide clean drinking water, or control flooding may ask the World Bank for a loan.

Loans from the World Bank have strings attached, however. Loans come with special conditions called "structural-adjustment programs." These have been used to force loan recipients to change some of their governmental policies. In the example of the dam building discussed above, the country may be forced to privatize the distribution of water once the dam is built. The World Bank is located in Washington, D.C. Some critics of the bank say that it is too closely tied to U.S. interests.

International Monetary Fund. The International Monetary Fund (IMF), like the World Bank, is located in Washington, D.C., and it too makes loans to governments around the world. The purpose of these loans is different, however. IMF's loans are made to help stabilize the *currency* (money system) of a country. Stable currencies help maintain order in world markets. Like the loans from the World Bank, the IMF's loans have special conditions, which some critics of the IMF say are unfair. In the former Yugoslavia, some critics point out, the IMF demanded privatization of publicly owned businesses, which were then taken over by speculators and foreign interests.

World Trade Organization. A third example of a multilateral financial institution is the World Trade Organization (WTO). The WTO replaced a similar, older institution in 1995. Over 145 nations belong to the World Trade Organization. Meetings are held every two years. The purpose of the WTO is to lower tariffs (taxes on imports) and eliminate any other barriers to free trade. The fundamental philosophy of the WTO is that free trade benefits all. But the WTO's critics say that its trade policies favor rich countries at the expense of poor ones.

In Genoa, Italy, protesters demonstrate against the World Trade Organization.

Group of Seven/Eight (G7/8)

The Group of Seven/Eight (G7/8) is not a formal institution. Beginning in 1975, the leaders of seven of the world's wealthiest nations have met annually at a summit meeting. The G/7 members are Canada, France, Germany, Great Britain, Italy, Japan, and the United States. In 1994, the leader of Russia began meeting with the G/7 leaders, thus the name G8.

The G7/G8 leaders do not have a set agenda for each meeting. Instead, they discuss whatever political and economic issues they think are important in a given year. Because they are the leaders of most of the world's wealthiest nations, any decisions that the G7/G8 leaders make can greatly impact world events.

Nongovernmental Organizations

The term *nongovernmental organization (NGO)* is used by the United Nations to refer to independent citizen-action organizations. One way to describe a nongovernmental organization is to call it an international interest group. Most NGOs are nonprofit, voluntary, and private. They often deal with quality-of-life issues such as health, hunger, poverty, the environment, and human rights. Examples of NGOs include Amnesty International, CARE, Greenpeace, and the International Committee for the Red Cross. NGOs use their power to persuade or influence independent nations and international organizations to take certain actions.

Test Yourself
What does the World Trade Organization have to do with globalization?

★ RELIGION ★

Missionaries often spread religion. They go to different countries to do good works and to teach the people the beliefs of a certain religion. Historically, there are many examples of missionaries converting people to a new religion.

Spread of Religion Through International Trade

Another way religion has spread is through casual contact among ordinary people. Traders, for example, take their religious practices with them when they travel to markets in different parts of the world.

Silk Road. Since the means of communication and transportation have always facilitated trade between different countries, they have contributed to the spread of religion as well. A good historical example of this is the Silk Road. In ancient times, Chinese silk cloth was highly valued for its strength, lightness, luster, and beauty. Silk was costly to make since a pound of silk required about 2,000 silkworms to spin their cocoons. The cocoons were then soaked in water, unraveled, and woven into cloth. Wealthy Romans especially liked to wear silk clothing, and a steady trade developed between China and the Roman Empire. The series of roads that connected these two ancient civilizations was known as the Silk Road. Other peoples, such as Indians, Persians, Greeks, and the nomads of Central Asia, also used this trade route to transport spices, gold, metals, precious stones, timber, and grains.

Religious ideas, too, traveled along the Silk Road. These included Buddhism, Christianity, and Islam. As caravans moved goods along the Silk Road, religious teachers helped convert people to new religions.

Spread of Religion in Modern Times. In today's world, modern technology helps spread religion, just as the Silk Road did in ancient times. People have easy access to other countries through improved forms of transportation, including the jet airplane. The world's major religions and even small religious sects have Web sites on the Internet. Radio and television stations often broadcast religious programs. Information about theology and religious practices is easily transmitted beyond political borders. All religions, in effect, have become global.

 Test Yourself
How has the Internet helped globalize religion?

> ▶ POINTS TO REMEMBER

- We live in a global society, but people do not agree whether globalization is a positive or negative force.

- Environmental problems can easily spread around the world.

- Collective security is the rule in international relations today.

- Because of technological advances, one country's popular culture can easily spread around the world.

- Major international organizations have been developed to promote economic globalization.

- Religions can spread farther and faster because of globalization.

EXERCISES

CHECKING WHAT YOU HAVE READ

1. The rapidly growing interdependence of the world's economies is known as

   A. diffusion
   B. McDonaldization
   C. globalization
   D. integration.

2. Which one of the following nations is not a member of the G7/G8?

   A. Spain
   B. France
   C. Japan
   D. Italy

3. What organization makes loans to support development projects in various countries of the world?

   A. WTO
   B. World Bank
   C. IMF
   D. NATO

4. NAFTA is a trade agreement the United States made with

   A. Canada and Mexico
   B. Western European nations
   C. Latin America
   D. India and China.

5. The term "outsourcing" refers to

   A. U.S. efforts to create more jobs than our competitors
   B. exploiting natural resources for industry
   C. cooperative global efforts to preserve the environment
   D. the practice of exporting jobs from developed countries to less-developed countries.

6. The process of globalization is more rapid when

   A. transportation and communication systems are improved
   B. governments pass tariffs
   C. the number of NGOs stay steady
   D. governments tighten security.

7. What effect have some foreign insects and animals like the emerald leaf borer and the zebra mollusk had on new countries in which they settled?

   A. They increased the new countries' standard of living.
   B. They improved air and water quality.
   C. They caused damage to their new environment.
   D. They had no effect.

8. The Warsaw Pact and NATO were both founded to be

   A. collective-defense systems
   B. collective-security organizations
   C. intergovernmental organizations
   D. balance-of-power associations.

9. The Columbian Exchange refers to

   A. a program of the World Bank
   B. efforts by the International Monetary Fund to strengthen the economies of poor nations
   C. the trading of foods, plants, and animals between the Old and New worlds in the century after the explorations of Christopher Columbus
   D. environmental hazards resulting from heavy industries in Europe and North America.

10. If you were shopping in an EU country, what would be the best money to have in your pocket?

   A. the German mark
   B. the French franc
   C. the euro
   D. the dollar

USING WHAT YOU HAVE READ

1. Find a roster of your favorite professional basketball or baseball team. Note the native country of the players on that team. Mark the locations on a world map and connect each location with the location of the team. What does your map tell you about globalization?

2. Assume you and your fellow classmates work for the Ohio Department of Agriculture. Form a committee of two to five people and brainstorm ideas for stopping the spread of the emerald ash borer. Make a list of your best ideas.

THINKING ABOUT WHAT YOU HAVE READ

1. Check the labels of your clothing at home. Write down the country of origin for each item of clothing. Note where your clothes were manufactured. Compare your list with those of your classmates and discuss the implications of your findings.

2. On a sheet of paper write the word "globalization." Create a web diagram on the subject. Be sure to include both causes and effects of globalization on your web.

SKILLS

Interpreting a Cartoon

Study the cartoon below. Then explain what the cartoonist is saying about American agriculture and foreign trade.

REPRINTED, WITH PERMISSION, FROM THE COLUMBUS DISPATCH

CHAPTER 9
REGIONS OVER TIME

BENCHMARK:

Analyze the cultural, physical, economic, and political characteristics that define regions and describe reasons that regions change over time.

To meet the requirements of this benchmark, you must understand how you can use data to make comparisons between and among countries. In particular, you must know how to interpret data on birthrates, death rates, infant mortality rates, education levels, and the per capita gross domestic product. In addition, you should be able to explain how differing points of view play a role in conflicts over territory and resources within and among regions. Finally, you must understand the factors that contribute to cooperation and conflict in regions, including political and economic conditions, resources, geographic locations, and differences in culture.

★ INTERPRETING DATA TO MAKE COMPARISONS ★

The world is made up of many diverse regions and countries. In today's global economy, the world's regions and countries have become increasingly dependent on one another. In order to understand how regions of the world interact, it is important to understand the similarities and differences among regions. Interpreting data will help you to make meaningful comparisons between places.

Data are facts and figures or, more broadly, information from which conclusions can be drawn. (*Data* is the plural form of *datum*.) Data may be statistics, which are often obtained from surveys, such as the U.S. Census, which is taken every ten years. Data may also be obtained from historical sources such as the birth and death records of a city or town. Data are often presented in the form of graphs, charts, and maps. Interpreting data is not just about reading numbers. You must be able to look at data and draw conclusions from what you see. Always keep in mind the source of any data you use, and be aware of any bias that might influence the presentation of data.

Data for Studying Different Regions and Countries

The kinds of data that will help you compare regions and countries include population statistics (birthrates, death rates, and infant mortality rates) and social and economic statistics (gross domestic product and education levels). These factors make up the *demographics* of regions. Although demographics also deal with indicators such as immigration, migration, and population distribution in a region, you need deal only with the indicators listed above.

Birthrate. *Birthrate* is the ratio of live births in a region in a specific time period. It is often calculated in terms of the number of live births per 1,000 people in one year. Countries or regions with high birthrates often have to deal with problems brought on by increased population. These countries must deal with issues such as feeding and housing people and providing them with adequate education and health care. A large population often leads to overcrowding in cities, poverty, and food shortages. Some countries, such as China, have tried to control the birthrate. China's population is so large (over 1.3 billion people) that its resources must be stretched thin to accommodate its population. As a result, China placed a one-child limit on couples.

High birthrate is often a problem in developing nations. Developing nations are characterized by little industry, low income per household or family, and low gross domestic product. *Gross domestic product (GDP)* is the value of the goods and services a nation produces in a given time period (usually a year). Often, cultural and social factors contribute to high birthrates in these nations. Although the governments may want to decrease birthrates, cultural values influence people to have many children. China is an example of a culture that has traditionally valued large families.

Developed nations (those that are wealthy, industrial, and technologically advanced), in general, have lower birthrates than developing nations. The *fertility rate* (average number of children born to each woman) is lower in these nations than in developing nations for the following reasons: (1) the availability of birth control methods, (2) the role of women in society, and (3) access to education. The widespread availability of birth control in developed nations allows

A large family in Orissa, India

families to limit the number of children they have. In developing nations, access to birth control is more limited and, because of cultural values, having fewer children may not be acceptable to many women. Often, in developing nations, women have lower social status than men. In these societies, women often have more children than women in developed nations, where women's standing is higher. In addition, the role of women in traditional societies is often restricted to bearing and raising children. Access to education also plays a part in fertility rates. In nations that have higher female literacy, women have lower fertility rates. *Literacy rate* is number of people over the age of 15 in a country who can read.

Table 1 Comparison of Birthrates and Literacy Rates in 2000

Country	Birthrate*	Fertility Rate**	Male Literacy Rate†	Female Literacy Rate†
Cambodia	33.5	4.82	80.8	59.3
Sudan	38.6	5.47	71.8	50.5
United States	14.2	2.06	97	97
United Kingdom	11.7	1.72	99	99

*per 1,000 people
**average number of children born per woman
†percentage of people over age 15 who can read

Test Yourself
Analyze Table 1.

1. Which country has the highest literacy rate and the lowest fertility rate?
2. What can you infer about the status of women in these nations, based on the statistics in the table?

Death Rate. *Death rate* is the number of deaths per 1,000 people in a given year. Generally, developing countries have a higher death rate than developed countries. Social and economic problems can develop if a high death rate in a developing country is not matched by a high birthrate. Then the population will decline. However, in developed countries, better health care has led to longer life and a larger percentage of older people in their population. Most developed nations have programs to assist their senior people. But if the birthrate is low, there are fewer young people to support high-cost programs to help the elderly, which can lead to economic difficulties.

Infant Mortality Rates. Like birthrates and death rates, infant mortality rates can be used to compare national and regional populations. *Infant mortality rate* is the number of children per 1,000 born each year who died under one year of age. Infant mortality rates worldwide have decreased over the years as a result of advances in medicine and health care, especially in developed nations. Infant mortality rates are often high in developing nations because they lack adequate health care for everyone. Table 2 shows the infant mortality rates for the countries in Table 1.

Table 2 Infant Mortality Rates	
Country	*Number per 1000 births*
Cambodia	76.37
Sudan	64.05
United States	6.63
United Kingdom	5.22

Test Yourself

Study Table 2 and answer these questions.

1. Which nation has the highest infant mortality rate?
2. Which nation has the lowest infant mortality rate?
3. What can you infer about these nations from the differences in infant mortality rates?

Per Capita Gross Domestic Product. In addition to population factors, you can examine a nation's per capita gross domestic product to understand its economic system and the standard of living of its people. As you read above, the gross domestic product (GDP) is the total value of goods and services a nation produces in a given time period, usually a year. It does not include the value of net income earned in other countries. *Per capita GDP* is the average income of each person in a country. To find the per capita income, divide the GDP by the number of people living in a nation. The per capita income in developed nations is much higher than in developing nations. In general, people in nations with a high per capita GDP have more money to spend on basics such as food, medicine, and health care, as well as on luxuries, such as vacations and leisure activities, than do people in nations with a low per capita GDP.

Just because a nation has a high per capita GDP, however, does not mean that *all* the people in that nation make that amount of money or are financially well-off. For example, the average per capita GDP of the United States in a recent year was approximately $31,000. This was over 23 times the per capita GDP of Cambodia, which was $1,350. But about 34.6 million people in the United States lived below the poverty threshold. The poverty threshold in the United States was an income of $18,850 for a family of four.

★ DIFFERENT POINTS OF VIEW ★

Within regions, conflict often arises over territorial boundaries and resources. This happens because different groups within a region often have different points of view on how to distribute and use territory and resources. *Boundaries* are borders. If you look at a globe, you can see the boundaries that divide the countries of the world. If you look at a map of Ohio, you can see the boundaries around the state and the boundaries around counties in Ohio. In addition, every town has boundaries, and every piece of property in that town has boundaries. What would happen if a group of people in Greentown broke away and formed their own, new town, called Bluetown? Most likely, there would be conflict. People in Greentown may not want to give up land. People in the new Bluetown may feel they have a right to that land and do not want to be part of Greentown, which has a culture different from theirs.

India and Pakistan

Conflicts over territory and resources have arisen throughout history. For example, India and Pakistan have been fighting over the region of Kashmir for more than 50 years. Kashmir lies between Pakistan and the northernmost region of India. Its population is composed of both Hindus and Muslims. In 1949, the UN established a line of control that separated Pakistani Kashmir from Indian Kashmir. To complicate matters, in 1962, China gained control of part of Kashmir, and the following year, Pakistan gave China another piece of land in Kashmir.

India, Pakistan, and disputed Kashmir

Causes of the Conflict Over Kashmir. The conflict in Kashmir stems from religious and ethnic differences between Muslim Pakistan and Hindu India. Pakistan claims that the population in Indian Kashmir is mostly Muslim, so the land should belong to Pakistan. India's government is secular, so India believes religion should not play a role in the division of territory. In addition, India believes violence in Indian Kashmir is spurred by Pakistani militants, not by a desire of the people to be free of Indian rule. Pakistan claims the violence is the normal process of a Muslim people who do not want to be ruled by Hindu India. Many Indian leaders believe that Kashmir would choose to remain part of India. Of course, Pakistanis believe Kashmir would choose to become part of Pakistan. Tensions escalated further when the two nations began testing nuclear weapons in the late 1990s. Fears of a nuclear war convinced both nations to take steps to cool tensions and end violence, but today, the conflict over Kashmir continues.

★ CONFLICT AND COOPERATION AMONG NATIONS ★

This indicator asks you to explain how political and economic conditions, resources, geographic locations, and cultures have all contributed to cooperation and conflict. How do these factors lead to conflict? Every nation has its own political and economic system. Differences in political beliefs can lead to conflicts among nations.

Conflicts

Throughout the 20th century, different political beliefs, religions, and ideologies caused prolonged conflicts between nations in many parts of the world. In recent years, the Middle East has been the scene of conflicts caused by claims to territory and by religious differences. For example, in the 1980s, Iran and Iraq fought a long, bloody war over the control of a critical waterway in the Persian Gulf. The war caused thousands of deaths, but it ended with neither side being able to claim victory. In 1990, Iraq invaded Kuwait, its oil-rich but weak southern neighbor, to seize its oilfields. Also in the 1990s, Iraq fought bloody battles with the Kurdish people, who claim territory in northern Iraq. In other areas such as Israel and Lebanon, claims over territory and differences between the Muslim and the Jewish populations have resulted in much bloodshed, and no lasting peace has been achieved. In Europe, religious and cultural differences ignited conflict between Northern Ireland, the Irish Republic, and England for decades. Terrorist attacks and bombings, and harsh measures to suppress dissidents, left thousands dead. Only in the late 1990s and early 21st century was some measure of peace attained, as the conflicting groups made concessions, a stable government was elected in Northern Ireland, and militants put down their weapons.

Cooperation

Political and economic conditions can also lead to cooperation among nations. For example, the United States is politically aligned with many nations in Europe and Latin America. These nations share the common bonds of democratic political systems, industrial economies, and similar cultures. Throughout history, these nations have often worked together to fight nations with different political and economic systems, such as the Fascist regimes of Germany and Italy, and military-controlled Japan during World War II.

European Union. As you read in Chapter 8, many nations in Western Europe belong to the European Union (EU), which has twin goals of political and economic cooperation for member nations. In 2002, all the EU nations, except Great Britain and Denmark, gave up their own currencies and switched to the *euro.* Using the same money system has led to more economic equality among member nations. However, although these nations cooperate economically and politically, they retain their individual national identities.

Organization of Petroleum Exporting Countries. Geographic locations and resources contribute to cooperation when regions band together to share resources or economic benefits from those resources. In 1960, oil-producing nations in the Middle East and Venezuela formed the Organization of Petroleum Exporting Countries (OPEC). By cooperating, these countries are able to set production quotas for member nations and to control world oil prices. Several times between 1973 and 1980 OPEC raised the price of oil dramatically. However, conflict over policies led some nations to drop out of OPEC in the 1990s.

Pipelines carry oil directly to a huge Saudi Arabian oil refinery.

Cultural Conflicts

Cultural conflicts are at the heart of many world conflicts. You read about Kashmir earlier in the chapter. This is an example of a cultural conflict as well as a territorial conflict.

A similar example is the conflict between Israel and nations of the Middle East. Israel was founded by the United Nations in 1947 as the Jewish homeland for World War II concentration camp survivors and any other Jewish people who wanted to live there. Israel was created by dividing Palestine into two parts. The Arab section of Palestine was taken over by Jordan. Israel's Arab neighbors have been in conflict with Israel over territory since 1948. This conflict has been marked by much violence. (See the historical background in Chapter 6.)

For a period of time, relations seemed to ease between Israel and some Arab nations, in part because of a desire of these nations to curtail violence in the region. Israel signed a peace treaty with Egypt in 1979, with Jordan in 1994, and with Mauritania (an Arab state in North Africa) in 1999. The violence between Israel and the Palestinians escalated after 2000. Efforts to ease tensions and improve relations were renewed in 2005 when a new Palestinian president took office.

The conflict between the Tutsis and Hutus in Rwandi in the 1990s was a cultural conflict. About a million Tutsis were killed by the Hutus. The ethnic cleansing of Muslims in Bosnia by the Serbs in the 1990s is another example. Each time the "crime" of the victims was that they were different from the people in power.

Test Yourself
What national conflicts over territory have caused international concern in recent years?

POINTS TO REMEMBER

- Data are facts and figures that can be used to compare countries and regions.

- Birthrate is the number of live births per year in a nation per 1,000 people. Death rate is the number of deaths per year in a nation per 1,000 people. Infant mortality rate is the number of children under one year of age that die per 1,000 each year.

- In nations with a high birthrate and high fertility rate, women often have a disproportionately low literacy rate compared to men.

- A low fertility rate correlates to the availability of birth control, the role of women in society, and women's access to education.

- Gross domestic product (GDP) is the total value of goods and services a nation produces in a given time period, usually a year. Per capita (per person) GDP is the total GDP divided by the number of people in a country.

- In general, people in nations with a high per capita GDP have a high standard of living, including greater access to good education and health care, than people in developing countries.

- Within regions, conflicts often arise over territorial boundaries and resources.

- Nations with similar political, economic, and social systems often exhibit cooperation. The creation of the European Union is an example of economic and political cooperation.

EXERCISES

CHECKING WHAT YOU HAVE READ

1. Which of the following conditions is often found in developing nations?

   A. high literacy rate
   B. low birthrate
   C. low death rate
   D. high fertility rate

2. Which of the following occurs if a high death rate is not matched by a high birthrate?

   A. Health care must be improved.
   B. Women have greater access to education.
   C. The population declines.
   D. Programs to aid the elderly are canceled.

3. The European Union is an example of

   A. a price-setting organization
   B. economic and political cooperation
   C. a humanitarian organization
   D. an international court.

4. Differences in culture and the desire for territory fueled conflict between Israel and

   A. Rwanda
   B. Arab nations
   C. Iraq
   D. Serbia.

5. The dispute between India and Pakistan over Kashmir involves

   A. the struggle for democracy
   B. oil-rich territory
   C. religious differences
   D. Christianity.

USING WHAT YOU HAVE READ

1. Choose one of the countries from Table 2 (on page 139) that has a low literacy rate for women. Why do you think the female literacy rate is so low? Research the country on the Internet or at the library to find out about the status and role of women in this nation. Write a paragraph to explain why women in this nation have a low literacy rate.

2. Are there territorial disputes where you live? Perhaps people are protesting the building of a shopping mall or housing development or the danger from a rundown, vacant building or lot. Research local newspapers to find out. What dispute did you find? Who is involved and why are they involved? What is the issue? Which side would you take? Write a short essay to answer the questions and explain your position.

THINKING ABOUT WHAT YOU HAVE READ

1. What can you tell about the equality of women in a society by looking at the ratio of female to male literacy?

2. In many of the world's nations, the elderly receive some form of pension or payment from the government, as well as medical and social services. Research a country (not the United States) to learn how it provides supplemental income and other services to the elderly. Find out how these services are paid for (by individual contributions over time, employers, the government, or a combination of these methods), and how income and services are distributed to the citizens. Which methods of financing and payment do you think are the fairest and the most reasonable for all citizens? Explain your answers.

SKILLS

Reading and Interpreting Tables

The table below lists five countries, A, B, C, D, and E. Analyze the information in the table and answer the questions that follow.

Population and Literacy

Country	Birthrate*	Fertility Rate**	Male Literacy Rate†	Female Literacy Rate†
A	12.2	1.2	99	99
B	26.5	4.6	78	38
C	14.3	2.1	99	99
D	30.1	5.4	70	40
E	25.3	4.3	50	50

*per 1,000 people
**average number of children per woman
†percent of population over 15 years old who can read

1. According to the table, which country has the highest birthrate?

2. The male and female literacy rates are equal to each other in which countries?

3. From the information in this table, which countries appear to be developing nations?

4. What can you infer about country E from this table?

CHAPTER 10

GEOGRAPHIC CHANGE AND HUMAN ACTIVITY

Analyze geographic changes brought about by human activity using appropriate maps and other geographic data.

This benchmark requires you to understand interactions between humans and their environment. You must be able to explain the causes and consequences of urbanization, in particular, the effects of economic development and population growth. You must also know how humans in cities affect the environment and understand the environmental consequences of urbanization.

★ URBANIZATION IN ANCIENT TIMES ★

Urbanization is the growth of cities and the movement of people to cities. Today, when you think of a city, you probably think of a modern city such as Los Angeles, Cleveland, or Chicago, but urbanization is not a modern phenomenon. Cities have existed since ancient times. Ancient cities differed in architecture and design from cities today, but like modern cities, they were centers of commerce, government, and culture.

Early Human Societies and the Development of Civilization

People have always lived in communities. For a long time in early human history, however, cities did not exist. At first, people banded together in groups in order to help one another hunt and gather wild food. Later in history, people learned to farm, and they settled down in permanent homes.

Nomads and Farmers. The earliest peoples were *nomads*. They wandered from place to place hunting wild animals and gathering plants for food. About 8,000 years ago, people leaned to *domesticate* wild plants and animals. They found that if they placed seeds and roots in the ground, new plants would grow from them. People also learned that they could tame certain animals and have a ready supply of milk and meat on hand. By raising crops and animals, people no longer had to roam in search of food.

The Growth of Civilizations

Farming communities led to the development of cities, and cities led to the development of civilizations. Large numbers of farmers settled in river valleys where the annual flooding of the river left behind rich soil for growing crops. To protect against the flooding of the rivers and to ensure water for irrigation, people learned to build dikes, dams, and irrigation channels. To facilitate such complex projects, people had to choose designers to plan the projects and leaders to organize them. The first known civilizations arose in an area called Mesopotamia, between the Tigris and Euphrates rivers. The development of irrigation projects provides a good example of how group cooperation for the common good helped bring about the necessary social structure for cities.

Development of Cities. Once people could control their food supply through farming, they were assured of a steady source of food. In time they began to produce a surplus, or more food than was needed, that they could store for future use. With a steady supply of food came an increase in the population. Over time, there were more people than were needed to grow crops and raise animals. This led to a *division of labor* in the settlements. Some people became crafts workers, others merchants or traders.

This is an artist's rendering of a 7th-century B.C. Assyrian king's palace, in the city of Nineveh in Mesopotamia. The city was in present-day Iraq.

Characteristics of Cities. Most of the settlements remained small villages, but over time some grew into cities. Ancient cities were characterized by large buildings and *social hierarchies*. The people built temples to their *deities* (male and female gods) and palaces to house their rulers. Rulers were at the top of society. Next came priests and warrior nobles. Merchants, crafts workers, and traders were the next largest portion of the population. The largest group were peasant farmers who lived outside the cities but helped support the city by supplying it with food and other farm products. In return, the city's rulers protected the farmers and provided them with a market for their goods. Many people in ancient civilizations had slaves.

City-States. Some ancient cities developed into *city-states*, cities that were independent of one another. Each city-state had its own ruler and set of deities. The economies of the city-states depended to some extent on trade with other city-states. Some city-states created empires by conquering their neighbors. An example is Babylon in Mesopotamia.

★ URBANIZATION AND THE MIDDLE AGES ★

The development of cities did not end in ancient times. Cities continued to grow, especially along trade routes. During the period of the Roman Empire (27 B.C. to A.D. 476), a number of cities in the empire became important centers of trade. The greatest of these were Rome, the capital of the western portion of the empire, and, Constantinople, the capital of the eastern portion.

Feudalism

After the Roman Empire in the West collapsed, the importance of cities in Western Europe declined. During the early Middle Ages (A.D. 500–1000), cities were replaced by a feudalistic social structure. *Feudalism* was a system of gov-

Italian city of Pisa, in the Middle Ages. Strong walls and defensive towers were needed to repel invaders.

ernment based on pledges of loyalty. Warriors swore loyalty to a lord in return for land and the protection of the lord's castle in times of war or natural disaster. The center of importance became the *manor*, the territory belonging to a lord. In the feudal system, most people settled on the manors of lords, for whom they worked in exchange for protection from outside attacks. The feudal system created a social hierarchy, with lords at the top and serfs, who were farmers bound to the land, at the bottom.

Cities Revive. In the 11th century, trade began to revive. This led to a revival of cities in Western Europe. Increased trade was partly due to a food surplus, which led to an increase in population. This in turn generated an increased demand for goods. Some cities grew up around the sites of *trade fairs*, which took place at major intersections of trade routes—both land and water routes.

Other cities began as towns created by merchants. The merchants would ask a local lord for a *charter* that guaranteed them the right to self-government in exchange for an annual payment. Eventually, some towns grew into cities as people migrated to them from manors. Many charters said that serfs who lived in the town for a year and a day were to be considered free. Some of these former serfs had been crafts workers on the manors. They earned their living in the new towns and cities by working as carpenters, blacksmiths, and other kinds of skilled workers. The Crusades, which lasted from 1095 to 1291, also added to the increase in trade and to the rise of cities, especially in Italy.

★ RAPID URBANIZATION AND THE INDUSTRIAL REVOLUTION ★

The Industrial Revolution began in England in the mid-1700s in the textile industry. As you read in Chapter 2, the Industrial Revolution was a period during which technological advancements led to industrialization, or the replacement of hand labor by machines. The Industrial Revolution in turn led to rapid urbanization and gave rise to many of the modern cities we know today.

Reasons That Industrialization Led to Urbanization

The industrialization of the textile industry in England caused rapid urbanization in two ways. First, prior to the introduction of factories, people who worked at home in rural areas spun thread and wove cloth. During the Industrial Revolution, machines took these jobs away from workers. The former textile workers migrated to cities in search of work.

Second, the *enclosure movement* ended small farming in large parts of Great Britain. Wealthy landowners found they could make more money by large-scale farming. They evicted their peasant farmers, the descendants of the manor serfs, and merged the small farms into large estates. With nowhere else to go, the displaced farmers and their families migrated to the new industrial centers in search of work. As industrialization continued to spread, cities grew. For example, the English city of Manchester, England, had a population of about 6,000 in 1685. By 1844, Manchester had become an industrial center, and its population had grown to almost 400,000.

In the United States, immigration contributed to rapid urbanization. After the Industrial Revolution spread to the United States in the early 1800s, it caused an explosive growth in the number and size of industrial cities, especially in the Northeast and Midwest. For example, Chicago had a population of over a million people in 1900, while New York City had over 3 million people. The population of Cleveland more than doubled, from some 160,200 persons in 1880 to nearly 382,000 in 1900.

In less than a century, Cincinnati grew from a small river city, in the 1830s (left), to a large metropolis, in the 1920s (below).

Problems of Urbanization

Overcrowding, poor sanitation, and crime were major problems in the rapidly growing industrial centers. Workers often lived in horrible conditions. They were crowded into tiny apartments in wooden tenement buildings. Often an entire family lived in one room. Because of the way in which tenements were built, apartments received little fresh air or sunlight. All the people on one floor shared a bathroom. Sanitation was poor, which led to the spread of diseases such as cholera. Working conditions were no better. Factory wages were low, and in many families, everyone, including children, worked in the factories six days a week, 10 or 12 hours a day.

Cities suffered environmental problems because of industrialization. The coal-burning factories of London in the 1800s regularly polluted the air. At noon, the sky was often so dark from smoke and soot that it looked like midnight. In addition, many factories dumped their waste into rivers. For example, the meatpacking industry in Cincinnati dumped unused animal parts into the Ohio River. In addition, the smell of rotting meat polluted the air.

★ URBANIZATION TODAY ★

After World War II, urbanization slowed down in most industrialized nations. Developed nations in Europe and North America began to experience *suburbanization*, the migration of people out of cities and into *suburbs*, the areas around cities. Cities and their surrounding suburbs are called *metropolitan areas*.

Suburbs

The growth of metropolitan areas has resulted in *suburban sprawl*—the spread of suburbs. The spread of suburbs has helped slow the growth of cities. Suburban sprawl also has some serious environmental consequences. One such consequence is the air pollution caused by the cars people drive to jobs in suburbs and cities. Then, too, as suburbs spread, housing developments replaced farmland and undeveloped areas. Undeveloped areas provide homes for wild plants and animals and places where people can exercise and enjoy nature.

Communication and Travel Between Cities

Cities in developed nations are closely connected by economic interests and sophisticated communication and transportation systems. For example, in England and the United States, businesses often have offices in several different cities in different parts of the nation. Information and people travel with ease between offices as a result of air travel, cell phones, the Internet, and other forms of communication. Because of the increasingly global nature of modern economies and businesses, cities are connected on an international level as well.

Cities in Developing Countries

Nations in Africa, Asia, and many parts of Latin America are referred to as developing nations, because they are still modernizing and industrializing their economies. Urbanization is occurring at a rapid rate in many of these nations.

Much of this urbanization is a result of the migration of large numbers of people from the countryside to cities. There is a shortage of work in the countryside, and young people are forced to move to cities in search of jobs.

Many people are drawn to cities, hoping for improved education and economic opportunities. Unfortunately, many rural migrants find city life to be hard. Jobs are few, and those that exist for unskilled workers pay poorly. With little money, most migrants live in areas known as *shantytowns*, with inadequate sanitation, overcrowding, and little access to education. Many rural migrants are trapped in these shantytowns. They cannot afford to go back to the country, and they lack the education and resources that would help them succeed in the city.

Many of the problems that these rapidly growing cities experience result from the huge increase in population. Cities often do not have adequate resources to support the influx of people from the countryside. The result is shortages of housing and employment opportunities, and city services such as police, sanitation, and schools are stretched thin. In this way, the problems of new urban areas are no different from the problems experienced by cities in North America and Europe as a result of the Industrial Revolution.

Megacities and Primate Cities

Modern urbanization has also seen the rise of the *megacity* and the *primate city*. Some experts define the megacity as a city that has a population of 10 million or more. Geographer Mark Jefferson developed the concept of the *primate city*. This kind of city is larger than the combined populations of the second and third largest cities in the same country. Primate cities typically dominate the culture, government, and economics of a country. London, Paris, and Mexico City are all examples of dominant primate cities. The United States, Canada, and India do not have such cities. Industrialized nations that lack primate cities usually have multiple large cities, none of which dominate the country.

Population of Largest Megacities in 2004 (millions of persons)	
City and Country	*Population*
Tokyo, Japan	26.7
São Paulo, Brazil	19.2
Mexico City, Mexico	18.7
Bombay (Mumbai), India	17.8
New York, U.S.	17.1
Dhaka, Bangladesh	15.1
Delhi, India	14.6
Calcutta, India	14.03
Los Angeles, U.S.	13.6
Shanghai, China	13.07
Jakarta, Indonesia	12.6

Two views of 21st-century urban problems: Inadequate housing forces people to build their own homes, in this Manila, Philippines, shantytown (left); severe overcrowding brings pedestrian and vehicle traffic almost to a halt in Bombay, India (below).

The Megalopolis

Some nations have seen the rise of the *megalopolis*. A megalopolis is an extensive, heavily populated area with many cities. The northeastern United States is a good example of a megalopolis. The cities of Boston, New York, Philadelphia, Baltimore, and Washington, D.C., and many smaller cities such as Wilmington, Delaware, and towns and villages in between spread along the Atlantic Coast in what seems like an almost unbroken chain of urban areas.

 ## Test Yourself
How does suburban sprawl affect the environment?

POINTS TO REMEMBER

- The first settlements developed from groups of people coming together to build and maintain dikes, dams, and irrigation systems in order to farm.

- A steady supply of food resulted in an increase in population, which, in turn, brought about an increase in the size of settlements and the development of cities.

- The Industrial Revolution led to the rapid urbanization of Western Europe and the United States.

- Urbanization is the growth of cities and the movement of people to cities.

- Pollution and construction in open spaces and former farmlands are environmental consequences of urbanization.

- Urbanization in developing nations in Latin America, Africa, and Asia is fueled by population growth, much of it coming from the movement of rural people to the cities. This process is similar to what occurred in Western Europe and the United States during the Industrial Revolution.

- Rapidly growing cities today suffer from a lack of adequate resources, such as housing, jobs, and public services, to take care of increasing populations. These are the same problems experienced by cities in the late 19th and early 20th centuries.

- Modern urbanization has seen the rise of the megacity, an urban area with a population of 10 million or more.

- Primate cities dominate the culture, government, and economy of a country.

- A megalopolis is an extensive area with large numbers of people spread over a number of cities.

EXERCISES

CHECKING WHAT YOU HAVE READ

1. What caused cities to decline in Europe during the early Middle Ages?

   A. better farming methods
   B. famine
   C. feudalism
   D. industrialization

2. What contributed to population growth in industrial cities in the United States in the late 19th century?

   A. immigration
   B. baby boom
   C. migration to suburbs
   D. environmental pollution

3. Which of the following is a consequence of the growth of suburban areas?

   A. poor sanitation
   B. air pollution from motor vehicles
   C. increase in open spaces
   D. increase in migration from rural areas to cities

4. Which city is an example of a primate city?

   A. New York
   B. Paris
   C. Calcutta
   D. Los Angeles

5. What contributes to urbanization today in developing nations in Africa, Asia, and Latin America?

   A. population growth
   B. agricultural advances
   C. government programs
   D. megacities

USING WHAT YOU HAVE READ

1. Urbanization today results in some of the same economic and environmental problems that urbanization caused in the past. Choose a city that grew rapidly as a result of the Industrial Revolution and one city that is experiencing rapid urbanization today. Research them at the library or on the Internet. What problems do these cities have in common? What problems are different?

2. In this chapter, you read about suburban sprawl. Think about the area where you live. Do you live in a suburb or a city? Are you part of a major metropolitan area? What problems does your community face today? What problems will your community face in the future? Do research by reading the local newspaper, listening to local radio stations, and watching the local TV news. Talk to adults and learn what they think. Write an essay to answer the questions.

THINKING ABOUT WHAT YOU HAVE READ

1. Why do you think the United States lacks a primate city?

2. In this chapter, you learned about the megalopolis that exists on the northeastern coast of the United States. Using the library or the Internet, find a megalopolis outside North America. How does it differ from the megalopolis in the northeastern U.S.? How is it similar?

SKILLS

Working With Maps

Look at the map below and answer the questions that follow. The map depicts cities with populations of over a million people.

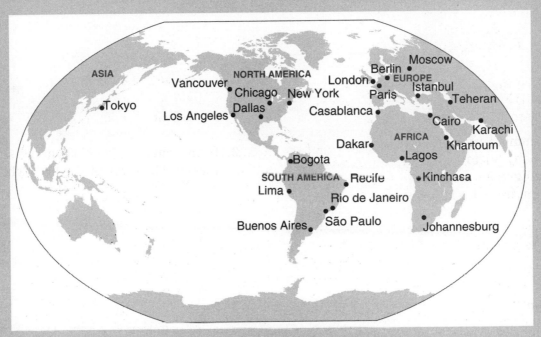

World's Largest Cities

1. Which city is in Africa?
   A. Lima
   B. Lagos
   C. Istanbul
   D. Vancouver

2. What do most of the cities in the Americas shown on this map have in common geographically?

3. Which is the southernmost city shown on this map in Africa?

4. On what continent is Recife located?

5. On what continent is Dakar located?

CHAPTER 11

PATTERNS AND PROCESSES OF MOVEMENT

BENCHMARK:

Analyze the patterns and processes of movement of people, products, and ideas.

For this benchmark, you must understand the causes of human migration now and in the past. You should also be able to recognize patterns of migration, such as the movement of people from rural to urban areas during the age of industrialization. Since the earliest times, humans have migrated from place to place. Migration includes moving within a country or region as well as immigration to another country. It is important that you understand the reasons behind human migration. For this benchmark, you should know the political, economic, and environmental factors that contribute to human migration.

★ WHAT IS MIGRATION? ★

Migration is the movement of people from one place to another. Sometimes, people move to cities from towns. Sometimes, they move to another country or another continent. Migrations change how population is distributed. Migration also changes the cultural landscape of places. People who migrate bring with them their language, customs, traditions, and religion. New cultures arise as the cultures of migrants blend with the cultures of the people already living in a place.

Reasons That People Migrate

People migrate for both voluntary and involuntary reasons. Voluntary migration occurs when people choose to leave one place for another. An example of voluntary migration is moving to Florida from the northeastern U.S. in search of warmer weather. Involuntary migration occurs when people are forced to move to a new place. Africans who were kidnapped and brought to the Americas as slaves are an example of involuntary migrants.

Push Factors and Pull Factors. The factors that drive people to migrate voluntarily are called push factors and pull factors. Push factors are reasons that cause people to migrate, such as famine, religious persecution, or political conflict. Pull factors are reasons that draw people to a new place, such as religious freedom, better economic opportunities, and cultural ties. Often, both factors play a part in the decision to migrate. People may be pushed to migrate by dissatisfaction with their own government and be pulled to a new country by their preference for its government.

Immigration, Emigration, and Internal Migration

When people leave one country for another, they are both emigrants and immigrants. In the nations they leave behind, they are referred to as *emigrants*. They are known as *immigrants* in the new country in which they settle. *Internal migration* takes place within regions and nations. The movement of people from towns to cities within a country is an example of internal migration. Migration also takes place on a local scale, within towns and cities. If you move to a new house in a different part of the town in which you already live, that is local migration.

Although there are universal factors that influence migration, people and groups have moved for different reasons throughout the history of the world. By understanding the reasons for migration, you will gain a greater understanding of how culture and ideas spread and change. Understanding migration will also help you understand why people live where they do. The remainder of the chapter discusses some examples of significant migrations in world history. Remember that human migration continues today, because it is an ongoing process.

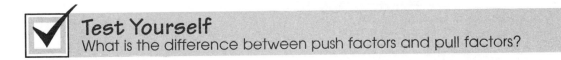

Test Yourself
What is the difference between push factors and pull factors?

★ EXAMPLES OF EARLY MIGRATIONS ★

The first inhabitants of the Americas came as a result of migration. Until recently, most archaeologists accepted the theory that during an ice age (perhaps 40,000 years ago), the first groups of hunter-gatherers crossed into the Americas from Asia. The theory claimed that they crossed along a piece of land that is now under the Bering Strait. Archaeological discoveries were made in the last part of the 20th century and the early part of the 21st century, however, that challenged former ideas about when and where the first migrations to the Americas occurred. Some now believe that people also migrated by ocean-going craft, from Asia and Polynesia, and settled along the coasts of the Americas.

Over thousands of years, the ancestors of modern Native Americans settled throughout North and South America. Archaeologists assume that the way in which they spread out was similar to the way in which other hunter-gatherers spread through an area. A group would settle in on place. Over time some members of the group would decide to move on. Perhaps the food supply began to run low because the number of members of the group was increasing. The new migrant group would find a new area for a camp. Over time, some of its members would split off and leave. The process was repeated over and over until the continents of North America and South America were populated.

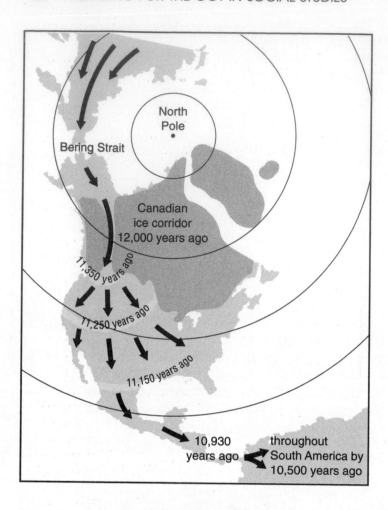

Prehistoric migration routes from Asia to the Americas

The Bantu Speakers in Africa

Another major migration was the spread of Bantu-speaking peoples in Africa, beginning sometime around 1000 B.C. and lasting until the 3rd or 4th century A.D. Bantu is a language family, not an ethnic group. Those who speak a Bantu language belong to many different ethnic groups with many different customs and traditions. Bantu speakers were first centered near the Niger River in West Africa. Over many centuries, their descendants migrated throughout sub-Saharan Africa.

No one knows why the first Bantu group migrated. Since they were farmers, it is likely that they migrated in search of better farmland. Over time, the descendants of the earliest Bantu migrants picked up and moved into new areas, probably because of expanding population. As they settled in new regions, the Bantu speakers had to adapt to their new environment. As a result, Bantu speakers in some areas became herders rather than farmers. It is believed that the Bantu-speaking people helped spread the technique of smelting iron and making iron tools throughout Africa.

 Test Yourself

What was probably the main reason why the ancestors of Native Americans and Bantu speakers migrated from one place to another?

The migration of Bantu-speaking people had, by the year A.D. 1000, brought them across the African continent.

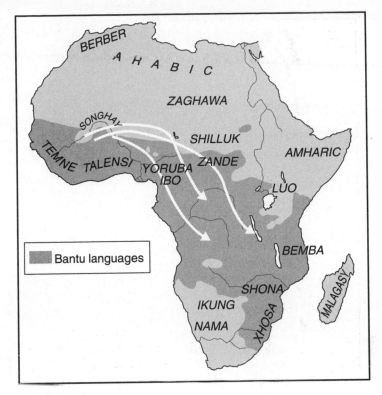

★ EXPLORATION AND MIGRATION ★

The 1500s saw the beginning of the European Age of Exploration. European nations began to look for new routes to Asia in search of gold, spices, and other luxury goods. By the mid-1500s, European nations began to set up colonies in the lands claimed by their explorers. The first immigrants were soldiers and adventurers intent on finding riches. (See map, pages 162–163.)

Later, employees of European trading companies established outposts in the colonies, especially on the islands in the Caribbean and in India and Southeast Asia. Families and single people moved to the English colonies in North America to start new lives. European missionaries went to many of the colonies to convert the native peoples to Christianity. Conflict often arose between these missionaries and the native peoples.

Spanish and English Colonization of the Americas

Spain and England were the main colonizing nations in the Americas. Spanish colonists settled in the southern and western parts of North America, the Caribbean islands, Central America, and South America. English colonists settled the northeastern part of North America.

Spanish Colonists. In Spanish America, the cultures of the colonizers and the indigenous people eventually blended. Few Spanish women migrated to the Spanish colonies. As a result, Spanish men married native women, and a new social class known as *mestizos* developed. These are people whose ancestry is

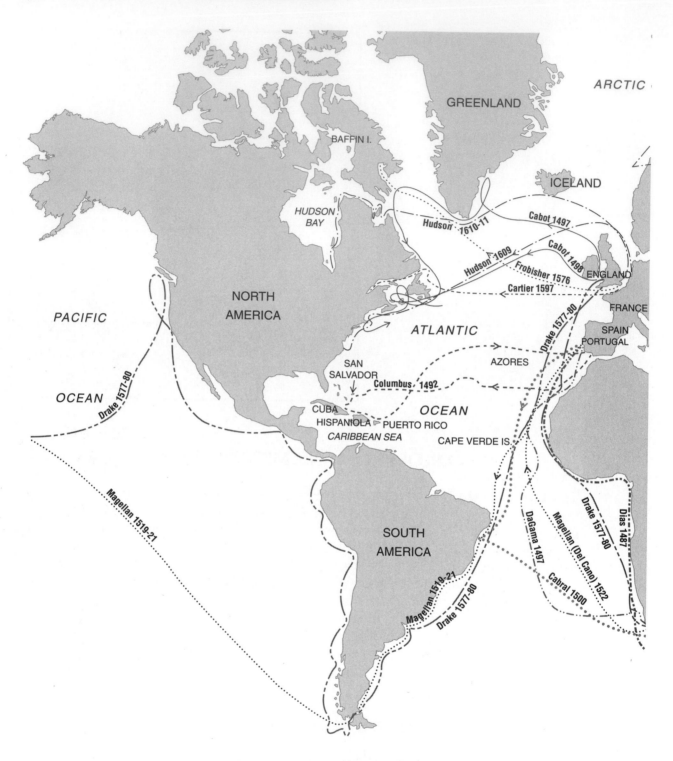

European Age of Exploration

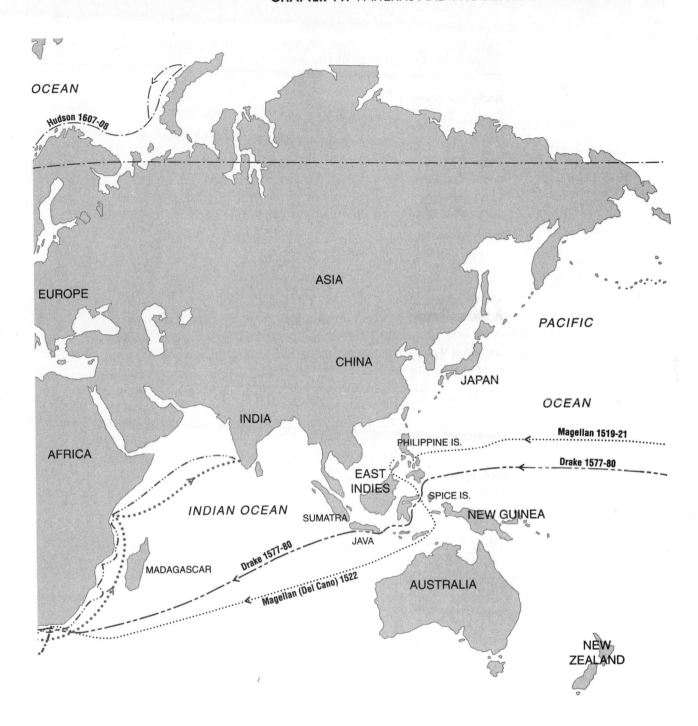

a mix of Spanish and Native American. In many nations in Latin America today, mestizos make up the majority of the population.

English Colonists. The British exploration of North America sparked migrations from Great Britain and other parts of Europe. Push factors for many of the early colonists to British North America were religious persecution and lack of economic opportunity. Pull factors were the ability to practice their religion freely and the promise of economic opportunity. Examples of those who came for religious reasons were English Puritans, Pilgrims, Quakers, Roman Catholics, and French Huguenots. Farmers who were pushed off their land in England because of the enclosure movement (see Chapter 10) came for land.

Forced Migrations

The major example of forced or involuntary migration occurred as a result of European colonization. The transatlantic slave trade transported millions of Africans against their will to the Americas. It is estimated that between the 1500s and 1800s, some 11 million Africans arrived in chains at British ports in the Caribbean and in mainland colonies. Millions more were shipped to the Spanish colonies. An unknown number of Africans died during the brutal passage from Africa to the Americas. The English slave trade began in the Caribbean as a way to populate sugar plantations with workers. Later, the slave trade became big business for English and colonial merchants as one leg

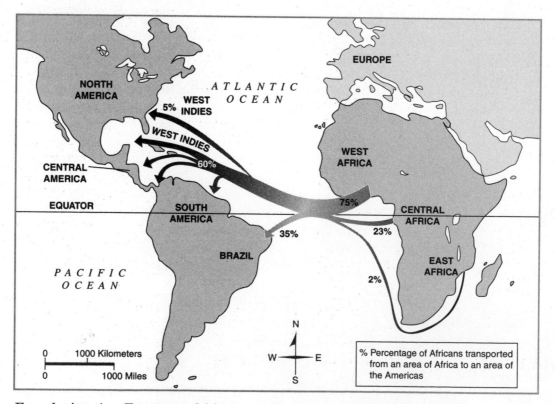

Forced migration: Transport of Africans to the Americas, 16th-18th centuries

of the triangular trade between England, Africa, and Caribbean and mainland colonies.

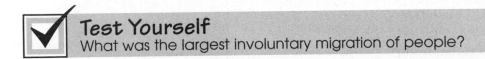

Test Yourself
What was the largest involuntary migration of people?

★ MIGRATION IN THE NINETEENTH CENTURY ★

The period between 1820 and 1920 saw more than 30 million Europeans immigrate to the United States. Like the original colonists, they came in search of a better life. Some believed that the streets were "paved with gold."

The Industrial Revolution

Beginning in the 1870s, the Industrial Revolution was a major pull factor in this international migration. The Industrial Revolution also contributed to massive internal migrations in industrializing nations such as England and the United States. The result was rapid urbanization. As you read in Chapter 10, urbanization is the movement of people to cities and the growth of cities. During the Industrial Revolution, millions of people migrated from rural areas to cities in search of work. This is a trend that continues today in industrializing nations in Africa, Asia, and Latin America.

Push and Pull Factors. Many Europeans who immigrated to the United States in the 1800s were pulled by the hope of a better life for themselves and their families. This better life might be defined in terms of better-paying work—or any work—and religious and political freedoms.

However, many push factors contributed to immigration as well. Two examples are Irish people and Jews from Russia and Poland. In the 1840s and 1850s, Ireland experienced a famine caused by the failure of its staple food crop, potatoes. A famine is a great shortage of food. To escape death by starvation and the political oppression of the British government, more than a million Irish people immigrated to the United States. Beginning in the 1880s, Jews emigrated from Russia and what had once been Poland to escape pogroms. *Pogroms* were attacks on Jews and the destruction of Jewish homes, towns, and businesses.

★ EFFECTS OF WORLD WAR I AND WORLD WAR II ★

The two world wars of the 20th century had opposite effects on immigration to the United States.

World War I

After World War I, immigration to the United States slowed greatly because of stricter policies. Anti-immigrant prejudice drove these policies. The

National Origins Act passed by Congress in 1924 limited the number of immigrants admitted annually to the United States to 150,000. The act limited the number of people of each national origin to a small percentage of the people of that nationality already living in the United States. The purpose of the act was to limit immigrants from Southern and Eastern Europe.

Migrations After World War II

Immediately after World War II, important migrations occurred throughout Europe, the United States, and Asia. In later decades, other factors and other events caused population shifts.

From Europe. Europeans who had fled their native countries to escape the bombings and other effects of warfare, or to escape fascism, tried to return to their homes. Some left Europe altogether in search of a more secure and prosperous place to live. Many came to the United States. In the aftermath of World War II, U.S. immigration policies were eased to admit displaced persons and refugees. *Displaced persons* were people who had no homes to return to. A great number of displaced persons entering the United States after World War II were Jewish survivors of the Holocaust. They had no homes, and in many cases, no families to return to. Other emigrants from Europe were *refugees*, fleeing newly formed Communist governments in Eastern Europe.

In Asia. During this same period, a mass migration occurred in South Asia. In 1947, the former British colony of India was partitioned into India and Pakistan. (See Chapter 9.) India is a Hindu nation, and Pakistan is an Islamic nation. This resulted in mass migrations, as Hindus migrated from Pakistan to India and Muslims migrated from India to Pakistan.

Migrations Today in Latin America, Africa, and Europe

Today, many nations in Latin America are experiencing mass migrations from rural areas to cities. Thirty percent of Brazil's population lived in cities in 1940. By the beginning of the 21st century, that number had risen to 75 percent. Much of the migration to cities in developing nations, whether in Latin America, Asia, or Africa, is fueled by population growth, which results in a shortage of jobs in rural areas. As you read in Chapter 10, the urban newcomers are looking for work.

Another factor that drives migration is civil war. In the 1980s and 1990s, several nations experienced civil wars. People in nations such as Somalia and Rwanda in Africa and Bosnia in Europe were forced from their home areas because of the fighting.

Migration today is facilitated by access to fast and relatively inexpensive means of transportation. But the reasons that people migrate today are similar to the reasons that have pushed and pulled people to move from place to place since earliest times.

Test Yourself
What are two reasons that people migrated in the 20th century?

POINTS TO REMEMBER

- Voluntary migration occurs when people migrate by choice. Involuntary migration occurs when people are forced to leave one place for another.

- Push factors are reasons that cause people to migrate. Pull factors are reasons that draw people to a new place.

- Archaeologists believe the earliest inhabitants of the Americas were hunter-gatherers who migrated from Asia, beginning perhaps 40,000 years ago.

- Bantu speakers moved east and south throughout Africa between 1000 B.C. and the 3rd and 4th centuries A.D., probably because of population growth.

- The establishment of European colonies beginning in the 1500s resulted in the migration of Europeans to most world regions.

- One of the largest involuntary migrations in world history was the transportation of more than 11 million enslaved Africans to the Americas as part of the transatlantic slave trade.

- The Industrial Revolution caused large internal migrations that led to urbanization in countries such as Great Britain and the United States.

- The Industrial Revolution also resulted in the immigration of more than 30 million Europeans to the United States.

- The partition of India into the nations of India and Pakistan in 1947 resulted in the mass migration of Hindus and Muslims.

- Today, developing nations in Latin America, Africa, and Asia are experiencing internal migrations as people move from rural areas to cities in search of economic opportunity.

EXERCISES

CHECKING WHAT YOU HAVE READ

1. Factors that force people to migrate are called

   A. pull factors
   B. voluntary factors
   C. immigration
   D. push factors.

2. Reasons why people are attracted to settle in new lands are called

   A. push factors
   B. involuntary factors
   C. pull factors
   D. emigration.

3. An example of involuntary migration is

   A. the exploration of the Americas by Europeans
   B. the transatlantic slave trade
   C. a move to a new town after graduating from college
   D. urbanization.

4. The migration of large numbers of Irish resulted from

   A. rapid urbanization
   B. pogroms
   C. a potato famine
   D. the Industrial Revolution.

5. Why did the United States ease immigration restrictions after World War II?

   A. to increase immigration from Canada
   B. to help Mexicans displaced by the war
   C. to increase emigration from all countries
   D. to aid displaced persons and refugees

USING WHAT YOU HAVE READ

1. Many countries in Latin America are experiencing rapid urbanization today. Using the library or the Internet, choose a Latin American country to study. Research the reasons that people in that country are migrating to cities. Then choose a specific city to study. What opportunities does the city offer to rural people? What happens to the rural migrants when they move to the city? How is the city affected by migration? Prepare a report answering these questions.

2. Several nations have experienced civil war since the 1980s. Use resources in the library or on the Internet to study one nation, such as Bosnia, Somalia, Rwanda, or the Sudan. Find out what the issues were in the civil war, who was displaced by the fighting, how many people were displaced, where they went, and what happened to them. Prepare a report.

THINKING ABOUT WHAT YOU HAVE READ

1. Why do you think countries pass laws restricting immigration? Research U.S. immigration policy on the Internet. Then, research the immigration policy of the European Union nations. What is different about the two sets of policies? Why do you think the differences exist?

2. The United States is a nation of immigrants. Where did your ancestors come from? When did they come to the United States? Why did they come? If you do not know the answers to these questions, ask older members of your family if they can tell you the story of how your family came to the United States.

SKILLS

Comprehending Reading Passages

Read the following excerpt from *The Jungle*, by Upton Sinclair, written in 1906, and answer the questions that follow.

. . . It was Jonas who suggested that they all go to America, where a friend of his had gotten rich. . . . Jurgis, too, had heard of America. That was a country where, they said, a man might earn three rubles a day; and Jurgis figured what three rubles a day would mean, with prices as they were where he lived, and decided forthwith that he would go to America and marry, and be a rich man in the bargain.

. . . So in the summer they had all set out for America. . . . They had a hard time on the passage. . . . It was in the stockyards that Jonas' friend had gotten rich, and so to Chicago the party was bound. They knew one word—Chicago—and that was all they needed to know, at least, until they reached the city. Then, tumbled out of the (railroad) cars without ceremony, they were no better off than before; they stood staring down the vista of Dearborn Street, with its big, black buildings towering in the distance, unable to realize that they had arrived, and why, when they said "Chicago," people no longer pointed in some direction, but instead looked perplexed, or laughed, or went on without paying any attention. They were pitiable in their helplessness. . . .

1. According to the passage, why did Jurgis want to go to America?

2. Why were the travelers bound for Chicago?

3. What is the implication of the following sentence from the passage? "They knew one word—Chicago—and that was all they needed to know, at least, until they reached the city."

4. Why did people laugh or look perplexed when the immigrants said "Chicago"?

5. Do you think the experience of this group of immigrants is typical of the experience of many immigrants to the United States? Why or why not?

CHAPTER 12

ECONOMIC SYSTEMS

BENCHMARK:

Compare how different economic systems answer the fundamental economic questions of what goods and services to produce, how to produce them, and who will consume them.

This benchmark requires you to understand how different economic systems work. In particular, you should be able to describe the costs and benefits of trade in relation to standard of living, productive capacity, the use of productive resources, and the infrastructure. You must also be able to explain how changing methods of production and a country's productive resources affect the ways in which it answers the fundamental economic questions of what to produce, how to produce, and for whom to produce. In addition, you must be able to analyze characteristics of traditional, market, command, and mixed economies with regard to private property, freedom of enterprise, competition and consumer choice, and government.

★ ECONOMIC SYSTEMS ★

People in different nations have developed different economic systems to help them make decisions about how best to obtain the goods and services they need and want. Goods are such items as houses, food, clothes, gadgets, and cars. Services are functions that people perform to help others. Some people who provide services are airline pilots, teachers, doctors, dishwashers, and those who work in hotels.

Benefits and Costs of Trade

Trade is the buying, selling, and exchanging of goods and services. Trade can be domestic (within a nation) or international (between nations). For nations, trade is a way to acquire goods, resources, and services that they themselves cannot produce or perform. Trade involves both costs and benefits.

Benefits. Some benefits of trade are (1) improved standard of living, (2) increased productive capacity, and (3) increased earnings for a nation.

Standard of Living. An important benefit of trade is its improvement of the standard of living by creating opportunities for countries to enjoy goods produced in other countries. *Standard of living* is the level of material well-being that a nation enjoys. Specialization makes this possible. *Specialization* is the producing and exporting of those goods that a nation is best suited to produce. Nations can *export* (send out and sell to other nations) goods they produce and *import* (bring in and buy) from other nations the goods they do not produce. For example, coffee and tea are difficult to produce in the United States. Therefore, the United States imports tea and coffee from nations in Asia, Africa, and South America. Since many Americans enjoy coffee and tea, importing those items improves their standard of living.

Infrastructure. People who engage in trade earn money (capital), that can be invested in business projects. The capital earned through trade can be invested in factories, transportation systems, education systems, and health care. A nation's system of public works, with their buildings, equipment, and workers, is known as its *infrastructure.* The infrastructure of a society keeps people healthy and provides them with opportunities to develop and prosper. Therefore, trade contributes indirectly but greatly to a society's standard of living.

Cost of Trade. *Cost* is the expenditure of something in order to achieve a goal. Sometimes the cost is clear and definite, such as the money invested or the labor and time used to produce goods. Other kinds of cost are more abstract. For example, if you use a piece of steel to make a girder for a bridge, then, obviously you lose the opportunity to use that piece of steel to make a railroad track. Therefore, the use of that resource, the piece of steel for the bridge, comes at the *cost* of losing the opportunity to use it for something else.

In world trade, using natural resources is an example of this cost. A country may earn money from exporting its natural resources, but once it has done so, it cannot use those resources for its own needs. A country must decide whether the benefit of trading its resources outweighs the cost of losing them for domestic consumption.

Economic Imperialism. Trade is usually mutually beneficial for the parties involved, but not in every case. When a colonizing country trades its colony's resources, the colonizing country often gets most of the benefits. In Chapter 3, you learned that Europe's African colonies were sources of raw materials and labor for the home countries. The colonies' resources were shipped to Europe's factories. The colonial powers benefited from this arrangement. They grew rich, while the African colonies suffered.

The European powers kept their colonies from developing industries and made them dependent on goods imported from the colonizing country. As a result, when these nations gained freedom, they had very weak economies. If the price on the world market for their cash crops, such as cotton and cocoa, dropped, they could not buy necessary goods from other nations. Even though the former African colonies won political independence, they remained economically dependent on industrial nations. This is known as *economic imperialism.*

Test Yourself
How does trade improve a nation's standard of living?

★ FUNDAMENTAL ECONOMIC QUESTIONS ★

Imagine that you and some friends want to start a manufacturing business. You are all hard-working people with drive, imagination, and a lot of money to invest. What do you need to know before you begin your enterprise? To find out you must answer three questions:

1. What should your company produce?
2. How and by whom should its products be made?
3. Who will buy and consume these products?

These three economic questions must be answered by anyone who runs a business. They must also be answered by all societies and all nations. Every nation has only a limited amount of resources. Ways must be found to convert those resources into goods and services.

Use of Productive Resources

Productive resources are any resources used to produce goods. Productive resources range from money, machines, land, and natural resources to human capital. *Human capital* is the body of knowledge that workers bring to a task. The availability of these resources to a nation or industry is its *productive capacity*. In other words, a nation's resources determine the kind of goods it can produce.

Making Changes in Productive Resources. When a change in productive capacity occurs, a country must reevaluate its use of productive resources. If

The kudzu vine overgrows everything in its path in this Oxford, Mississippi forest.

an agricultural nation wanted to change to an industrial nation, it would have to decide what to produce, how to produce it, and for whom to produce it. The answers that the newly industrializing nation would give to these questions would be entirely different from the answers it gave to the same questions when it was an agricultural nation.

Industrialized Countries. Countries that are already industrialized must also make changes in their use of productive resources from time to time. For example, one of the United States' important productive resources, lumber, has become scarce. Conservationists are always trying to find ways to protect the forests that produce lumber.

One of the many environmental threats to trees is a vine called kudzu. It was brought to the United States from Japan. The warm, humid climate in the southeastern United States was ideal for the growth and spread of kudzu. This strong, healthy vine took over the habitats of other plants. When it grew in forests, it twined around trees and killed them by cutting off their light and air.

When scientists examined this plant, they discovered that they could use it to make pulp, from which cardboard and other paper products are manufactured. Substituting kudzu for trees in making pulp accomplishes two goals: it transforms a destructive weed into a productive resource and reserves those trees that had once been used to make pulp for other purposes, such as lumber. Kudzu, which grows very quickly even in poor soil, has turned out to be a cheap and versatile productive resource. It is a very nutritious food for both humans and cattle and is believed to have medicinal properties. It continues to crowd out other plants, however. Conservationists caution people to keep its cultivation under strict control.

★ CHARACTERISTICS OF MAJOR ECONOMIC SYSTEMS ★

Every nation has tried to develop an economic system that fulfills the needs of its population. The economic systems you should study to meet the requirements of this benchmark are (1) traditional, (2) market, (3) command, and (4) mixed.

Traditional Economy

In a *traditional economy*, the fundamental economic questions are answered according to custom and religious beliefs. This system is typical in places that have not yet industrialized. The traditional economy is self-sustaining because everything that people in such an economy do is based on what their ancestors did. Most people in a traditional economy are farmers. Sometimes the land is owned by the community. Sometimes it is privately owned. In the latter case, heads of families usually pass on to their children a piece of land and the way in which that land is used. If a boy's grandfather was a soybean farmer, then his father was a soybean farmer, and the boy, too, will be a soybean farmer. Today, there are areas in Asia, Africa, and Latin America that still have traditional economies.

Market Economy

A *market economy* is an economic system that is controlled not by the government but by privately owned businesses. It is also called *capitalism* or, sometimes, a *free-market system*. Under capitalism, individual businesses have the freedom to decide what they will produce and sell to consumers (the people who buy and use products and services). This is called *free enterprise*. Consumers have the freedom to choose what they want to buy and what they do not want to buy.

Profit. Capitalists are motivated by profit. A business makes a *profit* when it earns more than it spends on expenses in doing business. The cost to business owners is the risk of losing money. The owners takes this risk, however, because of the potential rewards of a successful business. Business owners hire workers who do not share in the profit of the business, but who also do not risk losing an investment if the business fails (although they would lose their jobs). Workers in a capitalist system are free to work where they want. They are not forced by the government or by tradition to work in a certain place or industry.

Shares of Stocks. In capitalist systems, businesses are privately owned. However, they are often financed by more than one owner. Many people in a capitalist system invest in a corporation by buying *shares of stock*. One share of stock is one *share* (part) of ownership in a corporation. When the business makes a profit, individual investors receive part of that profit as dividends.

Competition. Competition and consumer choice play vital roles in capitalism. Although private business owners are free to choose what to produce, consumer choice and demand strongly influence their decision. A company cannot make a profit selling a product that few or no consumers want to buy. Competition forces businesses to make higher quality products.

For example, there are many sneaker companies in the world. If a new company introduces a new sneaker, its owners must make consumers want to buy that sneaker. The company's new sneaker must be one that consumers like better than the older sneakers on the market. Otherwise, the new company will go out of business. If consumers like the new brand better, then to stay in business, other sneaker companies must improve their product to compete with the new sneakers.

Supply and Demand. The theory of supply and demand also plays a significant role in a market economy. *Supply* is the amount of a good that is available. *Demand* is the desire of consumers to buy that good. According to the theory of supply and demand, when supply goes up, prices go down. When demand goes up, prices go up. Increased competition created by the ready availability of goods forces companies to compete on price. However, when demand for a product rises, companies can charge a higher price because people really want the product. For example, suppose that a pair of suede boots costs $50. A celebrity wears the boots, and suddenly, everyone wants a pair. The company then raises the price of the boots to $100, and people buy them because the demand is high. When those boots go out of style, and demand drops, the company will have to drop the price again.

Production line techniques make it easier and cheaper to supply the demand for doughnuts.

Command Economy

A *command economy* differs greatly from a market economy. A command economy is controlled by the government. The government owns the *means of production*, which includes everything people use to produce wealth, such as machines, tools, buildings, and land. In a command economy, there is no freedom of enterprise. Because businesses are owned by the government, the government makes all the economic decisions. *Socialism* is an example of a command system.

Socialism. In socialism, the government makes all decisions regarding industry and manufacturing. Socialists believe that governmental control of businesses ensures fair wages and work hours, and job security for everyone. The government decides what businesses will produce. In some Socialist countries, people may not have a choice about where they work or what work they do. The government decides. The government controls not only the means of production, but also the education system. Through its education system, the government can develop the kind of workers it needs.

Communism. Ideally, a Socialist government would create a society in which all citizens share equally in the ownership and control of economic resources. In practice, this has seldom happened. *Communism* is a form of socialism sometimes called authoritarian socialism. Communism has regularly led to government abuses. Such a Socialist government cares more about revenue for government projects than about the standard of living of its workers. The former Soviet Union is an example of a Communist state. The people had little freedom of choice. They also suffered from low wages, lack of consumer choices, shortages of goods, and a low standard of living.

Mixed Economies

In reality, no country today has an economy that is solely a market economy or solely a command economy. Almost all economies are mixed economies—economies that have features of both a market economy and a command economy. Some countries lean more toward one or the other, and so they are labeled according to which system controls the majority of their economic activity.

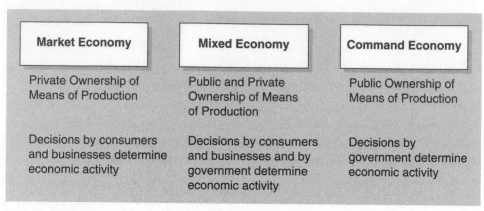

Market Economy	Mixed Economy	Command Economy
Private Ownership of Means of Production	Public and Private Ownership of Means of Production	Public Ownership of Means of Production
Decisions by consumers and businesses determine economic activity	Decisions by consumers and businesses and by government determine economic activity	Decisions by government determine economic activity

How production decisions are made in different economic systems

United States. Many people consider the United States economy the prime example of capitalism. However, it is not a pure capitalist economy. The U.S. government exercises some control over industry and business. In addition, although almost all farms, factories, and stores in the United States are privately owned, the U.S. government carries on many public enterprises, such as delivering the mail across the country and aiding citizens in disaster relief.

Sweden. Sweden is an example of a country with a mixed economy. Sweden has a system of *democratic socialism*. It is democratic, because Swedish citizens freely elect their government leaders. It is Socialist, because the government controls several major industries, such as railroads and electric-power plants. However, Sweden also has a large number of privately owned, profit-seeking industries. In this way, freedom of enterprise and freedom of consumer choice exist alongside government-owned business.

Like Sweden, most nations termed "Socialist" today have only a few government-run industries. Their national standard of living is relatively high. Many economists believe that pure socialism is a less practical economic system than capitalism. Even in China, where the Communist party still rules and the people cannot freely elect their leaders, the government has allowed people to open their own businesses and sell goods and services for a profit.

Test Yourself
Mixed economies include features of which two economic systems?

POINTS TO REMEMBER

- Trade is the buying, selling, and exchanging of goods within and between countries. The benefits of trade always come at a cost.
- Trade increases the standard of living, because it creates opportunities for countries to enjoy goods produced in other countries.
- Trade and specialization encourage efficient use of productive resources, such as money, machines, land, natural resources, and human capital.
- All nations and societies must answer the basic economic questions of what to produce, how to produce, and for whom to produce goods and services.
- In a traditional economy, the fundamental economic questions are answered according to custom or religious beliefs.
- In capitalism (a market economy), individual businesses have the freedom to decide what they will produce and sell to consumers, who have the freedom to choose what they want to buy and what they do not want to buy.
- A command economy is one that is controlled by the government, which owns the means of production, including machines, tools, buildings, and land. In a command economy, businesses do not have freedom of enterprise.
- Most economies today are mixed economies—economies that have features of both a market economy and a command economy.

EXERCISES

CHECKING WHAT YOU HAVE READ

1. The availability of resources that a country uses for trade or industry is called
   A. human capital
   B. productive capacity
   C. supply and demand
   D. economics.

2. A traditional economy is based on
   A. outside influence
   B. nomadic travel
   C. past practices
   D. the will of the government.

3. Which of the following is a feature of a market economy?
   A. freedom of enterprise
   B. government control
   C. publicly owned businesses
   D. lack of industry

4. Which is an example of a command system?
   A. capitalism
   B. anarchism
   C. mercantilism
   D. socialism

5. Most economies in the world today are

A. Socialist
B. traditional
C. mixed
D. Communist.

USING WHAT YOU HAVE READ

1. Look through a magazine or newspaper for an advertisement that you think is a clear example of some traits of capitalism. Cut it out and write a paragraph explaining how the advertisement shows these characteristics.

2. You learned about means of production in this chapter. Make sure you understand the definition. Then choose a piece of property in your community that is an example of a means of production. Write about how this land demonstrates capitalism at work.

THINKING ABOUT WHAT YOU HAVE READ

1. What strengths and what weaknesses do you see in capitalism?

2. What strengths and what weaknesses do you see in socialism?

3. Look on the Internet or in your local library for information about the fall of the Soviet Union. Make a list of reasons for its collapse. Think about how its command economy contributed to the collapse. Write an essay describing the collapse of the Soviet Union and the role of its command economy in this collapse.

SKILLS

Comparing Conditions in Two Countries

Ever since the end of World War II, the Korean people have lived under two separate and hostile governments. Those living in North Korea have a government that is controlled by the Communist party. North Korea's factories, farms, and other means of production are publicly owned. In contrast, Koreans living in South Korea have an economy in which most of the means of production are privately owned. In short, North Korea practices socialism, whereas South Korea practices capitalism. Which system has been more successful in producing various goods and services? The statistics in the following table give some facts about the two Koreas in the recent past. As you examine the statistics, keep in mind that they give only a partial picture. Even so, you can draw some conclusions about the quality of life in the two nations.

Examine the table and then answer the questions that follow.

North and South Korea, Selected Data

	North Korea	South Korea
Total population (2004)	22,698,000	48,199,000
Life expectancy at birth	male 68.1 years female 73.6 years	male 71.7 years female 79.3 years
Infant mortality rate (2003)	25.7	7.3
Literacy rate (%)	95 (1997)	age 15 and over, 97.9 (2001)
Imports (2001; value of	U.S. $1.8 billion	U.S. $141 billion
Exports (2001); value of	U.S. $826 million	U.S. $150.4 billion
Airports with scheduled flights	1 (2001)	14 (1996)
Food: daily per capita caloric intake	2,142 (2002)	3,055 (2001)
Televisions (2000)	1.1 million	17 million
Radios (2000)	3.3 million	48.6 million
Consumption of electricity (2000)	32.8 million (kilowatts per hour)	295 million kilowatts per hour
Gross National Product (GNP)	U.S. $9.9 billion (1999)	U.S. $576 billion (2003)
Military expenditure as a percentage of GNP (1999)	18.8	2.9

1. According to the table, which nation, North Korea or South Korea, has the larger population?

2. Which economy allocates the larger percentage of its GNP to military expenditures?

3. Based on information in the table, which nation is more likely to be a closed society?

4. Which nation has the larger amount of exports in U.S. dollars?

5. In which nation are people more likely to live longer?

CHAPTER 13

THE U.S. GOVERNMENT AND THE ECONOMY

BENCHMARK:

Explain how the U.S. government provides public services, redistributes income, regulates economic activity, and promotes economic growth and stability.

This benchmark requires you to understand the role the United States government plays in the domestic and international economy. You should be able to describe how the government promotes economic growth and stability as well as how it provides public services and redistribution of income. You must also understand the economic costs and benefits of protectionism, tariffs, quotas, and international trade blockades.

★ THE ROLE OF THE U.S. GOVERNMENT IN THE ECONOMY ★

The U.S. government plays a role in the domestic economy by regulating the economy for the welfare of its citizens.

Regulating Public Services

One way the U.S. government tries to ensure the welfare of its citizens is by regulating public services. *Public services* are functions that benefit the public, such as providing electric power or public transportation. The companies that provide these services are often *monopolies*. A monopoly is the exclusive control of a particular service or good by one company. For example, an area may have only one electric supplier. With no government regulation, the power company could charge any price it chooses because it has no competition from other companies that can offer the same service at a lower cost. By regulating public services, the government makes sure that prices remain fair.

Redistribution of Income

Another economic function of the federal government is the redistribution of income. To *redistribute* is to divide something up in different ways or in different proportions and then dispense it among members of a group.

A wind farm in Mexico generates electricity that is sold to power companies in Southern California.

The government redistributes income when it uses tax revenues to fund programs to help those in need. Examples of such programs are social security, unemployment benefits, and Medicare. These are called income-transfer programs because money is transferred from one group to another. In 1935, Congress introduced the payroll deduction, which is a system to withhold income taxes from wages. The Internal Revenue Service (the agency of the U.S. Treasury Department that collects taxes) takes payroll deductions to pay for such programs as unemployment benefits and social security benefits. Taxes taken from people who are currently working provide money for people who are entitled to receive social security or unemployment benefits.

Subsidies

The U.S. government also promotes economic growth and stability. Providing *subsidies* is one method that the government uses to encourage the growth of domestic industries. A subsidy is a grant, or gift, of money from the government to private groups or industries. An example is the use of subsidies to farmers to help them withstand changes in the prices of their crops.

The Federal Reserve System

The activities of the *Federal Reserve System* are the chief way that the federal government helps to stabilize the nation's economy and promote economic growth. The Federal Reserve System is the central banking system of the

United States. It consists of a board of governors and 12 regional Federal Reserve Banks. All national banks are required to belong to the system. The Federal Reserve regulates the nation's money supply and sets interest rates based on current economic conditions. The goal of the actions of the Fed, as it is called, is to keep the economy stable and growing.

Test Yourself
What is the chief way that the U.S. government promotes economic stability and growth?

★ PROTECTIONISM, TARIFFS, QUOTAS, AND BLOCKADES ★

The U.S. government intervenes in international trade as well as in domestic economic matters. Protectionism, tariffs, quotas, and blockades are some of the measures it takes to keep the economy of the United States sound.

Protectionism

Protectionism is an economic policy that imposes high duties (taxes) on imported goods that compete with similar domestic goods. Imported goods that are cheaper than comparable domestic goods will cause the sales of domestic goods to drop. In addition, imported goods increase the supply of total goods in a nation, which may, in turn, force domestic manufacturers to lower the prices of their competing domestic products. If the competition is too great and the loss of income for domestic businesses too large, they may go out of business, throwing thousands of people out of work. Therefore, governments practice protectionism with the goal of protecting domestic industries and jobs.

When there is lessened competition for domestic goods because of protectionism, domestic businesses are able to keep the prices of their goods relatively high. Without lower-priced competing goods, consumers tend to buy the domestic goods and manufacturers stay in business. However, protectionism can also hurt the domestic economy. In the 1980s, the United States limited the number of Japanese cars that could be imported. The sale of inexpensive Japanese cars was thought to be hurting the U.S. auto industry and threatening the jobs of autoworkers. Since the number of Japanese imports was limited, the price of cars made in the United States went up. However, when U.S.-made autos became more expensive, people bought fewer cars. This resulted in job losses in the U.S. auto industry, which is what the protectionist policy was supposed to avoid.

Protectionism has negative effects on the global economy. The global cost of protectionism is the decreased availability of goods in the world market. Trade conducted without protectionist policies is called *free trade*. Free trade tends to benefit the global economy by making available many different kinds of goods in large numbers.

Quotas

When the United States limited the number of cars that could be imported from Japan, it placed *quotas* on them. Quotas help industries in a number of ways. First, they can protect a domestic industry from a large inflow of competing foreign goods. Second, quotas can also ensure that a nation does not export too large a quantity of its own domestic goods. This becomes a problem when the domestic demand for a good is equal to the amount of that good that a nation produces. By limiting the export of such a good, the government can make sure that there is an adequate supply for the domestic market. In addition, by limiting the export of certain goods, the government can make sure the price of the good on the world market does not drop because of oversupply.

Costs of Quotas. There are also economic costs of quotas. If more of a good were available on the world market, the price would drop. This would be fine for world consumers but could be bad for the countries that produce these goods. They would make less money from the export of their goods.

Quotas also limit domestic choice. As a result of a quota, domestic consumers may not have the choice to buy a foreign product that may be better than the domestic one. Competition from a superior product can also lead to improvements in similar domestic products. An example is the U.S. auto industry. Faced with competition from small, fuel-efficient Japanese cars, U.S. automakers in the 1980s began to develop comparable small, fuel-efficient cars.

A German automaker produces this model of car, which it manufactures only in the United States.

Tariffs

Tariffs are taxes. Most often, the word tariff is used to refer to taxes levied by a nation on imports and exports. Tariffs are also a part of protectionist economic policy, and they work much like quotas in their effect on the domestic economy.

Political Consequences of Tariffs. Historically, the imposition of tariffs has had serious political consequences. For example, during the nation's colonial period, England imposed tariffs favorable to itself on its North American colonies. They were unfavorable to the colonies, however, and they were a major contributing factor to the War for Independence. During the period before the U.S. Civil War, Southerners were angered when tariffs were passed that hurt their region but were favorable to Northern industrialists.

Effect of Tariffs on International Trade. Tariffs can hinder international trade. In the 1920s and 1930s, many nations, especially the United States, used tariffs in an effort to protect their own economies. Unfortunately, these tariffs slowed the international economy and made the Great Depression worse. In the years after World War II, many nations, realizing the economic costs of protectionism, sought to build international cooperation.

General Agreement on Tariffs and Trade; World Trade Organization. In 1948, the General Agreement on Tariffs and Trade (GATT) was signed by the United States and more than 20 European nations. The goal of GATT was to increase international trade and reduce discriminatory trade practices such as tariffs. In 1995 GATT was replaced by the World Trade Organization (WTO). Its more than 150 member nations agree to abide by WTO rules of fair trade.

Free Trade Agreement; North American Free Trade Agreement. In 1987, the United States and Canada entered into the Free Trade Agreement (FTA), with the goal of removing trade restrictions between the two nations. This agreement was replaced in 1994 with the North American Free Trade Agreement (NAFTA), which also includes Mexico. NAFTA calls for the elimination of all trade barriers between and among the three nations over a period of 15 years. It is important to note that even though the federal government entered into the trade agreement, not everyone agreed with the policy of free, or freer, trade. Many people in the United States—both business owners and workers—did not favor NAFTA but wanted more protectionist policies. The fear was that NAFTA would result in the loss of U.S. jobs and hurt the U.S. economy.

Blockades and Embargoes

Blockades and embargoes are two barriers to trade that have political as well as economic goals.

Blockade. A blockade shuts off a nation from outside trade by preventing access to and from the nation's ports. During the U.S. Civil War, Union ships

California workers protest jobs lost because U.S. companies moved to less expensive foreign countries.

blockaded Southern ports so that the Confederacy could not ship its cotton to England. The blockade also prevented the ships of other nations from entering Southern ports.

Embargo. A nation imposes an embargo when it refuses to import goods from or export goods to another country. A nation will sometimes try to influence another nation's policies by imposing an embargo, hoping the economic pressure will force a change in policy. In this way, embargoes are used as economic sanctions.

An example of an embargo is the U.S. embargo of Cuban sugar and Cuban cigars. Angered by Fidel Castro's acceptance of communism, the United States refused to allow Cuban sugar to be imported into the United States. The government hoped that the economic hardship caused by the embargo would turn the Cuban people against Castro and they would overthrow him. The embargo has lasted for more than 40 years and so has Castro's government. Today, the United States and the United Nations often use embargoes against countries that attack other countries or groups within their own countries. An example is the embargo placed on Iraqi oil after the invasion of Kuwait in 1990.

Test Yourself
What did Canada, Mexico, and the United States intend to accomplish in the North American Free Trade Agreement (NAFTA)?

POINTS TO REMEMBER

- In the United States, and many world nations today, the government regulates public services, such as electric and gas utilities and telephone companies, in order to ensure that these services are fairly priced.

- The federal government redistributes income through income-transfer programs such as social security and unemployment benefits.

- The government uses subsidies to encourage U.S. economic growth and helps to stabilize the economy through the actions of the Federal Reserve System.

- Protectionism is an economic policy that imposes high duties on imported goods that compete with domestic goods.

- Quotas and tariffs are tools of protectionism.

- Quotas place limits on quantities of imported and/or exported goods.

- Tariffs are taxes on imports and/or exports.

- Blockades and embargoes limit a nation's ability to trade and are used for political as well as economic reasons.

EXERCISES

CHECKING WHAT YOU HAVE READ

1. What is one way quotas can help an industry?

   A. They make imported goods less expensive.
   B. They provide competition in a market.
   C. They lead to decreased demand.
   D. They can decrease the inflow of competing foreign goods.

2. Which is an example of an income-transfer program?

   A. social security
   B. the Federal Reserve System
   C. NAFTA
   D. World Trade Organization

3. Why are some people in the United States opposed to NAFTA?

   A. They do not believe in blockades.
   B. They think it will cause Americans to lose jobs.
   C. They support free trade.
   D. They prefer the WTO.

4. What kind of trade policies might have a negative effect on the global economy?

   A. the lifting of tariffs and quotas
   B. free trade policies
   C. the payroll tax deduction
   D. protectionist policies in Europe and the United States

5. In which U.S. industry in the 1980s did protectionist policies backfire?

   A. agricultural industry
   B. banking industry
   C. auto industry
   D. fishing industry

USING WHAT YOU HAVE READ

1. Research NAFTA on the Internet or in the library. After you have completed your research, make a two-column table listing what you think are the pros and the cons of the agreement. Do you agree that NAFTA is a good idea? If not, why not? How do you think NAFTA might benefit or harm the economy? Write a brief essay addressing these questions. Use your table to support your opinion.

2. The United States still has an embargo in place against Cuba. Today, many people think the embargo should be lifted. Research the embargo of Cuba. What are the economic effects of the embargo on the Cuban economy? What are the effects on the U.S. economy? What are the arguments in favor of eliminating the embargo? What are the arguments against it? Prepare a report answering these questions.

THINKING ABOUT WHAT YOU HAVE READ

1. How does the World Trade Organization operate? Look up the WTO on the Internet or in the library. What effect does the WTO have on the economies of member nations? Do you think the United States benefits from membership in the WTO? What rulings against U.S. trade practices have occurred in the last five years? Prepare a report on U.S. membership in the WTO.

2. What do you think would happen if the United States or any nation decided not to trade with other nations? How do you think that would affect its economy?

Would prices rise? Would there be a shortage of goods? Would there be a lack of certain types of goods? What would the social and cultural impact be?

Consider that Japan did something similar to this when it shut out the outside world from the 1600s through the mid-1800s.

SKILLS

Analyzing Primary Sources

Read the following passage and answer the questions that follow. The passage is an excerpt from President Bill Clinton's State of the Union address in January 1998.

. . . As we enter the twenty-first century, the global economy requires us to seek opportunity not just at home, but in all markets of the world. We must shape this global economy, not shrink from it. In the last five years, we have led the way in opening new markets, with 240 trade agreements that remove foreign barriers to products bearing the proud stamp "Made in the U.S.A." Today, record high exports account for fully one-third of our economic growth. I want to keep them growing, because that's the way to keep America growing and to advance a safer, more stable world. . . .

I know there is opposition to more comprehensive trade agreements. I have listened carefully and I believe that the opposition is rooted in two fears: first, that our trading partners will have lower environmental and labor standards, which will give them an unfair advantage in our market and do their own people no favors, even if there's more business; and, second, that if we have more trade, more of our workers will lose their jobs and have to start over. I think we should seek to advance worker and environmental standards around the world. I have made it abundantly clear that it should be a part of our trade agenda. But we cannot influence other countries' decisions if we send them a message that we're backing away from trade with them.

1. According to President Clinton, what accounted for one-third of U.S. economic growth?

2. What opposition to comprehensive trade agreements does President Clinton acknowledge?

3. What did President Clinton make "abundantly clear" should be a part of the trade agenda?

4. Why does President Clinton want to keep trade agreements going?

5. In the following quotation, what "decisions" is President Clinton referring to?
   "But we cannot influence other countries' decisions if we send them a message that we're backing away from trade with them."

CHAPTER 14

FORMS OF GOVERNMENT

BENCHMARK:

Analyze the differences among various forms of government to determine how power is acquired and used.

To meet the requirements of this benchmark, you must understand how power within human governments is created and maintained. As you read in Chapter 1, when people give up some of their freedom to a government in exchange for peace and security, they are entering the social contract. There are various opinions about which form of government is best suited to maintain law and order. This chapter discusses the following types of government: absolute monarchies, constitutional monarchies, parliamentary democracies, presidential democracies, dictatorships, and theocracies. It explains how governments acquire, use, and justify their power.

In this chapter, you will also learn how representative democracy compares with other systems, such as a monarchy in Saudi Arabia or a dictatorship in Cuba. You should be able to distinguish among various forms of government around the world today.

★ THEORIES ON GOVERNMENT ★

You learned in Chapter 1 that Thomas Hobbes believed that people, being selfish by nature, need a strong government, such as an absolute monarchy, to make them obey laws. John Locke, on the other hand, felt that a government should not only keep order but also ensure the rights of its citizens. Locke's ideas influenced political thinkers in the 18th and 19th centuries to advocate revolt against their nations' monarchs. Those nations then established democracies. Some of these democracies were more successful than others. This chapter discusses in some detail the differences among these and other kinds of governments.

★ MONARCHIES ★

There are two basic types of monarchies: absolute and constitutional.

Absolute Monarchies

Centuries ago, most governments were headed by a single person—a monarch. The exact title of the monarch differed from one society to the next. There were kings and queens, emperors and czars, sultans and pharaohs. Whatever the title, it usually belonged to just one family—the royal family. A monarch's crown (the symbol of his or her power) was passed down through generations, usually to the monarch's eldest or most trusted son. An absolute monarch is a ruler who completely controls the government and its laws. The people either obey the monarch's laws or suffer harsh penalties for disobeying.

At the time of the American Revolution (the 1770s), absolute monarchs governed most of Europe and much of the rest of the world. Since then, however, one royal family after another has been forced to surrender power.

A few monarchies do still exist. Examples of powerful monarchs in today's world may be found in the Middle Eastern nations of Kuwait and Saudi Arabia. Other powerful monarchs rule in the African nation of Swaziland and the Asian nations of Nepal and Brunei.

Saudi Arabia. The world's leading producer of crude oil, this nation is ruled by a family descended from the first Saudi king, Ibn-Saud. The present ruler is King Abdullah, the half-brother of the previous king, who died in 2005. As in most absolute monarchies, opposition to the king is not tolerated. Citizens are not free to speak out against the government. Nor can citizens take part in elections to choose public officials. All Saudi officials are appointed by the king, not elected by the people. Members of the royal family fill many of the government positions.

Brunei. Brunei is a small, oil-rich nation on the island of Borneo, in Southeast Asia. Brunei was politically powerful between the 15th and 17th centuries,

King Abdullah, ruler of Saudi Arabia

Sultan Hassanal Bolkiah, leader
of Brunei

after which it fell into decline. In 1888, Brunei became a British protectorate. Independence was granted in 1984.

The absolute monarch of Brunei is Sultan Hassanal Bolkiah. As sultan, he inherited his power from his father, who was one in a long line of rulers over several centuries. He is not only the sultan, but is also the prime minister, defense minister, and finance minister of Brunei. In addition, he is Brunei's religious leader.

Because Brunei is rich in petroleum and natural gas, the standard of living is very high. Its population of about 300,000 people do not pay taxes. They receive free education and free health care, and they are provided free sports and recreational facilities. Most citizens have high-paying jobs.

In exchange for their prosperity, the citizens of Brunei are expected to be loyal to their sultan. They are expected to obey the law and not to question the ruler's actions.

Constitutional Monarchies

Not all monarchs have total, or absolute, power. Constitutional monarchs serve more as representations of their nations' ideal characteristics. They usually preside over countries with basically democratic governments.

Great Britain. The power of Queen Elizabeth II of Great Britain is extremely limited. She is a living symbol of the British nation and its long history and traditions. As such, she serves to give stability to the British government and national pride to the people. In terms of real political power, however, Queen Elizabeth does little more than ratify (approve) the decisions of officials who

Queen Elizabeth II opens the British Parliament.

are elected to office by the British people. The British type of government is known as a *constitutional monarchy*, or limited monarchy. In such a government, real power belongs to elected officials, not the king or queen.

Queen Elizabeth opens Parliament, the country's legislature, every year with a speech. She attends public events and travels around the world representing the government and people of Great Britain. Once a week, she meets privately with the prime minister to discuss domestic and foreign policy. She also occasionally meets with other *ministers* (top officials) in the government.

Japan. Another example of a constitutional monarch is Emperor Akihito of Japan. He became the emperor of Japan in 1989. He is descended from a long line of emperors, going back to the 6th century B.C.

The title "emperor" is not really accurate. It is an English translation of a Japanese term "tenno" which means "heavenly sovereign." Akihito's reign (the years of his rule) is referred to as "Heisei," which means "the achievement of complete peace on Earth and in the heavens." Traditionally, the emperor is not mentioned by name. So in Japan, Emperor Akihito is referred to as Heisei Tenno. The chrysanthemum is the emperor's personal symbol.

Emperors of Japan have never had absolute power, although some have been more politically powerful than others. Most have simply been a symbol of the government's power, which traditionally was believed to have come from heaven. The Japanese constitution specifically states that the role the emperor is to be "the symbol of the State and the unity of the people, deriving his position from the will of the people in who resides sovereign power." Emperor Akihito has far fewer official duties than Great Britain's Queen Elizabeth II or other constitutional monarchs.

Real power in Japan rests in a number of governmental institutions. Executive power is held by the prime minister and the cabinet. Laws are made

Japanese Emperor Akihito delivers a speech to the parliament.

by the national legislature, which is called the Diet. There is a separate judiciary branch with its own powers.

Other nations that have constitutional monarchies include Spain, Denmark, Norway, Jordan, Nepal, Sweden, and the Netherlands.

Advantages and Disadvantages of Absolute Monarchies

Compared with other forms of government, an absolute monarchy has certain advantages. At its best, it can be a relatively stable form of government. People know that one person, the monarch, will continue to rule for the rest of his or her life. If the monarch is a capable leader and in good health, people are assured of the benefits of good government for many years.

On the other hand, when an absolute monarch dies, there can be much trouble over the question of who will be next on the throne. At the time of the ruler's death, the appointed heir might be only a child. Ambitious persons then have the opportunity to challenge the young ruler. Rival contenders for the throne might tear apart the kingdom in a civil war.

Another disadvantage to absolute monarchy is that an absolute monarch cannot be questioned. The freedoms of individual citizens are often limited. Rights that Americans often take for granted, like freedom of speech and freedom of the press, are not guaranteed in an absolute monarchy. There are few checks on the authority of the monarch.

Test Yourself
What type of government has a powerful parliament and a weak king?

★ DICTATORSHIPS ★

More common than monarchies in today's world are governments known as dictatorships. Unlike a monarch, a dictator does not sit on a royal throne or wear a royal robe and crown. Nor does a dictator usually inherit power from a parent. In one respect, however, dictators of modern times do resemble absolute monarchs. A dictator, like an absolute monarch, has total control of his or her nation's political system. No law can be passed without the dictator's approval. All officials in government take orders from the dictator.

How a Dictator Seizes Power

A dictator usually takes power by means of military force. This person could be a high-ranking army officer who, for a time, pretends to be loyal to the existing government. Or the person could be a commander of rebel armies that openly oppose the government. We might call this military leader "the general." When he thinks he can succeed, "the general" may declare a "national emergency" and announce that he is taking over the government. (If he is a rebel commander, his armies would first have to defeat the government's forces.) "The general" typically orders his troops to arrest the top leaders of the old government. This military takeover is called a *coup d'état*, or simply a *coup*. The new government organized by "the general" would be a military dictatorship.

How a Dictator Remains in Power

Once in office, the dictator usually pretends to be a great patriot and champion of the people. To show that the people support a dictator's government, elections may be held. But elections organized by a dictator are neither fair nor free. The *ballot* (list of candidates) usually gives only the names of the loyal supporters of the dictator. The police force, which is under the dictator's control, may use threats and actual force to stop anyone from saying anything against the dictatorship. Thus, time after time, the dictator and his or her party win elections by a nearly unanimous vote.

Cuba. The island nation of Cuba is a country that has been ruled by a dictator for decades. The present dictator, Fidel Castro, came to power in 1959 in a military coup overthrowing the dictator Fulgencio Batista. Castro and his supporters in the Communist party rule the nation without organized opposition. Many of Castro's opponents have been imprisoned. The Communist party is the only political party allowed in Cuba. Even though elections are held regularly, the Cuban people have no choice but to vote for the persons that Castro picks for different elective positions. There is an elected legislature, or lawmaking body. But it does nothing more than pass the laws that Castro wants.

North Korea. One of the world's most mysterious rulers is Kim Jong Il of North Korea. This country has very little contact with the rest of the world. Kim Jong Il was named to be his father's successor in 1980. He became the dictator of North Korea after his father died in 1994. He is secretive, rarely making public appearances. He has built a huge tower that dominates the skyline

Kim Jong Il, ruler of North Korea

of Pyongyang, North Korea's capital. The tower is called a monument to "self-reliance" and has become a symbol of North Korea's isolation from the rest of the world.

Within North Korea, Kim Jong Il has an almost cult status among many North Koreans. Supposedly, his birth was marked by the appearance of a double rainbow and a new, bright star in the sky. The media refer to him as "peerless leader." Some outside observers view Kim Jong Il as ruthless, shrewd, and willing to use any force necessary to stay in power. He has been accused of supporting terrorism in other countries.

In 2005, North Korea announced that it had developed nuclear weapons. If this is true, North Korea poses a grave threat to other East Asian countries and to world security.

Advantage of a Dictatorship

A dictatorship like Castro's may seem to Americans to be all bad because it deprives people of liberty. Moreover, people's rights are not guaranteed. But there is one main advantage to a dictatorship. When one leader completely controls a government, he can act quickly and decisively in an emergency. In the 1920s, for example, the Italian dictator Benito Mussolini came to the rescue of Italy's troubled economy by imposing his will on both business and labor. By contrast, democracies are often slow to act in an economic crisis because disagreements among rival political parties cause delays in passing laws or prevent their passage.

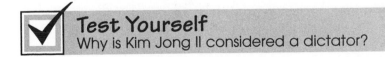

Test Yourself
Why is Kim Jong Il considered a dictator?

★ THEOCRACY ★

The term "theocracy" comes from the Greek language. It means "rule by the deity (God)." A *theocracy* is a form of government in which the leader of the dominant religion of a country also serves as the dominant political leader. Secular laws (laws of society) are the same as religious laws. The leader claims that God gave him or her the authority to govern.

History gives us many examples of theocracies. In ancient times, the Egyptian pharaohs were worshipped as both kings and gods. Kings of ancient Mesopotamia claimed divine power. In Mexico, the ruler of the Aztecs also served as a priest. The Puritan settlers of Massachusetts Bay Colony established a theocracy. The government of Massachusetts Bay was based on religious law. A present-day example of theocracy is Iran.

Iran

Iran is officially the Islamic Republic of Iran. The elected legislative body is called *Majlis*, which has been translated as both the Council of Experts and the Islamic Consultative Assembly. The vast majority of the 270-member Majlis are Muslims, but Zoroastrians, Jews, and Assyrian Christians have one seat each in the legislature. Two seats are reserved for Armenian Christians.

Laws passed by the assembly are reviewed by the 12-member Council of Guardians. The council is made up of six Muslim clerics (religious experts) and six Muslim attorneys. These 12 people have veto power over laws. They make sure that laws passed by the Majlis are consistent with religious law.

Iranian Council of Experts at the opening of its annual general assembly

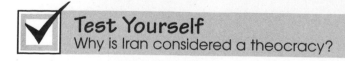

Test Yourself

Why is Iran considered a theocracy?

★ PARLIAMENTARY AND PRESIDENTIAL DEMOCRACIES ★

A *democracy* is a political system that gives average citizens the opportunity to influence the making of laws for their own society. There are two kinds of democracies—direct and representative.

People who live in some small towns in the Northeast can make laws directly through *town meetings*. They meet periodically in the local town hall. There they can discuss and decide upon public issues by majority vote. For example, they may decide whether or not to approve a neighbor's idea for controlling traffic on the town's main street, repairing a local bridge, or solving another local problem. Town meetings are an example of *direct democracy*.

Town residents give their views on a proposed landfill in a New York town.

Unlike a small town, a large city, a state, or a nation is usually much too large for direct democracy to be practical. No auditorium is big enough for thousands of citizens to sit down together to make laws. Instead, in a *representative democracy*, laws are made by a small number of officials who are elected by a vote of the people. The elected officials of large cities, states, and the nation represent the interests of the people who elect them.

Four characteristics are especially important to representative democracy:

● *Consent of the governed.* Laws are approved by the people's elected representatives. Indirectly, at least, the people have given their consent to these laws because a majority of their representatives voted for them.

- *Freedom to criticize and oppose.* Those wishing to change or do away with unwanted laws have the opportunity to express their views freely. They can criticize the government's actions and vote the leaders out of office at the next election. Government leaders therefore must pay attention to the people's views.

- *Rule by law.* A constitution sets boundaries, or limits, on what officials can and cannot do. The government is limited by a constitution, which is the supreme law of the land. This supreme law is a protection against abuse of power.

- *Guaranteed rights and liberties.* The rights of citizens are protected. For example, the Bill of Rights guarantees to every citizen of the United States the freedoms of speech, religion, assembly, and petition.

Parliamentary Democracy

Many of the world's democratic countries have a *parliamentary democracy*. This is true of the United Kingdom, France, India, Canada, Israel, and Australia. In these countries, the citizens elect representatives to the parliament. Members of parliament are expected to represent the best interests of the people.

Once elected, the members of the parliament elect a chief executive and cabinet to run the government. The chief executive, or prime minister, is a member of the parliament and is usually the head of the majority political party. He or she and the appointed members of the cabinet run the executive branch of government. They also sit in the national legislature, where they are responsible for making the laws that govern society.

Parliamentary Government in Canada. Because Canada was once a British colony, the queen of England is viewed as its head of state. The queen, though, has no power in the Canadian government. Although an official called the governor general symbolically represents her interests, he or she is actually chosen by Canada's prime minister and is only a symbol of the power of government. The governor general serves for five years. The post is alternated between an English-speaking citizen and one who is French-speaking. This is done to honor the dual cultures of Canada's people.

Canada is divided into 308 federal electoral districts called *ridings*. All citizens 18 and older are eligible to vote. Elections are held at least every five years (sooner in some cases) for members of the Canadian House of Commons. In each parliamentary race, the candidate with the most votes wins. Since Canada has a multiparty system, up to 12 political parties can sponsor candidates to run in each election.

The Canadian Parliament is *bicameral*. This means that there are two parts, or houses: the House of Commons and the Senate.

The House of Commons has 308 members. The parliament chooses one of its members to be the prime minister, or chief executive of the government. The prime minister, in turn, chooses members of parliament to serve in the cabinet. If the parliament is controlled by a majority party, this process runs smoothly. If there are several parties elected to the parliament with no majority party, then choosing the prime minister and cabinet (the process of "forming the government") is much more difficult. Members of different parties must

Canadian House of Commons members listen to a speech by the prime minister.

form a consensus of opinion in order to proceed. Compromise is necessary to form a government under these circumstances.

The Senate has 105 members who represent the various Canadian provinces and territories. Senators are appointed by the governor general based on the recommendation of the prime minister. The Senate approves or disapproves bills passed by the House of Commons. It also has committees to study economic and social issues.

The prime minister and cabinet carry out the laws passed by parliament and run the various ministries (departments) of government. The prime minister has two staff organizations for support. (1) The members of the Privy Council Office (PCO) give nonpartisan advice (advice not influenced by a political faction) to the government and its agencies. (2) The Prime Minister's Office (PMO) is the leader's personal staff. It is partisan (political) and gives advice on both policy matters and political issues.

The parliament and prime minister normally remain in power for at least five years. After five years, a new election is held. An election is scheduled sooner if there is a nonconfidence vote of the parliament. When the parliament votes down a tax or spending bill sponsored by the prime minister's party, it is said to be a vote of nonconfidence. The government "falls," and a new election is held. This is more likely to happen when the governing party has fewer than 154 members in the House of Commons—that is, fewer than half the total 308 members.

Presidential Democracy

Presidential democracy is the style of government in the United States. Unlike a parliamentary democracy, in which parliament chooses the prime minister, all eligible U.S. citizens can vote to decide who becomes the president of the United States. Therefore, the president has a national constituency. This means that the president must answer directly to the people, not to the legislative branch. The president's term is four years. He or she can serve only two terms. If for any reason the president cannot serve his/her term, the vice president will take his/her place. The vice president also serves for four years.

As chief executive, the president's major duty is to run the government. Like the Canadian prime minister, the U.S. president is assisted by a cabinet of advisers. The members of the cabinet are appointed by the president. The president executes, or enforces, the laws that are passed by the U.S. Congress, a separate branch of government. The president also has the power to veto bills. Although the president can influence lawmakers, he or she is not a member of Congress and cannot make laws.

Like Canada's parliament, the U.S. Congress is bicameral. This legislative body consists of a Senate and a House of Representatives, both elected by citizens 18 years and older. The Senate consists of 100 members. Senators serve for six years. The House of Representatives has 435 seats. Each representative serves for a two-year term.

The United States is a multiparty country. Throughout U.S. history, however, two major parties, the Democrats and the Republicans, have had the most influence on the U.S. government.

Pluses and Minuses of Representative Democracy

Compared with monarchies and dictatorships, representative governments offer people the greatest amount of protection from harsh and unjust laws. People are doubly protected against harsh rule by the rights guaranteed in a written constitution and by the power that they have as voters. Officials at all levels of government must continually earn the voters' trust. If a high official is corrupted by power, both a free press and political opponents can usually expose his or her wrongdoing.

Strong as it is, however, representative democracy does not guarantee good and effective government. First, because many competing groups and political parties disagree about what government should do, there may be long delays before needed laws are passed. Second, a democratic system depends for its success on millions of people being interested enough in public affairs to vote intelligently. If people lose touch with their representatives or cease to care about political issues, the quality of democratic government may decline. A democracy can remain healthy only so long as citizens make an effort to stay informed and to vote accordingly.

 Test Yourself
How is a direct democracy different from a representative democracy?

POINTS TO REMEMBER

- An absolute monarch gains power through heredity, rules without consulting a legislative body, and is not subject to elections.

- In a constitutional monarchy, the monarch is not the most powerful political force and may be only a figurehead. A constitution curtails the power of the monarch and gives rights to the people.

- A dictator is like an absolute monarch, but he or she usually comes to power through military force.

- A theocracy is a form of government whereby one or more leaders of the dominant religion rule the country.

- A democracy can be either direct or representative. It can take the form of a parliamentary system or a presidential system.

EXERCISES

CHECKING WHAT YOU HAVE READ

On a separate sheet of paper, write the type of government that each word or phrase below describes. Write either AM for absolute monarchy, DICT for dictatorship, or REP for representative democracy.

1. headed by king or queen

2. Cuba's system

3. limited by a constitution

4. consent of the governed

5. free elections involving competing parties

6. Saudi Arabia's system

7. only one political party

8. power passed down from a parent to a child

9. guaranteed rights for individual citizens

10. lawmakers acting on behalf of the voters

USING WHAT YOU HAVE READ

1. Create a poster about a dictator from history or from the present. Your poster should tell how and when the dictator came to power, give examples of his or her use of power, and evaluate his or her rule. Your poster should contain at least one graphic illustration (photograph, drawing, table, or symbol). Share your poster with your classmates.

Here are some possible choices to research:

Hafez al-Assad	Saddam Hussein
Idi Amin	Ruhollah Khomeini
Fulgencio Batista	Nikita Khrushchev
Josip Broz (Tito)	Vladimir Ilyich
Ngo Dinh Diem	Lenin
Samuel Doe	Ferdinand Marcos
François Duvalier	Slobodan Milosovic
Francisco Franco	Robert Mugabe

Benito Mussolini   Joseph Stalin
Manuel Noriega   Hugo Banzer
Juan Peron   Suarez
Augusto Pinochet   Ahmed Sukarno
Pol Pot   Kim Il Sung
Muammar Qaddafi   Afredo Stroessner
Antonio Salazar   Rafael Trujillo
Mobutu Sese Seko   Ne Win
Anastasio Somoza

2. On a separate sheet of paper, copy the following table. Fill in each section with as many positive and negative characteristics as you can.

Comparing Types of Governments

	Representative Democracy	Absolute Monarchy	Dictatorship
Positive Characteristics			
Negative Characteristics			

THINKING ABOUT WHAT YOU HAVE READ

1. Research an absolute monarch from the past. Then create a report card for this person. Think of categories to evaluate his or her performance as a ruler. These categories may include use or abuse of power, accomplishments while in power, protecting human rights, and promoting peace and economic prosperity. Give the monarch a grade in each category and an overall grade. Share your report card with the class. Be prepared to justify the grades you gave the monarch.

2. In a few sentences, explain how you think an absolute monarchy, a dictatorship, and a representative democracy would respond to the following issues or problems:

   a. A riot erupts in a major city. Shops are looted, and buildings are set on fire.

   b. A newspaper criticizes the government's leaders and policies.

   c. Postal workers go on strike.

SKILLS

Interpreting Political Cartoons

A. The cartoons that you might find on the editorial pages of a newspaper are called political cartoons or editorial cartoons. They are often funny, but humor is not their main purpose. Cartoonists express their views on political issues through their cartoons. In so doing, they are trying to influence your views. Study the cartoons below and answer the questions that follow.

"I want General Carter to run for Secretary of Defense; Colonel Jones to run for Secretary of Agriculture..."

"Do your civic duty and vote for the people the General chose!"

Decision making in a Dictatorship

1. What do these two cartoons have in common?

2. What does the cartoon on the left say about the electoral process in a dictatorship?

3. What does the cartoon on the right say about the electoral process in a dictatorship?

4. How might either of the above cartoons be redrawn to depict an election in a representative democracy?

5. How would a cartoonist be likely to show the power of an absolute monarch?

B. Kim Jong-Il is the dictator of Communist North Korea. The United States has accused North Korea of developing nuclear weapons, a charge Kim Jong-Il strongly denied until 2004. Study the cartoon below. Then answer the questions that follow.

The two faces of North Korean leader Kim Jong Il

1. What political statement is referenced by the cartoon?

2. How does Kim Jong Il appear on the left?

3. How does Kim Jong Il appear on the right?

4. Although the cartoon uses humor to make a statement, the statement is very serious. What is the cartoonist saying about North Korea and Kim Jong Il?

CHAPTER 15

GOVERNMENTAL CHANGE

BENCHMARK:

Analyze ways people achieve governmental change, including political action, social protest, and revolution.

For this benchmark, you must be able to analyze and evaluate the influence of various forms of citizen action on public policy. In particular, you should understand the role of citizen action in events such as the French Revolution, the international movement to abolish the slave trade and slavery, the Russian Revolution, the independence movement in India, the fall of communism in Europe, and the end of apartheid in South Africa.

You should also be able to describe and compare opportunities for citizen participation under different systems of government, such as absolute monarchies, constitutional monarchies, parliamentary democracies, dictatorships, and theocracies. Finally, you should be able to analyze how governments and other groups use propaganda to influence public opinion and behavior.

★ THE INFLUENCE OF CITIZEN ACTION ON PUBLIC POLICY ★

Imagine that the government in your community passes a law that you do not agree with. You and a group of friends want to change the law. How would you go about it? Would you write letters to local government officials? Would you run for public office? Would you stage a peaceful protest? Would you turn to violence? Would you start a revolution? These are all types of citizen action. Citizens take action to try to change a policy, law, social system, or government with which they are unhappy.

Actions for Political or Social Change

There are many examples throughout history of different groups trying to bring about change by taking action, either through political action, social protest, or revolutionary action. *Political action* occurs when a person or group attempts to make governmental changes using political means such as lending support and raising money for elected candidates who support their views. *Social protest* is an attempt to enact social change.

Political Action. Often, political action is taken by groups that have the money or power to try to enact change through political channels.

Social protest: Women in Florida march against domestic violence.

Social Protest. Social protest is often undertaken by underrepresented groups or those that are discriminated against and lack the power to bring about change through traditional political channels. *Civil disobedience*, in which a group of people violates a law in order to draw public attention to and sympathy for a cause an or injustice, is a form of social protest. Often, social protest has a goal of enacting political as well as social change. An example of civil disobedience as social protest is the civil rights movement in the United States in the 1950s and 1960s. The Rev. Dr. Martin Luther King, Jr., who was one of its leaders, advocated civil disobedience. The social protest of the civil rights movement led to government legislation that protected African Americans' civil rights.

Revolutionary Action. At times, protest can lead to *revolutionary action*, in which a government may be overthrown or drastically altered through either violent or nonviolent revolution. The French Revolution of 1789–1794 and the Russian Revolution of 1917 are two examples of revolutionary change.

The French Revolution

The French Revolution was a ten-year, often violent struggle for a more democratic and fair government and society.

Three Estates. As you read in Chapter 1, the population of 18th-century France was divided into three estates, or social classes. The First and Second estates were made up of clergy and nobles, respectively. The First Estate included both very wealthy church leaders and poor village priests. The Third Estate included about 98 percent of the French population. It included the

Revolutionary action: In the city of Bishkek, Kyrgyzstan, protesters with sticks chased riot police, in March 2005.

growing middle class of merchants, bankers, and such professionals as doctors and lawyers, as well as the poorest people, such as farm laborers and urban workers.

Third Estate's Grievances. The First and Second estates paid no taxes. The Third Estate paid all the taxes that supported both the lavish life style of the French monarchy and foreign wars. The increasingly wealthy middle class in the Third Estate resented this burden. They also resented that the French king was an absolute monarch; that is, he governed without consulting the people.

The Third Estate first tried political action to reform the French government. In 1789, King Louis XVI called a meeting of the Estates General in an attempt to calm the tension between the classes. In the Estates General, each estate had one vote. The First and Second estates usually voted together, giving them a majority. The Third Estate demanded that each member of all three estates be counted as one vote, which would give them the advantage.

The National Assembly. When this demand was not granted, the Third Estate, along with members of the other two estates who were sympathetic to their cause, refused to cooperate. They formed the National Assembly and drafted a constitution. On July 14, 1789, the revolution turned violent when urban workers in Paris stormed the Bastille, a French prison, and released the prisoners. At the same time, revolts against the nobility broke out across France.

Declaration of the Rights of Man and of the Citizen. In August 1789, the National Assembly adopted the *Declaration of the Rights of Man and of the Citizen*, inspired in part by Enlightenment ideals and the U.S. Declaration of

Debate in the French National Assembly, 1789, leading up to the revolution

Independence. Other reforms included limiting the power of the monarchy and eliminating various special privileges of the nobility. The revolution grew more violent during the period called the Reign of Terror (1793–1794), which began after the execution of the royal family. A *republic*, a government in which voters elect representatives to govern, replaced the monarchy. All male citizens were given the right to vote, and the nobility was abolished. The revolutionary period ended when Napoleon Bonaparte rose to power and became emperor.

Russian Revolution of 1917

The Russian Revolution of 1917 is an example of revolutionary protest and change. It was discussed in Chapter 4. Like French monarchs, Russian czars were absolute rulers. The Russian Revolution of 1917 was the second time that discontented Russians engaged in revolutionary action. The first one, in 1905, had been unsuccessful.

End of Czarist Rule. A second and successful revolution began in early March 1917 when women workers staged a march to protest food shortages. Together with other workers, they called for a general strike. The strike, along with the food shortage and shortages of fuel, caused riots. When ordered to fire on the protesters, Russian troops refused. Realizing that he no longer had military support, the czar stepped down on March 15. A provisional (temporary) government was set up.

Bolshevik Takeover. Vladimir Lenin and the *Bolsheviks*, a radical group in the Russian Socialist party, wanted more than the end of the czar's rule. They wanted to establish a Communist government based on the Socialist teachings of Karl Marx. The Bolsheviks promised to redistribute land to peasants and to transfer factories to workers. The Bolsheviks staged a coup on November 6, 1917, and ousted the provisional government. A civil war followed from 1918 to 1921, with Communists (Reds) fighting anti-Communists (Whites). The Communists won. The revolution ended with the formation of the Union of Soviet Socialist Republics in 1922.

The Movement to Abolish Slavery

The international movement to abolish slavery is an example of social protest that affected public policy. The *abolitionist movement* was aimed at social reform, namely, the end of African slavery and the emancipation of enslaved Africans. The abolitionist movement began in mid-18th-century Britain, with the spread of Enlightenment writings on freedom and equality. Some religious leaders also began to believe slavery was immoral; they could not reconcile it with Christian beliefs. *Abolitionists*—those who worked to abolish slavery—began a slow but steady campaign to end slavery in the United States and in the British Empire.

Abolitionists in Great Britain. Abolitionists in Great Britain began by pushing for an end to the transatlantic slave trade. In 1807, parliament ended British participation in the international slave trade. In 1833, parliament abolished slavery in the British Empire.

Abolitionists: In Great Britain, William Wilberforce (left) fought for the abolition of the slave trade and of slavery in the British Empire. In the United States, Angelina and Sarah Grimké (center) fought for the abolition of slavery and later established schools for the newly freed people; William Lloyd Garrison (right) published an abolitionist newspaper and founded an abolitionist society in Boston.

Abolitionists in the United States. In the United States, beginning in the 1830s, abolitionists used social protest as well as political action to seek to abolish slavery. Abolitionists formed the *Underground Railroad*, which helped enslaved Africans escape to the North and to Canada. Harriet Beecher Stowe's novel *Uncle Tom's Cabin*, published in 1852, is considered a social protest novel, because it brought attention to the evils of slavery and the need to end the practice. Abolitionist newspapers and publications written and edited by people like William Lloyd Garrison and Frederick Douglass were another tool of social protest. An example of political action was the formation of political parties, such as the Free Soil party and the Republican party, that supported candidates who opposed slavery.

A 19th-century U.S. abolitionist poster

The Independence Movement in India

Earlier, you read about the modern independence movement in India. This movement is another example of social protest as a means to achieve a political goal. Beginning in the mid-1700s, Great Britain had taken control of India and made it a colony. By the late 1800s, Indian nationalists, people who wanted independence from Great Britain, were organizing into political parties and calling on Great Britain to give India self-rule. Little was accomplished, however. Review the 20th-century events leading to India's independence, discussed in Chapter 6.

The Fall of Communism in Europe

The fall of communism in Europe (discussed in Chapter 5) also demonstrates how social protest and political action can help to bring about political change. The beginning of the end of communism can be traced to Poland.

Solidarity Party. In 1980, Solidarity, an anti-Communist political party in Poland, used huge strikes to force the Communist government to recognize it. In 1985, Mikhail Gorbachev, the Soviet premier, allowed Communist nations in Eastern Europe to have more control over their governments. As a result, Poland's Solidarity party candidates ran for national election in 1989 and won.

They took control of the government. It was the first democratic government elected in Eastern Europe in almost 40 years.

Fall of the Berlin Wall. People in East Germany and East Berlin were inspired by the events in Poland and began protests of their own. Later in 1989, East Berliners tore down the Berlin Wall that had separated them from West Berlin and West Germany. It had stood since 1961 as a symbol of Communist domination.

Disintegration of the Soviet Union. When the Berlin Wall was down, more Eastern Europeans rose up against their Communist governments and took to the streets in protest. The Communist leader of Romania was overthrown as a result of popular protests. Protests in Czechoslovakia caused the Communist government to step down. Eventually, these changes, along with the serious decline of the Soviet economy, led to the fall of communism in the Soviet Union as well.

The End of Apartheid

The end of apartheid in South Africa was also achieved by citizen action. As you learned in Chapter 6, apartheid was the South African government's policy that segregated nonwhites and discriminated against them legally, economically, and politically. South Africa was a former colony of Great Britain that had gained its independence in 1910. Whites were in a minority, and many whites were Afrikaners, descendants of Dutch settlers.

Reactions to Apartheid. When large numbers of black Africans began to move to South African cities after World War II, the Afrikaners decided to take action. In 1948 they passed laws setting up strict segregation of black Africans. Black Africans and sympathetic whites protested. For the most part, they used boycotts, strikes, demonstrations, and other forms of nonviolent protest. However, some activists turned to violence. Often, protestors were harshly punished. In addition to internal protest, many nations like the United States and Great Britain instituted economic sanctions against South Africa in the mid-1980s in an effort to try to force the South African government to end apartheid.

Removal of Apartheid Laws. As a result of internal and international pressure, President F. W. de Klerk and the South African government began to remove apartheid restrictions in the early 1990s. Nelson Mandela, who had been in prison for 28 years for his part in antiapartheid protests in the early 1960s, was elected the country's first black African president in 1994. This election was the first free election—the first in which black South Africans could vote—the country had ever held. (Review the discussion of apartheid in Chapter 6.)

Test Yourself
What is civil disobedience?

★ CITIZEN PARTICIPATION UNDER DIFFERENT SYSTEMS OF GOVERNMENT ★

Different types of government offer people different opportunities for citizen action. As you review these different types, you will be able to understand why, under some governments, citizens can change unfair laws and social practices.

Absolute Monarchy

As you read in Chapter 14, absolute monarchies are governments in which the kings or queens rule with total power. Absolute monarchs make all the laws. They may recognize some human rights, but not all. By definition, absolute monarchs do not recognize their subjects' right to change their government.

The king of France before the French Revolution is an example of an absolute monarch. As shown by the French Revolution, peaceful protests and demonstrations often do not work to bring about change under an absolute monarch.

Constitutional Monarchies

Constitutional monarchies are different from absolute monarchies in the degree of power that the monarch holds. In a constitutional monarchy, a king or queen is the head of state, but the power of the monarch is limited by the country's constitution. England is an example of a constitutional monarchy. The queen is a figurehead. The British Parliament, which is a representative law-making body, and the prime minister actually govern the country.

In constitutional monarchies, citizen action has the same role as it does in democratic nations. People use political action to try to change laws and government policies, and social protest to affect social change. Both are possible because most constitutions under a constitutional monarchy guarantee basic rights. Other examples of modern constitutional monarchies today are Denmark, Norway, and Sweden. In most modern constitutional monarchies, people are free to speak their mind and express their views, including dissatisfaction with the government.

Democracies

Democracies, including parliamentary democracies and presidential democracies, also present opportunities for citizen action. Under these systems, people are free to seek political action or speak out for social change.

Dictatorships and Theocracies

Two systems under which citizens have little or no opportunity for citizen participation are dictatorships and theocracies.

Dictatorship. A dictatorship does not foster citizen participation. People who speak out against dictators are usually severely punished or even killed. Saddam Hussein was the dictator of Iraq until he was removed during the Iraqi war in 2003.

Theocracy. A theocracy is a government ruled by religious leaders. The Islamic Republic of Iran is an example of a modern theocracy. Most of Iran's laws are derived from the religious teachings of the Qur'an, the Islamic holy book. But not all the laws cover religious practices. Many deal with aspects of daily life. Theocracies typically do not allow other religious groups a voice in running the government.

★ PROPAGANDA ★

The final part of this chapter's benchmark requires you to understand how governments and other groups use propaganda to influence public opinion or behavior. Propaganda is information spread by a government or group to promote or discourage a policy or cause. Propaganda often contains misinformation that is deliberately spread with the purpose of injuring a cause or a group. Propaganda can take many forms, including posters, slogans, and government directives.

During wartime a government will use propaganda to generate or maintain public support for its side. Often, propaganda depicts opposing forces as evil and glorifies the government that is spreading the propaganda. U.S. propaganda during World War I showed Germans as semibarbaric and called them Huns, thus identifying them with warlike invaders of Europe in the 4th and 5th centuries A.D. A political party, a political action committee, or any organization trying to influence public opinion may use propaganda to make the opposition seem evil. Propaganda is like advertising, but it promotes a political agenda rather than a commercial product.

Test Yourself
What two kinds of government offer the least opportunity for citizen action?

POINTS TO REMEMBER

- Citizen action is action taken by citizens to try to change a policy, law, social system, or government with which they are unhappy.
- Groups with money or power take political action to try to enact change through political channels.
- Groups that lack the power to bring about change through traditional political channels usually engage in social protest.
- The French Revolution of 1789 and the Russian Revolution of 1917 are examples of change brought about by revolutionary action.

- The abolition of the slave trade and slavery, the independence movement in India, the fall of communism in Europe, and the end of apartheid in South Africa involved varying degrees of political action and social protest.

- Both internal citizen action and external international pressure led to the end of apartheid in South Africa.

- The opportunity for citizen participation varies depending on the type of government under which citizens live. Constitutional monarchies, parliamentary democracies, and presidential democracies afford the most opportunity for citizen participation, while dictatorships and theocracies offer the least.

- Governments and groups often use propaganda to generate support for a cause or policy.

EXERCISES

CHECKING WHAT YOU HAVE READ

1. Political action attempts to enact change through

    A. dictators
    B. revolution
    C. social protest
    D. political channels.

2. *Uncle Tom's Cabin* is considered a novel of

    A. social protest
    B. political action
    C. government propaganda
    D. revolution.

3. What happened in Poland to draw world attention to the non-Communist Solidarity party?

    A. television ads
    B. strikes
    C. genocide
    D. civil war

4. People have no opportunity for citizen action in which type of government?

    A. constitutional monarchy
    B. presidential democracy
    C. dictatorship
    D. parliamentary democracy

5. Which of the following is an example of a modern theocracy?

    A. Islamic Republic of Iran
    B. People's Republic of China
    C. Cuba
    D. Israel

USING WHAT YOU HAVE READ

1. Many people in the world today use social protest to gain support for their cause. Some groups fight for the protection of animals or the environment. Other groups fight for rights of certain groups, such as women's rights, gay rights, rights of accused persons, human rights, minority rights, or for causes such as social justice and equality. Research one of the groups that engage in social protest. What are the goals of the organization? What types of social protest does it use? Do you think its protests are effective? What kind of propaganda does the group use? Prepare a report to answer these questions.

2. Two modern dictatorships are North Korea and Cuba. Use the library and Internet resources to do research on these two nations. How are they different? How are they similar? What are the opportunities for citizen action in each? Prepare a chart to compare the two nations.

THINKING ABOUT WHAT YOU HAVE READ

1. Choose an issue in your community, county, or state that you feel strongly about. What organizations can you find that support your view on the issue? How does each group try to enact change? If you cannot find a group, how would you start one?

2. Go to your local library or look on the Internet for information about the end of apartheid. What kinds of protest did people in South Africa use? What kinds of violent action did they take? How do you think these affected the government's decision to end apartheid? Do you think international pressure played a greater role in the end of apartheid than did internal pressure?

SKILLS

Analyzing Primary Sources

Read the following excerpt from a reporter, Web Miller, telling an incident in the Indian people's protest against the salt tax in 1930. The protest's leader, Mohandas Gandhi, had been arrested before this incident took place.

Mme. Naidu called for a prayer before the march started and the entire assemblage knelt. She exhorted them, "Gandhi's body is in (jail) but his soul is with you. India's prestige is in your hands. You must not use any violence under any circumstances. You will be beaten but you must not resist; you must not even raise a hand to ward off blows." . . .

In complete silence the Gandhi men drew up and halted a hundred yards from the stockade. A picked column advanced from the crowd, waded the ditches, and approached the barbed-wire stockade, which the police surrounded, holding their clubs at the ready. Police officials ordered the marchers to disperse under a recently imposed regulation which prohibited gatherings of more than five persons in any one place. The column silently ignored the warning and slowly walked forward. . . .

Suddenly, at a word of command, scores of native police rushed upon the advancing marchers and rained blows on their heads with their steel-shod (clubs). Not one of the marchers even raised an arm to fend off the blows. They went down like ten pins. . . . The survivors without breaking ranks silently and doggedly marched on until struck down. . . .

1. What kind of protest are the people in the passage practicing?

2. What law were the protestors breaking?

3. Why do you think the men continued to march, even as their fellow marchers were struck down?

4. Why do you think Gandhi and his followers believed in nonviolent protest?

CHAPTER 16

SOCIAL STUDIES SKILLS
AND METHODS

BENCHMARKS:

(A) Evaluate the reliability and credibility of sources.
(B) Use data and evidence to support or refute a thesis.

This chapter prepares students to meet the two benchmarks in the Social Studies Skills and Methods standard listed above. This standard focuses only on skills, not on specific content. Questions on the OGT may use content from any of the other standards to assess the skills addressed in these two benchmarks.

For benchmark A, you must be able to detect bias and propaganda in primary and secondary sources of information. In addition, you should be able to evaluate the credibility of sources for logical fallacies, consistency of arguments, unstated assumptions, and bias. You must know how to analyze the reliability of sources for accurate use of facts, adequate support of statements, and date of publication.

For benchmark B, you must understand how to develop and present a research project, including collecting data, narrowing and refining the topic, and constructing and supporting, or refuting, a thesis.

★ DETECTING BIAS AND PROPAGANDA ★

This standard asks that you be able to detect bias and propaganda in primary and secondary sources of information.

Primary and Secondary Sources

Primary sources are records from the past, such as letters, speeches, photographs, cartoons, and personal writing such as journals and essays. Primary sources come from the original author, speaker, or creator. Primary sources are important because they offer a glimpse of an era through the eyes of people who lived during that time.

Secondary sources are restatements of events written by a second-party author, such as a textbook, a biography, a book about a historic event, or a newspaper article. Secondary sources often offer analysis or an interpretation of an event. Most often, authors of secondary-source documents will use primary sources in their research. However, both primary and secondary sources can reflect opinions as well as facts.

Primary source and secondary source

Bias and Propaganda

It is important to be able to detect bias and propaganda when you use sources, because, by understanding the motives of the speaker or the author, you can assess the validity of the information in the source.

Bias. *Bias* is preference for one thing over another. For example, in a sports event, you may think one team is better than the opposing team because some of your friends are players on that team. Basing your evaluation of a team on your personal liking for its players rather than on its past performance is an example of bias.

A biased evaluation of a sports team will cause you to make poor predictions about the outcome of a game. In the same way, biased accounts of a his-

Example of "innocent bias"

toric or recent event will lead to poor judgment about its significance. Therefore, you must be able to tell whether or not an account or a source is biased. Ask yourself if the source contains facts that you can verify. Does it give only one side of the story? Biased sources contain more opinions than facts. In addition, they usually offer only arguments in favor of one position and leave out arguments that might support the other.

Propaganda. Propaganda stems from bias. It is the dissemination of information or material in support of a cause or policy by the people who support that cause or policy. Therefore, propaganda is biased information. Propaganda is often used during wartime to generate support for fighting the war. For examples, posters produced by the U.S. government against Germany in World War I used exaggerated depictions of German soldiers.

This World War I U.S. propaganda poster portrays the enemy as "Huns."

Identifying Bias and Propaganda

You cannot properly evaluate a source unless you know the position and motivation of its writer or creator. A textbook, for example, is often an unbiased source of information, because textbook companies try to make sure that they present facts and various points of view. However, if you find a biography titled *Tony Blair: A Weak Prime Minister*, you should recognize that the author is probably biased against British Prime Minister Blair. He or she may have distorted facts to fit an opinion or simply not have included facts that might contradict it.

Primary sources especially need to be analyzed for bias and propaganda. People who lived at the time of an event were probably either directly or indirectly affected by it. Therefore, they may have strong opinions about it. Their opinions will influence the way they present their views. To detect bias and/or propaganda, ask yourself the following questions:

1. Who is the author or creator of the information, and what is his or her background? What are the author's qualifications to write about this subject?

2. Does the source contain opinions (statements that cannot be proven)?

3. Does the source contain only one point of view, or facts for only one side of an argument?

It is important to remember that a biased source is not unusable or unimportant. As long as you recognize the bias or propaganda and analyze the source carefully, biased sources allow you to understand different points of view of events. You may not agree with a particular point of view, but it will help you understand how other people feel or felt about the topic.

Test Yourself
What are some drawbacks of a biased source?

★ CREDIBILITY OF SOURCES ★

When you use sources, it is important that your sources be *credible*, that is, trustworthy and believable. Although you can use a biased primary source to get a feel for one side of an argument, you must make sure your research is balanced. You need to be sure to include *factual* (true) information in the research that you do. You need trustworthy sources.

What specifically should you look for when evaluating sources? The standards list four characteristics that identify credibility. In analyzing a source, ask yourself the following questions:

1. Does the source contain logical fallacies?

2. Are the arguments in the source consistent?

3. Can you detect any unstated assumptions?

4. Is the source or author of the source biased?

Logical Fallacies. A *logical fallacy* is a flaw in the logic, or reasoning, of an argument. The *premise*, or basis, of the argument may not necessarily be incorrect, but the reasoning used to arrive at that conclusion is false. There are literally thousands of types of logical fallacies, but to simplify the discussion, think of a logical fallacy as an argument that just does not make sense. The following are two examples of common logical fallacies:

• The use of reasoning that appeals to emotion or popularity. "Everyone else wears red, so you should too."

- The use of an incorrect cause-and-effect sequence. Just because something happens after something else does not mean that the first thing *caused* the second thing to happen. "Reese became a basketball player before Jamie; therefore, Jamie became a basketball player because Reese did." This is a logical fallacy because you do not know that Jamie became a basketball player because Reese did.

Consistency of Arguments. When you look at the *consistency* of an argument, you need to look for two things. First, you have to determine if the author adequately supports his or her argument, preferably with *verifiable facts*. These are facts that can be proved to be true. In addition, you must determine if the argument contains any contradictions. If the argument contains contradictory information, then the argument is not consistent. In particular, the conclusion drawn in the argument must be consistent with the premise. For example, if the argument is "All apples are red," and the conclusion then states "Therefore, most apples are green," the argument is inconsistent.

Unstated Assumptions. An unstated assumption can weaken an argument. *Unstated assumptions* are accepted as true without proof. Therefore, if a source contains an assumption that is not adequately backed by facts, the argument is weak. An example of an unstated assumption would be as follows: *I hear that our new classmate is an A student. He (or she) must be boring.* This argument contains two hidden assumptions. One is that that all A students are boring. The other is that the speaker's idea of what is boring is universally accepted. Neither of these assumptions can be proved.

Bias. In evaluating the credibility of sources, you must also consider bias. Is there evidence of bias in the source? To determine the answer, consider who the author is and what the author's possible motives might be in writing the piece. (See the first section of this chapter for a more detailed discussion on how to detect bias.) If you detect bias in a source, the source is not necessarily invalid. However, you must decide if the bias damages the credibility of the source. You must also make sure that you take the bias into account when you interpret the source and that you find sources that balance the biased one.

Test Yourself
What are the four things you should look for in determining the credibility of sources?

★ RELIABILITY OF SOURCES ★

The standard also requires that you be able to analyze the reliability of sources. Reliability is similar to credibility. In evaluating reliability, you are determining how trustworthy the source of information is. For this standard, there are three characteristics you should use to determine the reliability of sources. Ask yourself the following questions:

1. Does the source supply and use accurate facts?
2. Does the source contain adequate support for its statements?
3. What is the date of publication?

Accurate Facts. The use of accurate facts is important because you cannot rely on facts that are not accurate, or correct. For example, if a source says that Christopher Columbus landed in the Americas in 1493, that is not an accurate fact. If a fact contained in a source is not accurate, it calls into question the accuracy of *all* of the facts in a source.

Supporting Evidence. If a source makes arguments or statements but offers no supporting evidence or statements, the source may not be reliable. With no supporting statements, you have no way of knowing where the facts in the source came from or why the author believes the facts to be true. A reliable source should offer factual information with sufficient supporting and explanatory information. In addition, you should look for evidence in a source of how the author arrives at his or her conclusions.

Date of Publication. Finally, the date of publication, when a work or source was published, is important in assessing the reliability of sources. This is particularly true of secondary sources. For primary sources, date of publication can serve as proof that the source is, indeed, primary. For secondary sources, it is often desirable to use the most recent date of publication you can find. Older secondary sources might also be reliable and contain valid information, but new information could have been discovered about a topic. Interpretations of historic events could have changed. Therefore, a recently published source is likely to have the most up-to-date information.

 Test Yourself
What are the three things you should look for in determining the reliability of sources?

★ DEVELOPING AND PRESENTING A RESEARCH PROJECT ★

This standard concerns your ability to communicate information through a research project. In a research project, you research a theme or topic and compile the information in a report that supports an argument that you choose. For this standard, you must understand three factors:

1. Collecting data on a topic
2. Narrowing and refining your topic
3. Constructing and supporting a thesis

Collecting Data on a Topic

When you begin a research project, you must first decide what you are going to research. In other words, you must choose a topic. Once you have chosen a topic, you must set about collecting data. Data can come in the form of textual information in primary and secondary sources as well as statistical information from credible and reliable sources. It is imperative that you determine the trustworthiness of your sources, because your sources will become the basis of your project, which you want to be correct.

Narrowing and Refining Your Topic

As you collect your data, you must set about narrowing and refining your topic. This means that you must narrow your focus. For example, suppose you choose the topic of "World War II" and begin looking at data. You have not spent very much time before you find that World War II is much too broad a topic for a five-page research project. There is simply too much information. So you focus in on one area to research, such as "the role of women in World War II." But this is also a large topic. You must narrow it even further. You might, for example, want to write about "the role of women on the home front during World War II" or "the role of women in the armed forces during World War II." By narrowing and refining your topic, you focus your argument and your research.

Constructing and Supporting a Thesis

Once you have narrowed your topic, it is time to construct a thesis. A thesis is the statement that will serve as the premise of your argument. A thesis is like a topic sentence in a paragraph, but a thesis must work for the whole essay or project. Everything in your project must support it. This is why narrowing your topic is important. To support a thesis, your topic must be narrow enough for you to construct an argument around it but broad enough so that there is enough information for you to write about.

Sample Thesis. A thesis can be one sentence or several sentences, but it should make a strong statement. The role of women in World War II might suggest this thesis:

> During World War II, women on the home front took jobs in factories when men went to war. The move to the labor force greatly changed women's view of themselves.

Supporting Your Thesis. Once you have a thesis, look for evidence to support it. The thesis above, for example, will work only if the rest of the research project contains adequate information to support it. As you collect more data, you may find that your thesis statement is untrue or that you cannot find enough evidence to support it.

If you find that you cannot support your thesis for either reason, revise it. You want your research project to be credible. Make sure that you use adequate support. Apply the criteria that you learned earlier in the chapter about the credibility and reliability of sources to evaluate your own project. There are various ways to present a research project. Your teacher may specify which one she or he prefers you to use. Some teachers ask that you prepare an oral presentation as well as a written presentation. Whatever presentation format you use, make sure your project supports your thesis.

Test Yourself
What are three steps in developing a research project?

POINTS TO REMEMBER

- Propaganda stems from bias, which is a preference for one thing over another. Propaganda is the dissemination of information or material in support of a cause or policy by the people who support that cause or policy. It is important to be able to detect bias and propaganda to evaluate a source.

- Logical fallacies weaken and invalidate arguments. The credibility of a source is called into question if it contains logical fallacies.

- A source that contains unstated assumptions and/or bias may not be credible. When reading or using such a source, you should take its assumptions and biases into account.

- Reliable sources use accurate facts and adequately support statements.

- Using a secondary source with a recent publication date helps ensure that you have the most up-to-date information and that your source covers more recent discoveries and interpretations.

- When constructing a thesis, remember to choose something that is narrow enough to focus your research but broad enough for you to find sufficient information to support the thesis.

- A research project you develop or present should have a strong thesis statement and provide adequate support for it. It should be free from any of the flaws in argument discussed in this chapter.

EXERCISES

CHECKING WHAT YOU HAVE READ

1. What characterizes propaganda?

   A. information from a neutral source
   B. a balanced argument
   C. a bias toward one side of an argument
   D. multiple points of view

2. If the conclusion of an argument contradicts the thesis, the argument is not

   A. consistent
   B. biased
   C. inaccurate
   D. propaganda.

3. Which is an example of a primary source?

   A. a textbook
   B. a biography
   C. a history book
   D. a recording of a speech

4. If a fact in a source is inaccurate, the rest of the facts in that argument are

   A. most likely true
   B. called into question
   C. probably untrue
   D. biased.

5. Everything in a research project must support

   A. the thesis statement
   B. some facts
   C. propaganda
   D. date of publication.

USING WHAT YOU HAVE READ

1. Imagine you are doing a research project. Choose a topic. Gather information in the library or on the Internet about the topic. Assess the credibility of the sources you find, using the guidelines you learned in this chapter. Are your sources credible? Why? Why not?

2. Go to the library and choose two books or one book and one magazine article on a topic in ancient history. Be sure one of your sources has a recent date of publication and the other an old date of publication. What differences in information can you find between the two? Does the newer work contain recent discoveries that the older one does not? Which source do you think is more valid? Why?

THINKING ABOUT WHAT YOU HAVE READ

1. Find a transcript online of a recent presidential campaign debate. What propaganda and bias can you detect in the candidates' answers? Can you find any logical fallacies and inconsistent arguments made by the candidates?

2. Look in your history textbook for primary sources. Practice what you learned in this chapter by analyzing the sources. After you have analyzed the sources, ask yourself if you think the sources are credible. Why? Why not?

SKILLS

Analyzing Primary Sources

Read the following source and then answer the questions that follow. The following was written by an Italian merchant in 1458.

In Praise of Merchants

The dignity and office of merchants is great and exalted in many respects, and most particularly in four. First, with respect to the common (good). For the advancement of the public welfare is a very honorable (purpose), as Cicero states, and one ought (to be willing) even to die (for it). . . . The advancement, the comfort, and the health of republics to a large extent proceed from merchants; we are always speaking, of course, not of plebeian and vulgar merchants but of the glorious merchant of whom we treat (and who is) lauded in this work of ours. And with respect to mercantile business and activity (we may say) this: Through trade, that ornament and advancement (of republics), sterile (unproductive) countries are provided with food and supplies and also enjoy many strange things which are imported from places where (other) commodities are lacking. (Merchants) also bring about an abundance of money, jewels, gold, silver, and all kinds of metals. They bring about an abundance of guilds of various crafts. Hence, cities and countries are driven to cultivate the land, to enlarge the herds, and to exploit the incomes and rents. And (merchants) through their activity enable the poor to live; through their initiative in tax farming they promote the activity of administrators in collecting taxes; through their exports and imports of merchandise, they cause the customs and excises of the lords and republics to expand, and consequently they enlarge the public and common treasury. . . .

1. Do you think this passage reflects bias? Why?

2. Do you think the facts in this passage are accurate? How could you determine if they are accurate?

3. What does the date of publication tell you about this passage?

4. Do you think this is a valid source?

5. Do you think the merchant adequately supports his statements?

PART II

United States History Since 1877

CHAPTER 17

INDUSTRIALIZATION

BENCHMARK:

Explain the social, political, and economic effects of industrialization.

This benchmark focuses on the effects of industrialization in the United States after 1877. In the course of learning about industrialization, you will also encounter its causes. Understanding the causes of industrialization will help you remember the effects. For the purposes of the Ohio Graduation Test (OGT), however, knowing the effects (results) of industrialization will help you be successful.

For this benchmark, effects of industrialization in the 19th century (1877–1900) include changes in work and the workplace, the impact of immigration and child labor, modernization of agriculture, urbanization, and the growth of the middle class and its effect on cultural life. Economic and political effects of industrialization in both the 19th and 20th centuries include the development of corporations, laissez-faire economic policies, monopolies, changes in the standard of living, and the growth of labor unions.

Reform movements in the late 19th and early 20th centuries were another response to industrialization, especially the Populists and the Progressives. The goals and achievements of these reform movements also are part of the story of industrialization in the U.S. They include urban reforms, the conservation movement, business regulation and antitrust legislation, the public school movement, and the regulation of child labor.

★ THE EFFECTS OF INDUSTRIALIZATION DURING THE 19TH CENTURY ★

In the 1870s, the United States experienced an unprecedented explosion of industrial growth. The Industrial Revolution, which was interrupted by the Civil War, reemerged with unparalleled vigor. A rapidly increasing workforce and the abundance of raw materials such as timber, iron, coal, and oil fueled the industrial boom. By 1900, the United States was the world's leading producer of manufactured goods.

Other factors helped the American economy outpace the rest of the world. Immigrants from around the world streamed into the United States looking for work. In addition to providing labor, immigrants purchased many of the products manufactured in U.S. factories. The improvement of transportation and communication systems and better machines and labor-saving devices all increased productivity. Talented business leaders invested in new processes and

By 1913, the United States had become the world's leading industrial nation.

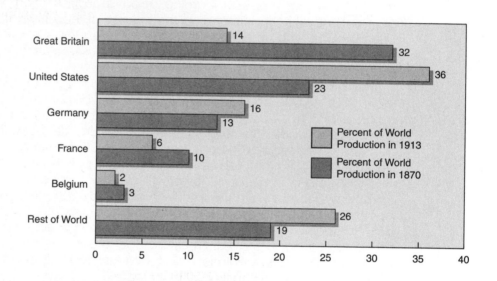

developed business organizations that resulted in the modern corporation. Industrial leaders enjoyed the support of a cooperative federal government that used tariffs to protect U.S. companies from foreign competition, while largely exempting the domestic companies from regulations and taxes on profits.

Work and the Workplace

Rapid industrialization changed the way Americans lived. Before the Industrial Revolution, factories in the United States were rather small operations, where owners and employees knew one another and worked side by side. That quickly changed as industry and manufacturing began to dominate the economy. Where people used to perform manufacturing tasks by hand, now they ran machines that did the work. Production and manufacturing processes also become much more complex, requiring more people to fill more jobs.

Growth of Urban Population. Between 1860 and 1900, due in large part to immigration from Europe, the U.S. population more than doubled. Until about 1915, the majority of people in the United States farmed or lived in small towns. By 1920, that balance had changed, with over 50 percent of the population living in urban areas.

Rural and Urban U.S. Population, 1860, 1900, 1920			
	1860	*1900*	*1920*
Total U.S. Population	31,443,321	76,212,168	106,021,537
Percent Living in Rural Areas	80.2	60.4	48.8
Percent Living in Urban Areas	19.8	39.6	51.2

Source: U.S. Census

Living Conditions in Cities. As more people moved from farms to cities to find jobs in factories, working and living conditions deteriorated. Before unions became influential, many workers often endured low pay, long hours, and unsafe conditions. The large labor force, which included immigrants, created fierce competition for jobs. The introduction of labor-saving machines in factories cost many workers their jobs. Depressions and "panics" periodically decreased consumer demand for goods, forcing businesses to cut production and lay off workers. In 1878, nearly a million people were unemployed as the result of a persistent depression. The economy improved for a while after that, but again in the mid-1880s, about 2 million workers were jobless. Most working

Photographer Lewis Hine captures child laborers working in a cotton factory in 1908.

people feared unemployment because they would be unable to support themselves and their families. At the time, the present-day safety net, which provides unemployment payments and other benefits, did not exist.

Women and Child Workers. Industrialization also increased the number of women and children who experienced poor working conditions in factories and mines for low wages. In order to survive, many families put mothers and children to work. By 1900, there were over one million women in the workforce, and about one out of every five married women worked outside the home. The pay for women was about half of what men earned for the same work. At the end of the workday, women still had to care for their homes and families.

In the late 19th century, more children entered the workforce. In 1880, approximately one out of every six children under the age of 16 worked. Some children as young as six or seven worked in the coal mines, textile mills, or sweatshops found in large cities. Like women, most children worked long hours for low pay in unhealthy conditions. Few of them were able to attend school. In the early 1900s, most states passed laws that regulated child labor. While these laws had some effect, they were often ignored or circumvented. Many families depended upon the meager wages of their children to put food on the table.

Test Yourself

How did industrialization in the United States affect family life? In what ways would working in a factory in the 1880s compare to working in a factory today?

★ ON THE FARM ★

The technological improvements of the Industrial Revolution in big cities helped modernize agriculture as well. As more and more Americans and immigrants moved into cities to work in factories, improvements in transportation and agriculture made it possible to feed these new urban laborers and their families.

Railroads. One of the most important advances was the expansion of the railroad, which shipped goods from rural areas to urban centers. In 1869, the Central Pacific and the Union Pacific railroads met at Promontory Point, Utah, creating the nation's first transcontinental railroad. By 1900, several transcontinental lines crisscrossed the United States. In 1880, about 93,000 miles of railroad track carried America's trains. Twenty years later, that figure had more than doubled to 193,000 miles.

Inventions. Other inventions contributed to the efficiency and productivity of rail travel. By 1875, refrigerated railroad cars allowed meatpackers to deliver their product virtually anywhere in the nation. In 1878, Andrew Chase developed an improved refrigerated car for meatpacking magnate Gustavus Swift

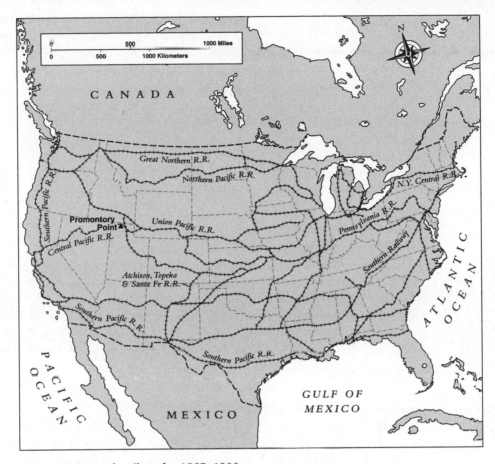

Transcontinental railroads, 1865–1900

that increased the shipping range for his perishable product. In addition to meat, perishable goods such as vegetables and milk could now be transported hundreds of miles to different markets.

The widespread use of improved agricultural technology allowed farmers to plant more crops on increased acreage and produce more food. The McCormick reaper, the thresher, and the steel-tipped plow enabled homesteaders to cultivate the vast tracts of the American heartland. In the 1880s, farmers began using combines, machines that reap, thresh, and clean grain crops. The use of silos helped to solve the grain storage problem, and barbed wire allowed the fencing of rangeland. Fertilizer, which allowed farmers to increase their yield per acre, also came in to greater use throughout this period.

All of these inventions, advances, and improvements, and many others allowed farmers to produce more food with less labor in a shorter period of time and ship that food almost anywhere in the nation on the expanding railroad network.

Test Yourself

How did agricultural tools and machines invented in the 19th century make it possible for American cities to grow rapidly in the late 1800s?

★ THE GROWTH OF CITIES ★

After the Civil War, business leaders built their factories in cities that had good seaports or railroad lines. As a result, U.S. cities grew rapidly during the late 1800s. The population shift to big cities produced two benefits. It provided workers for the factories, and it also provided a market for many of the manufactured goods.

The Urban Poor

In the late 1800s and early 1900s, the migration of Americans from small towns and rural areas to cities changed the face of the United States. In 1900, about 60 percent of Americans still lived in rural areas. By 1915, the balance leveled to about 50 percent rural and 50 percent urban. The 1920 Census revealed that for the first time in American history more people lived in urban areas than in rural areas. In addition to European immigrants, a significant number of people moving from the countryside to cities in the late 1880s and early 1900s were African Americans. By 1930, nearly one million African Americans had moved from the rural South to Western and Northern cities in search of jobs and to escape Jim Crow laws.

Urban Problems. The increase in urban population created several problems. Many cities were not prepared for fast-paced growth. Inadequate housing led to overcrowding. New city dwellers crowded into existing apartments and houses in poor, working-class neighborhoods, which turned into slums. In addition to substandard living conditions, urban slums were often plagued with violent crime.

Photographer Jacob Riis shows a family living in a crowded tenement apartment.

The lack of adequate sanitation was another problem faced by urban residents in the late 1800s. Cities typically did not have sewage systems that could handle the increased population. Cities often dumped sewage into the same lakes or rivers that provided drinking water, which often resulted in outbreaks of diseases such as typhoid fever and cholera. Many slum dwellers usually did not have the luxury of running water or bathtubs and had a difficult time keeping clean. This added to the problem of disease, as did air pollution from nearby factories.

Diseases such as cholera were a danger for people living in urban slums.

 Test Yourself
What kind of problems did workers living in cities face?

The Middle Class

While the poor suffered and struggled in slums, life for many middle-class Americans also changed as a result of the Industrial Revolution. The growth of large corporations created the need for more managers and office workers, who are often referred to as white-collar workers. By contrast, factory workers and laborers became known as blue-collar workers. Industrialization also created the need for other types of employees such as engineers and sales representatives. Wages for middle-class workers also increased during the latter years of the 19th century, raising their standard of living.

The growing middle class had the luxury of income to spend on more than just the food, clothing, and shelter necessary for survival. While low-wage laborers worked long hours for six or seven days a week, increasing numbers of middle-class Americans enjoyed more free time. Many Americans pursued recreational activities during their free time. Baseball, football, boxing, and horse racing became more popular spectator sports that drew large crowds. Bicycle riding also became popular. Theaters in large cities drew patrons who enjoyed vaudeville shows featuring a variety of singing, dancing, comedy acts, plays, and operas. Traveling circuses were welcomed by large crowds in towns and cities across the nation. One- and two-cent newspapers, in addition to dime novels (inexpensive paperbacks), sold well. In 1880, Thomas Edison invented moving pictures, and eventually thousands of people were enjoying movies at local theaters.

Industrialization changed the lives of millions of people in many ways. The changes benefited some people but made conditions worse for others. Industrialization drew immigrant and U.S.-born workers to cities and helped spawn some of the worst slums imaginable, but it also turned the United States into the world's leading manufacturing power and created whole new industries dedicated to leisure time activities. Industrialization, immigration, and urbanization were all part of a historical process that drastically changed how Americans lived and worked over a very short period of time.

Increased leisure time allowed more middle-class families to enjoy spectator sports such as baseball.

★ INDUSTRIALIZATION AND THE RISE OF THE MODERN CORPORATION ★

The construction of transcontinental railroads after the Civil War made mass distribution of consumer goods possible. The railroads enabled people across the United States to buy all sorts of formerly unavailable products. As the number of consumers grew, production increased to meet the demand.

Corporations. Business leaders needed capital (money) to build new factories. They had to construct buildings, buy raw materials, pay workers, and ship their goods to the marketplace. Forming a corporation is one way to raise the necessary capital. Many corporations sell shares of their business, called stock, to the public. Investors who buy stock in a corporation are actually buying part ownership of the company. If a corporation makes a profit, it gives some of the profit back to shareholders in the form of dividends. If the company does well and the price of its stock increases, shareholders can sell their shares and earn a profit. Stocks are bought and sold at financial exchanges such as the New York Stock Exchange.

In the United States, railroads were the first industry to form large corporations. Many other businesses and industries eventually incorporated. In addition to raising the necessary capital, corporations organized the manufacturing processes and business practices so that companies could control all aspects of an industry, including obtaining raw materials, production, and sales. By the late 1800s, large corporations such as the Standard Oil Company dominated the U.S. economy. Immediately after the Civil War, there were only a few very large factories such as the McCormick Company in Chicago, which manufactured farm machinery. By the end of the century, however, there were over 1,000 large factories that employed at least 500 workers. In 1900, the General Electric Corporation employed 11,000 workers at a plant in Massachusetts and 15,000 in a New York factory.

The rise of the corporation separated the owners from the people who managed the factory and did the work. Owners were no longer involved in the day-to-day operations of the business. They were interested in earning stock dividends and in the price of stocks they owned rather than in managing the company. As the United States moved into the 20th century, more people worked for large corporations rather than for small businesses or themselves.

In the late 19th century, business leaders increasingly faced the problem of intense competition, which forced them to lower prices to attract consumers and resulted in lower profits. To address the problem, some business leaders sought ways to reduce competition. One way was to merge several competing companies into a larger corporation. Another approach involved developing trade associations, in which competing corporations promised to abide by a mutually agreed-upon set of rules. Throughout the 1870s and 1880s, increasing numbers of businesses became less competitive as they merged or combined to form larger corporations, often referred to as *monopolies*, or "trusts." A monopoly occurs when one company or person effectively controls an entire industry. The Standard Oil Company became one of the earliest monopolies.

A criticism of the powerful Standard Oil Company, one of the first monopolies

Other industries such as steel manufacturing also became monopolies. By the early 1900s, about 300 huge corporations effectively controlled nearly 40 percent of manufacturing investment. U.S. Steel was the largest such combination, cobbled together from 150 smaller companies, with over $1 billion in capitalization and employing over 165,000 people. It also controlled about 60 percent of steel manufacturing in the United States.

Laissez-Faire Policies

One reason the United States was able to industrialize at such a rapid rate after the Civil War was its economic system, which was based on the principle of free enterprise. In the late 1880s, most American business leaders favored *laissez-faire* economic policies. Laissez-faire is a French term which means, in context, to let people do as they choose. Laissez-faire advocates argued that government should not interfere with the free market. The only roles government should have are to maintain law and order, enforce contracts, and protect property rights. According to the theory, government regulation increased costs and hindered the operation of the free market, which hurt society in the long run. A laissez-faire economy depends upon supply and demand to set prices and wages, which results in greater efficiency and more wealth to spread around. It also favors low taxes so that more money is in the hands of private citizens rather than the government.

In the late 1800s, the economy of the United States followed a laissez-faire course. Wages and working conditions were unregulated. Men, women, and children worked excessively long hours for low pay in extremely dangerous conditions with no unemployment or health insurance. When government stayed out of economic affairs, the theory argued, competition motivated businesses to offer better goods and services at the lowest possible prices. Many 19th-century business leaders and industrialists advocated laissez-faire to legitimize their business practices, but at the same time they accepted government subsidies and benefited from high tariffs on imports, which made their goods more competitive in the United States. There were no environmental regulations to protect air quality, water purity, or wildlife. Railroads were

"King Monopoly" demands tribute from his captive subjects.

given huge tracts of land along proposed train routes that they could sell to settlers to help pay for building track. They believed that government regulations were bad, but government subsidies and protections were beneficial.

In the 1880s, laissez-faire policies enable the rise of monopolies, which destroyed the competition that laissez-faire supporters argued their system fostered. In response, Congress in 1890 approved the Sherman Antitrust Act, which made monopolies illegal and gave the federal government the authority to bring litigation and even criminal charges against companies that engaged in anticompetitive practices and illegally restrained interstate trade.

Test Yourself
Why did corporations favor laissez-faire policies?

Standard of Living

Industrialization in the late 1800s raised the standard of living for many people, especially entrepreneurs, the middle class, and managers. Although some workers experienced increased wages and improved living conditions, they paid the heaviest price when economic times were bad. Ten- to 12 hour workdays and six-day weeks were the rule. Workers had no protection and could be laid off or fired for any reason. When recessions hit, workers often lost their jobs.

The different lives of the rich and the poor during the late 1880s

★ THE RISE OF LABOR UNIONS ★

The growth of industrialization in the United States was matched by the rise of organized labor unions. In the late 1800s, laissez-faire policies resulted in a largely unregulated workplace. Unsafe, unsanitary, and dangerous conditions were common. For many workers, wages were low and hours were long. In response, some workers attempted to organize labor unions in the hope of bargaining collectively with business owners for improved wages, hours, and working conditions. Owners resisted these attempts, sometimes with violence and often with government assistance.

Knights of Labor

One of the earliest unions to organize was the Knights of Labor, which began in 1869 as a secret society of tailors in Philadelphia. In the 1870s, a decade of recession and hard times, the Knights welcomed members from all industries. In 1877, railroad workers went out on strike across the nation to protest wage cuts. The strike turned violent, and President Rutherford B. Hayes ordered the use of federal troops to restore order. Over a hundred people were killed during the course of the strike, which increased worker militancy. The Knights of Labor benefited, and its membership rose sharply.

The Knights of Labor campaigned for an eight-hour workday, regulation of child labor, equal pay for women, a graduated income tax, and worker-owned factories. The Knights also pushed for restrictive legislation to protect American workers from competition by immigrants. It supported the Chinese Exclusion Act of 1882. At that time American unions were unfriendly to immigrants because they feared newcomers would take away jobs from their members.

When Terence V. Powderly took over leadership in 1879, the membership of the Knights of Labor boomed. By 1886, the Knights had about 700,000 members. Each chapter of the union accepted workers from an entire industry regardless of skill or job, and it welcomed African Americans and women. Powderly abolished the rules of secrecy and focused on obtaining rights and benefits for workers. At first, the Knights favored the use of arbitration and boycotts rather than strikes. By the 1880s, however, strikes had become part of the union's list of tactics, and they enjoyed some success in reversing wage cuts in the railroad industry.

Haymarket Riot. The Knights' demise came after the devastating Haymarket riot in Chicago, Illinois. In the mid-1880s, American labor leaders decided on an eight-hour work day as the primary goal for the movement. They organized a nationwide strike for May 1, 1886, to rally public support for the idea. Several strikes occurred in cities around the nation on that day, including Chicago. Two days later, a fight at the McCormick Harvester Plant led to a shooting, and the police killed one of the demonstrators. On May 4, union members met in Chicago's Haymarket Square to protest the shooting. The police attempted to disperse the crowd, and someone threw a bomb that killed 12 people. Eight police officers, who were seriously wounded by the bomb, eventually died as well. Despite the lack of evidence, the authorities quickly blamed the crime on anarchists, some of whom had spoken at the meeting earlier in the day. No one ever identified the bomber, but the jury found eight rally organizers guilty. Seven of them were sentenced to death. The guilty verdicts caused a sensation in the international labor movement, and protests were organized in many parts of the world. One of the convicted men committed suicide in jail, and the state of Illinois hanged four others. In 1893, three men were eventually pardoned by Governor John Altgeld, who reopened the case.

Several people who participated in the Haymarket riot were members of the Knights of Labor. They participated despite Powderly's objections. The Knights of Labor and unions across the nation suffered because of the violence associated with the Haymarket riot. Newspapers and politicians painted labor activists as extremists who engaged in violence against the government and desired anarchy. Government repression and adverse public opinion helped opponents of organized labor mount a successful campaign that set the labor movement back several years. The Knights of Labor, like most union organizations, took a severe hit. In only four years, the organization lost about 600,000 members.

American Federation of Labor

In 1886, workers met in Columbus, Ohio, and founded a labor organization that became one of the most important and lasting in American history. They organized the American Federation of Labor (AF of L) as an association of trade unions.

The AF of L grew out of an earlier union called the Federation of Organized Trades and Labor Unions, which was founded in 1881. Samuel Gompers, the president of the AF of L until 1924, and its other founders believed that industrial unions such as the Knights of Labor were too disorganized and undisciplined to withstand opposition from both management and the government. The AF of L was an association, or federation, of craft or trade unions, each of which accepted only members who were skilled workers in a particular trade. Gompers believed that unions should work within the system and concentrate on bargaining with management for the best deal they could negotiate. When

Samuel Gompers, the founder of
the American Federation of Labor
(AF of L)

negotiations broke down, the AF of L resorted to strikes and boycotts. The union also opposed radical politics and supported candidates from the two major parties who worked on behalf of labor issues.

Gompers' approach brought the AF of L into the mainstream. By 1904, its membership topped 1.5 million. In 1920, that number stood at 4 million members. The American Federation of Labor became the leading voice of unionism in the United States up to and beyond the New Deal years.

Formation of the CIO. As a confederation of trade unions, the AF of L did not address the problem of unskilled workers in mass-production industries who were not members of a trade union. In the 1930s, some AF of L members tried to expand their federation to include unskilled workers. Efforts at both the AF of L conventions in 1934 and 1935 failed to convince its membership that organizing unskilled workers was beneficial. Dissident AF of L members took action after the 1935 failure. David Dubinsky of the International Ladies Garment Workers Union, Sidney Hillman, the leader of the Amalgamated Clothing workers, John L. Lewis, the head of the United Mine Workers, as well as leaders of the Textile Workers and the Typographers unions founded the Committee for Industrial Organization within the AF of L to represent the unskilled workers of America. The committee gained strength within the AF of L and created a split among its leadership. In 1937, AF of L leaders, unable to reach consensus, expelled the committee from the union. The committee then became the Congress of Industrial Organizations (CIO). The two organizations remained separate until 1955, when they reunited to form the AFL-CIO, which for many years was the most powerful labor union in the United States.

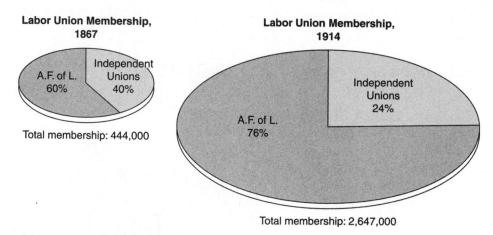

Labor union membership in 1867 and 1914

Test Yourself

How did the Knights of Labor and the American Federation of Labor differ?

★ REFORM MOVEMENTS: POPULISM AND PROGRESSIVISM ★

Two reform movements grew out of the dramatic change that accompanied industrialization—Populism and Progressivism. The two movements were distinct and reacted to problems in different ways.

Populism

Populism was primarily an agrarian movement. Despite industrialization and advances in agricultural technology, farmers in the late 19th and early 20th centuries experienced periods of economic hardship. Technology changed American agriculture but also led to overproduction. In addition, as the Great Plains opened up for settlement, more acreage came under cultivation. Overproduction and the availability of more farmland increased yield and drove prices down. Farmers grew more crops but earned less for them.

Farmers also faced the unpredictability of the weather and soil exhaustion. As farmers moved west to the Great Plains, they relied on railroads to transport their crops to market. Protective tariffs forced many farmers to pay high prices for American-made equipment instead of imported equipment, which was less expensive. All of these factors put farmers ever more deeply in debt.

Granger Movement. The Granger movement was the first attempt to address the problems that many farmers encountered. U.S. Department of Agriculture employees organized the first Grange meetings in 1867, meetings primarily as social gatherings to alleviate the isolation experienced by many rural farm families. After the economic recession caused by the Panic of 1873, Granges grew rapidly, becoming more than social organizations. Granges developed stores, cooperatives, processing plants, and factories as a way of helping farmers become more competitive and profitable. Grangers also became politically active, and some agricultural states enacted "Granger laws" that attempted to regulate railroad shipping and storage fees.

A farm family

Farmers' Alliance. Despite its limited success, the Granger movement began to decline in the 1880s. Many farmers, however, continued to experience problems. The Farmers' Alliance movement took up the cause. By 1890, Farmers' Alliances could claim about 1.5 million members. The Alliances were more political than the Grangers had been, and they developed detailed agendas for action, calling for strict regulation—even nationalization—of the railroads, monetary policies that would cause inflation, which would make it easier for farmers to pay off debts, a government agency that would offer low-interest loans, and government-run storage facilities. Farmers needed storage for wheat and other crops awaiting shipment on trains to processors.

Populist Party. Several droughts in the Great Plains during the 1880s increased hardships faced by farmers. By 1890, many farmers were desperate, and Farmers' Alliance leadership decided to increase its political efforts. Joining with Southern Democrats, some labor unions, and a few small reform parties, they organized a new political party called the Populist Party. The Populists quickly enjoyed success in the South and West, where they captured political control of several states and elected members to both the House and Senate.

At their national convention in 1892, Populist delegates examined strategies to make the government and political system work in their favor. Populists believed that Congress, indeed all branches of government, were controlled by industrial trusts, banking, and Eastern commercial interests. Referring to the vast gap between the rich and poor in America, the Populists' party platform maintained that

> corruption dominates the ballot-box, the legislatures, the Congress, and touches even the ermine of the bench [i.e., the courts]. . . . From the womb . . . of governmental injustice we breed the two great classes—tramps and millionaires.

The Populist platform also called for reforms in transportation, particularly railroads, land distribution and use, and in finance, especially the coinage of silver. Debt was a constant problem for many farmers, who borrowed in the spring to purchase seed and equipment with the hope of paying off their debts in the fall after a successful harvest. Declining farm prices in the 1870s and 1880s, as well as natural phenomena such as drought, made constant debt even more burdensome. The Populists viewed the coinage of silver as a way to increase inflation, which would allow farmers to pay their debts more easily.

In the 1892 elections, Populists again did well in Western and Southern states, and their candidate for president received over a million votes. The silver issue dominated the campaign. Populists in the West and South, with the support of organized labor, urged unlimited coinage of silver. They were convinced of the need for more money in circulation to inflate the currency. Inflation allowed borrowers to pay back their debt with cheaper money. By contrast, business leaders and bankers favored monetary stability, feared inflation, and wanted to stick with the gold standard.

The Panic of 1893 exacerbated the situation. Unemployment increased, several banks failed, and crop prices dropped. As the 1896 election approached, Populists picked up support as they increased their call for silver coinage. The Democrats nominated William Jennings Bryan, a silver supporter, for president, and the Populist Party endorsed him as well.

A powerful orator, William Jennings Bryan, the Democratic and Populist candidate for president in 1896, delivers his famous "Cross of Gold" speech.

With Populist support, Bryan and the Democrats carried the South and much of the West. They could not, however, overcome Republican strength in the North and East. William McKinley, a former representative and governor of Ohio, won a narrow election victory. The Populist Party was unable to gain additional support. The economy began to improve, and the Spanish-American War diverted attention from economic issues. Many Populist issues and ideas, however, lived beyond the party and were later enacted into law. These included the federal income tax, the eight-hour workday, the direct election of U.S. senators, and the abandonment of the gold standard.

The Progressive Movement

The Progressive Movement was an urban, middle-class reaction to social and economic dislocations fostered by the growth of the United States as an industrial power.

Progressive Reformers. Progressivism was not an organized political movement. It was, instead, an idea or a way of looking at the United States and the problems it experienced as it underwent the transformation from a previously rural nation to an industrialized world power. Progressives were reformers who did not challenge the basic principles of capitalism but who wanted to improve social conditions in the United States and strengthen its political system by fighting corruption and making it more inclusive. They tackled business abuses, corrupt city governments, and substandard living conditions for working people and immigrants in cities. Some Progressives became the first environmentalists, who were then called conservationists. Progressives also wanted to reform the political system by allowing women to vote and through other reforms such as the recall, referendum, initiative, and the direct election of U.S. senators. (At the time, senators were chosen by state legislatures.)

Progressives came from many walks of life but were overwhelmingly middle class and well-educated. They believed that they could apply the scientific method, education, and moral values to the problems faced by many Americans in the late 1800s and early 1900s.

Muckrakers. The Progressive Era saw the rise of a new kind of journalism. The *muckrakers* were journalists and writers who uncovered corruption and abuses in society; they "raked up the muck" to expose what went on below the surface of American business and politics. In 1904, Ida Tarbell wrote an exposé of the Standard Oil Company and its business practices. Lincoln Steffens published *The Shame of Cities* (1904), which uncovered political corruption in city governments. One of the most famous muckraking books was Upton Sinclair's *The Jungle* (1906), a novel that revealed unsanitary conditions in the meatpacking industry and the mistreatment of workers.

Theodore Roosevelt's Square Deal. In national politics, President Theodore Roosevelt and his wing of the Republican Party represented the Progressive spirit. After he became president following McKinley's assassination in 1901, Roosevelt (often called "TR") used the "bully pulpit," the prestige of the presidency, to encourage change where he believed it was needed. When he ran for president in 1904, Roosevelt called his administration the Square Deal because he wanted fair and equal treatment for all people. Roosevelt embraced several Progressive reforms. He added two departments to the Cabinet: Labor and Commerce. He lobbied vigorously for passage of the Hepburn Act (1906), which strengthened the Interstate Commerce Commission (ICC). TR also prosecuted a railroad monopoly using the Sherman Antitrust Act. The resulting *Northern Securities* case ended with the Supreme Court ordering the monopoly dissolved. When a coal strike in 1902 nearly paralyzed the nation, Roosevelt ordered the mine owners and the union leaders to the White House where he threatened to use troops to keep the mines open. The owners reluctantly backed down and agreed to bargain with the union. This brought an end to the strike. Additionally, Roosevelt pushed the Pure Food and Drug Act, which required accurate labeling and established regulations to improve food safety.

Roosevelt was a great outdoorsman, who had spent a large part of his youth in the West. He was interested in conservation and the effort to save natural resources from unnecessary destruction by mining and timber interests. During his administration, millions of acres were added to the national forests, which were then protected from logging. He increased the power of the U.S. Forest Service, under the direction of Gifford Pinchot, who instituted pro-

President Roosevelt fought to dissolve "bad trusts" but approved of "good trusts."

grams to plant trees and harvest them. The Roosevelt administration also oversaw a program of dam and canal construction that helped establish an irrigation system for farmers and ranchers.

Government Reforms. The Progressive Era is also remembered for attempts to clean up state and city governments, which were often riddled with crime and corruption. Many cities were under the control of "machines." These were political organizations run by bosses who controlled city or state legislatures and the awarding of lucrative government contracts. Progressives advocated the use of city commissions and city managers, professionals hired to run some small cities, to replace elected mayors and city councils. Tom Johnson, who served as mayor of Cleveland from 1901 to 1909, was a reform-minded Progressive. He battled corporate power and machine bosses. During his time as Cleveland's mayor, Johnson built parks, lowered streetcar fares, and made the city more sanitary. During Johnson's administration, Cleveland earned the reputation as the country's best-governed city.

Progressives fought for reforms on the state level as well. Robert La Follette of Wisconsin was elected governor and then U.S. senator and earned the support of farmers and unions for his attacks on railroads and corporations. La Follette and many Progressives favored electoral reforms. He championed direct primaries, which prevented political machines from controlling nominations for office. Progressives supported the *initiative*, which allowed voters to "initiate" laws by way of petitions, and the *referendum*, which enabled voters to accept or reject laws passed by the state legislature. The Progressive agenda also included the *recall*, which gave voters the power to remove from office officials who were deemed ineffective or corrupt.

Progressive reformers such as Jane Addams addressed the problems faced by immigrants through settlement houses in city slums. They helped immigrants learn English and adjust to life in the United States. The Progressives promoted health codes, health facilities, and improved sanitation systems for cities. They also pushed for child labor laws and temperance legislation to deal with the problem of alcoholism. Many Progressives favored the passage of the 18th Amendment to the Constitution, which prohibited the manufacture, sale, and transportation of alcoholic beverages.

Education. Many Progressives believed that education was the key to improving the system. In fact, public schooling became an important focus of Progressive reform efforts. John Dewey, Jane Addams, and Henry Barnard led the Progressive push to expand and improve public school education.

Child labor legislation occupied an important part of the Progressive agenda. As the United States moved to a predominately urban, manufacturing economy, more children were employed in factories and mines. They could be paid a lower wage than adult workers, and many children worked long hours for very little pay in unsafe conditions. Many never had an opportunity to attend school. In 1900, between 1.5 and 2 million children worked outside the home in factories or mines. In 1906, the muckraking journalist John Spargo raised public awareness when he published *The Bitter Cry of the Children*, which detailed the terrible conditions faced by thousands of children across the nation.

In the 1890s, Governor Altgeld of Illinois was one of the first public officials to address the problem of child labor. He persuaded the state legislature to pass laws controlling the employment of children, restricting them to an eight-hour day. He also appointed inspectors to help enforce the law. Business interests, however, were able to get the law repealed.

In 1904, Progressives founded the National Child Labor Committee to lobby Congress to pass laws that regulated child labor. Jane Addams was one of the committee's leaders. In 1908, Addams engaged a photographer, Lewis Hine, to visually document the plight of children in the workplace. Hine's photos are a graphic documentation of the harsh conditions in which many children worked.

Child Labor Legislation. Progressive reformers lobbied for the creation of a federal agency to address the problems of child labor. In 1912, President William Howard Taft established the Children's Bureau to "investigate and report upon all matters pertaining to the welfare of children and child life among all classes of our people." In 1916, Congress passed the Keating-Owen Act, which attempted to regulate child labor by forbidding the interstate transportation of products made in factories or businesses that employed children under 14 years of age or mines that employed children under 16 years of age. It also outlawed interstate transportation of products manufactured by any business that employed children under 16 who worked at night or who worked more than eight hours a day. In 1918, the Supreme Court declared the Keating-Owen Act unconstitutional.

In response to the Supreme Court's ruling, Congress enacted another child labor law, which levied a 10 percent tax on the profits of factories employing children under the age of 14 and on mines that employed children under the age of 16. In 1922, the Supreme Court struck down the law.

Progressives lobbied for the passage of a constitutional amendment giving Congress the power to regulate child labor. The amendment passed in Congress, but backers failed to obtain the necessary number of states to ratify it. In 1938, Congress approved the Fair Labor Standards Act, which outlawed child labor in industries that produced goods that were transported across state lines. The law established a minimum age of 14 for working outside of school hours in nonmanufacturing jobs, 16 for working during school hours, and 18 for hazardous work. The Supreme Court upheld the law.

The trust-busting championed by Roosevelt forced industrialists to change some business practices and pay attention to public opinion. Consumers gained some protection with the passage of food and drug legislation. The Federal Reserve System and the income tax helped to redistribute wealth so that people who needed it received help. Progressives were able to address some problems created by industrialization, but they did it in a way that did not fundamentally challenge the system that created such wealth and wealth disparities in the first place.

POINTS TO REMEMBER

- In the 1870s and 1880s, the United States experienced an unprecedented explosion of industrial growth.
- Industrialization was made possible by the rise of modern corporations.
- Beginning in the period between 1910 and 1920, more people lived in urban areas than in rural areas for the first time in U.S. history.
- One effect of industrialization was to bring more women and children in the workforce.
- In the late 1800s and early 1900s, farmers could grow more food because of improved agricultural technology.
- Urbanization accompanied industrialization. Living conditions for working people and immigrants in many American cities were substandard.
- The Industrial Revolution helped establish a new middle class in the United States.
- Laissez-faire economic policies helped lead to the development of large corporations and trusts.
- While many people suffered and the gap between the rich and poor was wide, the overall standard of living rose in the United States between 1880 and 1920.
- Labor unions, Populism, and Progressivism were all responses to the effects of industrialization.

EXERCISES

CHECKING WHAT YOU HAVE READ

1. Laissez-faire theory argued that

   A. poverty was natural and unavoidable
   B. the market was self-regulating
   C. government intervention was necessary
   D. corporations required regulation.

2. Generally, farmers of the late 19th century blamed their economic problems on

   A. railroads and banks
   B. poor farming practices
   C. rising costs created by mechanization
   D. outdated agricultural technology.

3. The Populist Party program

   A. was so impractical that none of it was ever enacted
   B. wanted to prohibit government intervention in the economy
   C. favored laissez-faire policies to help corporations
   D. favored regulation of railroads and coinage of silver.

4. The Progressive movement is best defined as

   A. an organized political party with a clear-cut set of goals
   B. an idea that favored government reform of social abuses
   C. probusiness and antiunion
   D. made up mostly of minorities and labor union members.

5. Populists wanted the free coinage of silver because it would

   A. lead to inflation
   B. lower equipment prices
   C. help the jewelry industry
   D. help railroads build more track.

6. Which of the following lasted well into the 20th century?

   A. Knights of Labor
   B. American Federation of Labor
   C. Granger movement
   D. Populist Party

7. Which of the following groups favored a civil service system?

   A. immigrants
   B. Progressives
   C. political machine bosses
   D. railroad owners

8. Between the late 1800s and early 1900s, the average standard of living in the United States

   A. stayed the same
   B. decreased
   C. increased
   D. could not be calculated.

9. Progressives generally believed that

   A. women were too emotional to vote
   B. women should have the right to vote
   C. corporations should not be regulated
   D. public education should be available only to those who can afford it.

10. At the state level, Progressive reformers

   A. opposed direct primary elections
   B. fought against direct election of senators
   C favored the initiative and referendum
   D. opposed public schools.

USING WHAT YOU HAVE READ

1. On a separate piece of paper, complete a Venn diagram like the one below, comparing the Populists and Progressives.

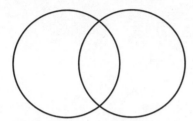

2. On a separate piece of paper, complete a concept map like the one below with as many effects of industrialization as you can identify.

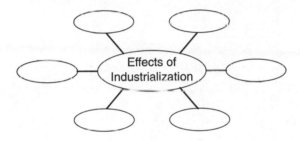

THINKING ABOUT WHAT YOU HAVE READ

Assume the role of a factory worker or a farmer in the 1880s. Write a letter to the editor in which you describe a serious problem facing either factory workers or farmers, why it is a problem, and suggest a way to solve the problem.

SKILLS

Interpreting a Primary Source

Read each of the following primary source documents about life in the later 1800s and early 1900s. Then answer the questions that follow.

"Honest Graft"

Everybody is talkin' these days about Tammany men growin' rich on graft, but nobody thinks of drawin' the distinction between honest graft and dishonest graft. There's all the difference in the world between the two. Yes, many of our men have grown rich in politics. I have myself. I've made a big fortune out of the game, and I'm gettin' richer every day, but I've not gone in for dishonest graft—blackmailin' gamblers, saloon-keepers, disorderly people, etc.—and neither has any of the men who have made big fortunes in politics.

There's an honest graft, and I'm an example of how it works. I might sum up the whole thing by sayin': "I seen my opportunities and I took 'em."

Just let me explain by examples. My party's in power in the city, and it's goin' to undertake a lot of public improvements. Well, I'm tipped off, say, that they're going to lay out a new park at a certain place.

I see my opportunity and I take it. I go to that place and I buy up all the land I can in the neighborhood. Then the board of this or that makes its plan public, and there is a rush to get my land, which nobody cared particular for before.

Ain't it perfectly honest to charge a good price and make a profit on my investment and foresight? Of course it is. Well, that's honest graft.

Or, supposin' it's a new bridge they're goin' to build. I get tipped off and I buy as much property as I can that has to be taken for approaches. I sell at my own price later on and drop some more money in the bank.

Wouldn't you? It's just like lookin' ahead in Wall Street or in the coffee or cotton market. It's honest graft, and I'm lookin' for it every day in the year. I will tell you frankly that I've got a good lot of it, too.

George Washington Plunkitt

Life in a Tenement

I counted the other day the little ones, up to ten years or so, in a Bayard Street tenement that for a yard has a triangular space in the center with sides fourteen or fifteen feet long, just room enough for a row of ill-smelling closet at the base of the triangle and a hydrant at the apex. There was about as much light in this "yard" as in the average cellar. I gave up my self-imposed task in despair when I had counted one hundred and twenty-eight in forty families. Thirteen I had missed, or not found in. Applying the average for the forty to the whole fifty-three, the house contained one hundred and seventy children. It is not the only time I have had to give up such census work. I have in mind an alley—an inlet rather to a row of rear tenements—that is either two or four feet wide according as the wall of the crazy old building that gives on it bulges out or in. I tried to count the children that swarmed there, but could not. Sometimes I have doubted that anybody knows just how many there are about. Bodies of drowned children turn up in the rivers . . . whom no one seems to know anything about. When last spring some workmen, while moving a pile of lumber on a North River pier, found under the last plank the body of a little lad crushed to death, no one had missed a boy, though his parents afterward turned up.

Jacob Riis, *How the Other Half Lives*

1. Who wrote each document?

2. What is the approximate date of the documents?

3. For whom was each written (the audience)?

4. What is the point of view of each document?

5. Summarize each document.

6. How do the two documents differ?

7. What does each document tell you about life in the United States at that time?

CHAPTER 18

IMPERIALISM

> **BENCHMARK:**
>
> **Analyze the reasons that countries gained control of territory through imperialism and the impact on people living in the territory that was controlled.**

This benchmark addresses reasons for the rise of imperialism after 1877 and the impact imperialism had upon the people living in the territories that came under United States control. Imperialism is a policy used by strong countries to gain social, political, and economic control over foreign territories. During these years, the United States, along with its rise as the world's industrial leader, became a major world power rivaling European nations such as Britain and Germany. In particular, it is important to understand American imperialism in regions such as the Far East, the South Pacific, the Caribbean, and Latin America. You will also need to understand the causes and results of the Spanish-American War and the impact imperialism had on people in territories controlled by other nations.

★ REASONS FOR IMPERIALISM ★

From the earliest years of nationhood, many Americans looked for ways to expand the United States, both territorially and economically. But why do some nations engage in imperialistic expansion, while others become the controlled territory? Why did the United States, in particular, become increasingly expansionist and imperialistic in the period after Reconstruction?

Before the Civil War, most territorial expansion occurred within the North American continent. Up to around the 1890s, most Americans embraced an isolationist approach to foreign affairs. The United States was protected on both sides by vast oceans, and American citizens generally wanted to keep the rest of the world at arm's length.

Economic Growth

Shortly after Reconstruction (1880s–1890s), however, things began to change. By then, most of the continental United States had been settled, and the nation experienced an explosive period of business and industrial growth. By the turn of the century, the economy of the United States was the world's strongest. As a result, many business leaders and industrialists became much more interested in the outside world. Industrial and agricultural output grew rapidly to the point where it became necessary for businesses to find foreign markets to sell their goods. Factory owners also needed to obtain certain raw materials not available in the United States for particular manufacturing processes.

Business leaders wanted the help of the United States government to expand their access to markets and raw materials. They hoped that through business dealings in foreign nations—supported by favorable economic and diplomatic policies—they would be able to continue to grow and prosper. In turn, politicians, often Republicans with close ties to business leaders, supported the use of foreign policy to achieve these goals. For example, both President Theodore Roosevelt and Senator Henry Cabot Lodge of Massachusetts endorsed the use of diplomacy in the service of economic expansion and new markets.

Test Yourself
What economic factors following Reconstruction helped cause the rise of imperialism in the United States?

In his book, *The Influence of Sea Power Upon History* (1890), Alfred T. Mahan, a naval officer and historian, supported the imperialistic beliefs and tendencies of several American leaders, including Roosevelt. Mahan argued that in order for a nation to have adequate access to markets and become a world power, it must possess a strong navy. Using the arguments of his influential book, military leaders persuaded Congress to provide funding for the strengthening of the United States Navy. They also encouraged government leaders to acquire islands to use as fueling and supply ports. Within ten years of the book's publication, the United States possessed the world's third largest navy.

Psychological Issues

Many Americans had other reasons, besides economic considerations, for supporting imperialism. Some people hoped that interest and involvement in foreign affairs would divert attention from worries and concerns about domestic problems.

Ideological Beliefs

Many people believed that the ideas of the British naturalist Charles Darwin (1809–1822), who developed the theory of evolution and natural selection to explain the origins of plant and animal species and human beings, could be adapted to address economic, social, and political problems. In the United States, a growing interest in *Social Darwinism* increased support for imperialistic adventures. Darwin's idea of the "survival of the fittest" was misapplied to nations. According to the theory, only the strongest nations could survive and prosper. The United States, supporters of this view argued, would have to become strong diplomatically, militarily, and economically, and acquire territories whenever and wherever possible.

In the 1840s, the idea of *manifest destiny* became part of the American political vocabulary. At that time, manifest destiny referred to the belief that it was the sacred duty of the United States to expand its institutions across the entire North American continent. John O'Sullivan, a magazine editor, coined the phrase in the mid-1840s when he wrote that "our manifest destiny is to overspread the continent allotted by Providence for the free development of our yearly multiplying millions." By the 1890s, imperialists were eager to apply manifest destiny to the rest of the world and to acquire territories in the Caribbean and Pacific.

Religious Beliefs

Religious reasons also contributed to the growing popularity of imperialism during the last decades of the 19th century. Many American Protestants such as the Reverend Josiah Strong believed that Anglo-Saxons (white, English-speaking people) had a responsibility to colonize beyond American borders in order to spread Christianity and the American way of life. They supported imperialism because they believed it was their duty to take the benefits of their "superior" American society to less fortunate people in the world.

Test Yourself
What beliefs associated with Social Darwinism caused some Americans to support imperialistic policies?

Influence of the Press

Newspapers and magazines also fueled imperialist tendencies by publishing sensationalistic articles that featured exotic, faraway places. Jingoistic, or intensely nationalistic, stories in newspapers such as William Randolph Hearst's New York *Journal* and Joseph Pulitzer's New York *World* advanced arguments for increased U.S. involvement in foreign affairs and the expansion of American territory.

Reasons Americans Supported Territorial Expansion Through Imperialism
Economic: Need for new markets and raw materials
Psychological: Diversion from domestic problems
Ideological: Social Darwinism misapplied to foreign affairs
Religious: Christian duty to spread Christianity and benefits of Western civilization

Political: Some politicians had ties to business interests that wanted new markets.

Strategic: Influenced by Mahan's book, military leaders wanted to build a strong navy and establish bases around the world.

Media: Newspapers that supported an imperialistic foreign policy influenced many readers.

★ THE SPANISH-AMERICAN WAR ★

The event that most clearly demonstrates the imperialistic tendencies of the United States at the turn of the century is the Spanish-American War. Cuba had been a colony of Spain since the 16th century. By the 1890s, however, the Spanish Empire was in decline, and independence movements developed in many of its colonies. In 1895, Cuban rebels initiated a revolt against Spanish rule. As rebel attacks became more numerous and violent, Spanish officials retaliated with brutal measures. Between 1896 and 1898, about 100,000 Cuban civilians were killed by Spanish troops.

Cuba

Imperialistic-minded Americans had long desired to expand American control over Cuba, located just 90 miles off the coast of Florida. Refugees fleeing the Cuban civil war came to the United States and circulated stories, some truthful and some exaggerated, about Spanish atrocities against Cuban rebels and civilians. Hearst's New York *Journal* and Pulitzer's New York *World*, competing for

U.S.-Spanish tensions on the eve of war

Divers investigate the wreckage of the *U.S.S. Maine.*

sales and circulation, printed lurid, sensational stories of atrocities in Cuba that outraged many Americans and inflamed public opinion against Spain. Public pressure to support the Cuban rebels increased throughout President Grover Cleveland's administration and continued when William McKinley took office in 1897. At first, the president resisted public opinion, which was incited by the "yellow" press, and refused to intervene.

"Remember the* Maine!"** On February 15, 1898, the American battleship *U.S.S. Maine*, anchored in Havana harbor, exploded, killing over 260 sailors. The press controlled by Hearst, Pulitzer, and others immediately blamed the Spanish for sinking the ship. To this day, the exact cause of the explosion remains unknown. President McKinley demanded that Spain agree to a cease-fire with the Cuban rebels, which it did. Many Americans, however, who were influenced by the yellow press, clamored for war. No longer able to resist public opinion, in April 1898, McKinley sent a war message to Congress that presented four reasons why the United States should provide military support to the Cuban rebels:

1. ". . . to put an end to the barbarities, bloodshed, starvation, and horrible miseries now existing there. . . ."
2. "We owe it to our citizens in Cuba to afford them . . . protection and indemnity for life and property. . . ."
3. "The right to intervene may be justified by the very serious injury to the commerce, trade, and business of our people and the wanton destruction of property and devastation of the island."
4. "The present condition of affairs in Cuba is a constant menace to our peace and entails upon this Government an enormous expense."

Congress responded on April 20, 1898, with a joint resolution authorizing the use of American force. Congress also passed the Teller Amendment, which stated that the United States would not annex or take political control of Cuba. The amendment promised that Cuba would have its independence after the fighting ended.

The Philippines

The fighting began not in Cuba but in the Philippines. In anticipation of hostilities, Assistant Secretary of the Navy Theodore Roosevelt had ordered the newly enlarged American navy to the Philippines, which had been a Spanish colony for nearly four centuries. Inspired by the battle cry, "Remember the *Maine!*," Commodore George Dewey and the American fleet steamed into Manila Bay on May 1, 1898, and quickly overwhelmed the Spanish navy. On land, American troops and Filipino rebels joined forces to attack the Spanish troops. With the fall of the city of Manila on August 13, the United States now controlled the Philippines.

Victory in Cuba. The U.S. invasion of Cuba encountered several difficulties. Composed largely of volunteers, American troops were poorly trained and ill-equipped. In fact, more American troops died from disease than in battle. Over 5,000 Americans died from diseases such as dysentery, typhoid, and malaria. Fewer than 400 died as a result of fighting.

The fighting in Cuba lasted over four months. In May, a Spanish fleet entered the harbor at Santiago. American ships moved in quickly to blockade the coast and trap the Spanish fleet in the harbor. One month later, American soldiers landed in Cuba, supporting Cuban forces that kept Spanish troops at bay. On July 1, American and Cuban troops, including Theodore Roosevelt's Rough Riders and African American troops from the Ninth and Tenth cavalries, defeated Spanish forces in the Battle of San Juan Hill. Two days later, the Spanish fleet attempted to break out of Santiago Bay and was destroyed by the American navy. Spain realized that it could no longer defend the island. The fighting ended in August, and Spain asked for terms of surrender.

Theodore Roosevelt (center with glasses) with the Rough Riders

Peace Terms. Spain and the United States signed a formal peace treaty in Paris on December 10, 1898, ending what Secretary of State John Hay called "a splendid little war." The treaty gave almost all of Spain's colonies—Cuba, the Philippines, Guam, and Puerto Rico—to the United States.

Revolt in the Philippines. The defeat of the Spanish in the Philippines sparked a contentious debate in the United States about what to do with the island. Imperialists in the United States wanted to annex the Philippines. By contrast, anti-imperialists believed that the United States should follow the principles of the Declaration of Independence and grant the Filipino people their independence. The Treaty of Paris called for annexation, but the United States Senate had to ratify the treaty with a two-thirds vote. Anti-imperialists mounted a spirited campaign to defeat the treaty, but the Senate narrowly approved it. The Philippines became an American territory.

Many Filipino citizens were outraged that the United States would free them from Spanish control but then annex the islands. Emilio Aguinaldo, who had fought with U.S. forces against Spain, led a guerrilla war against the new occupiers. Americans were not prepared for the stiff resistance of Aguinaldo's Filipino rebels. Before they finally defeated the Filipino forces in 1902, thousands of American and Filipino guerrillas died.

Test Yourself
Why did Filipinos resist American occupation of their nation?

U.S. troops occupied Cuba until 1909. The Teller Amendment eventually allowed Cuba to gain its independence. Congress, however, approved the annexation of Puerto Rico, the Philippines, and Guam, making the United States a world power rivaling the strongest European powers. The Philippines later became independent, but Guam and Puerto Rico remain territories of the United States today.

Test Yourself
Why did Cuba gain its independence after the war, while the Philippines and Guam became U.S. territories?

★ THE ANNEXATION OF HAWAII ★

In the 1820s, American missionaries arrived in the Hawaiian islands in order to spread Christianity. The islands' good harbors and strategic location attracted Americans involved in the whaling industry. About a decade later, American business leaders introduced sugarcane farming and gradually developed large plantations, bringing in thousands of Japanese and Chinese laborers. Before long, American interests owned much of the land and came to have great influence in Hawaiian business and political affairs.

Although the United States recognized Hawaii as an independent nation in 1842, American influence in its affairs continued to grow. When the American government allowed the importing of Hawaiian sugar into the U.S. with no tariffs, profits from sugar production in the islands increased rapidly, and American plantation owners in Hawaii benefited enormously. In 1887, the United States negotiated with Hawaiian officials to obtain permission to build a naval base at Pearl Harbor in exchange for renewal of the favorable no-tariff agreement. Since many Hawaiians depended on plantation work for their livelihood, Hawaiian leaders agreed to the arrangement.

In the 1890s, American-based sugar producers, who had to compete against growers in Hawaii, persuaded Congress to end the tariff exemption. The growers now had to pay tax on the sugar they shipped to the United States. In order to be competitive in the American market, they dropped the price they charged for their sugar. Their profits also fell, and they faced financial ruin.

The growers looked for a solution, and they devised a plan to make Hawaii part of the United States. If the islands were an American territory, they would not have to pay the sugar tariff, and their profitability would be restored. In 1893, the sugar planters—with support of U.S. Marines—led a revolt against Queen Liliuokalani, who had started to take away some of the power held by Americans in the islands. American business leaders set up a provisional government headed by Sanford Dole, which was quickly recognized by the chief American diplomat in Hawaii. This new Hawaiian government wrote a treaty of annexation, hoping that the Congress would approve it and make Hawaii a territory of the United States. President Grover Cleveland opposed the treaty. When William McKinley became president in 1897, he pushed for the treaty's ratification. In addition to supporting American business interests in the islands, McKinley believed that Hawaii's strategic location in the Pacific and the naval base at Pearl Harbor were important to the defense of the United States. Anti-imperialists were able to delay ratification for over a year, but in 1898, Congress voted in favor of the treaty and annexation. In 1900, Hawaii officially became a territory of the United States. It became a state in 1959.

★ THE OPEN DOOR POLICY IN CHINA ★

American imperialists also eyed the Far East for expansion of trade and influence. Secretary of State John Hay feared that other nations, especially European powers, were gaining too much power in China. Throughout the 1890s, France, Germany, Great Britain, Russia, and Japan established centers of trade in China called *spheres of influence*. Each nation had the power to control trade and commerce within its particular sphere or region. Hay worried that these nations would gain an economic advantage by preventing the United States from sharing in the very profitable Chinese trade.

In 1899, Hay sent a diplomatic note to nations that had spheres of influence in China. He asked those nations to agree to an "Open Door" policy for all nations in China. This Open Door policy meant that all nations would share equal trading privileges in China. The nations that received Hay's note did not want to accept a proposal that would benefit the United States at their expense, but they did not reject the policy outright.

The Boxer Rebellion

At the beginning of the 20th century, Chinese nationalists led by members of the Society of Harmonious Fists, also known as the Boxers, staged a revolt against foreigners in China. They killed several Christian missionaries and attacked foreign settlements throughout the nation, trapping hundreds of Westerners in the city of Beijing. In August 1900, foreign troops, including some from the United States, defeated the Boxers and rescued the people trapped in the city. Victorious foreign governments forced the Chinese to sign favorable trade agreements and pay indemnities to insure against any future damages.

Animals representing different nations want their piece of China.

Fearing that foreign troops in China might try to occupy the nation, Hay sent a second Open Door note to the invading nations. In the note, he stated that China's independence and territorial borders should be respected, and that the United States still supported the policy that all nations have access to "equal and impartial trade with all parts of the Chinese empire." These Open Door notes set U.S. policy in China for several administrations after McKinley's.

★ "BIG-STICK" DIPLOMACY ★

On September 6, 1901, nearly six months after his second inauguration, President McKinley was shot by an anarchist during a visit to the Pan American Exhibition in Buffalo, New York. McKinley died eight days later. Vice President Theodore Roosevelt became the nation's leader. Roosevelt, a hero of the Battle of San Juan Hill in Cuba, was a proponent of American expansionism. He once said that the United States in foreign policy should "speak softly and carry a big stick." The press quickly attached the "big-

Illustration depicting the fatal shooting of President McKinley in 1901

stick" label to his administration's foreign policy. Roosevelt believed the United States should be a world power, and his aggressive foreign policy made American imperialists happy. Anti-imperialists, by contrast, wanted the United States to maintain its tradition of not being involved in global affairs.

★ THE PANAMA CANAL ★

Many people wanted to build a canal through Central America that would connect the Caribbean Sea with the Pacific Ocean. Such a canal meant that ships in the Atlantic Ocean would not have to sail around the South American continent to reach the Pacific. In 1878, a French company began building a canal across the isthmus of Panama, but disease and engineering problems forced it to abandon the project. Now that the United States owned territories ranging from the Philippines in the Pacific to Puerto Rico in the Caribbean, Roosevelt believed it was a strategic necessity to revive the canal project and provide more rapid travel to the nation's most remote bases.

At first, Roosevelt's plans were frustrated because Colombia controlled Panama at that time and refused to reach an agreement with the United States on building a canal through its territory. In 1903, frustrated by lack of progress in negotiations with the Colombian government, Roosevelt provided American support to an uprising in Panama. The Panamanian rebels quickly succeeded in freeing their nation from Colombian control and established an independent government. In 1903, the government signed the Hay–Bunau-Varilla Treaty with the United States, giving the Americans control of a canal zone through the isthmus. Construction on the canal began in 1904, and the project was completed ten years later. It remains one of the world's great engineering feats.

President Roosevelt (center) oversees construction of the Panama Canal.

While many Americans applauded Roosevelt's efforts to build the canal, anti-imperialists and Latin Americans resented his aggressive tactics. In 1925, Congress voted to pay Colombia $25 million for the loss of Panama.

★ THE ROOSEVELT COROLLARY TO THE MONROE DOCTRINE ★

Latin America was the scene of other examples of Roosevelt's big-stick approach to foreign policy. In the early 1900s, several Central American nations suffered from financial woes and owed debts to European creditors. In 1902, the British sent a warship to Venezuela to collect what was owed to them. Another financial crisis brewed in the Dominican Republic (then called Santo Domingo) in 1904, and it appeared that other European nations might send forces there. Roosevelt believed such actions by European nations would violate the Monroe Doctrine (1823), which held that European nations could not establish colonies or intervene in the Western Hemisphere. In December 1904, Roosevelt issued a policy that became known as the Roosevelt Corollary to the Monroe Doctrine. This policy stated that the United States would exercise "international police power" in response to chronic misconduct by any nation in the Western Hemisphere. Roosevelt threatened to send troops to collect taxes in Central American nations for other nations until the debts were paid.

Over the course of the next two decades, based on Theodore Roosevelt's big stick diplomacy, William Howard Taft's "dollar diplomacy," and Woodrow Wilson's "moral diplomacy," the United States sent forces into Nicaragua, Honduras, Haiti, and the Dominican Republic. Many people in these Latin American nations resented U.S. intervention in their affairs, and these actions fostered poor relations throughout the region for many decades to come.

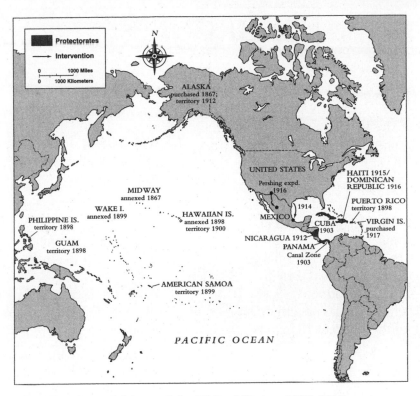

Territorial acquisitions of the United States, 1867–1917

POINTS TO REMEMBER

- There are several reasons in addition to economic considerations that led to the rise of American imperialism, including ideological, religious, political, strategic, and humanitarian.

- Many Americans were anti-imperialistic and opposed U.S. efforts to gain territory overseas.

- The United States became a world power following the Spanish-American War, possessing territories such as the Philippines, Guam, and Puerto Rico.

- Many citizens in territories controlled or acquired by the United States resented their loss of freedom and self-determination. Some violently resisted, such as the people in the Philippines.

- American business interests engineered the acquisition of Hawaii as a U.S. territory.

- Theodore Roosevelt's "big-stick" diplomacy led to the building of the Panama Canal and to interventions in several Central American nations' affairs.

- Secretary of State John Hay's "Open Door" notes to nations that held spheres of influence in China set U.S. policy there for many years to come.

EXERCISES

CHECKING WHAT YOU HAVE READ

1. What change in the United States after Reconstruction was a factor in the rise of imperialism?

   A. Thousands of people were killed in the Civil War.
   B. Business and industry suffered a severe decline.
   C. Businesses required foreign sources for raw materials and markets in which to sell their products.
   D. People feared that European nations were an imminent threat to invade the United States.

2. In his book *The Influence of Sea Power Upon History* (1890), Alfred T. Mahan argued that

   A. the United States was so well protected by both oceans that a strong navy was unnecessary
   B. most powerful empires relied upon armies rather than naval power
   C. the U.S. Navy in 1890 was already strong enough and should not be enlarged
   D. to become a world power, a nation must possess a strong navy.

3. Which idea associated with Social Darwinism led to increased support for imperialism?

   A. survival of the fittest
   B. self-determination
   C. self-government
   D. anticolonialism

4. Supporters of imperialism would be most likely to use which of the following ideas to argue in favor of territorial acquisition?

   A. universal suffrage
   B. manifest destiny
   C. self-determination
   D. freedom of religion

5. Which of the following provided for Cuba's independence after the Spanish-American War?

   A. the Teller Amendment
   B. the Hay–Bunau-Varilla Treaty
   C. Social Darwinism
   D. manifest destiny

6. What event caused American intervention in Cuba against Spanish colonial rule?

   A. the Battle of San Juan Hill
   B. the Battle of Manila Bay
   C. the passage of the Teller Amendment
   D. the sinking of the battleship *Maine*

7. Which U.S. president was associated with "big-stick" diplomacy?

   A. William McKinley
   B. Theodore Roosevelt
   C. Grover Cleveland
   D. Woodrow Wilson

8. Which of the following clearly demonstrated resentment and resistance of colonized people against an occupying nation?

   A. the signing of the Hay–Bunau-Varilla Treaty
   B. the American-led rebellion in Hawaii
   C. the rise of the "yellow press" in the late 1890s
   D. Aguinaldo's actions in the Philippines after the Spanish-American War

9. John Hay's Open Door notes are most closely associated with

   A. spheres of influence in China

B. exemption from sugar tariffs for Hawaiian growers

C. the Teller Amendment on Cuba

D. the Panama Canal Zone.

10. The Roosevelt Corollary was an expansion of the

A. Bill of Rights

B. Teller Amendment

C. Monroe Doctrine

D. Treaty of Paris (1898).

USING WHAT YOU HAVE READ

1. Describe a scenario in which an American president might invoke the Roosevelt Corollary today.

2. Do an Internet search for "imperialism." In what context is the term used today?

What references are made to the United States regarding imperialism? Make a list of topics.

THINKING ABOUT WHAT YOU HAVE READ

1. Write a letter to the editor in which you take a position on going to war in Cuba or on the acquisition of the Philippines as a U.S. territory following the Spanish-American War. State your view and support it with arguments based on events of the time.

2. If you were a Filipino living in the Philippines in 1900, how would you have felt about Emilio Aguinaldo's revolt against American occupation troops? Explain your answer.

SKILLS

INTERPRETING A POLITICAL CARTOON

Study the cartoon below and answer the questions that follow.

1. Who does the large figure represent?

2. How is the large figure dressed?

3. What is he holding in his right hand, and what does it represent?

4. What is the message of the cartoon?

CHAPTER 19

WORLD WAR I AND THE ONSET OF WORLD WAR II

BENCHMARK:

Connect developments related to World War I with the onset of World War II.

This benchmark addresses the connection between the two world wars. Regarding World I, this chapter focuses on the United States' decision to enter the war, President Woodrow Wilson's Fourteen Points, the Treaty of Versailles, and the nation's eventual decision not to participate in the League of Nations. Regarding World War II, the emphasis is on the impact of U.S. involvement on the war's outcome, the change from isolationism to internationalism, and the reaction to the Japanese attack on Pearl Harbor. The actual conduct of either war is *not* an emphasis of this benchmark. For purposes of the Ohio Graduation Test (OGT) in Social Studies, questions assessing this benchmark will involve the *connection between the two wars*. It is important to understand how the events following World War I led to the outbreak of World War II.

★ CAUSES OF THE GREAT WAR ★

On June 28, 1914, Gavrilo Princip, a Bosnian Serb nationalist, assassinated Archduke Franz Ferdinand, the heir to the throne of the Austro-Hungarian Empire, in Sarajevo, Bosnia. This was the immediate event that sparked the outbreak of hostilities in Europe. Many other long-term factors, however, created a situation in Europe in which a single political assassination could lead to a devastating war of previously unimaginable death and destruction.

Nationalism

What were these roots of war in Europe? For several years prior to the assassination, *nationalism* had been on the rise in Europe. Smaller kingdoms and regions joined together in Germany and Italy to form larger nations with central governments. Over time, nations such as Germany, Italy, Britain, France, and Russia pursued and established colonies overseas. As territories to colonize became scarcer, rivalries among the colonizing powers intensified, and they moved to protect their interests by increasing their military strength. Consequently, an arms race developed.

The Alliance System

At the same time, the most powerful European nations began to create alliances with one another in order to strengthen their relative positions. Nations entered into these alliances with the belief that in order to avoid conflict they had to maintain a "balance of power" in the world. Two major alliances developed. The Triple Alliance consisted of Germany, Austria-Hungary, and Italy. The Triple Entente included Great Britain, France, and Russia. By entering into these *entangling alliances*, member nations agreed that an attack on one member was an attack on all, and that they would defend one another. Nationalism, colonial rivalries, the arms race, and this complex system of alliances created a volatile mix. One spark could easily ignite a catastrophic inferno. Franz Ferdinand's assassination provided that flashpoint, and the world was soon at war.

Beginning of the War

Following the assassination in Sarajevo, the government of Austria-Hungary issued an *ultimatum*, a set of conditions that must be accepted, to Serbia, which it blamed for the killing. The Serbian leadership refused to agree to the demands, and on July 28, 1914, Austria-Hungary—with Germany's support—declared war on Serbia. The alliance system that had developed in the previous years rapidly pulled other nations into the conflict.

Russia quickly went to the defense of Serbia. In August, Germany, supporting Austria-Hungary, declared war on Russia and its ally France. On August 4, 1914, Germany invaded neutral Belgium on its way to attack France. The German invasion of Belgium triggered Britain's declaration of war against Germany, because the British had pledged to protect the Belgians. World War I was on.

In the war, the Allied Powers included Great Britain, France, and Russia. Italy joined the Allies in 1915, rejecting its earlier role in the Triple Alliance. The Central Powers consisted of Germany and Austria-Hungary. The Ottoman Empire (Turkey) eventually joined the Central Powers as a defense against Russia. Bulgaria also entered the war, siding with the Central Powers.

After some initial advances by both sides, the war settled down into a stalemate based on trench warfare. Both sides were dug in and holed up in long trenches across from each other. The land between them was known as "no-man's land." For almost three years, the war dragged on this way. Casualties were high due to new technologies such as tanks, poison gas, machine guns, and airplanes. Despite occasional breakouts, neither side made much headway.

★ THE UNITED STATES AND THE WAR, 1914–1917 ★

When war erupted in Europe, many Americans opposed any efforts to involve the United States. Agreeing with President Wilson, public opinion generally favored U.S. neutrality. Most Americans at the time viewed the war as Europe's problem. In fact, a popular song of the day was entitled "I Didn't Raise My Boy to Be a Soldier."

As the war dragged on, however, more Americans began taking sides. Some favored the nation of their ancestry. By 1915, about 8 million people of German or Austro-Hungarian descent lived in the United States. There were also 4.5 million Irish Americans, most of whom hated the English. Based on historic ties to England and ethnic ties to France or Russia, many other people sided with the Allies. At this point in the war, however, neutrality was still the United States government's official policy.

Both the Allies and the Central Powers used propaganda with varying degrees of success to influence public opinion in the United States. Entry of the United States on either side would make a major difference in the outcome.

Trade With the Belligerent Powers

Another factor that drew the United States toward entry into the conflict was trade. American businesses made huge profits trading with European nations that needed food and war materials. Business leaders wanted to maintain neutrality and trade with both sides. The British naval blockade of Germany, however, made it difficult to trade with any of the Central Powers. The bulk of U.S. trade went to England and France. Trade with the Allies accelerated rapidly. In 1914, American merchants conducted about $8.25 million in business with the Allies. By 1916, that increased to over $3 billion. Moreover, Allied governments borrowed money from U.S. banks to help pay for the goods. These business arrangements helped further persuade many Americans to support the Allied side. The American economy prospered as a result of war trade.

Unrestricted Submarine Warfare by Germany

The Germans resented American trade with the Allies. The United States was officially neutral, but due to the British blockade, American ships were unable to reach the Central Powers. By February 1915, Germany was desperate to cut supply lines to the Allies, and announced it would use its U-boat (submarine) fleet to attack any ships entering or leaving English ports. The U.S. government strenuously objected, and President Wilson warned the Germans that they would be held accountable for any deaths of Americans. Despite the warning, Germany carried out its threat.

***Sinking of the* Lusitania.** On May 7, 1915, a German U-boat attacked the British ship *Lusitania* just off the coast of Ireland. The ship sank quickly, and about 1,000 passengers, including over 100 Americans, died. At first, it was thought that the *Lusitania* carried only civilian passengers. Later, the public discovered that it also carried war supplies. Nevertheless, an outraged American public called for retribution. Some American leaders such as Teddy Roosevelt called for a declaration of war. Wilson vigorously protested and denounced the attack, sending three communiqués to the German government, but he stopped short of initiating any military action.

A newspaper drawing depicting the survivors of the *Lusitania*

The Sussex Pledge. A few months later, a German U-boat attacked the unarmed French ship *Sussex*, injuring several American citizens. Wilson threatened again to break off diplomatic relations with Germany. The German government, fearful of bringing the United States into the war on the Allied side, backed off. It agreed to compensate Americans who were injured and issued the *Sussex Pledge*, which promised to warn neutral and passenger ships before any attack.

As the United States approached the 1916 presidential election, disagreement among Americans over whether or not to prepare for war increased. Pacifists believed that if the U.S. government strengthened the military, the nation would be more likely to enter the war. Those favoring "preparedness" argued that a military buildup was necessary to protect and defend the nation. Wilson maintained his hope for neutrality but eventually sided with those who favored preparedness. In the summer of 1916, Congress approved the funds necessary to double the size of the army and build new warships.

Despite the military buildup, support for neutrality remained high. Many Americans hoped that the United States would be able to avoid joining the conflict in Europe. In fact, both presidential candidates campaigned for neutrality. In the election, Wilson narrowly defeated his Republican opponent, Charles Evans Hughes, using the campaign slogan "He Kept Us Out of the War."

In late January 1917, Germany reversed its policy on unrestricted submarine warfare. The Germans announced that they would attack any merchant vessel, armed or unarmed, entering or leaving Allied ports. German leaders took the chance of forcing the United States into war, but they believed that they could win the war before the U.S. had a chance to mobilize its forces and get them to Europe.

Zimmermann Note. In response to the German announcement reinstituting unrestricted submarine warfare, President Wilson broke diplomatic relations with Germany on February 3, 1917. About a month later, another incident

Unrestricted submarine warfare by Germany

pushed the United States closer to war. British agents intercepted a telegram from German Foreign Minister Arthur Zimmermann to the German ambassador to Mexico. In the telegram, Zimmermann instructed the ambassador to persuade Mexico to enter the war against the United States and recapture lost territory in New Mexico, Texas, and Arizona. The press published the telegram, and the American people were outraged.

Events in Russia also helped to sway people in the United States in the direction of entering the war. In March 1917, a revolution overthrew the old czarist regime, and a new democratic government replaced the monarchy. Many Americans thought the U.S. should support the new Russian government. Around the same time, German U-boats sank four American merchant ships without warning, killing several people. Wilson concluded that it was no longer possible for the United States to remain neutral.

★ THE UNITED STATES ENTERS THE WAR ★

On April 2, 1917, Wilson went before a special session of Congress to ask for a declaration of war. In his speech, Wilson said:

> The world must be made safe for democracy. Its peace must be planted upon the tested foundations of political liberty. We have no selfish ends to serve. We desire no conquest, no dominion. We seek no indemnities for ourselves, no material compensation for the sacrifices we shall freely make. We are but one of the champions of the rights of mankind. We shall be satisfied when those rights have been made as secure as the faith and freedom of nations can make them.

Four days later, Congress overwhelmingly passed the declaration of war. The vote in the Senate was 82 to 6 in favor of the declaration, and 373 to 50 in the House.

The U.S. government encouraged volunteers to enlist and serve the nation during World War I.

The job of raising and training a fighting force became a top priority. In May, Congress passed the Selective Service Act, authorizing the government to draft men into the armed forces. By the end of the war, just under 2 million men were drafted out of about 24 million registered. Another 2 million men volunteered. Within a few months, the army increased from about 200,000 to nearly 4,000,000 soldiers. For the first time, women also joined the armed forces in noncombat roles. Between 300,000 and 400,000 African American troops joined the army. They served in segregated units and were often given menial jobs. About 100,000 African American troops saw combat. The French decorated one African American regiment for bravery. Henry Johnson, an African American soldier, was the first American to receive the Croix de Guerre.

Henry Johnson, an African American soldier, became a highly decorated war hero.

It was a time of eagerness and optimism for those joining the military. "Over There," a popular song by George M. Cohan, caught the the spirit of the times:

> Over there, over there,
> Send the word, send the word over there
> That the Yanks are coming,
> The Yanks are coming,
> The drums rum-tumming everywhere

American Troops Help Turn the Tide

The first troops of the American Expeditionary Force (AEF) reached Europe in the summer of 1917, but the majority did not arrive until 1918. The Allies desperately needed reinforcements. Trench warfare had taken a frightful toll on Allied troops. The entry of U.S. forces produced immediate effects. The United States Navy moved quickly to counteract German U-boats. Employing a convoy system, Americans were able to increase the amount of food and military supplies that got through to the Allies. Not one single American soldier bound for the war in Europe died as a result of a submarine attack.

The need for troops to bolster Allied forces became even more important due to events in Russia. In a second revolution in November 1917, Bolshevik Communists led by Vladimir Ilyich Lenin overthrew the democratic government established after the previous revolution. Lenin wanted to get Russia out of the war so he could concentrate on establishing a government along Communist principles. He signed the Brest-Litovsk Treaty with Germany in March 1918. The treaty enabled Germany to move its troops from Russian territory in the Eastern front to the Western front against the British, French, and Americans.

Road to Victory. Between March and June 1918, the Germans began a major offensive. Without American troops to help stop the German push, the Allies might have lost the war. The *doughboys*, as American troops were called, led by General John J. Pershing, helped contain the Germans at Château-Thierry, Belleau Wood, Saint Mihiel, and the Argonne Forest, a battle which raged on for almost seven weeks. When Allied troops finally defeated the Germans at the Argonne, German leaders realized that victory was no longer possible. In early October, they asked the Allies for an armistice. The German government accepted all of the Allies' cease fire demands in November. The war was over.

★ THE STRUGGLE FOR PEACE ★

Attention turned to constructing the peace. Throughout the war, Wilson maintained his hope of establishing a "peace without victory," meaning that he did not want to punish the defeated nations. Instead, Wilson wanted to create a structure by which nations could avoid future wars. When the fighting ended, Wilson pursued that hope vigorously. The president's peace plan, known as the

Fourteen Points, offered proposals that he hoped would be embraced by Allied leaders. Reflecting Wilson's belief in self-determination for ethnic peoples, eight of the fourteen points concerned the reshaping of territorial borders and the creation of new nations. Other points referred to the readjustment of overseas colonies, freedom of the seas, an end to secret alliances, opening up global trade, disarmament, and the establishment of a world peace organization to settle disputes among countries, the League of Nations.

Wilson's Fourteen Points

1. No more secret treaties; "open covenants, openly arrived at"

2. freedom of the seas

3. free trade; removal of barriers to free trade among nations

4. arms reduction; cutbacks and limitations on military arms

5. peaceful settlements of disputes over colonies; interests of colonized people to be considered

6-13. national self-determination; new nations proposed; adjusted national boundaries

14. proposal for the League of Nations; world organization to settle international disputes

The Big Four

Wilson traveled to Europe in late 1918 to personally negotiate with leaders of the Allied governments. He was the first U.S. president to visit Europe during his term in office. Neither Russia nor Germany was invited to the conference. All over Europe, cheering crowds greeted Wilson enthusiastically. Despite his popularity, Wilson faced a daunting challenge. The other heads of state—Britain's Prime Minister David Lloyd George, French Premier Georges Clemenceau, and Italian Prime Minister Vittorio Orlando—were not in a forgiving mood. The war had taken a terrible toll. England, France, Russia, Germany, and Austria-Hungary each lost between one and two million people. Some estimates put the number killed—soldiers and civilians—in World War I at 15 million, with another 20 million wounded. The European economy was in ruins. Millions were homeless and suffering from hunger, malnutrition, and disease. Wilson's idea of "peace without victory" fell on deaf ears. Lloyd George, Clemenceau, and Orlando were determined to punish the Central Powers, especially Germany.

New Nations and Reparations. At the conference, Clemenceau wanted to carve up Germany into a number of smaller states. He wanted to insure that Germany would never again be strong enough to invade France. Clemenceau and Lloyd George also wanted the defeated nations to pay huge reparations, or compensation, for damages. After months of negotiations, the Allied leaders remained firm, and Wilson had to compromise on several points. The treaty that eventually emerged from the conference was harsh on Germany, causing

The Big Four at the Versailles Conference (from left to right)—David Lloyd George (Great Britain), Vittorio Orlando (Italy), Georges Clemenceau (France), and Woodrow Wilson (United States)

deep resentment among Germans that would surface years later on the eve of World War II. Wilson was able to weaken some of the harshest demands, and the treaty included his proposal for a League of Nations. Wilson, however, did not achieve his vision of a treaty aimed at reconciliation.

Versailles Treaty

In June 1919, at the conclusion of the conference, the final treaty called for Germany to disarm and to give up all its overseas colonies. It also demanded that Germany pay huge sums to France and Great Britain in reparations. In the "guilt clause," Germany was forced to admit that it was responsible for the war. The Versailles Treaty and treaties signed with the other defeated Central Powers redefined boundaries throughout Europe. Areas once under the control of Russia, Austria-Hungary, and Germany were taken away. As a result, Czechoslovakia and Yugoslavia became new nations, and Poland, Finland, Latvia, Estonia, and Lithuania were granted their independence. These and other border changes resulted in conflict later on.

Wilson's Fight for Treaty Ratification. On his return to the United States, Wilson had to convince the Senate to ratify the treaty. Wilson submitted the Treaty of Versailles to the Senate on July 10, 1919. In order to ratify it, the Senate had to approve the treaty by a two-thirds majority. Many senators, however, had serious concerns and reservations about the treaty. The Republicans enjoyed a two-vote majority in the Senate. As a Democrat, Wilson faced an uphill battle.

New nations and new borders in Europe after World War I

Some opponents of the treaty believed that it was too harsh on Germany, but most of the opposition centered on the League of Nations. They believed the League would take away authority from the U.S. government and draw the nation into future wars. Senate Republicans, led by Henry Cabot Lodge of Massachusetts, demanded certain changes to the League's charter before he would vote in favor of ratification. Wilson refused to make any changes. He chose to fight Lodge and the Republicans rather than compromise the charter.

Wilson believed that he could sway the Senate by marshaling public opinion for the treaty. In September 1919, he went on a speaking tour in the hope of gaining needed public support. He traveled by train through the Western United States, covering some 8,000 miles in three weeks and giving about ten speeches a day. On September 25, the exhausted president collapsed after a speech in Colorado. He suffered a stroke that left him severely debilitated and from which he never fully recovered.

U.S. Senate Rejects the Treaty. When the Senate voted in 1920, Wilson could have achieved ratification if he had agreed to the changes demanded by Lodge and his colleagues. From his sickbed in the White House, Wilson directed his supporters to refuse any compromise, and the treaty was eventually defeated. The United States never joined the League of Nations. In 1921, after Wilson left office, the United States negotiated separate peace treaties with Germany and the other Central Powers, officially ending the war.

Provisions of the Treaty of Versailles

- Germany must accept responsibility for causing World War I; "war-guilt clause"
- Germany required to pay large amount as *reparations*—payments for war damages
- Germany must disband armed forces; promise to keep future army under 100,000 soldiers
- Germany forbidden from manufacturing or importing war materials
- Alsace-Lorraine region returned to France
- German coal-mining region (Saar Basin) under French control for 15 years
- Poland restored as an independent nation with access to Baltic Sea
- Germany must give up all its overseas colonies
- Creation of world peacekeeping organization; League of Nations

★ CONNECTIONS TO WORLD WAR II ★

Harsh conditions imposed on Germany by the Treaty of Versailles contributed to the outbreak of a second world conflict just two decades later. World War II resulted in even more deaths, about 40 million, than World War I. Over half of those killed in World War II were civilians, many of them victims of the Nazi regime.

Resentment of the Versailles Treaty

The Treaty of Versailles dictated severe terms to Germany, which as the defeated nation, had no choice but to accept. Stripped of its colonies and territory, forced to disarm, and required to pay huge reparations, Germans came to deeply resent the treaty and the Allies. The treaty's "guilt clause" also angered the German people. Throughout the 1920s and 1930s, many Germans nurtured a desire for revenge. Adolf Hilter and his National Socialist (Nazi) Party exploited that resentment and anger to seize power in Germany with a promise to restore the nation to its former glory.

Although it fought with the victorious Allies in World War I, Italy was also disappointed by the Treaty of Versailles. The Italians desired territory in what became Yugoslavia but they never received it. Their disappointment coupled with terrible economic conditions following the war, led many Italians to embrace Benito Mussolini and his Fascist Party as an answer to their problems.

Japanese Imperialism in Asia

Following World War I, Japan also turned to a militaristic and totalitarian government as a response to economic and political problems. In 1931, Japan invaded Manchuria in China and set up Manchukuo, a puppet state. The League of Nations was ineffective in opposing Japanese aggression. Japan pushed further south into China, and later into Indochina. The League's promise of collective security and mutual defense came to be seen as empty.

Worldwide Depression

In addition to the weakness of the League of Nations, which was aggravated by the refusal of the United States to join, the world experienced a devastating economic depression in the 1930s. Following the stock market crash in New York City in 1929, the United States experienced a sharp decline in the production of manufactured goods and increased unemployment. Investment and foreign trade, which was hindered by high U.S. tariffs, also suffered. Nations that traded with the United States began experiencing the economic downturn, the economies of most of the world's nations were quickly devastated. By 1931, tens of millions of people around the world were unemployed and struggling to survive the Great Depression.

Most nations responded to these troubles with manifestations of nationalism. Great Britain tried to gain economic advantage by abandoning the gold standard and establishing preferential trade policies with British Commonwealth nations. The United States also gave up the gold standard and declined to enter into an agreement that would have stabilized exchange rates. In Italy, Mussolini established strict economic controls. He addressed the problem of unemployment by increasing the size of Italy's armed forces. Under Hitler and the Nazis, Germany went further than the Italians. Fascism and Nazism were militaristic, totalitarian responses to the problems the emerged after World War I. After strengthening their military forces, both Mussolini and Hitler viewed war as a legitimate means of achieving their goals. Both nations embraced aggressive foreign policies in order to build empires and return their nations to the status of world powers.

Two dictators, left to right, Benito Mussolini receives Adolf Hitler in Venice, Italy, in 1934.

Prelude to World War II

Germany's resentment of the Versailles Treaty, Allied guilt over the treaty, the ineffectiveness of the League of Nations, isolationism in the United States, a global economic depression, and the rise of nazism, fascism, and communism all helped create the conditions that led to the outbreak of a second war in Europe.

German Expansion. After consolidating his power at home, Hitler began moving aggressively in foreign affairs. He openly violated the Versailles Treaty by reintroducing the draft in 1935 and remilitarizing the Rhineland in 1936. Unwilling to risk another war, both Prime Minister Stanley Baldwin of Great Britain and Premier Édouard Daladier of France failed to take military action against Germany. In 1935, Mussolini invaded Ethiopia and won an easy victory. Although the League of Nations condemned Italy's aggression, the League refused to enact an oil embargo against Italy, which would have severely impacted its economy. During the Spanish Civil War, which broke out in 1936, both Hitler and Mussolini sent General Francisco Franco substantial aid in his effort to overthrow Spain's democratically elected government. In 1938, German troops marched into Austria unopposed.

Appeasement. Emboldened by his success and the weakness of Great Britain and France, Hitler turned his attention to the Sudentenland, a German-speaking region of Czechoslovakia. Hitler threatened to seize the Sudentenland by force if Czechoslovakia refused to surrender it to Germany. Baldwin's successor as prime minister, Neville Chamberlain, believed that Germany had been the victim of an injustice because of the harsh Versailles Treaty. Chamberlain thought that further aggression by Germany and another war could be avoided by appeasing Hitler. In an effort to resolve the crisis, Chamberlain, Daladier, Mussolini, and Hitler met at a conference in Munich, Germany. In September 1938, they reached an agreement, the Munich Pact, that ceded the Sudetenland to Germany in exchange for Hitler's assurance that he would not seek additional territory. Upon his return to Great Britain, Chamberlain triumphantly declared that the pact had preserved "peace for our time." Six months later, however, Hitler violated the Munich Pact and seized the rest of Czecho-

"Peace for our time." Neville Chamberlain displays the Munich Pact after returning to England in 1938.

slovakia. Recognizing the failure of appeasement, Chamberlain and Daladier now realized that they could no longer trust Hitler and vowed to declare war against Germany if it invaded Poland, which also had territory that the German dictator wanted.

In August 1939, Germany signed a 10-year nonaggression pact with the Soviet Union. The pact's secret protocols gave the Soviet dictator Joseph Stalin a free hand to act against the Baltic nations of Lithuania, Latvia, and Estonia, and in eastern Poland. The pact cleared the way for Hitler to invade Poland and, at least in the short term, avoid a war with the Soviet Union. On September 1, 1939, Germany invaded Poland. Soviet troops also occupied Eastern Poland. Both Great Britain and France declared war on Germany. A second world war in Europe had begun.

In the Far East, Japan's militaristic government sought to expand its empire. The Japanese wanted to secure new sources of raw materials so they would be less reliant on other countries, especially the United States. Despite protests from the League of Nations, Japan seized Manchuria in 1931 and later occupied more Chinese territory. (In fact, Japan withdrew from the League in 1933.) After the fall of France to Germany in 1940, Japan invaded Indochina, which was then a French colony.

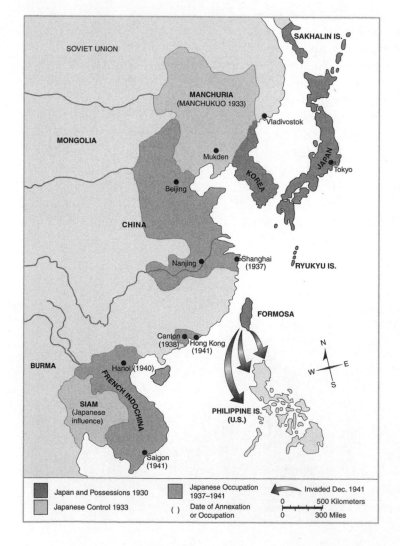

Japanese aggression during the 1930s

President Roosevelt and Japanese Aggression

President Franklin Delano Roosevelt decided that he must respond to Japanese aggression. His approach was to punish Japan with economic sanctions. In July 1941, after he learned of the Japanese invasion of Indochina, Roosevelt froze all Japanese assets in the United States. As a result, trade between Japan and the U.S. ceased. Since the United States was a major supplier of oil to Japan, the Japanese economy suffered. The Japanese government offered to pull out of Indochina in return for aviation fuel supplies from the United States. China's leader, Chiang Kai-shek, and Britain's Prime Minister, Winston Churchill, who had succeeded Chamberlain, strongly opposed the deal and convinced Roosevelt to reject it. Having been rebuffed in their effort to reach an agreement with the United States, Japan again pushed into Indochina in November 1941. Roosevelt sent an angry protest to the Japanese government, which they viewed as insulting and disrespectful. Thinking that the United States would eventually enter the war, Japan decided to strike first and destroy the U.S. Pacific fleet.

Pearl Harbor. At 7:55 on the morning of December 7, 1941, Japanese planes attacked the United States naval base at Pearl Harbor in Hawaii. About an hour later, a second wave of aircraft attacked the unprepared Americans. In less than two hours, the Japanese had crippled the U.S. Pacific fleet. The attack sank four battleships, the *U.S.S. Oklahoma*, the *U.S.S. Arizona*, the *U.S.S. California*, and the *U.S.S. West Virginia*, and heavily damaged four others. Three destroyers and three cruisers suffered extensive damage and nearly all of the military aircraft on the island were destroyed. (The navy's four aircraft carriers were spared because they were out to sea.) Nearly 2,400 Americans died in the surprise Japanese attack.

The *U.S.S. Arizona* sinks after being destroyed by Japanese planes during the surprise attack on Pearl Harbor.

On December 8, the day after the Japanese attack, Roosevelt addressed a joint session of Congress and asked for a declaration of war. In his speech, President Roosevelt called December 7 a "date which will live in infamy." Only one member of Congress voted against the declaration. Three days later, Germany and Italy, allies of Japan, declared war on the United States. Congress responded with a declaration of war against the two Axis nations. The United States had entered World War II.

★ THE U.S.: FROM ISOLATIONISM TO INTERNATIONALISM ★

In the years between World War I and World War II, the United States had returned to a policy of isolationism. Over many decades, Americans generally wanted to keep out of European conflicts and avoid any kind of "entangling alliances." This view, however, never argued for complete isolation from the rest of the world. In fact, many isolationists saw nothing wrong with commercial or financial expansion—backed by military force—especially in the Pacific and Caribbean areas. As the United States became more industrialized and as transportation and communication systems improved, the nation's economy came to depend more on foreign trade and isolationist sentiment began to decline.

Even after the United States broke with tradition and entered World War I, isolationism did not die. Many rural and small-town Americans remained committed to isolationism. After World War I, leaders from farm states such as Robert La Follette of Wisconsin and William Jennings Bryan of Nebraska opposed the Versailles Treaty and the League of Nations.

While the Nazis were marching through Europe and brutally persecuting Jews and other groups during the 1930s, the United States remained strongly isolationist. Between 1935 and 1937, Congress passed several neutrality laws. By 1940, however, many Americans were beginning to reconsider their opposition to entering the war. Germany's crushing defeat of France in 1940 and the Battle of Britain caused many Americans to have second thoughts. Japan's aggressive behavior in the Far East and the threat to America's future security alarmed many people. Economic sanctions were still the preferred method of defense, but the mood began to shift more toward military action. Pearl Harbor ended the debate. Earlier arguments were quickly shelved as the United States prepared for war. By the end of the war, whether it wanted to be or not, the United States was the most powerful nation on the globe.

POINTS TO REMEMBER

- The assassination of Archduke Franz Ferdinand was the immediate cause of hostilities that resulted in World War I.

- Long-term causes of World War I included nationalism, colonial rivalries, a military arms race, and a system of entangling alliances.

- The Allied Powers included Great Britain, France, Russia, and Italy. The Central Powers were composed of Austria-Hungary, Germany, the Ottoman Empire (Turkey), and Bulgaria.

- Despite new war technologies, the first years of World War I became a stalemate due to trench warfare.

- Most Americans were initially isolationist and opposed involvement in World War I. Americans tried to trade with both sides of the conflict.

- Germany's use of unrestricted submarine warfare ultimately led to U.S. entry into World War I.

- The entry of the United States into World War I was decisive in the defeat of Germany and the Central Powers.

- Wilson favored a nonpunitive peace and offered his Fourteen Points to achieve that goal.

- Other Allied leaders wanted revenge and a harsh peace plan; the Versailles Treaty reflected their views.

- President Wilson was unable to obtain ratification of the Versailles Treaty in the U.S. Senate; the United States never joined the League of Nations.

- Harsh terms of the Versailles Treaty, Allied guilt over the treaty, U.S. isolationism, worldwide economic depression, nazism and fascism, communism, and Japanese aggression in the Far East created the conditions that eventually led to the outbreak of World War II and U.S. involvement.

- Isolationism was dominant prior to both World War I and World War II. It took significant acts of aggression against the United States to reverse that sentiment.

- The attack on Pearl Harbor ended the debate between isolationism and internationalism. After World War II, the United States became the leading power in the world.

EXERCISES

CHECKING WHAT YOU HAVE READ

1. The single most important factor in causing the entry of the U.S. into World War I was

   A. Britain's naval blockade
   B. the assassination of Archduke Franz Ferdinand in Sarajevo
   C. unrestricted submarine warfare by Germany
   D. the sinking of the *Sussex*.

2. Which factor guaranteed that a war between Britain and Germany would involve other nations?

   A. the system of entangling alliances
   B. new war technologies such as poison gas and airplanes
   C. the assassination of Archduke Ferdinand in Sarajevo
   D. the rise of nationalism

3. Which of the following was a part of Wilson's Fourteen Points?

   A. German reparations to the Allies
   B. maintenance of national boundaries as they existed when World War I began
   C. a "guilt clause" for Germany
   D. the establishment of a League of Nations

4. Which of the following statements is most accurate?

   A. The U.S. Senate approved the Versailles Treaty with reservations.
   B. The U.S. Senate rejected the Versailles Treaty.
   C. The U.S. joined the League of Nations after the Versailles Treaty was rejected.
   D. Wilson's Fourteen Points rejected of the idea of a League of Nations.

Match the term in the left-hand column with the appropriate answer in the right-hand column.

_____ 5. Central Powers

_____ 6. Germany

_____ 7. Britain

_____ 8. Allies

A. naval blockade of Germany

B. unrestricted submarine warfare

C. Britain, France, Italy, Russia, United States

D. Austria-Hungary, Germany, Turkey, Bulgaria

USING WHAT YOU HAVE READ

In what ways did World War I lead to the outbreak of World War II? Support your answer with evidence.

THINKING ABOUT WHAT YOU HAVE READ

Prior to the entry of the United States into World War I, two views prevailed. One favored preparedness, increasing our military strength to be ready for war. The other opposed military buildup and advocated pacifism. Pacifists argued that if the United States prepared for war, it was more likely to use the weapons that had been developed. Choose one of the points of view and write a position statement that explains the reasons for your opinion.

SKILLS

Creating a Propaganda Poster

Study the propaganda poster on page 274. To what emotions does the poster appeal? Design a propaganda poster that either supports or opposes the entry of the United States into World War I.

CHAPTER 20

WORLD WAR II, THE COLD WAR, AND CONTEMPORARY CONFLICTS

BENCHMARK:

Analyze connections between World War II, the Cold War, and contemporary conflicts.

This benchmark addresses the connections that exist among World War II, the Cold War, and more contemporary conflicts such as the Korean and Vietnam wars. As with the previous benchmark, the emphasis is on the *connections*. In discussing United States history, the focus is the Cold War. How did World War II influence the beginnings of the Cold War? And what impact did Cold War policy have on later conflicts? Specific events that might be used in OGT questions include the Marshall Plan, the strategy of containment, the Truman Doctrine, the Berlin blockade, the Cuban missile crisis, and both the Korean and Vietnam wars. OGT items will not address the conduct of either of those wars, but rather the connections that may exist among those conflicts, World War II, and/or the Cold War.

Just as following World War I the victors created conditions that led to a second global conflict, leaders of the nations that defeated Germany and Japan in World War II—driven by economic, philosophical, military, and political rivalries—shaped a world that produced another kind of conflict, a "cold war." The two great superpowers that emerged from World War II represented antagonistic political and economic systems. Each side was determined to protect and advance its view of the world. World affairs for the next forty-plus years would be shaped by this rivalry—the Cold War—between the United States and the Union of Soviet Socialist Republics (U.S.S.R.).

How events are connected.

★ ORIGINS OF THE COLD WAR ★

The U.S.S.R. suffered severe losses during World War II. Over 7 million Soviet citizens and 11 million soldiers died, thousands of towns and villages were leveled, and millions of homes were destroyed. At the end of the war, about 25 million Soviet people were homeless and hungry. Leaders of the U.S.S.R. wanted to protect its borders from any further invasion, especially from Western Europe. During Napoleon's reign in France in the early 1800s, as well as in both world wars of the 20th century, invaders entered Russia (later, the U.S.S.R.) from the west. After Hitler's defeat in World War II, Soviet leaders moved to make sure that Germany would pose no future threat. To protect against future attack, Soviet leaders established a buffer zone of satellite nations around its western flank.

The Soviets were also desperate to rebuild their war-ravaged economy. Hunger and homelessness were immediate concerns that Soviet planners needed to address. They hoped to create an industrial giant to rival the United States in world trade and, subsequently, in global influence.

The situation was different for the United States after World War II. Although hundreds of thousands of Americans died in the course of defeating Germany and Japan, the United States did not experience an invasion or any devastation. In fact, the United States was stronger than ever at the end of the war. Business was booming. Economists estimated that the nation controlled about half of the world's wealth. Americans glimpsed a future different from that envisioned by Soviet Communists. Americans, for the most part, believed that the rest of the world should model itself after the United States. That is, they envisioned a world in which other nations would adopt the democratic, capitalistic way of life that U.S. troops had died to protect—a world where free trade, free elections, and business expansion were the norm.

A Clash of Systems

These two opposing worldviews—undemocratic socialism in the Soviet Union versus democratic capitalism in the United States—were the foundations of diplomacy and global politics for the next several decades. Most nations of the world, willingly or not, lined up with one side or the other. And, until the collapse of the Soviet Union in 1991, the Cold War between these two opposing camps defined international relations. The war was "cold" because it did not involve actual combat between the U.S. and the U.S.S.R. Rather, both sides used military threats, espionage, propaganda, economic influence, and politics to achieve their goals. Most importantly, after 1949 both sides possessed nuclear weapons, and on several occasions the world was perilously close to nuclear war. The Cold War did not produce the massive loss of life that World War II had, but it did result in heightened tensions and huge military expenditures to defend against the opposing side. Moreover, limited and "proxy" conflicts—such as Korea and Vietnam—arose out of Cold War tension and perceived threats. For over 40 years, the Cold War defined much of what went on among nations around the globe.

Test Yourself
Explain how the worldviews of the United States and the Soviet Union differed.

Yalta Conference. In February 1945, the "big-three" leaders—President Roosevelt, Soviet Premier Joseph Stalin, and British Prime Minister Winston Churchill—met at Yalta on the Black Sea. The purpose of the meeting was to make decisions about what the world would look like after World War II. The victors wanted to create "spheres of influence" and establish national borders that would work to their advantage. At that time, Soviet armies were moving swiftly across Eastern Europe on their way to Germany. Churchill, on the other hand, hoped to save as much of the British Empire as possible, and President Roosevelt sought to advance U.S. interests, including the spread of democracy and favorable trade relationships. Roosevelt also needed Soviet cooperation once the European war ended, to help defeat Japanese forces in the Pacific. During the talks, the three leaders agreed that the Soviet Union would join the fight against Japan in return for territory in Asia. Stalin further agreed to support the establishment of the United Nations.

Sitting, left to right, Winston Churchill, Franklin Delano Roosevelt, and Joseph Stalin at Yalta in February 1945

The cooperation experienced at Yalta was short-lived. The issue of what to do with Germany and Eastern Europe presented irreconcilable differences among the three nations. The Soviets wanted to impose heavy reparations on Germany. Britain and the United States realized that the defeated Germans would not be able to make exorbitant payments, and were afraid of being pressured into providing financial support to help Germany meet its obligations. Instead of reparation payments, the leaders agreed to divide Germany. Each victorious nation would control the part of Germany that it occupied at the war's conclusion.

Soviet control over the Eastern European nations posed an equally difficult problem. By war's end, the U.S.S.R. already controlled many of the nations along its western border, and Stalin insisted that Britain and the United States agree to permit Soviet domination in Czechoslovakia, Hungary, Austria, Bulgaria, Romania, and Poland. Roosevelt and Churchill objected to Stalin's demands, but there was really little they could do to remove Soviet forces from these nations. Roosevelt still had the war against Japan in the Pacific to fight, and he was in no position to pressure the Soviets. Eventually, Churchill and Roosevelt agreed to Soviet domination in the area, but demanded that free elections be held at the earliest possible date. In October 1945, the United Nations signed off on the Yalta accords, giving the U.S.S.R. control over most of Eastern Europe.

Potsdam Conference. In April 1945, shortly after the Yalta talks, President Roosevelt died. Vice President Harry S. Truman was sworn in as president. Truman was inexperienced in foreign affairs. His foreign policy advisers were becoming increasingly worried about continued Soviet expansion and pushed for Truman to take a hard line against Stalin. In July 1945, Truman, Stalin, and the new British Prime Minister Clement Attlee, who had just ousted Churchill in the national election, met in Potsdam, Germany, to settle unresolved issues from Yalta. By then, tensions between the United States and the Soviet Union had increased significantly. At the meeting, Truman took a tough stance. At that time, the United States was the only nation in possession of the atomic bomb, and Truman believed he could negotiate from a position of strength. At Potsdam, the three leaders reached agreement on Germany. The Germans were to completely destroy their war industries and totally disarm. Germany would remain divided, and each occupying nation could require war reparations from its own zone. (The French also occupied a fourth German zone.)

The Potsdam talks settled the German question for the time being, but over the next few months distrust between Truman and Stalin continued to grow. The Soviet Union imposed harsh regimes on the nations it controlled in Eastern Europe. Several opposition leaders were executed after show trials, and the promised elections were anything but "free" or democratic. In February 1946, just a year after Yalta and seven months after Potsdam, Stalin proclaimed that capitalism, and by implication the United States, threatened world peace. He further predicted that capitalism and communism were on a collision course. The U.S.S.R., he announced, would discontinue trade with Western nations and would develop weapons systems with which it could defend itself. Stalin's *saber rattling* was a clear message that the U.S.S.R. planned to develop atomic weapons.

Test Yourself
Compare the Yalta talks with the talks in Potsdam. How were they alike? How were they different?

During a trip to the United States shortly after Stalin warned the West of his intentions, Churchill made a famous speech in Missouri in which he said that in Eastern Europe "an iron curtain has descended across the continent." The democratic nations of the West, Churchill urged, must join forces to combat the threat of Soviet expansion throughout the world. The United States must take the lead in combating Soviet Communist influence and aggression around the globe. The Cold War was clearly under way.

Containment and the Truman Doctrine

Early in 1946, George F. Kennan, a U.S. diplomat stationed in Moscow, developed a strategy to deal with Stalin and the Soviet threat. He sent his ideas to President Truman and publicized them in an article for *Foreign Affairs*, and they soon became the basis of U.S. foreign policy in the Cold War. Kennan's basic premise was that the U.S.S.R. must be confronted and contained whenever and wherever it sought to extend its influence. Soviet leaders, Kennan argued, were averse to risk-taking; they were cautious and reluctant to engage in confrontation. When faced with firm resistance, they would back off. Kennan did not think that the Soviets could be ousted from Eastern Europe, but that they should be contained everywhere else.

Truman agreed with Kennan's appraisal, and the *containment policy* quickly evolved into the Truman Doctrine, which would soon be put to the test. In 1946, civil war broke out in Greece between Soviet-backed Communist rebels and the Greek government, which was allied to Britain. In early 1947, Britain, still recovering from the devastation of World War II, looked to the United States to help the Greeks combat the rebels. Truman wanted to support the anticommunist Greek government, but Congress did not want to increase taxes to pay for additional expenditures. At the same time, the U.S.S.R. was trying to force Turkey into granting it access rights to the Dardanelles, the straits that connect the Black Sea to the Mediterranean Sea. Truman reacted to these threats with a forceful speech to Congress in which he asked for $400 million to aid the Greeks and Turks. Thus, the Truman Doctrine was born, and it proved to be successful. In 1949, the Greek Communists were defeated, and U.S. aid helped the Turks resist Soviet pressure. For the next two decades, containment, embodied in the Truman Doctrine, became the driving force in U.S. diplomacy and foreign policy.

Harry Truman, the first Cold War president

Test Yourself
How was the Truman Doctrine related to the policy of containment?

The Marshall Plan

Two years after the end of World War II, much of Europe remained economically depressed. As nations worked to rebuild factories, roads, and power systems, people struggled to find work, housing, and food. Millions were sick, hungry, and homeless. In France and Italy, Communist parties, appealing to people's frustration over economic hard times, grew in strength. Truman and his advisers worried about the growth of communism in Europe, but they also realized that military power was not always the answer. U.S. businesses and industries needed Europe as a market for their goods. A strong U.S. economy depended upon an economically revitalized Europe.

Under the leadership of Secretary of State George Marshall, the United States developed a plan to help the European nations rebuild their economies. Between 1948 and 1951, the Marshall Plan provided over $13 billion in assistance to 16 European nations. In order to obtain monetary assistance under the plan, the nations had to use the funds to buy American goods. U.S. officials invited the U.S.S.R. and its satellites in Eastern Europe to participate, but Stalin denied them permission. The Soviets objected to the plan because they believed it was intended to enable the United States to dominate Europe and weaken Soviet influence there.

The Marshall Plan achieved its objectives, exceeding the most optimistic predictions. By 1952, Western European industrial output had increased nearly 65 percent. American businesses prospered as well. Moreover, as Western European economies improved, the appeal of communism declined. In this respect, the Marshall Plan was clearly successful.

The Berlin Crisis

This did not mean, however, that Cold War tensions decreased during these years. On the contrary, relations between the U.S.S.R. and the United States worsened as the Marshall Plan succeeded. Germany, and more particularly Berlin, became the center of increased tension. The United States desired an economically strong Germany that could contribute to the recovery of Western Europe and at the same time help contain the threat of Communist or Soviet expansion. The United States, France, and Britain planned to rebuild Germany's infrastructure in their zones so that a new Germany could contribute to Europe's economic recovery. The ultimate goal was to build a democratic German nation in which nazism, fascism, or communism would have no appeal. The U.S.S.R. felt threatened by these efforts. When the United States, Britain, and France announced a new currency for their zones, the Soviets were outraged. They saw it as a step toward merging three zones into one stronger entity. In June 1948, the Soviets blocked all roads and railways to Berlin. They also cut off electrical power to West Berlin. The Soviets hoped either to force the Allies to leave Berlin or drop their plan for unifying West Germany into one nation. The 2 million inhabitants of West Berlin were literally trapped. They had no supply routes, no way to get food, clothing, fuel, or medicine.

Berlin Airlift. How did President Truman respond? His options were limited. He could have tried to open transportation routes into Berlin with military

Divided Germany, divided Berlin, and Soviet satellites in Eastern Europe, after World War II

force, but this would have risked all-out war with the U.S.S.R. He could have allowed the Soviets to take control of Berlin, but that would have violated his containment policy and given the U.S.S.R. a huge victory in the Cold War. Truman's advisers developed a different and daring plan that called for a massive airlift of supplies to the people of West Berlin. This avoided a direct mili-

A U.S. military cargo plane delivers food and supplies to the people of West Berlin.

tary confrontation with the Soviets. For 324 days, C-47 and C-54 cargo planes flew vital supplies around the clock into Berlin's Templehof airfield. During that time, some 277,000 flights ferried in about 2 million tons of supplies. The success of the Berlin Airlift became an embarrassment to Stalin and a huge propaganda victory for the United States. Finally, in May 1949, Stalin relented and canceled the failed blockade.

Shortly after Stalin lifted the Berlin blockade, the United States, France, and Britain agreed to form the Federal Republic of Germany (commonly referred to as West Germany). The strong West German state that Stalin hoped to prevent through the blockade became a reality. Not long after that, Stalin retaliated by forming the German Democratic Republic, which was popularly known as East Germany. Throughout the rest of the Cold War, divided Germany and Berlin became a metaphor for the American-led struggle against Communist expansion.

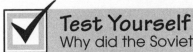

Test Yourself
Why did the Soviets cut off access to West Berlin?

Throughout the late 1940s and 1950s, the Cold War intensified. In 1949, two important events caused a heightened sense of urgency. In August, the Soviet Union detonated its first atomic bomb. By the end of 1949, a long civil war in China resulted in the establishment of a Communist government. Not coincidentally, the United States, Canada, Britain, and nine other European nations formed the North Atlantic Treaty Organization (NATO) to defend the West against Soviet aggression. NATO was a mutual defense agreement in which nations promised to consider an attack on one member the same as an attack on all. NATO nations would go to the aid of any member that was attacked. In 1955, the U.S.S.R. and its allies formed a counteralliance called the Warsaw Pact, thereby increasing fear and anxiety during the Cold War.

National Security and the Arms Race

An important and costly feature of the Cold War was an intense and sustained arms race between the United States and the Soviet Union. In 1950, President Truman authorized a secret, comprehensive review of United States military strength. The report, *NSC-68: United States Objectives and Programs for National Security*, maintained that the United States should operate under the assumption that the U.S.S.R. had a "design for world domination." NSC-68 also warned that to guarantee its security, the United States had to increase its nuclear arsenal and enlarge its capacity to fight conventional wars against Soviet aggression. According to the report, the United States should

> develop a level of military readiness which can be maintained as long as necessary as a deterrent to Soviet aggression, as indispensable support to our political attitude toward the U.S.S.R., as a source of encouragement to nations resisting Soviet political aggression, and as an adequate basis for immediate military commitments and for rapid mobilization should war prove unavoidable.

Korean War

To implement the NSC-68 recommendations, the United States would have to triple its defense budget. Truman had the difficult job of convincing a reluctant Congress that a tax increase was necessary to insure America's military preparedness. In June 1950, just as Truman was about to approach Congress with his budget requests, some 75,000 troops from Communist North Korea pushed across the 38th parallel in a surprise attack on South Korea, an American ally. Korea had been divided after World War II, and the North Koreans wanted to reunite the nation under their Communist government. Two days later, Truman ordered naval and air support for South Korea, and he sought assistance from the United Nations Security Council. Soviet representatives on the Security Council were absent and therefore unable to veto the U.S. request. The Security Council passed a resolution condemning the invasion and authorized the use of military force to expel North Korean troops from South Korea.

The Korean War lasted until 1953. At the end of the fighting, Korea remained divided at the 38th parallel, and the negotiated armistice called for a demilitarized zone (DMZ) on both sides of the border. Despite spending over $64 billion and losing over 54,000 American soldiers in the conflict, the United States did not emerge as a clear-cut winner, nor did the war resolve issues in Asia. It did, however, result in the huge military buildup called for in NSC-68, and it prompted the founding of SEATO, the Southeast Asia Treaty Organization, patterned after NATO in Europe. Despite the fact that Congress never officially declared war in Korea, the American public generally supported the war as necessary to combat the threat of Communist aggression and expansion. The Korean War also set a precedent for later limited and undeclared conflicts, such as U.S. intervention in the Dominican Republic in 1965 and the Vietnam War.

Cuban Missile Crisis

Following World War II, nationalism energized many people in Latin America. For many years, U.S. mining and agricultural corporations had been wringing enormous profits out of various Latin American countries. Workers and their families, however, shared little in the wealth they helped produce. Leaders of nationalist movements used this resentment against American business leaders and corporations to foment unrest and revolution.

In Cuba during the 1950s, U.S. business interests held tremendous power over the economy. Great numbers of Cubans lived in dire poverty. In 1958, a young lawyer named Fidel Castro led a revolt against the Cuban government, then headed by Fulgencio Batista, a dictator friendly to the United States and American business interests. Castro's goal was to overthrow Batista and nationalize foreign businesses. Castro succeeded in ousting Batista in 1959, and by 1961, had seized all U.S. businesses. President Dwight Eisenhower broke off diplomatic relations with the Castro government. Castro, a Communist, signed a trade agreement with the U.S.S.R.

In 1961, John F. Kennedy became president. Like Eisenhower, Kennedy was concerned about having a Soviet ally so close to the United States. (Only

Fidel Castro, a Communist, seized power in Cuba and aligned himself with the Soviet Union, which alarmed the United States.

90 miles separate Cuba from the tip of Florida.) In April 1961, Kennedy decided to act. He approved an invasion on the Cuban mainland by an anti-Castro Cuban group trained by U.S. military personnel. They landed at the Bay of Pigs in Cuba with the intent of igniting an uprising against Castro. The invasion failed miserably. U.S. officials were embarrassed, and the United States appeared weak and ineffective.

Kennedy, however, kept pressure on Castro. Despite the Bay of Pigs fiasco, he still wanted to force the Cuban leader out of office. Using Central Intelligence Agency (CIA) operatives and other covert means, the Kennedy administration attempted to disrupt Cuban trade, trained more Cuban exiles to conduct raids, and even plotted to assassinate Castro. None of these efforts were successful. They did succeed in angering Castro and Nikita Khrushchev, the Soviet leader. Khrushchev wanted to protect his foothold in the Caribbean, while Castro felt threatened by the military might of the United States. Consequently, they decided to install Soviet missiles in Cuba that could easily strike the United States if war broke out.

In October 1962, U.S. spy planes taking surveillance photographs of Cuba discovered the missiles. During the following tense week, Kennedy administration officials met to set an appropriate response. Some advisers wanted to attack Cuba and destroy the missiles, risking Soviet retaliation and nuclear war. Acting on the advice of his Secretary of Defense, Robert McNamara, Kennedy chose a different strategy. He decided to impose a naval blockade of Cuba in order to block any further shipments of missiles. He also demanded that Khrushchev remove the missiles already in place or American forces would destroy them. Kennedy made his decision public on national television just eight days after the discovery of the missiles. He dispatched 180 ships to cut off shipping lanes and ordered the air force to keep bombers in the air. U.S. military forces were on the highest alert. The United States and the Soviet Union were closer to war than any time previously during the Cold War. After four nerve-wracking days, Khrushchev backed down and agreed to remove the missiles from Cuba. In return, he demanded that the United States promise never to attack Cuba and to remove missiles it had stationed in Turkey. Kennedy agreed never to attack Cuba and remove the U.S.'s missiles in Turkey that were obsolete anyway. The crisis ended.

Test Yourself
What event precipitated the Cuban missile crisis?

While the Cuban missile crisis brought the United States and the Soviet Union to the brink of war, its aftermath witnessed some relaxation of Cold War tensions. The two countries remained adversaries, but the crisis helped their leaders recognize that communication and negotiation were important to avoid hostilities that could lead to nuclear war. Despite that realization, however, the arms race actually heated up after the Cuban crisis. The Soviets responded to their humiliation in Cuba with increased weapons production, and the U.S. government and American public viewed the stand-off as a rationale for maintaining military and nuclear strength, as well as confirmation of the policy of containment.

"Let's Get A Lock For This Thing"

After the Cuban missile crisis, John F. Kennedy and Nikita Khrushchev realized they had to work together to defuse tensions that could lead to nuclear war.

—from *Straight Herblock* (Simon & Schuster, 1964)

Vietnam War

Not long after the resolution of events in Cuba, another major conflict grew out of Cold War antagonisms and distrust. Since the end of World War II, the French had been waging a civil war with nationalist rebels in the Southeast Asian nation of Vietnam. The Communist rebels, led by Ho Chi Minh, wanted to drive the French out of their homeland. Fighting continued for several years, and the United States helped finance French operations against the rebels. In 1954, President Eisenhower explained his support for anticommunist regimes like the French in Vietnam on the basis of the *domino theory*. If one country in Southeast Asia fell to communism, Eisenhower explained, others would be sure to follow, just like a row of dominos when the first one is knocked over. The domino metaphor was a twist on the idea of containment.

Test Yourself
Explain the domino theory and its relationship to containment.

In 1954, Vietnamese forces defeated the French at Dien Bien Phu. Following this victory, diplomats from several nations met in Geneva, Switzerland, to negotiate a peace. The resulting treaty temporarily divided Vietnam at the 17th parallel, with the Communists controlling the northern half. National elections were to be held in 1956 to reunite the country under one government. Although the United States participated in the talks, it never signed the treaty. Fearful that the Communist rebels would win, Ngo Dinh Diem, the South Vietnamese leader, canceled the promised elections. The rebel groups formed the National Liberation Front (NLF) to lead a resistance movement.

The NLF, or Vietcong, used guerrilla tactics against the South Vietnamese government, assassinating hundreds of officials. The NLF had close ties to Ho Chi Minh in North Vietnam, who helped supply Vietcong forces in the South. Communist China also provided aid to Vietcong rebels. President Kennedy believed it was important to contain the spread of communism in this part of the world, but he was reluctant to support Diem's corrupt government in the South. Eventually, Kennedy demanded that Diem undertake reforms to clean up his government in return for U.S. aid and military training. By 1963, about 16,000 U.S. military advisers were in Vietnam, training South Vietnamese forces.

Despite his assurances to U.S. officials, Diem did not institute serious reforms. South Vietnamese government officials regularly stole much of the aid sent by the U.S. to support Diem's fight against the Vietcong. Moreover, the South Vietnamese troops were unsuccessful in fighting Vietcong forces. In 1963, a group of South Vietnamese army officers, with the support of the CIA, staged a coup and took control of the government, killing Diem in the process. Three weeks later, Lee Harvey Oswald assassinated President Kennedy in Dallas, Texas. Lyndon Johnson, the vice president, was sworn in as the new president. Vietnam was now his problem.

Like Kennedy, Johnson believed that Communist rebels in Vietnam were a threat to the global balance of power. But Johnson needed the support of Congress to increase troop strength in Vietnam. In early August 1964, he used reports of an alleged North Vietnamese attack on two U.S. ships in the Gulf of Tonkin to make his appeal. On August 7, Congress approved the Gulf of Tonkin Resolution. The resolution gave the president the power to take "all necessary measures to repel any armed attack against the forces of the United States, and to prevent further aggression." Johnson now had the authority he needed to expand the war against the Vietcong and North Vietnamese. It was not until several years later that the public found out that the two U.S. ships attacked were actually helping South Vietnamese troops conduct a raid on North Vietnamese islands in the gulf.

Over the next 11 years, until the fall of Saigon in 1975, about 58,000 American military personnel died in Vietnam. Four presidents—Eisenhower, Kennedy, Johnson, and Nixon—tried to prevent rebels from gaining control of Vietnam and reuniting it under a Communist government, but they all failed. In the end, Cold War–inspired fear of Communist aggression spawned a controversial war that resulted in large-scale, sometimes violent, protests at home, and over a million deaths, including the Vietnamese, on the battlefield.

POINTS TO REMEMBER

- The Cold War arose out of differing worldviews among the superpowers after World War II. The Soviet Union was a Communist, undemocratic nation; the United States was democratic and capitalist.

- United States foreign policy during the Cold War was based upon the policy of containment.

- The policy of containment accepted Soviet domination of Eastern Europe but favored confrontation with communism everywhere else.

- After World War I, both the Truman Doctrine and the Marshall Plan were an outgrowth of containment.

- The Soviet Union refused to participate in the Marshall Plan.

- The Marshall Plan succeeded in restoring and strengthening the economies of Western Europe and the United States.

- The Marshall Plan succeeded in weakening the appeal of communism in Western Europe.

- The United States found a nonviolent way to resolve the Berlin crisis: a massive airlift of supplies to the people of West Berlin.

- Government report NSC-68 called for a massive buildup of the U.S. military and nuclear weapons. The Korean War helped President Truman win congressional approval for the plan.

- Feeding on nationalistic, anti-American sentiment, Cuban rebel leader Fidel Castro rose to power in 1958 and allied Cuba with the Soviet Union.

- The Cuban missile crisis brought the world closer to nuclear war than at any other time. The crisis was defused when Khrushchev backed down and removed the missiles from Cuba.

- The Vietnam War was partly a result of U.S. government leaders' belief in the "domino theory" and the need to contain communism in Southeast Asia.

EXERCISES

CHECKING WHAT YOU HAVE READ

Connect the name in the left column with the appropriate term in the right column.

1. World War II
2. Berlin
3. Greek rebels
4. Marshall Plan
5. NATO
6. NSC-68
7. Khrushchev
8. Vietnam War

A. first test of Truman Doctrine
B. aided economic recovery in Europe
C. Yalta talks
D. airlift of supplies
E. missile crisis
F. Gulf of Tonkin Resolution
G. mutual defense pact
H. U.S. report advocating military and nuclear strength

USING WHAT YOU HAVE READ

Interview someone in your community who served in the Vietnam War. Ask how the person felt about the war at the time, and whether that view has changed. If the view has changed, ask how and why. Write a brief report of your findings.

THINKING ABOUT WHAT YOU HAVE READ

Use the library or the Internet to do further research about the Potsdam Conference. Compare and contrast the concerns and interests of the "Big Three" leaders—Truman, Attlee, and Stalin—who attended the Potsdam talks. Use a table like the one below to make your comparison.

Truman	Attlee	Stalin

WRITING A PERSUASIVE LETTER

You are a State Department official in the late 1940s. Write a letter to President Truman to persuade him to use the policy of containment in dealing with the Soviet Union. Use specific examples in your arguments.

SKILLS

Creating a Web

Use a web similar to the one below to show connections between World War II, the Cold War, and other contemporary conflicts such as Korea and Vietnam. Use arrows to show cause and effect when appropriate. One connection is provided as an example. Make as many other connections as you can by adding additional bubbles.

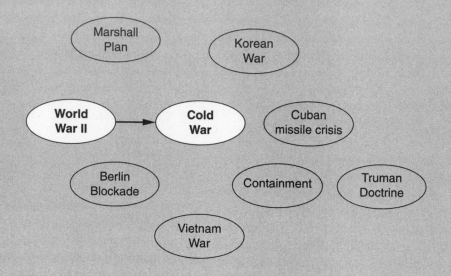

CHAPTER 21

TWENTIETH-CENTURY DOMESTIC AFFAIRS

BENCHMARK:

Identify major historical patterns in the domestic affairs of the United States during the twentieth century and explain their significance.

This benchmark requires you to know the important domestic affairs of the United States after World War I. You will be expected to analyze events and trends that took place in the United States from the 1920s through the 1970s.

This chapter will prepare you to discuss the key issues during those six decades. It covers the post-World War I Red Scare, McCarthyism, the space race, and other events of the Cold War. It analyzes economic changes such as stock market speculation during the 1920s and the 1929 stock market crash, agricultural problems in the Dust Bowl, the Great Depression, the New Deal, industrial mobilization for World War II, wartime changes in the workforce, the prosperity that followed World War II, and the migration of African Americans from the South to the North.

This chapter also covers various civil rights issues. These include denying women the right to vote before 1920, immigration restrictions, nativism, race riots, the Ku Klux Klan, and the internment of Japanese-Americans during World War II. It describes the actions taken to address these problems such as the successful women's suffrage movement, the Supreme Court's 1954 *Brown* v. *Board of Education of Topeka* decision, which outlawed racial segregation in U.S. public schools, and the civil rights movement of the 1950s and 1960s. Finally, this chapter looks at some of the artistic trends of the Roaring Twenties, such as the Harlem Renaissance, and major events of the 1960s and 1970s, such as the anti–Vietnam War protests and the counterculture movement.

★ THE ROARING TWENTIES ★

The decade of the 1920s is often portrayed as a period of prosperity and frivolity. It is remembered for Prohibition, flappers, flagpole sitters, ragtime music, the Harlem Renaissance, and gangsters. While many Americans enjoyed prosperity, the good life did not reach everyone. Despite the popular Hollywood images of the decade, the 1920s were, in fact, marked by conflict and turmoil.

During that period, some Americans welcomed change. Others did not. Many Americans rejected people with new ideas about society and politics and developed an exaggerated fear of immigrants, radicals, and minority groups.

Red Scare

Immediately following World War I, people in the United States became intensely suspicious of radicals—especially those from foreign nations. The Bolshevik Revolution in Russia in 1917 led to fear of a similar uprising in the United States. Fear of communism, political violence, and labor unrest became known as the Red Scare.

After World War I, factories that made armaments and other war supplies closed, throwing many people, especially new immigrants who could get only factory jobs, out of work. Consequently, labor unrest increased. As some people began to see immigrants, labor activists, and political radicals as threats, they felt that government officials should respond harshly to strikers and other workers who demonstrated dissatisfaction with labor conditions.

International Workers of the World (IWW). One incident involving a labor group called the International Workers of the World (IWW) exemplifies this intolerant attitude. The IWW was strongly influenced by the Socialist Party. Most of its leaders had objected to World War I and had refused to comply with the draft. This caused many Americans to consider them unpatriotic and deepened their suspicion that IWW members were plotting against the U.S. government. On January 21, 1919, the workers in a Seattle shipyard went out on strike, which set off a series of other strikes in the same area. Newspapers all over the United States covered these strikes and exaggerated the impact they were having. The citizens of Seattle became fearful that the strikes would shut down their city and unleash the forces of anarchy.

Although the leaders of the IWW were not responsible for the situation, the general public blamed them. Remembering that the IWW had Socialist leanings, people claimed that its leaders were reds, left-wing radicals who wanted to overthrow the U.S. government and establish a Communist country. In 1919–1920, U.S. Attorney General A. Mitchell Palmer directed federal agents to arrest more than 150 leaders of the IWW. Many of these leaders were tried, convicted, and sentenced to lengthy prison terms. Palmer also deported thousands of aliens suspected of having radical views. In Indiana, hatred of political radicalism was so intense that a jury acquitted the killer of an immigrant who had shouted, "To hell with the United States."

Sacco and Vanzetti. The most controversial case against immigrant radicals took place in Massachusetts. In 1920, the South Braintree police arrested two Italian immigrants, Nicola Sacco and Bartolomeo Vanzetti, who were also admitted anarchists, for robbery and murder. Some observers noted that the pair's political beliefs prejudiced members of the jury, who convicted them of the charges. Several appeals for a new trial were denied, and Sacco and Vanzetti were executed in 1927. Thousands of people around the world protested the verdict and executions, believing that they were motivated by ethnic, class, and political prejudice against the two men.

Nativism. Fear of and antagonism toward foreigners—often referred to as nativism—also manifested themselves in increasingly restrictive government immigration policies. Prior to World War I, immigration to the United States from Europe was open. There were no quotas and very few restrictions.

Nicola Sacco (right) and
Bartolomeo Vanzetti during
their trial

Business and factory owners wanted cheap labor to run their factories and
build their railroads. After the war, however, sentiment in favor of restricting
immigration increased. While the war was being fought, immigration to the
United States slowed to a trickle. With the end of hostilities and the return of
troops to the United States, some Americans began to fear that immigrants
would take jobs away from returning soldiers. Unions such as the American
Federation of Labor (AF of L) supported restrictions on immigration in order
to protect postwar jobs, while business leaders favored restrictions because
they feared the importation of political radicalism from Europe.

By 1920, immigration rates were on the rise again, approaching prewar levels. Responding to the growing nativist opposition to immigration, in 1921,
Congress passed the Quota Act, which put a 350,000-person cap on annual
immigration from a single country. It restricted the proportion of immigrants
coming from countries in the Eastern Hemisphere to 3 percent of the number

"The Only Way to Handle It,"
a cartoon arguing in favor of
immigration quotas during
the 1920s

of people from those countries who had been living in the United States in 1910. Since the U.S. immigrant population of 1910 had consisted mostly of people from Northern and Western Europe, most of the immigrants allowed into the United States in 1921 were also from those regions.

In 1924, Congress tightened restrictions even further by passing the National Origins Act, which reduced the total number of immigrants per year to just 150,000 from a single country. Quotas were also reduced, to 2 percent of each nationality's proportion of the population in 1890. This change severely restricted immigrants from Southern and Eastern European nations such as Italy and Russia, which many Americans believed were breeding grounds for radicalism. This act totally excluded Asians. Like the Quota Act of 1921, the National Origins Act favored immigrants from Western European nations such as England and Germany.

Test Yourself
What caused the Red Scare of the 1920s?

The Great Migration and Racial Tensions

Another demographic phenomenon of the 1920s was the migration of African Americans from the rural South to industrial cities in the North. Before World War I, the vast majority of African Americans lived on farms in the South. During the war, factory jobs drew African Americans northward, and the migration continued after the fighting ceased. Over a million African Americans left the South after the war, eager to escape racism and poverty resulting from the system of sharecropping. Most Southern African Americans were *share-croppers*—tenant farmers who gave their landlords a share of their crops in exchange for use of the land and the equipment to farm it. Many African Americans were forced into sharecropping because they were poor and unable to pay rent to lease farmland and buy farm equipment. This system kept them trapped in poverty. Between 1910 and 1920, the African American population in Cleveland increased over 300 percent, and in Detroit it rose over 600 percent. Most Northern industrial centers experienced similar increases.

Racial Tensions. Many white American troops returning from World War I saw the African Americans who had served with them and those who were migrating from the South as rivals for jobs and housing. Tension and conflict often resulted from this rivalry. Some cities adopted residential segregation laws that restricted where African Americans could live. After the Supreme Court found those discriminatory ordinances unconstitutional in 1917, whites inserted clauses into deeds that restricted the sale of property to African Americans. As a result, African Americans were forced to live in ghettos or segregated neighborhoods. The most famous example of an African American ghetto was Harlem in New York City. It quickly became the center of African American culture in the United States and hosted a movement of African American art and literature that became known as the Harlem Renaissance.

Race Riots and Lynchings. The racial tension between whites and African Americans occasionally escalated into violence. Race riots, in which white mobs attacked African Americans in their neighborhoods, took place in several U.S. cities, including Washington, D.C.; Chicago, Illinois; Longview, Texas; Knoxville, Tennessee; and Omaha, Nebraska. In 1921, white mobs razed as many as 40 city blocks in Tulsa, Oklahoma, destroying over 2,000 homes, businesses, and public buildings and killing a number of African Americans. Even small towns fell victim to mob rage. In 1923, a mob searching for an accused rapist completely burned down the little town of Rosewood, Florida, killing at least eight people and injuring dozens.

Violence against African Americans also took the form of lynching. Between 1920 and 1930, hundreds of African Americans were lynched in the United States. The exact number will never be known because many were never reported or recorded. Although lynching did not disappear entirely for many years, public opposition to lynching and attempts to pass federal anti-lynching laws in the 1920s helped to focus attention on the practice, and the number of lynchings decreased in the subsequent decades. The last known lynching in the United States took place in Mississippi in 1964.

Ku Klux Klan. The 1920s also witnessed a revival of the Ku Klux Klan (KKK), a racist organization originally founded during Reconstruction by white southerners. The Klan reemerged in great strength in several places across the United States. In became particularly strong in the South, in Midwestern states such as Indiana and Oklahoma, and in many cities, including Detroit, Atlanta, and Chicago. In 1923, one Klan rally in Indiana drew over 10,000 people. At the height of its power in the early 1920s, the Klan claimed over 5 million members nationally.

The Ku Klux Klan marches in Washington, D.C., in 1925.

Klansmen claimed that the organization stood for Christian values and true Americanism. In reality, the KKK fed upon hate and fear. KKK members feared change and anyone who was not white and Protestant. They feared and reviled immigrants, Catholics, Jews, and African Americans. When the Klan reached its pinnacle of power in the early 1920s, a number of U.S. senators and representatives, and hundreds of state and local officials, were KKK members. During its peak, the KKK sponsored elaborate cross-burning rallies and marched openly in parades dressed in their white hoods and sheets. On occasion, they also resorted to violence in order to intimidate their enemies.

In the second half of the decade, Klan membership declined sharply due to criminal activities and scandals involving its leadership. Several KKK officials were indicted and tried for a variety of crimes. Declining immigration rates also contributed to the Klan's demise. By 1930, Klan membership fell to about 30,000 members nationwide.

Test Yourself
Why did Ku Klux Klan membership increase in the 1920s?

Popular Culture and the Harlem Renaissance

The 1920s are popularly remembered as a time when people rebelled against decorum and styles. Manners became more relaxed and less formal. Fashion became more comfortable and revealing. Pastimes were deliberately silly and flamboyant. Artists, writers, and musicians experimented with new ideas and styles.

The Flapper. In 1920, Americans ratified the Nineteenth Amendment to the U.S. Constitution, which gave women the right to vote. Ratification marked the successful end to a long, hard struggle by advocates of women's suffrage. In addition to representing an important milestone in women's history, the amendment's ratification symbolized new freedom for women. The decade came to be symbolized by the *flapper*, a modern young woman who rejected the strict values of the past and advocated more open attitudes toward lifestyle, fashion, and sex. Flappers were the kind of women represented by the character of Daisy in the novel *The Great Gatsby* (1925), and other works by F. Scott Fitzgerald. In reality, a relatively small percentage of women in the United States during the 1920s were flappers. Most women conducted their lives much as women had in the decade or so before the 1920s. But the flapper became the popular image of that time, reinforced by movies, literature, and the press.

The Economy of the 1920s. During the 1920s, many, but not all, Americans enjoyed relative prosperity. Fueled by phenomenal growth in the automobile industry, the economy expanded rapidly. By the end of the decade, the number of cars on America's roads had almost tripled, and American industry in general enjoyed higher productivity, earnings, and profits. Thousands of goods flooded the market, and consumers snapped them up. Mass consumption, which is taken for granted today, largely originated in the 1920s. It was the result of business practices such as marketing, advertising, and selling goods on credit or installment plans.

Popular Entertainment. Mass communication significantly altered American popular culture during the "Roaring Twenties." Commercial radio originated in 1920 with broadcasts from Pittsburgh's KDKA. Both NBC and CBS radio networks went on the air in the 1920s. In 1922, only about 60,000 homes had radios, but by the end of the decade, radios were in more than 10 million homes. Networks provided programs funded by commercial advertisers to local stations, which in turn increased demand for consumer goods.

Movies also became increasingly popular during the 1920s. The films were silent with subtitles and performed by such actors as Douglas Fairbanks, Sr., Mary Pickford, and Charlie Chaplin. Theaters sprang up in cities and towns across America, creating a mass entertainment sensation. In 1927, the first *talkie*, *The Jazz Singer*, a film with a synchronized soundtrack, hit the theaters, making the movies even more popular in the ensuing years.

Harlem Renaissance. African Americans also contributed to the rich cultural and artistic life that marked the 1920s. The Harlem Renaissance—named after a predominately African American section of New York City—was a period marked by an explosion of talent and works from a remarkable group of African American intellectuals, writers, musicians, artists, and scholars. The movement was a self-conscious expression of African American cultural identity and pride. Writers such as Jean Toomer, Langston Hughes, Countee Cullen, Zora Neale Hurston, and Claude McKay put their stamp on American cultural and literary history during the Harlem Renaissance and helped to pave the way for a wider appreciation of black literature and art.

Langston Hughes, a leading poet of the Harlem Renaissance

Prohibition. One feature of the 1920s was the general defiance of Prohibition. In 1919, the Eighteenth Amendment to the Constitution prohibited the manufacture, sale, and transportation of alcoholic beverages in the United States and their import or export. Millions of people either made their own liquor or smuggled it into the United States from other countries. Some people, called *bootleggers*, made a living by selling alcoholic beverages illegally. Many bootleggers were members of gangs. This amendment, which had been intended to improve society, actually increased criminal activity.

A federal agent breaks open a barrel of alcohol during Prohibition.

Stock Market Speculation and the Crash of 1929

The 1920s began with hope, optimism, and prosperity, but the decade did not end that way. In fact, the last major event of the decade ushered in the worst economic depression in American history. Throughout much of the decade, however, most U.S. businesses were highly productive, churning out large quantities of goods and reaping large profits. Most Americans were confident that the economy would keep expanding. Buoyed by a belief in continued expansion, many people invested heavily in the stock market, often buying stock on credit (called buying on margin). Despite warnings from some bankers and economists, "the boundless commercial romanticism of the American people, inflamed by year after plentiful year of Coolidge Prosperity," could not be checked. Stock market speculation had become a kind of "national mania," wrote Frederick Lewis Allen in *Only Yesterday: An Informal History of the 1920s* (1931).

This was not a problem as long as stock prices continued to rise, and during the latter half of the decade, that is exactly what happened. Between 1925 and

1929, stock values more than doubled. But in September 1929, the tide turned, and stock prices began to drop sharply. On October 24, which became known as Black Thursday, prices plummeted as panicky investors sold their holdings. Then on Tuesday, October 29, the market plunged further, dropping 43 points. A record 16 million shares were sold that day. Brokers who had sold stocks to investors on credit (margin) called in their debts, but few could pay because they had been forced to sell their stocks at huge losses. By the end of October, thousands of people had lost everything.

Test Yourself
How did Prohibition increase criminal activity?

★ THE GREAT DEPRESSION YEARS ★

The stock market crash of 1929 ushered in a decade in which millions of people suffered through unemployment and poverty. The nation's leaders, who were once so optimistic, lost their confidence and became stricken with fear and doubt.

Effects of the Great Depression

Just three years after the stock market crash, the nation's total economic output had declined by nearly 50 percent. While the crash brought on the Great Depression and shook people's confidence in the economy, it was not the Depression's primary cause. Prior to 1929, economic warning signs had begun to materialize. Some segments of the population did not enjoy the prosperity that many others experienced during the 1920s. Farm income was down, and particular industries such as railroads, mining, and lumber saw their output drop. Construction projects and automobile purchases declined. As a result, businesses laid off workers, and consumer buying power declined. It became a vicious cycle. As consumer spending decreased, demand dropped, production declined, and businesses laid off employees, who then had no money to spend on goods.

Crop prices also fell. Immediately following World War I, a bushel of wheat in Idaho sold for about $2.50. In 1932, that same bushel went for only 26 cents. Some farmers destroyed their crops in an attempt to decrease supply and thereby force prices up. By 1933, about a quarter of the nation's workforce was unemployed, and many others had their wages cut. Thousands of people in cities across the nation had to stand in bread lines or visit soup kitchens to feed their families. Some were forced to build shacks out of scrap materials and live in shantytowns, called Hoovervilles, after President Herbert Hoover.

Banking and Credit. A banking and credit crisis added to the nation's problems. When people who had borrowed money could not pay it back, banks were

Life during the Great Depression: a Hooverville in Central Park in New York City (left) and a mission distributing bread to poor people.

unable to give depositors their money, and many banks were forced to close their doors. During the 1920s, many people bought goods on credit. Farmers bought equipment, consumers bought cars, and investors bought stocks—all on credit. As business declined, more and more people lost their jobs or had their wages cut and were unable to make their payments, often defaulting on their loans. Between 1930 and 1933, over 9,000 banks went out of business, and millions of depositors lost their savings.

Gap Between Rich and Poor. Another sign of trouble in the economy was the gap between the rich and the poor. During the 1920s, that gap widened. The rising tide of prosperity did not benefit everyone equally. In 1929, just one percent of the population owned about one-third of the nation's wealth. Conversely, nearly three-quarters of the American people lived on the edge of personal disaster. When bad times hit, these people were the first to be laid off and often lost their homes and life savings.

The Dust Bowl

In addition to suffering through economic woes, residents of the Great Plains states—Oklahoma, Kansas, New Mexico, and parts of Texas and Colorado—were hit by a severe drought that led to an ecological disaster. New farming technology such as tractors and disc plows allowed farmers to clear and plant millions of acres of wheat and other crops in this area. For thousands of years, sod, clumps of grass roots, had kept the soil in place on the windy open plains, but since the mid-1800s, U.S. farmers plowed the sod up in order to plant their crops. The drought that began in 1931 killed many of the crops and dried out the soil. In turn, windstorms, called *black blizzards*, blew the soil away. The drought and this process of wind erosion continued for several years, and the entire area became known as the "Dust Bowl." Experts estimated that a single storm in 1934 carried off about 300 million tons of soil. In 1935, an Oklahoma woman described living in these conditions:

> In the dust-covered desolation of our No Man's Land here, wearing our shade hats, with handkerchiefs tied over our faces and Vaseline in our nostrils, we have been trying to rescue our home from the wind-blown dust, which penetrates wherever air can go. It is almost a hopeless task, for there is rarely a day when at some time, the dust clouds do not roll over. Visibility approaches zero and everything is covered again with a silt-like deposit, which may vary in depth from a film to actual ripples on the kitchen floor.

Millions of people were forced to leave their homes and farms in the Dust Bowl. The region's devastated economy simply could not support the people living there. By 1940, about 2.5 million people had migrated out of the Dust Bowl in search of a livelihood. Nearly 200,000 people headed for California. As one Kansan put it in 1936, "The land just blew away; we had to go somewhere."

Attempts to Alleviate the Depression

In 1928, when times were still good, American voters elected Herbert Hoover president. Hoover's firm belief in a limited role for government, especially in relation to the economy, had seemed to make sense during prosperous times. The president's views, however, limited his responses to the Depression of the 1930s. Rather than providing relief for impoverished citizens, Hoover's efforts focused on trying to increase jobs. He believed that direct relief such as welfare would undermine Americans' work ethic and lead to dependency on the government. Hoover believed that local charities and churches could and should meet the immediate needs of homeless and starving Americans.

As the Depression worsened and local funds to meet the needs of the poor dried up, Hoover began to use government resources to fight unemployment. He encouraged business leaders to reduce layoffs and labor leaders to forgo strikes. Hoover attempted to increase employment with huge government construction projects such as the Grand Coulee, Hoover, and Boulder dams in the West. In 1932, he created the Reconstruction Finance Corporation (RFC) to provide loans to businesses. In that same year, Congress passed the Emergency Relief and Construction Act, which sent money to states for relief and offered funds for local public works projects. To keep foreign goods from competing with U.S. goods, Hoover signed the Hawley-Smoot Tariff, which raised taxes on imported goods.

Bonus Army. Despite Hoover's efforts, many Americans blamed him for the Depression. Hoover, for his part, refused to take any responsibility for the disaster. As times continued to get worse, his popularity plummeted. One event in particular added to the growing anti-Hoover sentiment. In 1924, Congress passed a law that authorized cash bonuses to be paid to veterans who had served their country in World War I. The law stated that the bonuses would be paid in 1945. In the spring of 1932, the so-called *Bonus Army*, consisting of thousands of veterans, marched on Washington, D.C., demanding that the bonuses be paid immediately to relieve their suffering. Congress refused to approve the early payments, and most of the Bonus Army returned home. Over 10,000 remained in Washington, D.C., however, to protest the government's decision. By July, Hoover ordered the removal of the bonus marchers. General Douglas MacArthur, supported by officers such as George Patton and Dwight Eisenhower, commanded the Americans troops to forcibly remove the marchers from the capital. The use of force against the war veterans infuriated many Americans and further damaged Hoover's chances for reelection in November.

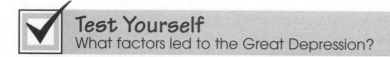

Test Yourself
What factors led to the Great Depression?

★ THE NEW DEAL ★

During his 1932 campaign for reelection, Hoover used optimistic slogans such as "Prosperity is just around the corner." He warned the electorate that his Democratic opponent, Franklin Delano Roosevelt (FDR), would destroy capitalism if elected.

Roosevelt, on the other hand, talked about a "new deal" for the American people. His campaign avoided specific proposals to deal with the Depression and consisted of vague promises to help American workers and their families. He promised to increase federal relief for families in need and to repeal Prohibition. The Roosevelt campaign slogan was "Happy days are here again." This cautious approach to campaigning paid off for FDR. He was elected in a Democratic landslide, with 57 percent of the popular vote. The Democrats also took control of both houses of Congress, giving Roosevelt a clear mandate to pass important legislation.

The Hundred Days

When Roosevelt took office in March 1933, he called a special session of Congress to pass legislation aimed at relieving the devastating effects of the Great Depression. The period between March 9 and June 16 became known as the *Hundred Days* because of the numerous important pieces of legislation passed by Congress in a relatively short period of time. Roosevelt's legislative program targeted the three R's: relief, recovery, and reform. He wanted to bring relief for people in need, recovery of American business and industry, and reform of the economic system, which had allowed the Depression to happen in the first place.

The Hundred Days (March 9–June 16, 1933)

Legislation/Program/Action	Description
Emergency Banking Relief Act (March 9)	Allowed fiscally sound banks to reopen. Gave the president broad discretionary powers over banking transactions involving gold, silver, credit, and currency.
Civilian Conservation Corps Reforestation Relief Act (March 31)	Established the Civilian Conservation Corps (CCC), which provided 250,000 jobs to unemployed men, ages 18 to 25, in reforestation and construction.
U.S. abandons gold standard (April 19)	U.S. abandons gold standard, which causes a decline in the exchange value of the dollar abroad and an increase in the prices of stocks, commodities, and silver in the American exchanges.
Agricultural Adjustment Act (May 12)	Paid farmers to grow fewer crops in order to reduce the supply and raise farm prices. (Struck down by the Supreme Court in 1936.)
Federal Emergency Relief Act (May 12)	Established the Federal Emergency Relief Administration (FERA), which provided grants to states and municipalities for relief to unemployed persons. The states and municipalities used the money to create jobs.
Tennessee Valley Authority Act (May 18)	Established the Tennessee Valley Authority (TVA), an independent public corporation, which built dams and power plants in the Tennessee Valley region, which covers seven states, to control flooding and promote the economic development of the area. The TVA competes with private companies by selling electricity and fertilizers.
Federal Securities Act (May 27)	Required the full disclosure of information regarding new securities issues to investors and the registration of all new issues with the Federal Trade Commission (FTC), and later with the newly formed Securities and Exchange Commission (SEC).
National Employment System Act (June 6)	Established the U.S. Employment Service, which provided matching funding for state employment services.

Home Owners Refinancing Act (June 13)	Established the Home Owners Loan Corporation (HOLC) to refinance home mortgages.
Banking Act (June 16)	Established the Federal Deposit Insurance Corporation (FDIC), which insured bank accounts up to $5,000. Extended membership of Federal Reserve system to savings and industrial banks.
National Industrial Recovery Act (NIRA, June 16)	Gave workers the right to unionize and standardized codes for minimum wages, maximum work hours, prices, production, and competition. Established both the National Recovery Administration (NRA), which enforced these codes, and the Public Works Administration (PWA), which allocated funding for the building of roads and public buildings. (Supreme Court struck down NIRA in 1935.)
Emergency Railroad Transportation Act (June 16)	Increased the federal regulation of railroads.
Farm Credit Act (June 16)	Provided refinancing of farm mortgages.

Critics of the New Deal. The New Deal had its opponents. Business interests generally opposed Roosevelt's efforts, thinking they would destroy capitalism and the free market. The American Liberty League, a newly formed conservative organization, advocated reduced federal spending and wanted the government to stay out of economic policy-making.

Criticism of Roosevelt and the New Deal came also from the left. Critics on the far left argued that the New Deal did not go far enough. They wanted the government to be more active. Francis Townsend, a doctor from California, advocated a monthly pension for older Americans. His idea was that older workers would give their jobs to young people if they had a pension that met their needs. Townsend's scheme garnered little serious interest in Congress, but it focused attention on the problems faced by elderly Americans. Townsend later claimed that his ideas formed the basis for the Social Security Act (1935).

Another New Deal critic from the left was U.S. Senator Huey Long, a Democrat from Louisiana. Although he supported Roosevelt at first, Long soon broke away from the president and the mainstream Democratic Party, espousing populist criticisms of the nation's wealthy. He proposed a wealth redistribution plan called Share-the-Wealth, which would substantially increase taxes on wealthy Americans and provide all citizens a minimum yearly income of $2,500. Long had presidential ambitions and took his message to the people in 1935. Roosevelt and Democratic leaders feared that Long's candidacy could draw enough votes away from the president in the 1936 election to allow the Republicans to win. Long never had the chance, however, to challenge Roosevelt. In September 1935, a political rival assassinated Long in Louisiana.

Second New Deal. Although New Deal policies and programs alleviated the suffering of many Americans and helped to improve the nation's economy to some degree, the Depression still gripped the United States in the mid-1930s. Roosevelt and the Democrats decided to take additional legislative action. In 1935, Congress passed the Revenue Act, which raised taxes on the wealthy and on corporations. They also established a new set of programs that became known as the Second New Deal. Between 1935 and 1941, the Works Progress Administration (WPA), administered by Harry Hopkins, provided construction jobs to about 2 million Americans. WPA projects included airports, bridges, highways, and public buildings such as courthouses and libraries.

The WPA also employed artists, writers, and musicians. Artists were commissioned to create public sculptures and murals. Playwrights wrote plays, and actors performed them in cities and towns across the nation. WPA writers conducted research and wrote about 150 volumes in the series *Life in America*. These books chronicled everyday life in the United States and included studies of ethnic and racial groups, such as *The Italians of New York* and *The Negro in Virginia*, and collections of folklore. WPA writers also produced state, city, and regional guides that were used by travelers for years. WPA musicians and singers staged operas and other musical productions at prices ordinary people could afford. WPA-sponsored companies also gave programs of folk songs and spirituals.

In 1935, Congress passed the Social Security Act, which established an income-support system for American workers and their families. It taxes workers and employers in order to provide pensions for retirees and insurance for the unemployed. The Social Security Administration also made funds available to the states for relief of needy families with dependent children under 18. The latter activity evolved into the modern welfare system.

Labor Movement Under the New Deal. Throughout the early 1930s, union membership had been on the rise. In 1934–1935, United Mine Workers president John L. Lewis and other labor leaders tried to include unskilled workers in the American Federation of Labor (AF of L). That effort failed, but Lewis and his supporters formed the Committee for Industrial Organization (CIO) to advocate the formation of a union for workers by industry that would benefit skilled and unskilled workers. In 1938, they broke with the AF of L and formed the Congress of Industrial Organizations. Roosevelt supported labor's right to organize and bargain. In 1935, the Democrats pushed the National Labor Relations Act, also known as the Wagner Act, through Congress. It recognized the rights of workers to form unions and to bargain collectively. The National Labor Relations Board was set up under the Wagner Act. This five-member agency regulates the process of collective bargaining between labor and management. The National Industrial Recovery Act (NIRA), passed in 1933, had also recognized workers' rights to organize, but the Supreme Court found it unconstitutional.

As shown by the Supreme Court's opposition to such legislation as the NIRA and AAA, Roosevelt's plans to implement his New Deal reforms encountered difficulty. In 1937, he also misread American public opinion in his ill-fated attempt to increase the size of the Supreme Court ("court packing") so that he could appoint justices who approved of New Deal legislation. The New Deal also failed to end the Great Depression. It took World War II to accomplish that. The New Deal did, however, provide work and relief for millions of Americans, and it established a precedent for a more activist federal government in times of economic distress.

Test Yourself
What were the three R's of the New Deal, and how did President Roosevelt address each one?

★ WORLD WAR II ★

On December 7, 1941, Japanese aircraft attacked the American naval fleet at Pearl Harbor in Hawaii. The next day, President Roosevelt called it "a date which will live in infamy." The United States was at war. But before American troops could engage in fighting, the economy had to produce the necessary weapons and supplies.

The Home Front

The nation's economy, which had struggled all through the 1930s, had to shift to wartime production. In order to speed up the process, the government created the War Production Board to oversee the conversion of industries to war production, and the Office of Price Administration to control prices and prevent rapid inflation. The government used the National Labor Relations Board to arbitrate labor disputes in this radically altered economy. The Office of War Mobilization acted as an intermediary, coordinating with other agencies to increase efficient operations.

Faced with previously unheard of demands for revenue to fund the war effort, Congress passed the Revenue Act (1942). This act raised corporate taxes, expanded the pool of people required to pay an income tax, and, to collect taxes in a timely manner, instituted a withholding system to deduct taxes from workers' paychecks. President Roosevelt called the Revenue Act "the greatest tax bill in American history."

The federal government also borrowed money from the public by selling war bonds. Bonds are a promise to repay the amount of purchase, plus interest, at a future date. Many people considered it their patriotic duty to buy war bonds to help the government finance the war. In 1941, Roosevelt bought the very first Series E U.S. Savings Bond. By the end of the war, Some 85 million Americans had purchased a total of more than $185 billion worth of bonds.

American industrial production exploded as the nation's industries converted to war production. The output was enormous. By the war's end in 1945, American factories and workers had produced thousands of ships, airplanes, and tanks. When factories were in full swing, production time dropped drastically. Some smaller ships were produced in just five days, while larger vessels took between two and three weeks to complete.

Propaganda

During World War II, the U.S. government instituted a sustained campaign to promote the war at home. In 1942, it created the Office of War Information (OWI), one of several agencies organized to promote public support for the war through propaganda. The OWI managed several campaigns to sell the war to the American public. Under the leadership of Elmer Davis, OWI produced advertising programs and attempted to make sure that movies offered a patriotic view of the war effort. OWI posters encouraged Americans to support their troops, while portraying the enemy as brutal barbarians. Many well-known artists, writers, and filmmakers took part in the government's efforts to win the hearts and minds of the American public. One of the most famous examples of government-sponsored propaganda was movie director Frank Capra's series *Why We Fight*. At the time, Capra was an officer in the Army Signal Corps. Army Chief of Staff General George C. Marshall ordered Capra to produce films that would explain United States policy to the troops. Soon the award-winning series of seven documentary films was being shown in theaters across the nation.

Women and Minorities in the Workforce

With millions of men and women serving in the armed forces and war-production demands increasing each year, nearly everyone back home could find work. The war did something that the New Deal could not. It restored prosperity to the United States. Workers had steady incomes, but with most factories retooled for war production, there were not many consumer goods to buy. In fact, many items, including food, were so scarce at home they had to be rationed. People were issued coupons by the government to buy goods such as meat, sugar, tires, and gasoline. To help target farm production for the war effort, many people planted "victory gardens" to help feed their families. They also collected scrap metal, which could be recycled to make weapons and equipment.

With lots of jobs available and much of the workforce overseas, opportunities opened up in factories for people who had previously been excluded such as African Americans, Hispanics, and women. A record number of women also joined the services. Although they did not serve in combat roles, members of the Women's Army Auxiliary Corps (called WACs) and the navy's female branch, Women Accepted for Volunteer Emergency Service (WAVES), performed bravely in both the European and Pacific theaters. At home, many women took jobs traditionally held by men. The artist Norman Rockwell created the image of Rosie the Riveter in 1943 as a tribute to the contributions made by working women to the war effort. The vast output of the defense industries during World War II was in no small part made possible by women taking jobs previously thought to be men's work. At the war's conclusion, however, most women lost their jobs to men returning from the war.

Minorities also benefited from the need for labor in America's wartime factories. The Great Migration of African Americans from the South to the North that started around the time of World War I picked up again during World War II. Even though work was abundant, early in the war African Americans still

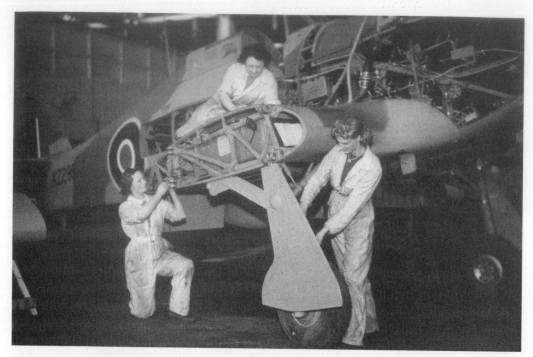

Women repair an aircraft engine during World War II.

experienced discrimination. African Americans also faced discrimination in the military. They were placed in segregated units, often commanded by white officers, and trained for menial jobs rather than for combat. Over 2.5 million African Americans, both men and women, served in all branches of the service. Despite the discrimination they experienced, African Americans served their country honorably and bravely.

Percentage of African Americans Living in the South, 1890–2000	
Year	**%**
1890	90
1900	90
1910	89
1920	85
1930	79
1940	77
1950	68
1960	60
1970	53
1980	53
1990	53
2000	54

In 1941, A. Philip Randolph, president of the Brotherhood of Sleeping Car Porters, and other civil rights leaders planned a march on Washington to protest the exclusion of African Americans from both the private sector and government workforces. Randolph and his colleagues canceled the march when President Roosevelt issued Executive Order 8802 in June 1941. The order prohibited discrimination on the basis of race, creed, color, or national origin in federal government jobs and in defense industries. Roosevelt also established the Fair Employment Practices Committee (FEPC) to enforce the order.

Pressure from African American leaders also helped bring about change in the armed forces. As the war continued, more African Americans were needed for combat duties. Perhaps the most famous African American fighters were the Tuskegee Airmen, the 332nd fighter group of the 99th Squadron, who flew combat missions in Europe. They were called the Tuskegee Airmen because most of the training was conducted at Tuskegee Institute, the school founded by Booker T. Washington, in Alabama.

As had happened in World War I, the migration of African Americans to the North during World War II created tensions that sometimes resulted in violence. Housing shortages heightened racial tensions in several cities across the nation. In 1943, a race riot in Detroit resulted in 34 deaths before the army could restore order. Mexican Americans, despite serving bravely in the war, also experienced prejudice and discrimination. During the same month as the Detroit riots, white sailors in Los Angeles randomly attacked and beat Mexican American youths.

Japanese American Internment

Although male and female Americans of all races performed many courageous acts during the war, the treatment of Japanese Americans at home produced one of the nation's darkest chapters. After the surprise Japanese attack on

Under military guard, Japanese Americans arrive at the Santa Anita Assembly Center before being transferred to internment camps.

Pearl Harbor on December 7, 1941, many Americans were gripped by fear and hysteria. Citizens on the West Coast were especially fearful of further attacks by Japanese forces. They put pressure on the government to relocate people of Japanese ancestry to inland areas. Many feared that, in the event of a Japanese invasion along the West Coast, Japanese Americans would assist the invaders by engaging in espionage and sabotage. President Roosevelt eventually yielded to the anti-Japanese hysteria and, in February 1942, signed Executive Order 9066. Japanese Americans were forced to leave their homes and businesses and move to internment camps located in Arkansas, Arizona, Utah, Wyoming, Colorado, Idaho, and California. Evacuations began in March 1942, and before they ended, the government had dispersed about 120,000 Japanese Americans—most of whom were born in the United States and therefore were citizens—to ten different camps, where living conditions were bleak and harsh. Many lost their homes or businesses permanently. The government took no similar actions against American citizens of German or Italian descent, prompting opponents of Japanese American internment to charge that the policy was racially motivated.

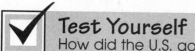

Test Yourself
How did the U.S. government pay for World War II?

★ AFTER THE WAR ★

The decade and a half following the end of World War II was a period of innovation, economic expansion, and prosperity. The standard of living crept steadily upward for many, but not all, Americans. Suburbs sprang up around cities, thanks in part to low-cost mortgages and increased affordability of automobiles, as well as the construction of the nation's interstate highway system. Television soon replaced radio as the primary form of home entertainment and dramatically changed the way Americans spent their leisure time. Air travel became more accessible, and families started having more children, signaling the beginning of the postwar baby boom.

Postwar Prosperity

Immediately after the war, the U.S. economy performed surprisingly well. Economists and government officials feared that the return of millions of servicemen and -women would trigger a wave of unemployment that could escalate into a depression. In the two years following the end of the war (1945–1947), the number of Americans in uniform dropped from over 12 million to just 1.5 million. All of those returning troops had to be absorbed into the workforce, and many were. One factor that helped alleviate the problem was the passage of the G.I. Bill of Rights, or Servicemen's Readjustment Act, in 1944. The G.I. Bill provided funds for servicemen and -women to go to college or get other forms of job training. It also provided health and unemployment benefits as well as housing loans. Over one million veterans took advantage of the G.I. Bill by pursuing an education instead of competing for jobs. At the war's conclusion, millions of women who worked in defense industries were either laid off or voluntarily quit. This opened up jobs for the veterans who were eager to resume their civilian lives.

Inflation and Labor Unrest. A more serious economic problem faced by the Truman administration in the late 1940s was inflation. Truman feared that a sudden end to wartime wage and price controls would spark a period of severe inflation. When Truman lifted the controls, his fears proved correct. People had money to spend and were hungry for consumer goods that had not been available during the war years. Prices shot up quickly. As prices rose, buying power declined, leaving many Americans unhappy. Their hard-earned money bought less than before. Unionized workers responded with a rash of strikes in 1946—they wanted higher wages to deal with inflated prices.

Truman dealt severely with striking unions. He ordered federal authorities to seize the coal mines when the United Mine Workers went on strike, and he threatened to draft railroad workers into the army if they went on strike. A Democrat, Truman suffered politically as a result of his actions against organized labor. In the 1946 congressional elections, Republicans won both houses of Congress, making it difficult for Truman to get his legislative agenda passed. In 1947, the new Republican-dominated Congress passed the Taft-Hartley Act, which curbed the power of unions, over Truman's veto. Taft-Hartley required unions to notify employers of their intent to strike and then wait 60 days. If strikes affected the national welfare, the law gave the federal government the authority to seek a temporary injunction against the union from striking for 80 days. The law also banned the *closed shop*, a workplace that would hire only union members.

Truman's First Full Term. As the nation moved toward the 1950s, the economy continued to improve and inflation fell. To many people's surprise, Truman won the presidential election in 1948, defeating Thomas Dewey. In his first full term, Truman tried to institute a legislative program called the Fair Deal. He signed legislation raising the minimum wage and extending Social Security benefits to more people. He also pushed through legislation that provided funding for low-cost housing and farm price supports. In other legislative initiatives, Truman was not as successful. He was unable to obtain enough support to pass civil rights legislation that would have expanded his executive order to desegregate the armed services and prohibit discrimination in federal hiring. The president failed in his efforts to persuade Congress to approve legislation to create a system of national health insurance and repeal the Taft-Hartley Act. It was only in foreign policy that Truman enjoyed bipartisan support for his policies.

New Red Scare

While the United States and the Soviet Union competed with each other around the world, the Cold War also affected life at home. Fear of Soviet aggression and subversion changed the way Americans saw both the world and one another. In 1949, the fear escalated when Chinese Communists seized control of China, and the Soviet Union successfully detonated an atomic bomb. The United States was no longer the only nuclear power on the globe. These fears produced an era of near-hysterical suspicion marked by accusations of disloyalty.

Federal Employee Loyalty Program (FELP). Critics of President Truman accused him of being "soft" on communism. In response, he toughened his administration's stance. In 1947, amid this climate of fear, Truman issued Executive Order 9835, which established the Federal Employee Loyalty Program (FELP). The program conducted security checks on over 2 million government employees, most of whom were cleared. People could be fired for simply being a potential threat, however, and although evidence against government employees was rarely found, a large number of employees resigned from their government jobs, and about 200 were fired. State and local governments soon followed the federal government's lead, often demanding that employees take loyalty oaths requiring them to swear that they had never been members of the Communist Party.

McCarran Internal Security Act. In 1950, Congress passed the McCarran Internal Security Act, which required Communist organizations and members to register with the attorney general. The law also prohibited defense industries from hiring known Communists, and it legalized internment of certain people during national emergencies. Truman vetoed the bill, arguing that it violated basic constitutional rights. Congress, however, overruled his veto, and the bill became law.

House Un-American Activities Committee. In 1938, Congress established the House Un-American Activities Committee (HUAC). In 1947, HUAC gained national attention by investigating allegations of Communist influence in the Hollywood movie industry. HUAC set out to prove that Communist members of Screen Writers Guild inserted subversive propaganda into Hollywood films. Although HUAC's accusations were never proved, their actions forced a number of people out of the film industry. The committee called both "friendly" and "unfriendly" witnesses. Friendly witnesses, including actor and future president Ronald Reagan, testified about their knowledge of Communists in the film industry. Ten unfriendly witnesses refused to testify, invoking their Fifth Amendment protection against self-incrimination. The so-called Hollywood Ten were found guilty of contempt of Congress and served up to 12 months in jail. The Hollywood Ten and a number of other writers and directors were also *blacklisted* by studios in the 1950s, making it impossible for them to find work in the U.S. movie industry.

In 1948, Whittaker Chambers, a journalist who had once been a member of the Communist Party, appeared before HUAC and testified that Alger Hiss, who had attended the Yalta Conference in 1945 and helped organize the United Nations (UN), had spied for the Soviet Union during the 1930s. Hiss denied the accusation, but he was indicted and tried for perjury. (Since the statute of limitations had expired, he could not be tried for espionage.) The 1949 trial resulted in a hung jury, but the government tried him again a year later. Hiss was convicted and sentenced to five years in prison. After his release in 1954, he continued to maintain his innocence until his death in 1996.

Joseph McCarthy. The man whose name came to be most closely associated with the post-World War II Red Scare was Joseph McCarthy. A relatively obscure Republican senator from Wisconsin, McCarthy exploited for political gain the fears held by many Americans about subversion and international communism. In 1950, McCarthy sparked a national frenzy by claiming that he had a list of 205 names of known Communists who were employed by the U.S. State Department. Although he never offered any evidence to back up his charges, which were eventually discredited, McCarthy remained the focus of media attention and developed a reputation as a heroic guardian of American freedom. Many people who disapproved of McCarthy's witch-hunt tactics did not publicly oppose him because of his popularity, and because they were afraid of being accused of disloyalty and sympathizing with Communists.

When Republicans took control of Congress after the 1952 election, McCarthy's power increased. The Senate Republican leadership named him chairman of the Senate's Government Operations Committee, and he used that committee's Permanent Investigations Subcommittee to pursue other alleged subversives. McCarthy's success was due in large part to increased public concern about subversion caused the recent trial for espionage of Communist Party members Julius and Ethel Rosenberg, and by the outbreak of the Korean War.

McCarthy's undoing began in 1954, when he investigated the U.S. Army. The Army–McCarthy hearings were televised, and over 20 million Americans watched McCarthy frequently interrupt witnesses and, without evidence, accuse people of disloyalty and being Communists. In December 1954, the Senate censured McCarthy for his conduct, and his influence finally came to an end. The climate of fear in the United States gradually declined, although it never disappeared completely. McCarthy died in 1957. The term *McCarthyism*, referring to demagoguery and making false allegations, soon entered the English language.

Test Yourself
What fueled Senator McCarthy's witch hunts?

Space Race

The space race between the United States and the Soviet Union was another manifestation of the Cold War. In October 1957, the Soviet Union shocked the world when it launched *Sputnik I*, the first manmade object to orbit the Earth. *Sputnik I* remained in orbit for three months. A month later, the Soviet Union launched *Sputnik II*, which carried a dog. The American public reacted with fear and dismay. On January 31, 1958, the United States finally made it into space by launching the *Explorer I* satellite. Between 1958 and 1961, the Soviets launched six more *Sputniks*, each larger than the one before. In 1958, President Eisenhower signed the National Aeronautics and Space Act, which established the National Aeronautics and Space Administration (NASA), a government agency that facilitated space exploration.

The most stinging blow to U.S. prestige and pride came on April 12, 1961, when the Soviet Union sent the first person into space. Yuri Gagarin, the Soviet cosmonaut, flew a rocket that circled the globe once and returned to Earth. Several weeks later, on May 5, 1961, Alan Shepard became the first American to travel into space. Shepard's flight lasted 15 minutes. On February 20, 1962, *Mercury 6*, which carried John Glenn, successfully orbited the Earth.

The U.S. Moon Landing. In 1961, President John F. Kennedy took the initiative, issuing a challenge to the nation. He said:

> I believe that this nation should commit itself to achieving the goal, before this decade is out, of landing a man on the moon and returning him safely to the Earth. No single space project . . . will be more exciting, or more impressive to mankind, or more important . . . and none will be so difficult or expensive to accomplish. . . .

Kennedy's challenge paid off, and the United States took the lead in the space race. In 1968, five years after Kennedy's assassination, NASA launched *Apollo 8*, the first manned space flight to orbit the moon. In July 1969, Neil Armstrong, Edwin "Buzz" Aldrin, and Michael Collins, the crew of *Apollo 11*, made their historic voyage to the moon. After successfully achieving orbit, Collins remained behind in the spacecraft, while Armstrong and Aldrin landed on its surface. When Armstrong took his first step on the moon's surface, he said, "That's one small step for a man, one giant leap for mankind." A worldwide television audience watched in awe as the first human beings walked on the moon. By the end of the Apollo program in the early 1970s, ten more Americans had landed on moon's surface.

Astronaut Edwin "Buzz" Aldrin on the moon

Immigration to the United States

In the first half of the 20th century, most of the immigrants to the United States came from Europe. Between 1900 and 1940, about 16 million people entered the U.S. from various European nations. After World War II, immigration patterns changed. Instead of Europe, more immigrants came from Latin America and Asia, where enormous population growth, wars, and economic problems forced many people to leave their homes. From 1970 to the end of the century, over 26 million people, mostly from Latin America and Asia, immigrated to the United States.

U.S. Immigration Laws and Policies, 1948–1990

1948 Displaced Persons Act: U.S. policy that permitted 205,000 fleeing refugees to enter the United States over two years (later increased to 415,000)

1950 Grounds for exclusion and deportation of subversives expanded; aliens required to report their addresses annually.

1952 McCarran-Walter Immigration and Nationality Act
Multiple immigration and naturalization laws combined into one:
(1) reaffirmed the national origins quota system
(2) limited immigration from Eastern Hemisphere nations; Western Hemisphere unrestricted
(3) established preferences for skilled workers and relatives of U.S. citizens and permanent resident aliens
(4) tightened security and screening standards and procedures

1953 Refugee Relief Act: 1948 law limit increased to admit over 200,000 refugees.

1965 Immigration Act: National origins quota system abolished; maintained principle of numerical restriction by establishing hemispheric and per-country ceilings and a preference system.

1976 The 20,000-per-country immigration ceilings and preference system applied to Western Hemisphere countries; separate hemispheric ceilings maintained.

1978 Separate ceilings for Eastern and Western Hemispheric immigration combined into one worldwide limit of 290,000.

1980 Refugee Act: Removed refugees as preference category; established clear criteria and procedures for their admission; reduced worldwide ceiling for immigrants from 290,000 to 270,000.

1986 Immigration Reform and Control Act (IRCA)—comprehensive reform effort:
(1) legalized aliens who resided in U.S. unlawfully since January 1, 1982
(2) established sanctions prohibiting employers from hiring or recruiting illegal aliens
(3) created new classification of temporary agricultural workers; provided for the legalization of certain workers
(4) established visa waiver pilot program allowing the admission of certain nonimmigrants without visas

1990 Immigration Act: Comprehensive immigration legislation:
  (1) increased total immigration under an overall flexible cap of 675,000 immigrants beginning in 1995
  (2) created separate admission categories for family-sponsored, employment-based, and diversity immigrants
  (3) revised all grounds for exclusion and deportation; rewrote political and ideological grounds and repealed some grounds for exclusion
  (4) authorized attorney general to grant temporary protected status to undocumented alien nationals of designated countries subject to armed conflict or natural disasters
  (5) revised and established new nonimmigrant admission categories
  (6) revised and extended Visa Waiver Program
  (7) revised naturalization authority and requirements
  (8) revised enforcement activities

Test Yourself
What event spurred the U.S. to speed up its space program?

★ SOCIAL PROTEST ★

The Vietnam War was another product of the Cold War. American policy makers in the 1950s and 1960s believed in the domino theory: If Vietnam fell to the Communists, the rest of Southeast Asia would follow. As war casualties and deaths mounted, many Americans, including draft-age college students, began to oppose the war. In fact, in the United States, the late 1960s and early 1970s were a time of protest and social turmoil.

The first antiwar demonstrations took place in early 1963, when most Americans could not even locate Vietnam on a map. By 1968, public opinion was bitterly divided between *hawks*, who supported the war effort, and *doves*, who opposed it. The assassinations in 1968 of Martin Luther King, Jr. and Senator Robert Kennedy substantially increased tensions. During the 1968 Democratic National Convention in Chicago, antiwar protesters disrupted the proceedings and clashed violently with the police, all of which were broadcast on television. After Richard Nixon's election as president in November, the protests continued. In 1969, a half million antiwar protesters marched in Washington, D.C., demanding an end to the war. In 1970, the killing of students protesting the war, and its expansion into Cambodia, at Kent State University in Ohio and Jackson State University in Mississippi, stunned the nation. As more troops were withdrawn from Southeast Asia during the early 1970s, and after the draft was abolished, the number of protests declined. Although the United States and North Vietnam officially negotiated an end to the war in 1973, feelings of bitterness and cynicism continued to affect many Americans into the next decade.

Opponents of the Vietnam War rally in Washington, D.C.

The Counterculture

The 1960s antiwar movement evolved into a broader movement that became known as the *counterculture*. No decade since the 1920s had experienced the degree of cultural change seen in the 1960s. About 75 million children from the post–World War II baby boom became teenagers and young adults in the 1960s. Fueled by Vietnam War protests, these young people wanted change in all aspects of society: lifestyle, education, values, laws, and entertainment. They felt that many members of their parents' generation supported the Vietnam War because of their irrational fear of communism and/or because of a desire for power and control. The young people of the counterculture began to believe that the minds of older people were shackled by material values and meaningless taboos and that their moral choices were shallow and even corrupt. A popular slogan among young people was, "Don't trust anyone over thirty." On the other hand, they thought people in their own age group were more able to see the world clearly and make good moral choices. They used the slang word *hip* to denote this superior way of knowing and seeing things. Hence they called themselves *hippies*.

The hippies of the counterculture movement wore their hair long and sported colorful, unconventional clothes. Some used mind-altering drugs such as LSD that caused hallucinations and feelings of rapture. Their favorite music was rock and roll. Musicians and rock groups such as Bob Dylan, Jefferson Airplane, the Grateful Dead, Janis Joplin, Jim Morrison, and Jimi Hendrix incorporated protest and social commentary into their songs. The 1969 Woodstock Festival, a three-day music festival in rural New York, became the symbol of the period. Attended by nearly 500,000 people, the festival captured the counterculture's spirit of rebellion and personal freedom.

Jimi Hendrix was one of the most popular musicians of the late 1960s.

Women's Liberation

An important manifestation of social and political protest and change in the 1960s was the reemergence of "feminism"—the movement to obtain equal rights for women. In its new phase, this movement was also called "women's liberation." Betty Friedan's book *The Feminine Mystique* (1963) brought the movement back to life. Friedan argued that there was more to life for women than just being housewives and mothers. Women should be free to pursue any goal they set for themselves. During the 1960s, many women took Friedan's advice and became involved in political and social movements, attended college, or pursued a career.

In 1966, feminist leaders organized the National Organization for Women (NOW) to work on issues such as workplace discrimination, equal pay for equal work, and day care for the children of working mothers. NOW members organized mass marches, rallies, and other forms of protest to raise public awareness about their issues. In the 1970s, NOW and other organizations advocating equal rights for women staged a campaign in support of the Equal Rights Amendment (ERA). The ERA did not win in the 38 states necessary for ratification, but the campaign brought women's issues to the attention of people across the nation. In 1973, feminist groups won a major victory when the Supreme Court ruled in *Roe* v. *Wade* that women had the right to an abortion during the first three months of pregnancy. Abortion foes quickly responded with a "right-to-life" movement to overturn *Roe* v. *Wade*, enact legal restrictions on abortion, and finally make abortion illegal again. Today, the women's movement is focused primarily on protecting legalized abortion and addressing issues of discrimination in the workplace, such as pay discrepancies and limits to their advancement.

Highlights of the Women's Rights Movement, 1957–1981

1957 Number of women and men voting is approximately equal for the first time.

1963 "Equal Pay" Act passed by Congress; promised equitable wages for the same work, regardless of the race, color, religion, national origin, or sex of the worker.

1964 Title VII of the Civil Rights Act passed; included prohibition against employment discrimination on the basis of race, color, religion, national origin, or sex.

1965 President Johnson signs Executive Order 11246; required federal agencies and federal contractors to take "affirmative action" in overcoming employment discrimination.

1966 National Organization for Women (NOW) founded.

1970 Equal Rights Amendment (ERA) reintroduced into Congress. (It had first been introduced in 1923.)

1972 Title IX of the Education Amendments; prohibited sex discrimination in all aspects of education programs that receive federal funds.

ERA passed by Congress; sent to the states for ratification.

1973 *Roe* v. *Wade*; U.S. Supreme Court declared that Constitution protects women's right to terminate an early pregnancy; made abortion legal in the U.S.

The Federal Home Loan Board ended discrimination against women applying for mortgage loans.

1974 Congress made credit discrimination against women illegal.

1976 Title IX took effect; opened way for women's increased participation in athletics programs and professional schools.

100,000-people march in support of the ERA in Washington, D.C.

1978 Pregnancy Discrimination Act banned employment discrimination against pregnant women.

More women than men enter college for the first time.

1981 Sandra Day O'Connor became first woman appointed to the U.S. Supreme Court.

The Civil Rights Movement

After World War II, African Americans continued to advance their movement for civil rights in the United States. President Truman had desegregated the armed forces by executive order in 1948, but much of the rest of American society remained racially segregated. In 1896, the U.S. Supreme Court had ruled, in *Plessy* v. *Ferguson*, that public facilities could be racially segregated just as long as they were equal. In reality, facilities for African Americans were seldom equal to those for whites. In 1950, the National Association for the Advancement of Colored People (NAACP) decided to challenge the *Plessy* ruling by attacking segregation in public schools. Thurgood Marshall, later the first African American appointed to the Supreme Court, was the NAACP lawyer who argued the case before the high court. Marshall argued that if schools were segregated, they were inherently unequal and, therefore, unconstitutional. In 1954, in the landmark *Brown* v. *Board of Education of Topeka* case, the Supreme Court unanimously declared that segregated schools were unconstitutional.

Little Rock, Arkansas. Several states complied with the ruling and desegregated their schools without incident. But in some states, especially in the South, opposition to desegregation was strong. Racist groups such as the Ku Klux Klan took advantage of the situation to increase their membership, and opponents of desegregation organized White Citizens Councils to mount organized resistance to the court order. In 1956, Southern members of Congress drafted and signed the Southern Manifesto, which demanded that "legal" segregation be restored. The most famous incident of defiance to the *Brown* ruling occurred in 1957 in Little Rock, Arkansas. Nine African American students were scheduled to enroll in Little Rock Central High School that September. Arkansas Governor Orval Faubus, a staunch opponent of integration, called out the Arkansas National Guard to prevent the nine students from attending Central High. A court order forced Faubus to withdraw his troops, but an angry mob turned the students away. In response, President Eisenhower sent federal troops to Little Rock to enforce the court order and protect the African American students as they attended classes. For the first time since Reconstruction, the federal government took action to advance the rights of African Americans. Moreover, the events in Little Rock were covered extensively on television and helped sway the opinion of many Americans against racism and in favor of civil rights.

Montgomery Bus Boycott. In 1955, an African American woman named Rosa Parks boarded a bus in Montgomery, Alabama, after a hard day's work. When told to give up her seat to a white person, Ms. Parks refused. She was subsequently arrested and fined. A young Baptist minister in Montgomery, Dr. Martin Luther King, Jr., helped organize a boycott of the bus company as a response to this unfair treatment. King was an advocate of nonviolence, and he wanted to use the boycott as an example of what could be accomplished using nonviolent tactics. African Americans made up a majority of the riders on Montgomery's buses, but the company refused to give in, despite losing a great deal of revenue. In 1956, unable to handle the economic impact of the boycott, the city of Montgomery agreed to desegregate its public transportation facilities. In the same year, the Supreme Court ruled that the segregation of public transportation was unconstitutional. In 1957, King became the head of the Southern Christian Leadership Conference (SCLC), which he helped found, and quickly became the recognized leader of the civil rights movement.

Sit-Ins and Freedom Riders. During the 1960s, the civil rights movement gathered speed and momentum. Students in Greensboro, North Carolina, staged a sit-in at a segregated lunch counter in 1960. Many similar nonviolent protests soon followed throughout the South. That same year, African American students at Shaw University in Raleigh, North Carolina, organized the Student Nonviolent Coordinating Committee (SNCC). In 1961, the Congress of Racial Equality (CORE) sponsored bus trips around the South testing the enforcement of the new law outlawing segregation in public facilities. These young people, both black and white, were soon called *freedom riders.*

Violent Backlash. The rest of the 1960s witnessed mostly turmoil and increasing violence against those who fought for civil rights. In 1963, Medgar Evers, an NAACP leader, was murdered in Jackson, Mississippi. Just over two months later, over 200,000 civil rights advocates participated in the peaceful March on Washington. (See Chapter 31.) Less than a month later, riots broke out in Birmingham, Alabama, where racists bombed a Baptist church, killing four young African American girls. As the decade wore on, violence on both sides of the civil rights movement escalated, culminating with the assassination of King in 1968. While his philosophy of nonviolence still resonated among many people, others believed that only violence would bring about change.

Events of the Civil Rights Movement, 1964–1971

1964	CORE and SNCC launched massive voter registration drive aimed at African Americans; known as the Freedom Summer.
	Civil Rights Act made segregation in public facilities and discrimination in employment illegal.
	Three civil rights workers in Mississippi killed by racists.
1965	Black nationalist leader Malcolm X assassinated in Harlem by Black Muslims.
	African Americans led by Martin Luther King, Jr. marched to Montgomery in support of voting rights; stopped by police blockade; several marchers injured after police use tear gas, whips, and clubs; known as "Bloody Sunday."
	Congress passed Voting Rights Act, which made it easier for Southern blacks to register; literacy tests became illegal.
1965–1968	Race riots in Los Angeles, Newark, New York, Cleveland, Detroit, and Chicago

1968	Martin Luther King, Jr., assassinated in Memphis, Tennessee.
	Civil Rights Act prohibited discrimination in the sale, rental, and financing of housing.
1971	Supreme Court decision *Swann* v. *Charlotte-Mecklenburg Board of Education* ruled that busing is a legitimate means for achieving integration of public schools.

As anti–Vietnam War protests heated up, the civil rights movement had to compete for more national attention. Although many issues remained unresolved for African Americans, as time went on, the public became distracted by events halfway around the world in Southeast Asia. But the civil rights movement never abandoned its work; its fight for equality for all Americans continue to the present day. Moreover, the battles waged by African Americans in the 1950s and 1960s encouraged other groups to address issues of equality. Hispanic Americans and Native Americans also waged campaigns to redress grievances and end the discrimination they had endured over the years. Indeed, the 1960s and 1970s were decades of turmoil and confrontation. It was a time that forced people from all walks of life to view their nation through different lenses, and it helped to define the issues that engage Americans to this very day.

Test Yourself
What was the effect of the *Brown* decision?

POINTS TO REMEMBER

- The Red Scare of the 1920s focused on political radicals and immigrants.

- In the 1920s, many African Americans moved from the South to the North in search of jobs.

- In the 1920s, the Ku Klux Klan's hatred focused on African Americans, Catholics, Jews, radicals, and immigrants.

- During the Harlem Renaissance of the 1920s, talented African American writers and artists lived and worked in Harlem in New York City.

- The Great Depression, the worst in the nation's history, gripped the United States from 1929 until 1941.

- Franklin Roosevelt's New Deal focused on relief for those in need, recovery for American business and industry, and reform of the economic system.

- After the Japanese attack on Pearl Harbor, U.S. industry quickly mobilized to make war supplies.

- Women played an important role in wartime industries.
- A second migration of African Americans from the South to the North occurred during and after World War II.
- The U.S. government forced many Japanese Americans to give up their homes and businesses and live in internment camps during World War II.
- The United States economy boomed in the 1950s.
- McCarthyism played on fears of communism and domestic subversion during the Cold War.
- The space race was a product of the Cold War.
- Vietnam was a Cold War conflict that turned hot.
- The civil rights movement of the 1950s and 1960s resulted in several victories for African Americans.
- The *Brown* decision found racially segregated public schools unconstitutional.

EXERCISES

CHECKING WHAT YOU HAVE READ

On a separate sheet of paper, construct a time line. Choose a 30-year span between 1920 and 1970 that you want to cover. Select at least ten events from that time span and place each of the ten events at the proper place on the time line. Next, circle the two events on your time line that you think are the most significant and in a short paragraph explain why.

USING WHAT YOU HAVE READ

On a separate sheet of paper, construct a table similar to the one below. Complete the table by characterizing each decade with descriptive words or phrases.

1920s	1930s	1940s	1950s	1960s

THINKING ABOUT WHAT YOU HAVE READ

1. In a paragraph or in a graphic organizer of your design, explain what the Red Scare of the 1920s, the Ku Klux Klan, internment of Japanese Americans during World War II, and McCarthyism all have in common. Support your explanations with examples.

2. What did the migration of African Americans in the 1920s from the South to Northern cities have in common with the African American migration from the South to the North in the 1940s and 1950s?

3. Think of a simile for one of the decades covered in this chapter. "The 1920s were like a _____," or "the 1930s were like a _____." Finish the simile and then explain why you selected it.

SKILLS

Writing a Persuasive Letter

In a representative democracy, citizens have the right and responsibility to express their opinions on public issues. One way to do this is by writing a letter to either a government official or the editor of a newspaper. Imagine that you are a citizen concerned about an issue described in this chapter.

Some suggestions are: the excesses of the 1920s Red Scare or the McCarthyism of the 1950s; internment of Japanese Americans during World War II, the Vietnam War or antiwar protesters, the civil rights movement of the 1950s and 1960s. You may also select some other issue. The letter might be to the U.S. president of the time, a public official, or a newspaper editorial page. In your library or on the Internet, conduct further research about your selected topic. Then compose a letter following the four steps outlined below.

The first step in writing an effective letter is to become well informed about your topic. The next step is to compose a draft of the letter. Make sure that you (1) identify the issue, (2) state your opinion on the issue, (3) give some examples, facts, statistics, or other kinds of support for your opinion, and (4) make a request for appropriate action. When you are satisfied that the letter's message is clear, complete the final draft and print it out.

CHAPTER 22

CULTURAL PERSPECTIVES

BENCHMARK:

Analyze the influence of different cultural perspectives on the actions of groups.

This benchmark asks students to analyze how the perspectives of different groups in American society affect their actions. Grade-level indicators direct students to describe how perspectives led groups to create political action groups, specifically the National Association for the Advancement of Colored People (NAACP), the National Organization for Women (NOW), the American Indian Movement (AIM), and the United Farm Workers (UFW). The benchmark also asks students to analyze group perspectives evident in African American, Latino, and American Indian art, literature, music, and the media. How do these contributions reflect culture in the United States, and how have they helped shape American culture?

★ POLITICAL ACTION GROUPS ★

Throughout the history of the United States, Americans have formed groups of like-minded people in order to work collectively to achieve their aims. Perspective—the way group members view their situation or place in the United States—dictates how a particular group or organization might approach a problem or issue. Often these groups look to the local, state, and the federal government for help. In order to convince government officials to support them, groups organize to take political action. These groups sometimes form *political action committees* (PACs)—independent organizations established to raise and contribute money to the political campaigns of candidates who agree, to an extent, with the views and aims of the group. PACs were founded because federal laws prohibit most interest groups from contributing money directly to political candidates. PACs also organize public awareness campaigns in order to inform people about their issues and concerns. In recent decades, minority groups have found this approach particularly successful. During the 20th century, the National Association for the Advancement of Colored People (NAACP), the National Organization for Women (NOW), the American Indian Movement (AIM), and the United Farm Workers (UFW) Union mounted political action campaigns that resulted in substantive social and cultural change.

National Association for the Advancement of Colored People (NAACP)

In 1909, an interracial group of about 60 people met in New York City. They came together in response to a recent race riot in Springfield, Illinois. White activists such as Oswald Garrison Villard, Mary White Ovington, William English Walling, and Henry Moscowitz joined with black leaders such as Ida B. Wells-Barnett, Mary Church Terrell, and W. E. B. Du Bois to chart a course of action for combating racial discrimination and violence. They were horrified by the violence committed against blacks in Springfield and many other places around the

Ida B. Wells-Barnett, one of the founders of the NAACP

nation. These founding leaders of the NAACP decided that they would work primarily through the legal system to achieve their goals, which were to secure equal protection of the law for all people and universal adult male suffrage. The NAACP's perspective can be seen in its current mission statement:

> The NAACP insures the political, educational, social, and economic equality of minority groups and citizens; achieves equality of rights and eliminates race prejudice among the citizens of the United States; removes all barriers of racial discrimination through the democratic processes; seeks to enact and enforce federal, state, and local laws securing civil rights; informs the public of adverse effects of racial discrimination and seeks its elimination; educates persons as to their constitutional rights and to take all lawful action in furtherance of these principles.

Moorfield Storey, a white lawyer, became the NAACP's first president, while W. E. B. Du Bois, a Harvard-educated sociologist and author, oversaw publications and research for the new organization. In 1910, Du Bois became the first editor of *The Crisis*, the NAACP's official journal, and within three years, the NAACP had established local chapters in cities such as Washington, D.C., St. Louis, Kansas City, Boston, and Detroit.

W. E. B. Du Bois, scholar, editor, author, and one of the founders of the NAACP

NAACP leaders decided early on that they would use the legal system to oppose social injustice and discrimination. A few years after its formation, NAACP lawyers experienced success with a Supreme Court victory in *Guinn* v. *United States* (1915), in which the Court overturned an Oklahoma law that denied the right to vote to some, mostly black, citizens.

The NAACP gained attention when it organized a campaign to protest D. W. Griffith's popular but racist film, *The Birth of a Nation* (1915), which was also known by its alternate title, *The Clansmen*. The substantial publicity that the NAACP's campaign against the film received led to an increase in its membership. The organization soon boasted 300 local chapters and by 1919, membership rose to 90,000, a tenfold increase. *The Crisis* became an important vehicle for writers and scholars of the Harlem Renaissance such as Du Bois, Langston Hughes, and Countee Cullen.

After World War I, the NAACP focused on the effort to end lynching. The organization campaigned in Congress for passage of the Dyer Bill (1918), which sought to punish lynchers and government officials who refused to prosecute lynch mobs. Congress did not pass the Dyer Bill, but the NAACP's long-running antilynching campaign helped decrease the number of lynchings.

Challenging "Separate-but-Equal." In 1930, Walter F. White became secretary of the NAACP. White led the organization through its period of successful legal challenges to racial discrimination. Under White's leadership, the NAACP took on several cases aimed at reversing the separate-but-equal doctrine established in *Plessy* v. *Ferguson* (1896). "Separate-but-equal" dictated separate facilities for blacks and whites just as long as they were equal. In practice, however, the facilities for blacks were seldom equal.

The NAACP also fought against economic discrimination, especially during the Great Depression and in the years immediately following World War II. In 1941, thanks in part to NAACP pressure, President Franklin Roosevelt established the Fair Employment Practices Committee (FEPC) to ensure fair hiring practices in defense industries.

NAACP membership continued to increase after World War II. By 1946, the NAACP claimed about 500,000 members. The growth in membership was due in large measure to the organization's campaigns against discrimination in both education and the workplace, and its voting rights efforts. The organization pushed for desegregation in the armed forces, which President Harry Truman ordered in 1948, and in public schools, which culminated in the 1954 *Brown* case. NAACP lobbying was influential in the passage of several important Civil Rights Acts in 1957, 1964, 1968, and the Voting Rights Act of 1965.

In 1954, the Supreme Court finally overturned the doctrine of separate-but-equal with landmark case of *Brown* v. *Board of Education of Topeka*. Thurgood Marshall, the NAACP's lead attorney in the case, convinced the Court that separate schools for blacks and whites were by their very nature unequal and unconstitutional. This case, which marked the beginning of the end of legal segregation in the United States, remains the NAACP's single most important victory and helped spark the civil rights movement led by the Reverend Dr. Martin Luther King, Jr.

After the 1950s and 1960s, the NAACP continued to focus on working within the system to pass legislation and seek judicial relief for injustices experienced by African Americans. Today, the organization remains a powerful voice for racial equality in all aspects of public life. While the NAACP's emphasis in recent years has shifted to economic advancement and educational equality for African Americans, the organization continues to play a vital role in fighting discrimination and reflecting the concerns and needs of an important segment of the American population.

Test Yourself
What was the focus of NAACP work in the early years of its existence?

The National Organization for Women (NOW)

Even though they outnumber men in the United States, women are considered a minority group in a historical and political context because of years of legal, political, economic, and social discrimination against them. For example, women in the United States could not vote until 1920, when the Nineteenth Amendment to the Constitution was ratified. Throughout American history, women were often paid less than men for the same kind of work.

In the 1960s, women made some progress toward legal equality with the passage of the Equal Pay Act (1963) and Title VII of the Civil Rights Act of 1964, which prohibited gender discrimination. Many leaders of the feminist movement, however, did not think these laws went far enough, and they did not believe that these laws were being adequately enforced.

Feminist Movement. In 1966, in Washington, D.C., 29 feminist leaders attending the National Conference of State Commissions on the Status of Women founded the National Organization for Women (NOW) to address issues and obstacles they perceived that stood in the way of equal rights and opportunity

Author Betty Friedan co-founded the National Organization for Women (NOW).

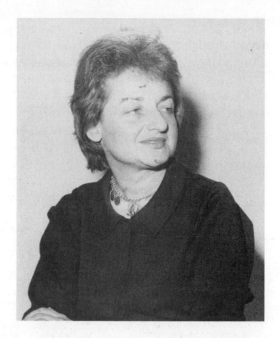

for all women. "It only took a few of us to get together," said founder Betty Friedan, "to ignite the spark—and it spread like a nuclear chain reaction." NOW quickly developed a "Bill of Rights for Women," in which the organization spelled out its goals. NOW's Bill of Rights for Women called for enforcement of existing laws such as Title VII, equal education and job-training opportunities, child care tax deductions, child care centers, maternity leave rights, and the passage of an Equal Rights Amendment (ERA) to the Constitution. In its statement of purpose, NOW declared:

> The purpose of NOW is to take action to bring women into full participation in the mainstream of American society now, exercising all the privileges and responsibilities thereof in truly equal partnership with men.
>
> We believe the time has come to move beyond the abstract argument, discussion and symposia over the status and special nature of women . . . ; the time has come to confront, with concrete action, the conditions that now prevent women from enjoying the equality of opportunity and freedom of choice which is their right, as individual Americans, and as human beings.

In just three years, NOW's membership increased to over 175,000, and its quick success spawned the organization of other feminist groups such as the National Women's Political Caucus (NWPC).

Equal Rights Amendment. In the 1970s, NOW focused on the passage and ratification of an Equal Rights Amendment (ERA) to the Constitution. Originally proposed in 1923, the ERA would guarantee that women and men would have the same rights and protections under the law. One of NOW's public relations strategies was a campaign button that read simply "59¢," a reminder of the wage gap between men and women at the time. Fifty-nine cents represented the average wage paid to women for every dollar paid to men. As a result of feminist political action, Congress passed the ERA in 1972. Throughout the 1970s, NOW led a national campaign to secure the ratification of at least 38 states, as required for the ERA to become part of the Constitution. In the same decade, conservative opposition to the ERA successfully frustrated NOW's efforts to obtain the necessary state votes.

Another key issue for NOW since the early 1970s has been its support for legalized abortion. In *Roe* v. *Wade* (1973), the Supreme Court ruled that women have the right to terminate a pregnancy in the first three months. NOW strongly supported the Court's decision, which was opposed by many religious and right-to-life organizations. NOW continues to argue in defense of legalized abortion today.

Test Yourself
What prompted the 29 founders of NOW to create the organization in 1966?

American Indian Movement (AIM)

American Indians (Native Americans) comprise another group of people whose political actions have been dictated by their perspective of the world and their place in it. In 1968, Native Americans who met in Minneapolis, Minnesota, organized the American Indian Movement (AIM) to combat the problems they faced. In 1992, Dennis Banks, one of AIM's leaders, explained:

> Because of the slum housing conditions; the highest unemployment rate in the whole of this country; police brutality against our elders, women, and children; Native Warriors came together from the streets, prisons, jails and the urban ghettos of Minneapolis to form the American Indian Movement. They were tired of begging for welfare, tired of being scapegoats in America and decided to start building on the strengths of our own people; decided to build our own schools; our own job-training programs; and our own destiny. That was our motivation for being. That beginning is now being called "The Era of Indian Power."

In addition to these issues, AIM focused on protecting treaty rights of the individual Native American tribes in the United States and preserving Native American culture.

"The Trail of Broken Treaties." In 1972, AIM sponsored a protest march in Washington, D.C., which it called "The Trail of Broken Treaties," to protest treaties broken by the U.S. government throughout the nation's history. In a position paper published to coincide with the march, AIM leaders explained their views and goals:

> We need not give another recitation of past complaints. . . . In 1832, Black Hawk correctly observed: "You know the cause of our making war. It is known to all white men. They ought to be ashamed of it."
>
> The government of the United States knows the reasons for our going to its capital city. . . . We go because America has been only too ready to express shame, and suffer none from the expression—while remaining wholly unwilling to change to allow life for Indian people. . . .

For our part, in words and deeds of coming days, we propose to produce a rational, reasoned manifesto for construction of an Indian future in America. If America has maintained faith with its original spirit, or may recognize it now, we should not be denied.

AIM listed many demands that served to focus the efforts of its members. Among other things, they called for:

- a commission to review treaty commitments and violations;
- relief against treaty rights violations;
- judicial recognition of Indians' right to interpret treaties;
- land reform and restoration of a 110-million-acre native land base;
- abolition of the Bureau of Indian Affairs;
- creation of an Office of Federal Indian Relations and Community Reconstruction;
- tax immunities;
- protection of religious freedom and cultural integrity;
- improved health, housing, employment, economic development, and education.

AIM's Victories. AIM was successful in achieving some of its goals. In 1972, Congress enacted the Indian Education Act and in 1975, the Indian Self-Determination and Education Assistance Act, which gave Indians greater control over the education of their children, thus allowing them to preserve their culture.

Members of the American Indian Movement (AIM) protest the mistreatment of their people.

In the 1970s and 1980s, federal courts also ruled on behalf of Indians who sued the government to regain land lost as a result of treaty violations. In 1971, the federal government gave over 40 million acres of land and paid the Inuit Indian people nearly $1 billion as a result of the Alaska Native Claims Settlement Act.

AIM's protests sometimes ended in violent confrontations with government officials or agencies such as at Wounded Knee, South Dakota, in 1973. The group's actions shed light on problems about which many Americans had been unaware. AIM continues its work to restore native lands to American Indians and to improve the lives of its members through political means, social protest, and public awareness and education campaigns.

Test Yourself
What two laws did Congress pass in response to AIM's activities?

United Farm Workers (UFW)

Like the NAACP, NOW, and AIM, the United Farm Workers (UFW) union organized when a group of people, in this case, migrant workers—who pick the crops that end up in America's grocery stores and supermarkets—perceived common grievances and sought relief through social and political activism. Many farmworkers, especially in the West and Southwest, were Hispanic Americans of Latin American descent, Puerto Ricans or immigrants from Mexico, the Dominican Republic, Guatemala, Cuba, and other nations in Central and South America. Their numbers grew rapidly during the 1960s, from about 3 million to 9 million by the end of the decade.

Throughout the 1960s, the number of Mexican workers employed at California farms also increased. For many years, these workers traveled from farm to farm, picking vegetables, fruits, and other crops. They often worked long hours for little pay and often endured difficult conditions such as low-quality housing.

In 1965, many grape pickers made an average of only 90 cents an hour, plus ten cents per basket picked. State laws regulating working conditions for pickers existed but were mostly ignored by the farm owners. Living conditions were unsanitary for the most part, and, despite child labor laws, many children worked in the fields alongside their parents. The life expectancy of an average farmworker was 49 years.

In response to these conditions, two organizations were formed. In 1959, the AFL-CIO, the largest labor union in the United States, founded the Agricultural Workers Organizing Committee (AWOC). It developed out of an earlier organization, started by Dolores Huerta, called the Agricultural Workers Association (AWA). Most of AWOC's membership consisted of African Americans, Hispanics, and Filipino workers. The Filipino workers in particular had experience organizing unions for pickers and holding strikes.

Dolores Huerta and Cesar Chavez. In 1962, Dolores Huerta, a former teacher, and Cesar Chavez established the second organization, the National Farm Workers Association (NFWA). Chavez grew up in a farmworker family and knew firsthand of the hardships most migrants suffered. He traveled the central valley of California for years trying to persuade farmworkers to join his fledgling union.

In the spring of 1965, two strikes, one led by NFWA and the other by AWOC, resulted in growers agreeing to increase wages for pickers. Later that summer, another strike occurred near Delano, California, where grapes were ripe and ready to be picked. Members of the AWOC went on strike against nine farms in an attempt to get the growers to increase pickers' pay to $1.25 an hour. The growers rejected the AWOC's demands and began to bring in "scabs"—

Dolores Huerta during the grape pickers' strike

nonunion replacement workers—to fill in for the strikers. The AWOC leaders then appealed to Chavez to persuade the NFWA to join the strike. On September 16, NFWA members voted unanimously to join the strike, shouting "Viva la Huelga!" (Hooray for the Strike!). The NFWA had more members than AWOC and took over leadership of the strike. Because it was difficult to set up pickets on farms spread out over hundreds of square miles, the NFWA organized roving pickets and a national boycott against buying table grapes. Chavez hoped to hurt the growers financially so that they would agree to raise wages. In an effort to increase their strength, the AWOC and the NFWA merged to form the United Farm Workers Organizing Committee (UFWOC). The boycott lasted five years. In 1970, however, the UFWOC negotiated a contract with grape growers that brought higher wages and better working conditions for pickers.

Cesar Chavez addresses supporters in New York City.

Test Yourself
What grievances drove Cesar Chavez and the NFWA to go on strike for five years?

★ AFRICAN AMERICAN, AMERICAN INDIAN, AND LATINO CULTURE ★

Just as political groups reflect particular perspectives about the United States and the rest of the world, so do artists from minority groups. The United States is a nation rich in diversity, and we can see that diversity reflected all around us in the cultural contributions of various groups. Each group's history and experiences have helped shape its music, art, and literature, which, in turn, have influenced the broader American culture in a number of important and lasting ways.

Music

Artists from different minority groups have played an immense role in the development of popular American music. The historical experiences of each group helped to define the music it created, and the resulting music has likewise contributed to the broader, diverse musical history of our nation. Today, there is a wide variety of "American" music that owes its origins to a particular cultural group, including bluegrass, Cajun, country, folk, gospel, and ragtime music. These styles are sometimes referred to as "roots music" because they formed a foundation for subsequent music styles such as rock and roll, rhythm and blues, jazz, and hip-hop.

Art

A similar process occurred in other areas of artistic expression such as literature and painting. Artists and writers who were influenced by their experiences as members of a minority group created art that reflected their personal histories. That art influenced later writers and painters who interpreted earlier works through their own lenses.

Literature

Many contemporary American writers owe a debt to African American writers who belonged to the Harlem Renaissance of the 1920s. Claude McKay, Zora Neale Hurston, Countee Cullen, and Langston Hughes wrote from the perspective of African Americans living in the United States in the 1920s. Their work significantly influenced subsequent poets and novelists. James Baldwin and Ralph Ellison, two African Americans who published books after World War II, were influenced by the Harlem Renaissance writers, and have, in turn, influenced others writing today.

Like their African American counterparts, many Hispanic and American Indian artists often borrow from their own perspectives, which are formed by their history and experiences as members of minority groups, when creating their art. In turn, their art has helped shape and influence the wider American culture.

POINTS TO REMEMBER

- Group actions result from the perspectives of its members and leaders.

- Groups sometimes form political action committees (PACs) in order to support candidates and officials who agree with their aims, and conduct public awareness and education campaigns.

- Over time, the focus of the NAACP's work changed as conditions changed.

- *Brown* v. *Board of Education of Topeka* (1954) was the NAACP's most famous and far-reaching legal victory after World War II.

- The National Organization for Women (NOW) was not able to achieve ratification of the Equal Rights Amendment (ERA), but it was successful in raising public awareness regarding issues of equal rights and opportunities for women.

- Two of the American Indian Movement's (AIM) primary goals remain to get the U.S. government to redress past treaty violations and to preserve Indian culture.

- The United Farm Workers (UFW) union grew out of the desire of migrant farmworkers in California to increase their pay, improve their working conditions, and gain access to better housing.

- African American, American Indian, Hispanic, and female artists were influenced by their experiences as members of a minority group in the United States. In the last century, their art has influenced the broader American culture and made lasting impressions on society.

EXERCISES

CHECKING WHAT YOU HAVE READ

Using information from this chapter, complete the following table on a separate piece of paper.

Group	Grievances	Group Actions
NAACP		
NOW		
AIM		
UFW		

USING WHAT YOU HAVE READ

Conduct a library or an Internet search on one of the political action organizations discussed in this chapter: NAACP, NOW, AIM, or UFW. Select an issue that has been important to the group in its history. Design a poster advocating for the position of the group regarding the issue that you selected.

THINKING ABOUT WHAT YOU HAVE READ

Select one of the political organizations discussed in this chapter. Choose an issue that has been important to that group throughout its history. Assume the role of a leader of that organization and write a letter to your U.S. senator requesting a new law that would address your group's grievance(s) regarding the selected issue. In your letter, describe the issue, provide support for your group's position on the issue, and suggest remedies that should be included in the new legislation.

SKILLS

Interpreting a Graph

Study the graph below.

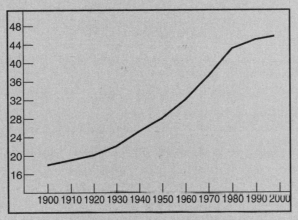

Women in the civilian workforce, 1900–2000
(as a percent of all civilian workers)

1. What does the graph show?

2. In which decade did the percentage of women in the workforce begin to level off after increasing in the previous decades?

3. How do you think NOW members or leaders might use this graph? Explain your answer.

CHAPTER 23

OPPRESSION, DISCRIMINATION, AND CONFLICT

BENCHMARK:

Analyze the consequences of oppression, discrimination, and conflict between cultures.

This benchmark focuses on the results of racial oppression, discrimination, and conflict in American society by looking specifically at legalized discrimination based on race in the form of the Jim Crow laws. It also asks students to analyze the struggle for racial and gender equality and its impact on the changing status of minorities since the late 19th century. Items on the Ohio Graduation Test will address the consequences, results, outcomes, and effects of oppression, discrimination, and conflict (but not the causes), specifically as the consequences relate to the Jim Crow laws as well as the struggle for racial and gender equality. A consequence that may be addressed in test items is the impact that struggle has had on the status of minorities since the later 19th century.

★ JIM CROW LAWS ★

Sometime in the 1830s or 1840s, a white minstrel show singer named Thomas Dartmouth "Daddy" Rice, blackened his face and imitated African American singing and dancing. One of the songs he performed was "Jump Jim Crow," in which he imitated an elderly African American man he had seen while traveling in the South. The song ended with the chorus:

> Weel about and turn about and do jis so,
> Eb'ry time I weel about I jump Jim Crow.

The name Jim Crow in the lyrics may have come from the owner of the slave whom "Daddy Rice" imitated. Soon the Jim Crow character was a staple of minstrel shows throughout the United States, and it became a stereotype of African American inferiority in the years before the Civil War. It was not long before the term "Jim Crow" became used as a racial slur to denigrate African Americans in general.

Discriminatory Laws After Reconstruction

"Jim Crow" also came to refer to the laws enacted in the 1870s in Southern states after Reconstruction, laws that created a legalized system of segregation based

A segregated water fountain in the South

on race. Many Northern states also enacted Jim Crow laws. After Reconstruction ended, whites took back control of Southern state governments from federal government officials and Northern carpetbaggers. In the 1870s and 1880s, these all-white legislatures enacted discriminatory laws that were intended to segregate whites and African Americans. Laws that established literacy tests, poll taxes, and grandfather clauses, for example, severely restricted the voting rights of African Americans. Poll taxes disenfranchised blacks, many of whom were poor. Literacy tests prevented many former slaves from voting because they were never allowed to learn to read or write. The grandfather clause stated that any male could vote if his father or grandfather had been eligible to vote before January 1, 1867. This law eliminated almost all African Americans who had been slaves prior to that date, and not eligible to vote.

Other typical Jim Crow laws outlawed marriage between blacks and whites and required businesses and public facilities to have separate areas or facilities for the two races. For example, several Southern states required bus companies to maintain segregated waiting rooms, ticket windows, and even drinking fountains. Railroads had to provide separate cars for white and black riders, and restaurants were strictly segregated—African American and white customers could not sit together. Separate restrooms for whites and blacks were common in public facilities throughout the South. Schools and housing were rigidly segregated. It was very difficult for African Americans to get bank loans in order to purchase a home.

An Alabama Jim Crow Law from the 1890s

It shall be unlawful to conduct a restaurant or other place for the serving of food in the city, at which white and colored people are served in the same room, unless such white and colored persons are effectually separated by a solid partition extending from the floor upward to a distance of seven feet or higher, and unless a separate entrance from the street is provided for each compartment.

It shall be unlawful for a Negro and white person to play together or be in company with each other at any game of pool or billiards.

Every employer of white or Negro males shall provide for such white or Negro males reasonably accessible and separate toilet facilities.

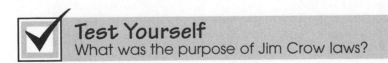

Test Yourself
What was the purpose of Jim Crow laws?

Challenging Jim Crow

In 1890, the Louisiana legislature enacted the Separate Car Act. It required all railroads in Louisiana to provide "separate-but-equal" accommodations for white and blacks. Anyone who violated the law by sitting in the wrong compartment could be fined or jailed.

In 1892, a Louisianan named Homer Plessy purchased a first-class ticket on the East Louisiana Railway. Plessy was one-eighth black, which meant that under the state's law he was considered black, and therefore required to sit in the "colored" car. Plessy challenged the law and sat in the car reserved for "white" passengers. Railroad officials tried to get him to move, but Plessy refused, and he was arrested.

In court, Plessy's lawyer argued that the Louisiana law violated both the Thirteenth and Fourteenth amendments of the U.S. Constitution. The Thirteenth Amendment abolished slavery, and the Fourteenth Amendment made anyone born in the United States a citizen and guaranteed "due process" to all Americans regardless of race. Due process means that the government must follow the law and treat everyone equally. Judge John H. Ferguson, who heard the case, found Homer Plessy guilty, declaring the Separate Car Act constitutional for trains running within Louisiana.

Plessy v. Ferguson. Plessy appealed the Louisiana court's decision to the U.S. Supreme Court. In 1896, the Supreme Court upheld the Louisiana court's ruling and the Separate Car Act, declaring that separate facilities for blacks and whites were legal as long as African Americans had access to equal public facilities. In effect, this ruling upheld the system of Jim Crow laws that had developed since the end of Reconstruction. In reality, however, public facilities and accommodations for African Americans were never equal. African American facilities such as schools were inferior because Southern state and local governments spent more money on facilities for whites than they did on those for African Americans.

Although the *Plessy* case dealt specifically with public transportation, states used the Supreme Court's decision to extend the separate-but-equal doctrine to most relations between whites and blacks. After the decision, governments could legally segregate public schools, theaters, train stations, restaurants, restrooms, and hotels. The *Plessy* decision enabled states to maintain Jim Crow laws until 1954, when the *Brown* decision overturned *Plessy* and outlawed racial segregation in public education.

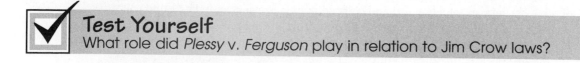

Test Yourself
What role did *Plessy* v. *Ferguson* play in relation to Jim Crow laws?

★ THE STRUGGLE FOR RACIAL AND GENDER EQUALITY ★

Previous chapters addressed the struggle of women and African Americans to gain equality. What has been the result of that struggle? Did the quality of life for them and other minority groups improve during the 20th century as a result of their efforts to secure civil rights and freedoms guaranteed to them in the Constitution?

Tangible Gains by African Americans and Women

The question may be answered by looking at the suburbanization in the United States. Throughout the period of Jim Crow, African Americans became increasingly concentrated in urban areas across the North and West. Throughout that same period, whites moved in greater numbers to suburban communities. If the civil rights movement was effective in eliminating segregation, reducing discrimination, and resulting in greater economic opportunity for members of minority groups, we might expect that more African Americans would move to affluent suburbs.

Housing. Statistics confirm this trend. Since 1970, there has been an increase in the number of African Americans who moved from inner-city neighborhoods to suburban areas. In suburbs such as Southfield, outside Detroit, Michigan, Prince George's County, Maryland, near Washington, D.C., and Mount Vernon, New York, which is north of the borough of the Bronx in New York City, the African American population increased in the last decades of the 20th century. This does not mean that discrimination against African Americans has vanished, but it does signal positive changes that can be traced back to the civil rights movement of the 1950s and 1960s.

Income. Median income is another indicator of whether or not minority status has changed over the decades. In a comparison of white and black families over the period encompassed by the modern civil rights movement (since the mid-1950s), white families still earn considerably more, but the gap has narrowed. In 1947, black families' median income (in adjusted 2001 dollars) was about 51 percent that of white families. In other words, middle-level white families earned about twice as much as middle-level black families. In 1960, the difference had narrowed slightly to 55 percent and in 1980 to 58 percent. In 2000, black families' median income was about 64 percent that of white families. This is clearly an improvement over a 53-year period, but a significant gap remains.

In the case of women, the earnings gap between men and women is an indicator of whether or not women have made gains over the past few decades. Between 1950 and 1980, married women entered the workforce in great numbers. During that period, the ratio of female-to-male earnings for full-time workers was about 60 percent. In the 1980s, however, the gap between the earnings of men and women started steadily to decrease. By the end of the decade, the ratio of female-to-male earnings had improved to about 68 percent. Currently, it is estimated that women who work full time through the year earn about 75 percent of what men earn for every hour worked. The narrowing of the earnings gap between men and women can be attributed to several factors, including more women achieving higher levels of education and greater work experience, and to legislation that forbids gender discrimination.

Test Yourself
Are there any indications that the struggles for racial and gender equality have improved the quality of life for any minority group?

POINTS TO REMEMBER

- Southern states began enacting Jim Crow laws shortly after the end of Reconstruction.
- Jim Crow laws were an example of legal racial segregation.
- The Supreme Court's ruling *Plessy* v. *Ferguson* found "separate-but-equal" constitutional and allowed Jim Crow laws to remain in place.
- The Supreme Court's approval of Jim Crow laws was not overturned until the *Brown* v. *Board of Education of Topeka* ruling in 1954.
- Since the 1970s, increasing numbers of African American families have moved from urban neighborhoods to suburban communities.
- In the years since the mid-1950s, the gap between median income in adjusted 2001 dollars for white and black families has decreased.
- Beginning in the 1980s, the earnings gap between men and women has narrowed.

EXERCISES

CHECKING WHAT YOU HAVE READ

1. How did Jim Crow laws get their name?

2. Why did Southern states begin enacting Jim Crow laws?

3. What are some examples of Jim Crow laws?

4. How did the Supreme Court's ruling in *Plessy* v. *Ferguson* affect Jim Crow laws?

5. How was the legal basis for Jim Crow laws ended?

USING WHAT YOU HAVE READ

Interview someone in your community who was active in the civil rights movement, women's movement, or who worked to gain equality for another minority group. Ask the person questions that will reveal what he or she thinks about how the status of their group has changed over the years. Write a brief report about your findings.

THINKING ABOUT WHAT YOU HAVE READ

Using information from this chapter, write a paragraph in which you explain how you think the status of African Americans or women has changed over the decades. Support your position with evidence from the chapter or from other sources. If you use other sources, be sure to cite them. Then predict how you think the status of the group you chose will change over the next two decades. Give reasons for your prediction.

SKILLS

Reading a Line Graph

Use the line graph below to answer the questions that follow.

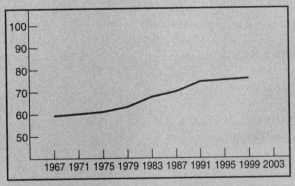

Earnings of female workers since 1967 (as a
percent of male workers' earnings)

1. What can you say about the earnings of female workers as a percent of male workers' earnings from 1967 to 1999?

2. According to the graph, in which decade did the earnings of female workers increase the most?

3. What factors could account for the gains that women have made in the workplace?

CHAPTER 24

CULTURAL EXCHANGES

BENCHMARK:

Analyze the ways that contacts between people of different cultures result in exchanges of cultural practices.

This benchmark focuses on the effects of immigration in the United States, and specifically on housing patterns, politics, the education system, and language. Questions on the Ohio Graduation Test (OGT) related to this benchmark will address only the effects of immigration, not the causes or patterns of immigration to the United States. The effects will be restricted to the areas listed above.

★ IMMIGRATION AFTER THE CIVIL WAR ★

In the years following the Civil War, when the nation's industrial output was increasing rapidly, immigrants began pouring into the country looking for new opportunities. Prior to the Civil War, most immigrants were from Western and Northern European nations such as England, Ireland, Germany, and the Scandinavian countries. In the 1880s, the source of immigration changed. More people came to America from Southern and Eastern European nations such as Italy, Poland, Russia, Greece, the Austro-Hungarian Empire, and the Ottoman Empire (Turkey). By 1907, about 80 percent of all immigrants originated in Southern and Eastern Europe. In the early 1900s, immigration from Asian nations such as Japan and China, and from Mexico, also increased. Between 1880 and 1900, about 9 million immigrants arrived in the United States, and from 1900 to 1914, about 13 million.

Difficulties Encountered by New Immigrants

While most of the "older" immigrants from Northern and Western Europe were Protestant, many of the newer immigrants were either Roman Catholic or Jewish. Because of their religions and the fact that few of them spoke English, these "new" immigrants faced a more difficult time fitting into American society. Consequently, the majority of the post-Civil War-era immigrants from the same country of origin stayed together in urban neighborhoods. Factory and other types of jobs also were more available in urban centers. In Western states such as California, immigrants often found work in the fields picking vegetables and other crops.

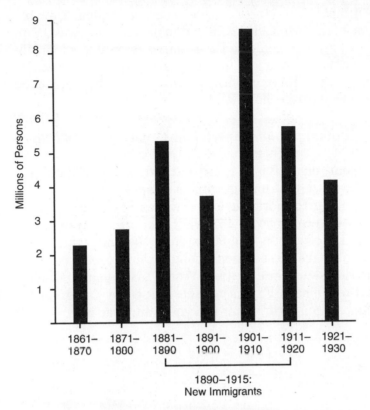

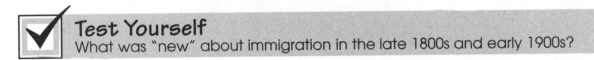

U.S. Immigration, 1861–1930

✓ Test Yourself
What was "new" about immigration in the late 1800s and early 1900s?

Problems in Cities. Immigrants settled in different areas when they arrived, depending upon when they came and their nation of origin. Following the Civil War, most Scandinavian immigrants (Norwegian, Swedish, Danish, and Finnish) gravitated to farming areas in the Midwest. Most Eastern and Southern European immigrants who arrived between the 1880s and early 1900s settled in large Eastern and Midwestern cities where they could find work in factories or as laborers. By 1910, about 80 percent of the residents of Chicago were either first- or second-generation immigrants, and in most major U.S. cities, immigrant families made up over half the total population. Between 1860 and 1910, the urban population exploded from around 6 million to over 42 million persons. Immigration was responsible for much of that increase. Housing and sanitation became severe problems in these cities. There simply were not enough places for the new immigrants to live. Many people had to crowd into small tenement apartments, where sanitary facilities were inadequate, and disease was rampant.

Immigrants faced enormous problems once they settled in American cities. Many of them had been farmers or agricultural workers in Europe. Working in a factory was a new way of life for them. Since many immigrants did not speak English, they tended to live together in neighborhoods with other immigrants from their native country. Italian, Polish, Russian, and Greek ethnic neighborhoods developed in most major cities. Many immigrants clung as much as they could to their old ways of life, celebrating ethnic holidays and reading newspapers in their native language. Because many immigrants were either Roman Catholic or Jewish, they attended churches or synagogues in their new homeland.

Backlash Against Immigrants. Many native-born Americans, mostly Protestant, reacted with fear and prejudice to the newcomers. Anti-immigrant sentiment, or nativism, grew as the number of immigrants increased. Some Americans viewed immigrants as competitors for jobs, and immigrants were often willing to work for lower wages in order to feed their families. Other nativists were motivated by religious prejudice or just disliked immigrants because of their languages and customs. One organization, the American Protective Association, lobbied Congress to restrict immigration. Similar nativist sentiment on the West Coast against Chinese immigrants resulted in the Chinese Exclusion Act. Passed by Congress in 1882, the act stopped Chinese immigration for ten years and was later extended.

Test Yourself
What kinds of problems did the "new" immigrants face upon arrival in the United States?

The Effect of Immigration on Politics

The flood of immigrants into American cities in the decades after the Civil War also affected the political scene. City governments had to grow as urban populations increased and as their problems multiplied—housing, sanitation, education, health, and transportation. Politics became a profession for some people in this new environment, and political machines sprang up in virtually every major city. A political machine is an organization that controls an urban political party. It provides services such as jobs to workers and favorable treatment to businesses in return for their support. As the number of immigrants grew, political machine operatives saw them as a source of votes and support. George Washington Plunkitt (1842–1924) was a well-known machine politician in New York City during the late 1800s. In 1889, he described how he maintained his support among the people in his district:

> . . . I've got a regular system for this. If there's a fire in Ninth or Tenth or Eleventh Avenue, for example, any hour of the day or night, I'm usually there with some of my election district captains as soon as the fire engines. If a family is burned out I don't ask them if they are Republicans or Democrats, and I don't refer them to the Charity Organization Society, which would investigate their case in a month or two and decide if they are worthy of help about the time they are dead from starvation. I just get quarters for them, buy clothes for them if their clothes were all burned up, and fix them up until they get things runnin' again. It's philanthropy, but it's politics too—mighty good politics. Who can tell me how many votes one of those fires

George Washington Plunkitt

brings me? The poor are the most grateful people in the world, and, let me tell you, they have more friends in their neighborhoods than the rich have in theirs.

. . . Another thing, I can always get a job for a deservin' man. I make it a point to keep track of jobs, and it seldom happens that I don't have a few up my sleeve ready for use.

Through their control of city government, machine officials gave jobs to many immigrants and their children, and in return expected their votes. Politicians were also able to garner the support of businesses by handing out contracts for services and other kinds of preferential treatment. The machine could then pressure these businesses to hire immigrants and other supporters. Political machines were usually corrupt and engaged in illegal or criminal activity. Immigrants unfamiliar with the political system and desperate for work or a place to live were often willing to trade their vote for a job or an apartment, no matter how low the wages or how dilapidated the housing.

Test Yourself
How did urban political machines take advantage of immigrants?

Immigration in the Late 20th Century

Today—just as in the years after the Civil War—the huge wave of immigrants places severe strains on the educational systems in most large cities.

In 1965, Congress passed the Immigration and Naturalization Act. The law increased the number of immigrants allowed to enter the United States, especially from Latin America and Asia, and it ended quotas that favored Europeans. In the 1970s, 1980s, and 1990s, immigrants from the former Soviet Union, China, Cuba, and Southeastern Asian nations such as Vietnam, Laos, Korea, and Thailand entered the United States, many as refugees from civil wars and political chaos in their homelands.

Education of Immigrants. As a result of this most recent wave of immigration, school enrollment increased, especially in large cities, where many immigrant groups settled. Classrooms often became overcrowded. Many immigrants' native language is not English, which makes it difficult for them to learn. Urban school systems, whose budgets are already tight, have had to spend large amounts of money for teachers of English as a second language to help these students.

Today, a good education is more important than ever in preparing for the workforce. Knowledge of English and greater technical skills are needed for more and more occupations. This places great stress on educational systems across the nation.

Test Yourself
How has immigration put strains on the educational system of the United States?

Learning the New Language

In one aspect of life in the United States, it is easy to recognize how immigration throughout its history has enriched our nation. English, as commonly spoken in the United States, has appropriated words from other languages. According to the 2000 Census, some 47 million residents above the age of five spoke a language other than English at home. (In 1990, that figure was about 32 million.) About half of those 47 million spoke Spanish. Other languages included Chinese, Korean, French, German, Italian, Russian, and Vietnamese. These languages have added richness to the American vocabulary.

Faster Assimilation. Many immigrants of the late 1800s and early 1900s never became very good English-speakers. Their children were more accomplished with the language and usually became bilingual. Their grandchildren often could speak only English. Today because of television, the Internet, and language programs, immigrants seem to be reducing the time period from immigration to assimilation from three generations to just two. This rich interaction among immigrants and native speakers over many decades has resulted in changes to "American" English that we take for granted today.

Loan Words. *Loan words* are words incorporated from one language—called the *source language*—into another. Thanks in large part to its rich immigrant experience, American English has borrowed many words from other languages. This is a prime example of *cultural exchange*. Since Spanish speakers have played a large part in American history, there are many examples of loan words from Spanish in American English. Alligator, bronco, cafeteria, cigar, cigarette, guerrilla, mustang, patio, and tornado are just a few of the many loan words from Spanish that we use in the United States every day. Besides thousands of place names, we have also adopted loan words from various Native

American Indian languages. Some examples are bayou, chipmunk, hickory, hominy, igloo, kayak, moccasin, moose, opossum, pecan, squash, tepee, toboggan, and tomahawk.

Test Yourself
What is an example of cultural exchange in the use of language in the United States?

The United States has been shaped by cultural exchanges from its very beginnings, starting with white settlers coming into contact with Native Americans in the 17th century and continuing through wave after wave of immigration, right into the 21st century. The United States has always been a nation of immigrants, and they have enriched American culture and contributed to its economy, as well as its way of life, in very important ways.

POINTS TO REMEMBER

- In the years after the Civil War, the pattern of immigration changed from predominately Northern and Western European to Southern and Eastern European and Asian immigrants.
- The "new" immigrants of the late 19th and early 20th centuries were mostly Roman Catholic or Jewish.
- Many immigrants clustered together in urban neighborhoods with others from their nation of origin.
- Most immigrants found work as urban laborers or factory workers; some settled on farms in the Midwest.
- Many native-born Americans feared and resented immigrants; nativism increased after the Civil War.
- Urban political machines recruited immigrants for political support by providing jobs and other services.
- Immigration has affected and will continue to affect the racial and ethnic makeup of the U.S. population.
- Educating immigrants and their children creates financial stress on the nation's educational system.

EXERCISES

CHECKING WHAT YOU HAVE HEARD

1. Why did many immigrants come to the United States in the decades following the Civil War?

2. Why did many immigrants cluster together with other people from their nation of origin in American cities?

3. What were some of the most severe problems faced by immigrants when they arrived in the United States?

4. Why did immigrants often cooperate with urban political machines?

5. What is an example of a cultural exchange that resulted from immigration to the United States?

USING WHAT YOU HAVE READ

Search a local newspaper or national newspaper over a two-week period or more for articles that discuss immigrants or immigration. Look for examples of the effects of immigration on the United States, either positive or negative. Make a table that lists the source of the article, the date, the immigrant group discussed, and the effect on the United States.

Source	Date	Immigrant Group	Effect on the U.S.

THINKING ABOUT WHAT YOU HAVE READ

Assume the role of the editor of a local newspaper in your community. Your community has recently experienced an influx of thousands of immigrants from a nation in which English is not the primary language. Most of the immigrants have little money and are uneducated. A U.S. representative from your district has proposed a federal law that would restrict immigration. Write an editorial for your newspaper in which you either support or oppose this proposed law. State your position clearly and explain the reasons for your opinion to your readers.

SKILLS

Understanding a Table

Study the table and answer the questions that follow.

Immigrants to the United States by World Region of Origin, 1971–2000 (thousands of persons)

Region	1971–1980	1981–1990	1991–2000
All Countries	4,493.3	7,338.1	9,094.4
Europe	801.3	705.6	1,311.4
Asia	1,633.8	2,817.4	2,892.2
North America	1,645.0	3,125.0	3,918.4
Canada	114.8	119.2	137.6
Mexico	637.2	1,653.3	2,251.4
Caribbean	759.8	892.7	996.1
Central America	132.4	458.7	531.8
South America	284.4	455.9	539.9
Africa	91.5	192.3	383.0

1. How has the number of immigrants to the United States changed over the past three decades?

2. How do you account for this change?

3. Which continent supplied the largest number of immigrants in the 1990s? Why do you think this was so?

4. Which region supplies the fewest number of immigrants? Why do you think this is so?

CHAPTER 25

REGIONS OVER TIME

BENCHMARK:

Analyze the cultural, physical, economic, and political characteristics that define regions and describe reasons that regions change over time.

This benchmark and the accompanying grade level indicator ask students to analyze characteristics of regions and to explain how those characteristics change over time, as well as how perceptions of regions change. Regions include urban areas, wilderness, farmland, and centers of industry and technology. A *region* is defined as an area with one or more common characteristics or features, which give it a measure of homogeneity and make it different from surrounding areas.

★ REGIONS OF THE UNITED STATES ★

Geographers study how people live on and use the surface of the Earth. Regions help them conduct that ongoing study. There are many regions within the United States, and they are defined in many different ways. Regions differ greatly in size and kind. Often the borders of a region are indistinct, and they change over time.

Regions can be based on landforms (mountains, plateaus), relative location (Northeast, Southwest), where people live (urban, rural, suburban), topography (desert, wetlands), economy (farming, industrial), religion (Amish), economic specialization (Corn Belt, Silicon Valley), language or ethnic group (Chinese, Hispanic), or other characteristics. By subdividing our nation into various kinds of regions, we can better understand the United States as a whole.

Metropolitan Statistical Areas (MSAs)

Other kinds of regions are characterized by their functions, such as school districts, cities, or counties. A Metropolitan Statistical Area (MSA) is another kind of region in this category. An MSA, according to the Census Bureau, consists of a central city with at least 50,000 people or more, the county that it is located in, and the surrounding counties in which jobs or commercial activity are linked significantly to the central city. The U.S. government currently lists 300 MSAs in the United States. Some are huge urban areas such as New York City, Chicago, and Los Angeles. Others are centered around smaller cities such as Dayton-Springfield, Ohio, or Erie, Pennsylvania.

Test Yourself
How are regions determined?

Urban and Suburban Regions

The vast majority of people in the United States live in an MSA, but that has not always been the case. It was not until between 1910 and 1920 that the majority of the U.S. population lived in urban areas. In 1870, nearly 75 percent of Americans lived in rural areas and were engaged in agriculture or businesses that supported farmers. In 1890, the percentage of people living in rural areas had decreased to about 65 percent. The 1920 Census was the first to reveal that more people were living in cities—51 percent—than in rural areas. This change was due in large part to the tremendous influx of immigrants between 1880 and 1920, most of whom lived and worked in urban areas. As more and more people lived in or had contact with urban areas, their perceptions of cities also changed. In the late 1800s and early 1900s, many Americans considered cities dirty and dangerous places that were breeding grounds for sin, crime, and disease. As travel became more affordable and available, and as more people moved to cities for work, the nation's perception began to change. As the United States moved into the 20th century, cities increasingly became centers of industry, technology, transportation, education, and culture. Once seen as ugly and corrupt, cities gradually became not only home to thousands of former country residents but also tourist destinations for many. During the Gilded Age (roughly the end of Reconstruction—1877—to the turn of the century), many cities witnessed the birth of large, elegant, and expensive hotels that attracted people from all over the nation.

The Move to Suburbia. After World War II, cities underwent another kind of change. Many people abandoned center cities for green pastures in the suburbs. Although many people still worked in the city proper, improved transportation systems made it affordable and possible for middle-income earners to commute from suburban homes to their jobs. Developers built millions of single-family homes in large tracts of land that had recently been rural areas. Soldiers returning from World War II used a government program called the G.I. Bill of Rights, which provided benefits to U.S. military veterans, to purchase suburban homes and attend college.

Areas such as the suburbs around Los Angeles, California, soon became home for large numbers of Americans who wanted to own a house. In the years after World War II, the center city became home for African Americans and immigrants, groups that could not afford to live in suburban areas. Throughout the 1970s and 1980s, many large cities suffered from declining tax revenues as people moved to the suburbs.

More recently, some cities have experienced a slight reversal of the trend toward suburbanization. Many cities have remained centers of culture and entertainment—with museums, theaters, and restaurants—to which younger people have returned. The substantial drop in crime in many large cities in the past two decades brought many people back. People have also returned to cities because of the high cost of suburban housing.

Farmland and Wilderness Regions

As urban and suburban areas grew, in a process sometimes referred to as *urban sprawl*, two other regions—wilderness areas and farmland—shrank. Especially in the years after World War II, when suburbanization accelerated, farmland increasingly fell victim to new housing tracts. In recent years, public concern over loss of farmland grew as urbanization and suburbanization appropriated more areas of fertile land. Some experts fear that this historical process could compromise the nation's capacity to produce food in the future. Many people have given up farming altogether. In 1981, a government study estimated that the amount of land converted from rural areas, usually farmland, to urban or suburban uses increased from about 1.1 million acres between 1958 and 1967 to over 2.3 million acres between 1967 and 1975. To make matters worse, much of this land was highly productive farmland. The problem is not simply that farmland is being converted to other uses. Another aspect of lost agricultural acreage is the kind of land that is being lost. Much of it is very fertile land that produced high crop yields.

This concern is not limited to the United States. Population experts today estimate that by 2025, the world's population will top 8 billion, a 38 percent increase. The number of acres of cropland in production, however, has not been increasing. In fact, due to urbanization, agricultural acreage has declined all over the world, especially in areas of high population growth such as several African and Asian nations. Despite the decline of agricultural acreage, however, improved technology and farming techniques have increased food production.

Test Yourself
Why has farm acreage declined over the past few decades?

Wetlands. Wetlands (swampy or marshy areas) are a particular kind of wilderness or wildlife region that provide habitat for fish, birds, and several kinds of small animals. In the early years of the 20th century, the drainage of wetlands increased rapidly due to population growth and industrial development. Land was needed for factories and housing. Improved construction technology and engineering capabilities made huge water projects possible. These types of projects, such as the Mississippi River dam system, have detrimental effects on surrounding wetlands. The land along the Mississippi River consisted of swampy areas consisting of thousands of small islands. Ponds and lakes were scattered throughout wooded areas along the riverbank, and the river channel changed frequently. Dams were built to create a navigable river system, increasing the water depth behind each dam and creating a lake. One result of the dam system was that it eliminated large fluctuations in the river's depth and helped control flooding. The project eliminated some wetlands and created new ones. The entire project lasted nearly 25 years.

Urban and suburban growth also drained wetlands, as did some agricultural businesses such as the timber industry. Wetlands were also drained in several places to create land that could be cultivated. Developers and farmers,

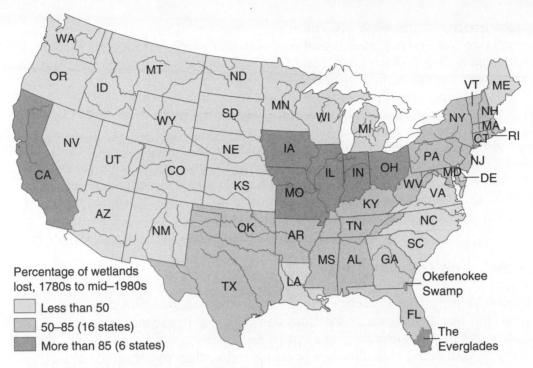

Percentage of wetlands
lost, 1780s to mid–1980s

☐ Less than 50
▨ 50–85 (16 states)
▧ More than 85 (6 states)

The loss of wetlands in the United States

for example, dug some 400 miles of canals that drained large areas of the Everglades, a huge swamp in southern Florida.

In the 1960s, Congress passed legislation that encouraged and supported wetland drainage for reasons such as flood control, farmland expansion, and housing. In the 1970s, however, with the development of the environmental movement, awareness of the importance of wetlands and their destruction increased, as did attempts to protect them. Congress responded with legislation such as the Emergency Wetlands Resources Act (1986), which helped limit wetlands destruction. In many places, efforts have been made to restore some wetlands, and National Wildlife Refuges have replaced projects to drain swamps or marshes. One notable example of wetlands restoration is in the Everglades, where about 60 percent of the remaining wetlands have been protected. Wetland loss has decreased, but it has not been eliminated.

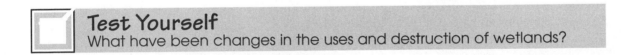

Test Yourself
What have been changes in the uses and destruction of wetlands?

Centers of Industry and Technology

Industrial centers have always been important regions in the United States, especially since the late 1800s. In recent years a new kind of region—a center of technology—has become significant to the U.S. economy. Thirty or 40 years ago, the technological revolution that resulted in the current information society based on computers and the Internet started in the area around Palo Alto,

California, now known as Silicon Valley. Stanford University in Palo Alto needed to raise money, so it leased part of the university to several technology companies. This was the beginning of the high-tech revolution. In 1971, Don C. Hoefler, a journalist, first coined the term "Silicon Valley." In that same year, Intel developed the first microprocessor, the computer chip. In 1976, Apple Computer produced the first personal computer, which helped introduce and popularize the new machines to ordinary people.

As the high-tech and Internet revolution advanced throughout the 1980s and 1990s, similar companies created centers of technology in other parts of the United States, such as Seattle, Washington; Portland, Oregon; Austin, Texas; Phoenix, Arizona; Boston, Massachusetts; and areas in the Midwest. High-tech regions can now be found in virtually every part of the United States.

The Rust Belt and the Sun Belt

Silicon Valley is an economic region. Another economic region is an industrial area that became known as the Rust Belt. Located in the midwestern United States, it consisted primarily of all or part of the states of Pennsylvania, Ohio, Michigan, Indiana, and Illinois. For many years, this area was the industrial hub of the United States, featuring steel mills, automobile factories, and many other heavy industries. Economic problems such as foreign competition, a shift from manufacturing to service industries, and aging buildings and equipment led to decline of Rust Belt industries. Many factories closed down, and many people who lost their jobs left the area looking for work elsewhere. The term *Rust Belt* became used in reference to the rusting machinery and abandoned plants that remained from more prosperous times. Many Rust Belt cities have revived, due in large part to the introduction of new service industries, high-tech companies, and other enterprises.

When people fled the Rust Belt in the 1970s, they often moved south or west to states such as California, Arizona, Texas, Florida, Georgia, North Carolina, and South Carolina. Many manufacturing companies moved their operations to take advantage of the better weather, fewer labor unions, lower taxes, and reduced labor costs. Many retirees also moved to the *Sun Belt*, as this region became known, to take advantage of the climate and lower costs of

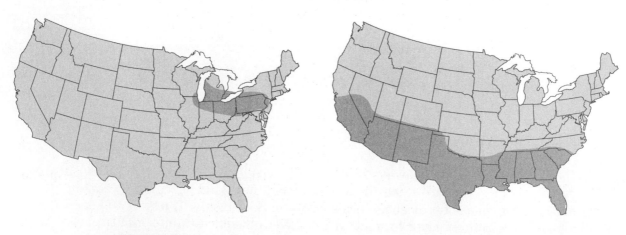

The Rust Belt   The Sun Belt

living. As a result, the Sun Belt states gained electoral votes and have become more important in the U.S. political scene.

 Test Yourself
How did the Rust Belt and the Sun Belt get their names?

POINTS TO REMEMBER

- Regions are defined in many ways, using different characteristics.
- Most Americans today live in a Metropolitan Statistical Area (MSA).
- A higher percentage of Americans lived in rural areas until around 1920.
- The general perception of cities has improved since the 1800s.
- The process of suburbanization increased after World War II, largely due to improved and affordable transportation.
- Recently, there has been a slight reversal of suburbanization.
- As cities and suburbs have grown, farmland areas have decreased.
- The number of wetlands also decreased after World War II.
- Recent legislation has helped to slow the loss of wetlands.
- The technological revolution that started in the 1970s fostered the development of high-tech regions throughout the United States.
- Many people left the Rust Belt in the 1970s to find work in Sun Belt states.

EXERCISES

CHECKING WHAT YOU HAVE READ

1. Why do geographers categorize places into regions?

2. What has been the most significant population change in the United States since the late 1800s?

3. What made the process of suburbanization possible in the United States?

4. What factors have influenced people to move back to cities?

5. How did the building of the Mississippi River dam system affect wetlands?

USING WHAT YOU HAVE READ

Assume the role of a public relations or marketing professional hired by an association of retirement centers in the Sun Belt states. Design a brochure that is intended to convince people to move from Rust Belt states to your retirement communities. Include both textual and visual elements. Make sure it provides reasons why people would want to move to the Sun Belt.

THINKING ABOUT WHAT YOU HAVE READ

Imagine you are watching a debate on a cable news station between an environmental activist and a commercial developer over the issue of wetlands. Based on what you have read in this chapter and from other sources such as the media and the Internet, list the arguments that the activist and the developer are likely to make on a separate piece of paper. Is it possible for them to compromise and reach a jointly beneficial solution? If so, explain how.

SKILLS

Critiquing Evidence Used to Support a Thesis

Read the article about urban sprawl from *USA Today* (August 28, 2003) and then answer the questions that follow.

Studies Tie Urban Sprawl to Health Risks, Road Danger

People living in sprawling American neighborhoods walk less, weigh more and are more likely to be hit by a car if they do venture out on foot or bicycle, suggests a series of studies out Friday.

Driving everywhere adds up on Americans' waistlines, and can be dangerous for their health. The studies are among the first reports to link shopping centers, a lack of sidewalks and bike trails, and other features of urban sprawl to deadly health problems. The studies appear in the September issues of the *American Journal of Health Promotion* and the *American Journal of Public*

Health. These reports come as more and more Americans are moving out to the suburbs—and walking less and less. Studies by the Federal Highway Administration show that Americans make fewer than 6 percent of daily trips on foot.

In the first report, Reid Ewing, a researcher at the University of Maryland, and his colleagues studied more than 200,000 Americans living in 448 counties in major metropolitan areas. The team assessed the degree of sprawl in each county and then looked at some key health characteristics. Team members found that people who lived in sprawling neighborhoods walked less and had less chance to stay fit.

These neighborhoods were built to accommodate cars and SUVs, not walkers, says Richard Jackson of the Centers for Disease Control and Prevention in Atlanta. People living in urban sprawl often can't walk because the shops are miles away, often in strip malls accessible only by high-speed roadways, he says.

Ewing's study shows that everyday driving trips to the store or to the corner bus stop can add up. People in sprawling neighborhoods weighed about six pounds more on average than the folks living in compact neighborhoods, where sidewalks are plentiful and stores and shops are close to residential areas.

The report also shows that people living in sprawling urban areas were more likely to suffer from obesity, which can put people at higher risk of cancer, diabetes, and a host of other diseases. Urban sprawl also put residents at a slightly higher risk of developing high blood pressure.

A second study, by John Pucher at Rutgers University in New Brunswick, N.J., suggests that urban sprawl poses another health hazard: It's dangerous to walk or bike in areas where cars rule the road. He found that American cyclists and pedestrians were two to six times more likely to be killed on the road than their German or Dutch counterparts. He says American cities could remedy that hazard by putting in more car-free zones, sidewalks and bike paths.

Some developers now sell planned communities with walking and biking paths. The Urban Land Institute, a group for developers and planners, says 5 percent to 15 percent of new development is designed with pedestrians in mind. If Americans don't get out of the car and walk more, experts worry that epidemic of obesity and disease will just get worse.

"What we're talking about are diseases that will become rampant among the baby boomers," Jackson says. "We've got to build neighborhoods that work for people."   (From *USA Today*, a division of Gannett Co., Inc. Reprinted with permission.)

—By Kathleen Fackelmann

1. What is the thesis of the article?

2. What statistical evidence is used to support the thesis?

3. What is the source of each statistic?

4. How credible do you think these sources and statistics are? Explain why.

5. Do you think the author used credible sources to support the thesis of the article? Why or why not?

CHAPTER 26

GEOGRAPHIC CHANGE AND HUMAN ACTIVITY

BENCHMARK:

Analyze geographic changes brought about by human activity, using appropriate maps and other geographic data.

This benchmark requires students to analyze the effect of human activity on geography—that is, their environment. In the history of the United States, how did advances in technology, communications, and transportation affect economic activity and the use of natural resources, human resources, and capital goods to produce goods and services? Students will be expected to analyze various forms of geographic data such as maps, charts, graphs, and tables, and draw conclusions based on their analyses.

★ HUMAN–ENVIRONMENT INTERACTION ★

Ever since human beings have lived on the Earth, they have been interacting with their environment. It was in the environment that prehistoric humans found food, clothing, and shelter. For the most part, they had to adapt to their environment in order to survive. Over thousands of years, however, people became increasingly able to alter their environments in ways that benefited them. The degree to which people changed the environment depended mostly upon the quality of their land, their technology, and their own ingenuity. Some environmental alterations took great effort and investment of capital resources, requiring the construction of dams or road systems. Natural disasters such as floods, tornadoes, hurricanes, earthquakes, and volcanic activity sometimes frustrated efforts by human beings to alter their environment.

The Development of the United States

By the end of the 19th century, the United States was one of the world's richest and most productive nations. An abundance of natural resources and human capital played a large role in that development. Laborers, entrepreneurs, investors, business leaders, scientists, engineers, and inventors all made contributions to the rapid increase of industrialization, innovation, and productivity. Although the development provided many benefits, it often came with a number of costs, many of which were unforeseen, such as air and water pollution and the overconsumption of resources.

On pages 374–375 is a time line of important advances in technology since the end of Reconstruction. As you read each development, event, or invention, think about the effect it had on the U.S. economy and environment. Predict some of the changes that might have occurred as a result of each one. How might it have changed economic activity? Did it alter the way people worked or where they lived? Did it use new resources or old resources in new ways? What were its consequences for American society?

★ USING GEOGRAPHICAL DATA ★

Geographical data are often presented in graphic form such as maps, charts, graphs, and tables. In this chapter you will find several graphic representations of data. Analyze what they demonstrate about economic activity and the use of productive resources in the United States.

Farms

In the second half of the 20th century, the number of farms in the United States declined sharply while the nation's population increased. Technological advances in farming made it possible for fewer farms to produce more food. Between 1950 and 1997, the number of farms decreased from 5.4 million to 1.9 million. This sharp drop in the number of farms was attributed to new machinery and better farming methods that increased productivity. During the 20th century, wheat yields per acre tripled, while the time needed to cultivate wheat declined dramatically. Corn production also experienced greater yields with less time needed needed for cultivation.

Technological innovations made these productivity increases possible. To cite several examples, tractors replaced horses and other farm animals. Fertilizers and pesticides increased crop growth rates and reduced losses to insects. Scientists produced disease-resistant seeds that yielded more per acre.

Farm operators (millions) in the United States, 1900–2000

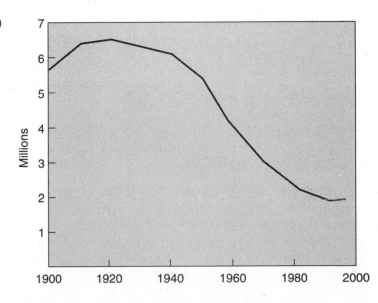

Technology Time Line, 1876–2004

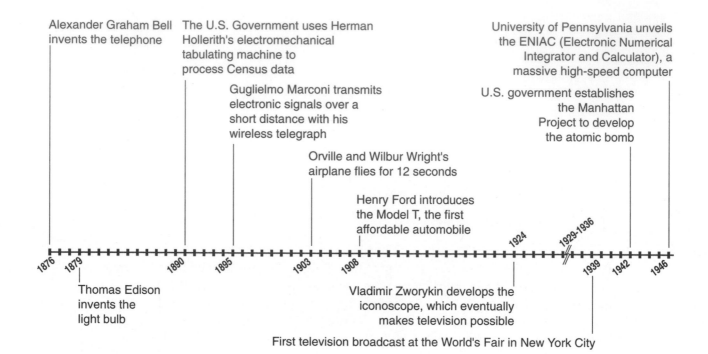

Alexander Graham Bell invents the telephone

The U.S. Government uses Herman Hollerith's electromechanical tabulating machine to process Census data

Guglielmo Marconi transmits electronic signals over a short distance with his wireless telegraph

University of Pennsylvania unveils the ENIAC (Electronic Numerical Integrator and Calculator), a massive high-speed computer

U.S. government establishes the Manhattan Project to develop the atomic bomb

Orville and Wilbur Wright's airplane flies for 12 seconds

Henry Ford introduces the Model T, the first affordable automobile

1876 1879 1890 1895 1903 1908 1924 1929-1936 1939 1942 1946

Thomas Edison invents the light bulb

Vladimir Zworykin develops the iconoscope, which eventually makes television possible

First television broadcast at the World's Fair in New York City

Guglielmo Marconi tests his wireless telegraph.

The Wright brothers test their air glider.

Microsoft Corporation's first version of the Windows operating system reaches the market

U.S. launches the first satellite in the Global Positioning System (GPS)

Development of prototype of first digital high-definition television

Physicists at Bell Telephone Laboratories invent the transistor, which revolutionizes the electronics industry

Apple Computer Company introduces the Apple II, the bestselling personal computer

U.S. Department of Defense's ARPANET system, the precursor to the Internet, links several different computer systems

Versions of Mosaic, the first graphical Web browser for Microsoft Windows, the Apple Macintosh, and certain Unix systems, are released

1957

1980

1996 1998 2001 2004

1948

1969

1985 1988 1991 1993

USSR launches Sputnik I, an artificial satellite into orbit

The Palm Pilot, a hand-held computer and personal organizer, reaches the market

Apollo Eleven astronauts Neil Armstrong and Buzz Aldrin walk on the moon

Development of the TCP/IP protocol for the transmission of data between computer systems which becomes the technological standard for the Internet

Work begins in Earth orbit to assemble the International Space Station (ISS)

Mars *Odyssey* space probe launched

Japanese computer scientists unveil Earth Simulator, supercomputer that performs millions of calculations per second

SpaceShipOne, first privately funded manned spacecraft, reaches altitude of nearly 70 miles

The ENIAC computer

Another result of these technological improvements was an increase in the size of farms. Small farms had a difficult time competing against large, corporate-owned operations, and many small farmers abandoned the occupation to work in cities. In the second half of the 20th century, the number of agricultural workers in the United States dropped by about 50 percent.

Education

Between 1910 and 1998, the percentage of people obtaining a high school diploma increased from 13 percent to 83 percent. The number of college graduates also increased significantly in the same period. New careers in technological fields required a better educated workforce.

Transportation

The means and amount of travel within the United States changed drastically over the course of the last century. Railroads were the most common method of travel in the late 1800s and early 1900s. After the 1920s, however, automobile use increased at the expense of rail travel. That trend has continued to the present. Rail travel also decreased in the later half of the 20th century as air travel became more affordable and available.

The Automobile. Perhaps the most significant transportation advance in the last century was the automobile. It has literally changed the face of America. In 1998, the United States had 4 million miles of roads, enough to circle the globe more than 155 times. In 1995, motorists drove personal vehicles over 2 trillion miles. Largely because of the automobile, the United States has become a predominately suburban nation, and the vast majority of Americans drive a personal vehicle such as a car, truck, or an SUV to work.

Means of Transportation to Work, 1960–2000					
	1960 (14 and older) percent	*1970 (14 and older) (percent)*	*1980 (16 and older) (percent)*	*1990 (16 and older) (percent)*	*2000 (16 and older) (percent)*
Automobile or other	64.0	77.7	84.1	86.5	87.9
Public Transportation	12.1	8.9	6.4	5.3	4.7
Walked Only	9.9	7.4	5.6	3.9	2.9
Worked at Home	7.2	3.5	2.3	3.0	3.3

Telephones

As the 20th century unfolded, the telephone became an integral part of life for most Americans. It made communication instantaneous, allowing people to talk over long distances at a relatively low cost. At first, telephones were used primarily by businesses, but by World War II, more American homes had them. In the 21st century hard-wired telephones are rapidly being replaced by cellular phones, which allow people to go virtually anywhere and maintain lines of communication.

Personal Computers

Like telephones, television, and automobiles, personal computers have changed the United States in many lasting ways. Although they were available in the late 1970s, sales of personal computers took off during the 1980s. A wide range of software programs, including games, spreadsheets, word processors, and financial tools, helped make personal computers popular with many families and businesses. Through the use of modems, personal computer users could communicate with one another and log on to online Bulletin Board Systems (BBSs), which were precursors to present-day Web sites.

The Internet. The mid-1990s witnessed the explosive growth of the Internet, an electronic network linking different computer systems around the world. The number of sites on the Internet's World Wide Web grew rapidly, offering users easy access to huge amounts of information. The Internet also revolutionized business and politics. New online businesses such as Amazon.com quickly became popular with many users. Many established corporations gradually turned to the Internet to market their products and services to new customers. Many politicians and candidates for office also set up Web sites to reach potential voters, publicize their campaigns, and raise money.

The Growth of Technology, 1920–2000

	Percent of Households with			Percent of TV households with		Commercial Television Stations		Cable Television		Daily Newspapers	
	Telephone Service	Radio	Television	Cable TV	VCRs	VHF	UHF	Systems (Number)	House-holds Served (millions)	Number	Circulation (millions)
1920	35.0	(NA)	(NA)	(NA)	(NA)	(NA)	(NA)	(NA)	(NA)	2,042	27.8
1930	40.9	39	(NA)	(NA)	(NA)	(NA)	(NA)	(NA)	(NA)	1,942	39.5
1940	36.9	73	(NA)	(NA)	(NA)	(NA)	(NA)	(NA)	(NA)	1,878	41.1
1950	61.8	91	9.0	(NA)	(NA)	98	0	(NA)	(NA)	1,772	53.8
1960	78.3	94	87.1	(NA)	(NA)	440	75	(NA)	(NA)	1,763	58.9
1970	90.5	99	95.3	6.7	(NA)	501	176	2,490	3.9	1,748	62.1
1980	93.0	99	97.9	19.9	1.1	516	218	4,225	15.2	1,745	62.2
1990	93.3	99	98.2	56.4	68.6	547	545	9,575	51.9	1,611	62.3
2000	94.6	99	98.2	68.0	85.1	567	721	10,243	68.6	1,480	55.8

(NA) not applicable

Source: U.S. Census Bureau, *Statistical Abstract of the United States: 2003*, p. 80.

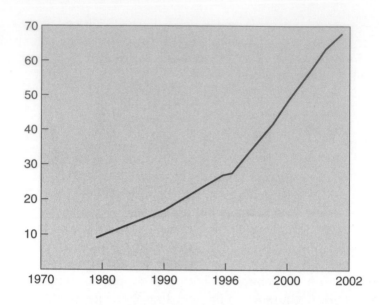

Percentage of households in the United States with a
personal computer, 1980–2002

Population Shifts

Advances in technology, communication, and transporation have led to many
changes in American life. Once a predominately rural nation, most Americans
lived in urban centers by 1915. During the 20th century, the automobile made
it possible for more people to move to the suburbs, where the majority of
Americans now live. The number of metropolitan areas (city and surrounding
suburbs) increased as well. In 1910, no state had 75 percent or more of its population living in metropolitan areas. By 2000, more than a third of the fifty
states had 75 percent or more of their population living in metropolitan areas.
In the latter half of the century, large population centers also shifted from the
Northeast and Midwest to the South and West.

POINTS TO REMEMBER

- People have always interacted with their environment in order to survive.
- Since the end of Reconstruction, the United States has become the world's
  leading industrial nation.
- The United States was able to lead the world economically in part because
  of advances in communication, technology, and transportation.
- Advances in communication, technology, and transportation resulted in
  changes to U.S. economic activity and its use of productive resources.
- Geographic and economic data are often presented in graphic form such as
  maps, charts, tables, and graphs.

- The number of farm operators in the United States declined sharply throughout the 20th century.

- The percentage of the population earning high school diplomas and college degrees has increased enormously since 1900.

- After 1950, railroad travel decreased while automobile and air travel increased.

- Telephones and computers have revolutionized communications since 1900.

- A majority of people in the United States now live in suburbs and metropolitan areas.

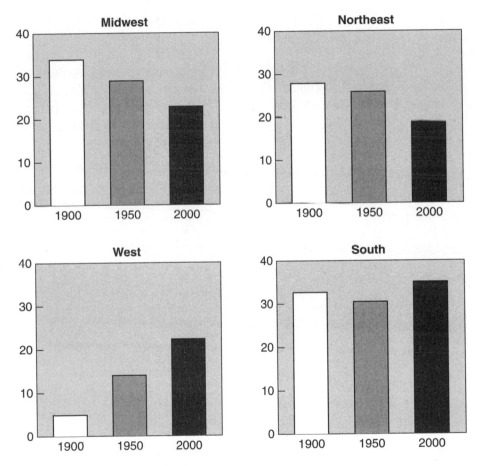

Population Shifts: Percentage of total population in each region, 1900–2000

EXERCISES

CHECKING WHAT YOU HAVE READ

1. What enabled the United States to become one of the richest and most productive nations in the world by the end of the 20th century?

    A. powerful military forces
    B. abundance of natural resources and human capital
    C. development of improved farming technology
    D. end of Reconstruction

2. Which of the following had the most direct effect on the transformation of the United States into a mostly suburban nation?

    A. automobile
    B. shopping malls
    C. air travel
    D. personal computers

3. What helped popularize personal computers with ordinary people during the early 1980s?

    A. Internet
    B. improved public transportation facilities
    C. better educated workforce
    D. wide range of software programs

4. Which of the following was most directly responsible for increased farm productivity during the 20th century?

    A. improved farming technology
    B. reduction in the number of farm operators
    C. favorable weather patterns throughout the century
    D. U.S. Department of Agriculture

5. Which two regions of the United States experienced the largest population growth during the latter half of the 20th century?

    A. Northeast and South
    B. South and West
    C. Northeast and Midwest
    D. Midwest and West

USING WHAT YOU HAVE READ

Using the time line on page 374–375 of the chapter, select five inventions, developments, or events you think are significant that have had an effect on economic activity and use of productive resources in the United States. Use those five inventions, developments, or events to complete the following table on a separate piece of paper.

Invention Development and/or Event	Year	One Effect on Economic Activity	One Effect on Use of Productive Resources

THINKING ABOUT WHAT YOU HAVE READ

1. Using the Internet and/or the local library, research your local community or a nearby town or city, comparing how it looks today with how it looked back in 1900.

2. Copy or download representative photographs of your community, both past and present. Compare the photographs and record your observations about categories such as transportation, architecture, communication, and technology used in everyday life.

3. Based on what you have learned about how technology, transportation, and communication alter economic activity and the use of productive resources, write an essay in which you predict how your community will look in 20 years and then in 50 years. Give evidence and reasons for your predictions.

SKILLS

Reading a Table

Study the table below and answer the questions that follow.

Percent of Population Living in Metropolitan Areas, 1910–2000

Area	1910	1920	1930	1940	1950	1960	1970	1980	1990	2000
United States	**28.4**	**34.0**	**44.6**	**47.8**	**56.1**	**63.3**	**69.0**	**74.8**	**77.5**	**80.3**
Northeast	54.6	60.6	74.1	75.8	78.7	80.4	81.5	85.0	88.2	89.6
Midwest	24.6	31.2	41.8	45.7	54.4	60.0	66.6	70.9	71.5	73.8
South	9.0	13.2	19.8	25.7	36.8	48.1	56.1	66.8	70.9	75.4
West	28.2	33.4	47.2	50.3	60.9	71.8	78.6	82.5	84.6	86.8

Source: U.S. Census Bureau, *Demographic Trends in the 20th Century*

1. What does the table show?

   A. the total number of people who lived in metropolitan areas between 1910 and 2000
   B. the percentage of the population that lived in metropolitan areas between 1910 and 2000
   C. the reasons why many people moved to metropolitan areas between 1910 and 2000
   D. the reasons why metropolitan areas decreased in size between 1910 and 2000

2. Which region of the United States had the largest growth of metropolitan areas between 1910 and 2000?

   A. Northeast
   B. Midwest
   C. South
   D. West

3. What was the first decade in which a majority of the U.S. population lived in metropolitan areas?

A. 1940s
B. 1950s
C. 1960s
D. 1970s

4. Which region of the United States experienced a decrease in the percentage of people living in metropolitan areas from 1910 to 2000?

A. Northeast
B. Midwest
C. all regions
D. none of the regions

5. Write a one-paragraph answer to this question: Can this table be used either to support or refute the thesis that the percentage of people living in metropolitan areas increased in all regions of the United States between 1900 and 2000 because of growth of automobile usage?

CHAPTER 27

PATTERNS AND PROCESSES OF MOVEMENT

BENCHMARK:

Analyze the patterns and processes of movement of people, products and ideas.

This chapter looks at the movement of people, products, and ideas in the United States after 1877, through the lens of patterns and processes. The focus is on the analysis of several geographic processes such as industrialization and postindustrialization, urbanization and suburbanization, and immigration. These topics have been addressed in other chapters, but this chapter approaches them from the perspective of patterns and processes, which will be the subject of questions on the OGT.

★ A POSTINDUSTRIAL UNITED STATES ★

Chapter 17 addressed the industrialization of the United States in the years after the Civil War and Reconstruction. This chapter focuses on how the United States has become what some people call a *postindustrial nation*. Review Chapter 17 before continuing with this chapter.

The industrial society that developed in the United States in the late 1800s owed its wealth to heavy manufacturing industries, railroads, and mining. The postindustrial society utilizes alternative ways to produce wealth and create jobs. In our postindustrial economy, communications, information technology, and service industries play a major role in the creation of wealth and jobs. Heavy industries still exist today, but they play a smaller role in the economy.

In 1973, Daniel Bell, a famous sociologist, published a book entitled *The Coming of Post-Industrial Society*. Bell predicted that the U.S. economy would shift its dependence from heavy industries to service industries and industries based upon scientific knowledge. The events of the last several decades have confirmed Bell's prediction.

Postindustrial Economy and Workplace Change

The change to a postindustrial economy has also changed the nature of work for many people. Many factory or assembly line jobs have been lost or replaced by machines. Today, more jobs are being created in postindustrial businesses, which require different skills such as knowledge of computers and software applications. In the industrial society, work required physical exertion and

This automobile plant uses machines to do most of the work that was once done by people.

effort. Jobs in the postindustrial society require technical training and knowledge. The United States still produces automobiles and steel, but the importance of those industries has gradually declined as communications and technology businesses have become more important in today's economy. High-tech information corporations such as Intel, Microsoft, Apple, and Time Warner play the same important role in the postindustrial economy that corporations such as Ford and U.S. Steel played in the industrial economy.

According to the Organization for Economic Cooperation and Development (OECD), by 2002, the nature of work had shifted dramatically not only in the United States, but also in Europe. The table below shows that most jobs in four European nations and the United States are now in service industries.

Percent of Workers Employed in Major Work Areas, 2002			
Nation	*Agriculture*	*Heavy Industry*	*Service*
United States	1.7	26.1	72.2
France	3.3	26.1	70.8
United Kingdom	1.3	28.8	69.9
Germany	1.3	32.1	66.6
Italy	3.1	30.4	66.5

Of all Western nations, the United States has experienced the greatest change from industrial to service work.

The Impact of the Computer Revolution on Society

The advent of the computer, especially the personal computer, has played a major role in the shift from an industrial society to a postindustrial one. The computer has impacted the lives of most Americans. Cable television, personal computers, cell phones, digital cameras, and many other products and services that were unimaginable a few decades ago are now common. The manufacture of these high-tech products has replaced in importance the heavy industrial production of earlier decades. Many companies that previously focused only on heavy industry have branched into service and information-based areas. For example, General Motors (GM) still manufactures cars, but, through a subsidiary, offers home mortgages as well.

Downsizing in the Postindustrial Age

During the industrial age, most things were large-scale—factories, labor unions, and the mining of raw materials. Big business did not refer just to profits or assets but also size. The opposite is true in postindustrial society. Businesses try to achieve greater production with increased efficiency and smaller scale. Over the past several decades, downsizing (reduction in a company's workforce) in American businesses has resulted in the loss of many jobs. The amount of human labor necessary to produce many consumer products has decreased significantly, resulting in a need for fewer workers. Many jobs previously performed by people are now performed by computer-controlled machines. Robots, for example, paint most of the automobiles produced today, a job that was performed by people a few decades ago.

Low-Paying Jobs. The growth of service industries over the past few years has created many jobs, but they are often low-paying. Moreover, they frequently do not provide benefits such as pensions or health insurance, which most large companies offered during the industrial age. Workers without health insurance can face bankruptcy if they or a member of their family are struck by a serious illness.

Postindustrial society has a lot to offer—cell phones, the Internet, satellite communications, and high-definition television—but it provides a host of problems that leaders in the public and private sectors will have to address in the future.

Test Yourself
How does postindustrial society differ from industrial society?

★ URBANIZATION AND SUBURBANIZATION ★

The process of urbanization and suburbanization is addressed in Chapters 17 and 26. Review those chapters for help with this benchmark.

In the years after the Civil War, the United States became the world's leading industrial nation. Accompanying the growth of industry, cities increased rapidly in size as large numbers of people, including many immigrants, came to urban centers to work in factories.

The Development of Suburbs, 1880s–1920s

In the 1880s, suburban communities existed, but there were relatively few of them, and most were inhabited by the wealthy. As the streetcar lines expanded, some people moved into single-family residences built along their path. Houses had to be within walking distance of the lines because people depended on the streetcars to get to work in nearby cities. Another factor that contributed to suburban growth during the later 1800s was the phenomenon of large industries building factories away from the central city. This was made possible by improvements in transportation and the increasing use of electricity. Some companies actually built towns near their plants. In 1890, Bethlehem, Pennsylvania, developed around the Bethlehem Steel Company. In 1907, U.S. Steel built Gary, Indiana, around its factory there. An increased number of high-paying managerial jobs during this period also made it affordable for more people to move into the suburbs.

From the end of the Civil War to the Great Depression of the 1930s, most suburbs housed the wealthy. New York's Tarrytown Heights (present-day Tarrytown) is a good example. Developed in the early 1870s, the community offered expensive lots that included a separate area where servants lived. In the 1920s, developers accommodated automobile owners with communities such as Shaker Heights, Ohio, near Cleveland, which provided expensive homes on large lots. In fact, between World War I and the beginning of the Great Depression, the United States experienced a mild suburban boom. Due mostly to affordable automobiles, the number of suburbs with single-family homes increased. World War II followed the Great Depression. During the period from roughly 1929 to 1945, very little housing was built. Few people could afford new homes. After the war broke out, many families were split up as the soldiers went to fight in Europe and the Pacific.

The Post–World War II Suburban Boom

After World War II, suburbanization became a mass movement in the U.S. Bedroom communities (where most of the employed persons commuted daily to city jobs) sprouted up around most urban areas. Between 1950 and 2000, the suburban population increased from about 27 percent to 50 percent. The 2000 election was the first in which half of the voters were suburbanites.

More affordable housing and improved highways as well as increased automobile ownership allowed more people to migrate to the suburbs. Beginning around the 1950s, developers bought large tracts of land at relatively low prices, and mass-produced houses. Large-scale, efficient production techniques resulted in homes that many middle-income families could afford. Mortgages guaranteed by the government, through programs such as the Federal Housing Administration (FHA) and the Veterans Administration (VA), made low-interest credit available to many people. In 1940, approximately 47 percent of Americans owned homes. By 2000, that figure was over 65 percent.

A change in the pattern of suburbanization occurred after World War II, especially in terms of quantity. When servicemen and -women returned from the war, the demand for consumer goods skyrocketed. During the war, most factories had converted to war production, and the manufacture of consumer goods decreased. With the return of peace, former military personnel and factory workers who saved money during the war because of the scarcity of consumer goods sparked high demand. Many couples got married, and the birthrate increased sharply. This marked the beginning of the so-called *baby boom*, which lasted from 1946 to 1964. Housing became a critical need for millions of people.

William Levitt, a New York builder, provided one answer to the postwar housing problem. Levitt used assembly-line methods to build in record time a suburb near New York City, which he named Levittown. He constructed rows of similar houses, which helped lower costs and speed up production. Levitt also included recreational areas such as swimming pools, baseball diamonds, playgrounds, and parks. By 1949, Levittown was home to about 17,000 families.

Levittown, New York, in 1954

Builders across the nation quickly adopted Levitt's techniques. Suburbs featuring single-family homes with modest yards sprung up around many cities throughout the nation in a very short time. Such rapid growth did not occur without problems. Development happened so fast that schools and commercial centers often lagged behind. Public transportation was often unavailable, forcing many suburbanites to drive and causing traffic congestion on streets and highways.

Housing starts are a statistic that refers to the number of new houses built each year in the United States. In the postwar period, single-family housing starts jumped sharply. From 1900 to 1945, the average number of single-family housing starts per year was about 280,000. Between 1946 and 2002, that average increased to over 1.1 million, a nearly fourfold rise, with the biggest jump occurring between 1945 and 1947.

Transportation

The Interstate Highway Act (1956) was both an effect of suburbanization and later a cause of suburban growth. The act sparked the construction of a national system of highways. The act established a trust fund by which the federal government paid for most of the highway system's construction costs. State governments had to cover about 10 percent. These new and improved highways contributed to the rapid growth of the suburbs.

The U.S. Interstate Highway System

Increased Mobility. As roads improved and as automobiles became more affordable, the inclination to move away from urban centers multiplied. Mobility made possible by the automobile eventually dominated life during the 1950s. It became less necessary for workers to live near their place of employment. Cars and freeways made shopping centers and malls possible. Drive-in theaters became a popular recreational activity. Because of the automobile and the growing dependence on it by most Americans, new housing developments eventually included garages, driveways, and parking spaces. From the 1960s to the present, newer suburbs have also featured larger homes. Suburbs built immediately after the war featured homes that were generally 1,500 square feet or less in size. They were often referred to as "starter homes," which implied an intention to move on to a larger place when possible.

Longer Commutes. Because of the automobile and suburbanization, the time it takes to get to work has increased nearly every decade since the 1950s. According to the U.S. Census in 1990, the average commute to work took about 22 minutes. In 2000, it had increased to 24 minutes. These figures establish that on average people spend about 48 minutes a day going to and from work. Increasing suburbanization is a major factor in the longer commute time. In large cities, the commute time may be even longer. Used by about 87 percent of commuters, driving is the most frequent means of traveling to and from work.

Changes in Suburban Life. While a few areas are experiencing a slight reversal of the process of suburbanization as some people move back to the central city, the process of suburbanization in the United States continues. Some aspects of suburban life have changed. A majority of the people living in suburbs now commute to other suburbs to work rather than to a central city. Automobiles are still the primary mode of transportation, and the cost of gasoline, which has risen over the past few years, has not discouraged many people from driving. Only the future can tell if that will change.

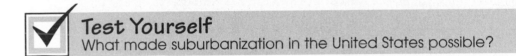

Test Yourself
What made suburbanization in the United States possible?

★ PATTERNS AND PROCESSES OF IMMIGRATION ★

Immigration into the United States is a process that has occurred since the beginning of the nation, but it is also an example of a historical pattern. More immigrants have come to the United States than any other country, some 50 million people. This process has not abated. More than one million immigrants arrive in the United States every year.

The fastest-growing ethnic group in the United States today are Hispanics, people from Spanish-speaking nations in Central and South America. There are currently about 6.5 times more Spanish-speaking people in the United States—about 27 million—than there were in 1950. Nearly half of them are of Mexican origin. The rest originated in Caribbean or Central and South American nations such as Cuba, the Dominican Republic, Guatemala, El Salvador, Venezuela, and Colombia. Many of today's immigrants also come from African and Asian nations.

Changes in Immigration Patterns

The origins of our most recent immigrants mark a change in the pattern of immigration to the United States. In the late 1800s and early 1900s, most immigrants were Southern and Eastern Europeans such as Russians, Poles, Hungarians, Czechs, Slovaks, Italians, and Greeks. These immigrants also represented a change from the pre–Civil War pattern of immigration. Because they represented a distinct change from previous newcomers, immigrants who arrived between the 1880s and the 1920s are often referred to by historians as the "new immigrants." Prior to the 1860s, most immigrants came from Northern and Western Europe, specifically England, Ireland, Germany, the Netherlands, Norway, Denmark, and Sweden. Many of them spoke English, and most were Protestant, with the exception of the Irish, most of whom were Roman Catholic. "New immigrants," on the other hand, were mostly Jewish or Roman Catholic, and they usually spoke little or no English. To many native-born Americans, they seemed strange because their languages, customs, and religion were alien. As a result, friction sometimes arose between the newcomers and native-born Americans, who also feared competition for jobs from immigrants willing to accept low wages.

Laws Change Immigration Patterns. In 1965, Congress passed a law that changed immigration patterns once again. The Immigration Act of 1965 abolished the quota system based on national origins and replaced it with a new quota system based on hemispheric standards. In the late 1970s, Congress replaced hemispheric quotas with an overall limit, but one that welcomed immigrants from all over the world. This helped shift the pattern of immigration away from Europe to other regions. In 1990, the ten top nations of origin for immigrants were, in order: Mexico, the Philippines, Vietnam, the Dominican Republic, Korea, China, India, the former Soviet Union, Jamaica, and Iran. The largest number of immigrants to the United States came from Latin America and Asia. That pattern continued throughout the 1990s. The United States welcomes more immigrants each year than any other nation. The number of foreign-born people in 1990 was about 20 million. In 2000, that number rose to nearly 28.5 million, about 10.4 percent of the population, with most of those from Central America and Asia.

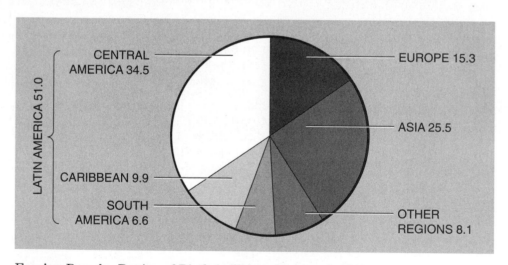

Foreign-Born by Region of Birth (millions of persons), 2000

Reasons for Emigration

What about the process of emigration? What makes a person or family decide to leave their home for a foreign land and take up residence in an alien culture? One way to explain this phenomenon is to look at the *push-pull factors*. This theory of emigration—or migration—holds that conditions in the nation of origin such as violence, persecution, or limited economic opportunities push some people out. Other places with certain attractions such as good living conditions, prospects for work, and respect for human rights pull those people. This way of viewing immigration helps us understand why many people came to the United States over the last three centuries.

Push Factors. In the late 1800s and early 1900s, the period of "new" immigration, push factors affected people living in Southern and Eastern Europe. Conditions such as unemployment, poverty, starvation, overpopulation, government oppression, and persecution pushed people out of their homelands. As the Industrial Revolution spread throughout Europe, many people suffered economic and demographic dislocation. Many European nations such as Italy experienced overpopulation, which intensified competition for jobs. There were not enough jobs for everyone, and land was often too costly or unavailable in most of these countries. Many young people raised on family farms had no opportunity to obtain land of their own. Political upheavals and religious or ethnic violence often served as push factors. In the 1880s and early 1900s, many Russian Jews were killed in violent attacks—known as *pogroms*—which were often orchestrated by the czarist government. Many Jews fled Russia to seek safety in America and other countries.

Pull Factors. The United States also provided several pull factors that attracted immigrants. The nation was rapidly developing as the world's industrial leader, and it needed workers. Many low-paying jobs were available to immigrants. In addition to work, the United States offered a democratic government and the Constitution, which officially prohibited religious and ethnic discrimination. Individual states also provided free public schools, where many young newcomers and the children of immigrants learned to speak English and became immersed in American culture.

Many people who came to the United States from 1965 to the present were pushed or pulled by those same factors. Details may differ from nation to nation and time to time, but basic push-pull factors remained relatively similar. People leave their homes to escape poverty, persecution, and violence, to

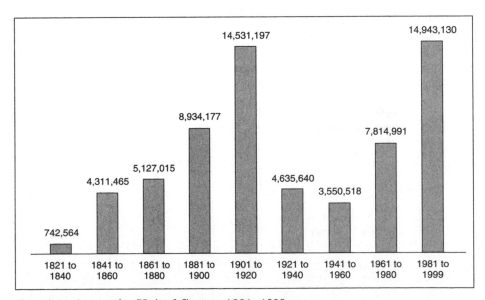

Immigration to the United States, 1821–1999

find work, and search for a better life. The United States offers a place to find work, even though many jobs taken by immigrants are often low paying, and it offers freedom from oppression. Democratic government, education, economic opportunity—all of these factors still draw immigrants to America.

Test Yourself

In what way have patterns of immigration changed over the course of U.S. history since the late 1880s?

POINTS TO REMEMBER

- U.S. history is replete with examples of patterns and processes of movement of people, products, and ideas.

- The postindustrial U.S. economy is based upon technology, service industries, and knowledge production, rather than upon heavy industries and manufacturing.

- The advent of the computer, especially the personal computer, was a major cause of the change to a postindustrial society.

- During the period of American industrialization, cities grew at a rapid rate.

- Between 1910 and 1920, more people lived in cities than in rural areas, for the first time in the nation's history.

- There have been several periods of suburban growth since the end of Reconstruction, but the greatest increase came after World War II.

- The growth of suburbs was made possible by improved transportation such as highways and affordable automobiles.

- Patterns of immigration to the United States, in terms of the nation of origin, have changed over time.

- Push-pull factors help explain the process of immigration to the United States.

EXERCISES

CHECKING WHAT YOU HAVE READ

1. How have jobs changed in the postindustrial economy?

2. What transportation system led to the growth of suburbs after World War II?

3. How did the government support the growth of suburbs after World War II?

4. How did the "new" immigrants of the late 1800s and early 1900s differ from earlier immigrants to the United States?

5. Where did most of the recent immigrants to the United States originate?

USING WHAT YOU HAVE READ

Interview your principal and leaders of local government in your area. Ask them to identify the immigrant group that has had the greatest impact over the last 20 years on your community. Ask them to describe the greatest contribution that the immigrant group has made to your community. Also, try to interview members of that immigrant group and ask them to describe why they came to the U.S. and your community and the biggest obstacles they had to overcome. Write a report describing your findings.

THINKING ABOUT WHAT YOU HAVE READ

Some people believe that the United States should enact legislation that would restrict immigration. Write a letter to the editor in which you either support such legislation or oppose it. State your position and then support it with arguments and evidence. Use the library or the Internet to gather evidence to support your position before you write the letter.

SKILLS

Interpreting a Bar Graph

Study the bar graph on page 391, Immigration to the United States, 1821–1999, and answer the questions below.

1. In what 20-year period did the greatest number of immigrants come to the U.S.?

2. In what 20-year period did the fewest number of immigrants come to the U.S.?

3. In what 20-year period did the second greatest number of immigrants come to the U.S.?

4. In what 40-year period did the greatest number of immigrants come to the U.S.?

5. In what 40-year period did the second greatest number of immigrants come to the U.S.?

CHAPTER 28

ECONOMIC SYSTEMS

> **BENCHMARK:**
>
> Compare how different economic systems answer the fundamental economic questions of what goods and services to produce, how to produce them, and who will consume them.

This chapter looks at fundamental economic questions related to the economy of the United States. First, how do trade, specialization, and interdependence affect the U.S. economic system? Second, how have labor unions, farm organizations, and business organizations developed, and what kind of economic effect have they had? Questions on the OGT will require knowledge of the U.S. economy in order to compare it to other systems. The development of labor unions was also addressed in Chapter 17. Review that section of Chapter 17 to help you understand concepts and subject matter in this chapter.

★ TRADE, SPECIALIZATION, AND INTERDEPENDENCE ★

International Trade

Why does the United States engage in trade with other nations? Why, in other words, do businesses in the United States either buy from or sell products to other countries? Doesn't the United States possess enough raw materials, produce enough goods and services, and grow enough food so that trade with other nations would be unnecessary? Looking around, you can see evidence of international trade everywhere. Much of the grain and other crops grown in the American heartland ends up on tables in other nations. Automobiles manufactured in Europe or Asia are in evidence on roads all across the United States. Most electronics equipment comes from Japan or other Asian nations. Much of the steel used to make American cars or erect buildings originates in foreign nations. Is all of that necessary? Why can't American companies manufacture those goods, thereby creating jobs in this country for our citizens?

Of course, we know that without international trade there are many products that would be unavailable in the United States. Americans would have to go without coffee, tea, bananas, chocolate, and many other items that cannot be produced in this country. Nations have different natural resources, as well as human resources, and they cannot always produce goods and services desired by their consumers. Additionally, they may not be able to produce them as efficiently as other nations.

Cost and Specialization

If a job pays $15 per hour for eight hours a day, the daily wage is $120. If someone who holds that job prefers to go fishing for a day rather than working, the opportunity cost of going fishing is $120. *Opportunity cost* is the value of the next best alternative when a choice is made. Trade involves opportunity cost, too. Business leaders and nations choose to produce particular goods and buy other goods from foreign countries because they make decisions based on opportunity cost. In other words, it is more efficient and therefore more profitable to produce the good or service with the lowest opportunity cost. That allows them to trade for other goods or services that have a higher opportunity cost.

Test Yourself
What does opportunity cost have to do with international trade?

Trade also involves other economic principles. One such principle is *absolute advantage*. If two countries possess the same resources, but one of the two is able to produce more of a particular good, due to increased efficiency, cheaper labor costs, or some other factor, it is said to have an absolute advantage. In that case, it makes sense for the nation that produces more of that good to specialize in its production and import other goods it needs. If the second country has an absolute advantage in producing a good that the first country wants, both will be better off if they specialize and trade. *Specialization* is production of a particular good that will, over time, result in efficiencies and reduced production costs, thereby making trade even more beneficial.

But even if one nation has an absolute advantage in production of several goods, trade in those goods may still be beneficial. A nation is said to have a *comparative advantage* in production of the good with the lowest opportunity cost. Countries have different opportunity costs because they possess different quantities or qualities of productive resources. Two nations might grow coffee, for example, but the climate and topography of one allows it to grow coffee more efficiently. It therefore has a lower opportunity cost for growing coffee than does the other nation.

Opportunity costs differ among nations and change over time. Human productive resources can improve with better training and education. Technology can improve efficiency and increase productivity. New raw materials can be discovered, or improved methods of extraction may be developed that make existing natural resources more cost-effective. Patterns of international trade shift as these opportunity costs fluctuate.

Interdependence

The United States has always engaged in international trade, but over the past three decades, this trade has assumed an even more important role in the U.S. economy. In order to stay competitive and profitable, U.S. companies must engage in global trade. Exporting businesses, for example, more than tripled between 1987 and 1999. This economic *interdependence* with other nations has had profound consequences for the American economy. Many U.S. corporations have closed down factories and plants in this country and moved their operations overseas where labor costs are lower, resulting in the elimination of many American jobs. On the other hand, consumers in the United States benefit from lower prices and greater choice in the marketplace.

Global Organization: The WTO. Since the end of World War II, U.S. economic policy has also reflected and encouraged increased international trade and global interdependence. Over 20 countries came together in 1947 to sign the General Agreement on Tariffs and Trade (GATT), which extended wartime tariff reductions and advocated the elimination of export quotas. In 1962, Congress followed up on GATT with the Trade Expansion Act, which authorized the president to enter into negotiations with nations to reduce additional tariffs. In the mid-1990s, the World Trade Organization (WTO) replaced GATT. WTO, of which the U.S. is a member, helps to enforce standing trade agreements, encourages trade talks and negotiations among governments, attempts to arbitrate trade disputes among member nations, and tries to help developing nations solve economic problems.

Regional Organization: NAFTA. The North American Free Trade Agreement (NAFTA) is a clear example of how the United States and other nations have become increasingly interdependent. Negotiations to establish a free-trade zone including Mexico, Canada, and the United States began in the early 1990s, during the George H. W. Bush administration. Congress passed the necessary legislation and President Bill Clinton signed it into law in 1994. The agreement eliminated restrictions on the trade of goods and services in North America. It abolished tariffs among the three nations, some immediately, others over time. Goods and services could flow freely throughout North America, which in effect has become one big market. NAFTA built upon a free-trade agreement between Canada and the United States that had been in

President Bill Clinton signs NAFTA in 1994.

place since 1989. The agreement protects trademarks, patents, and copyrights (referred to as intellectual property rights) and established procedures to settle disputes. NAFTA also includes provisions intended to address environmental concerns.

THE NAFTA PREAMBLE

The Government of Canada, the Government of the United Mexican States and the Government of the United States of America, resolved to:

- strengthen the special bonds of friendship and cooperation among their nations;
- contribute to the harmonious development and expansion of world trade and provide a catalyst to broader international cooperation;
- create an expanded and secure market for the goods and services produced in their territories;
- reduce distortions to trade;
- establish clear and mutually advantageous rules governing their trade;
- ensure a predictable commercial framework for business planning and investment;
- build on their respective rights and obligations under the General Agreement on Tariffs and Trade and other multilateral and bilateral instruments of cooperation;
- enhance the competitiveness of their firms in global markets;
- foster creativity and innovation, and promote trade in goods and services that are the subject of intellectual property rights;
- create new employment opportunities and improve working conditions and living standards in their respective territories;
- undertake each of the preceding in a manner consistent with environmental protection and conservation;
- preserve their flexibility to safeguard the public welfare;
- promote sustainable development;
- strengthen the development and enforcement of environmental laws and regulations; and
- protect, enhance and enforce basic workers' rights . . .

NAFTA and the growth of free trade have not been without controversy. Most U.S. labor unions and other workers' groups opposed NAFTA and similar agreements because they feared the loss of jobs to nations where lower wages prevailed, especially Mexico. Mexican farmers opposed the trade agreement because the U.S. government's subsidies to American farmers gave them an unfair advantage. Environmental activists also opposed NAFTA because they believed its environmental provisions were weak, and they thought existing protections were inadequately enforced.

Test Yourself
What does NAFTA do?

★ LABOR UNIONS, BUSINESS ORGANIZATIONS, AND FARM ORGANIZATIONS ★

Labor Unions

Throughout American history, various organizations have attempted to affect the nation's economy in ways that will benefit their members. Labor unions are one example of this kind of organization. Unions were formed by workers, often in the face of fierce resistance by business owners and government officials, to improve wages and working conditions and to correct perceived wrongs or imbalances in the economy. Unions are associations organized to have an impact on the economy. Traditionally, they have sought to raise wages as high as possible and to improve safety and other working conditions on the job. To the extent that unions are successful, they add to the cost of doing business. In companies or industries where unions were firmly established, they developed, in essence, significant control over the workforce. The impact that unions have on a particular company, or industry, or an economy in general, can be either positive or negative, depending upon the observer's point of view and can change over time.

Impact of Unions. Unions produce a positive impact for members when they negotiate higher wages and/or improved working conditions. On the other hand, fewer jobs are then available because the business has less to spend on labor. Another way to look at it is that the law of supply and demand works in labor as well as in the rest of the economy. As the price of labor increasees, business managers hire fewer workers. From the union members' perspective, however, it is in their best interest to keep other people from working for lower wages. What it means to consumers is that higher labor costs are passed on in the form of higher prices. Union supporters argue that their organizations are good for everyone. They seek to keep the standard of living high and the economy healthy. Their members earn enough money to buy the consumer goods produced in America, and that they have the opportunity to lead happy and secure lives.

Unions are able to organize and bargain with business because they are supported by the legal system. Over the years, union leaders and supporters have used both the legislative and judicial systems to establish rights, privileges, and protections. (On balance, however, U.S. courts have not been favorable to unions.) Companies are required by law to bargain in "good faith" with unions. When a union such as the AFL-CIO or the Teamsters wins the right to represent workers in a particular business or industry, it becomes the sole bargaining agent, and it can require union dues from all employees. Members' dues are used to pay salaries to union officials who negotiate with management regarding contracts and grievances. Like business and farm organizations, unions also get involved in the political process by supporting candidates who agree with their positions and priorities. Ultimately, unions can use strikes, or work stoppages, to attempt to persuade management to come to agreement. Over the years, strikes have sometimes been successful, both in the short and long term, and sometimes not.

Declining Membership. For various economic and political reasons, the percentage of unionized workers in the United States has declined in recent decades, especially in private sector businesses and industries. In 1983, for example, union membership stood at just over 20 percent of wage and salary workers in the United States. By 2007, only about 12 percent, or 15.7 million workers, belonged to unions. One reason union membership has declined is that many businesses have moved operations overseas where labor is cheaper, thereby eliminating many union jobs in the United States. Downsizing in American companies is another reason. In recent decades, the trend in American business has been to smaller companies, where unions have a more difficult time organizing. The increasing number of high-technology companies, which employ highly trained technical and professional workers, has also contributed to the decline of unions in the United States. Despite this decline in numbers and influence, unions continue to have a significant impact on the American economy through their role in setting wage levels, as well as in determining the amount businesses must spend on benefits such as health insurance and pensions.

Test Yourself

Why has the percentage of labor union members as part of the entire workforce declined recently?

Business Organizations

Other organizations impact the American economy by pursuing their own interests. *Business organizations,* like unions, try to influence government, the courts, and the public in ways that will benefit their members—in this case business owners and operators, and ultimately their stockholders or investors. A company or corporation is a business organization. Some of the largest ones, such as General Motors, Microsoft, General Electric, and Wal-Mart, have special departments that lobby legislatures, argue legal cases in the courts, and support the election of politicians favorable to their positions.

National Association of Manufacturers (NAM). In other instances, companies—large and small—often join together to share resources and form industry-wide organizations to accomplish the same goals. One such organization is the National Association of Manufacturers (NAM), the nation's largest industrial trade association. According to NAM, its goals are

> to enhance the competitiveness of manufacturers by shaping a legislative and regulatory environment conducive to U.S. economic growth [and] to increase understanding among policymakers, the media and the general public about the vital role of manufacturing to America's economic future and living standards.

NAM dates back to 1895, when the leaders of several companies met in Cincinnati to talk about common problems and concerns. The United States was mired in a depression, and association members wanted to find new markets for their products, especially overseas. President William McKinley, an Ohioan, addressed NAM's initial gathering. Members' objectives were to

- retain and supply home markets with U.S. products and extend foreign trade

- develop reciprocal trade relations between the U.S. and foreign governments

- rehabilitate the U.S. Merchant Marine

- construct a canal in Central America

- improve and extend U.S. waterways

As NAM grew and developed, it expanded its initiatives. It sent representatives overseas to encourage foreign trade, lobbied for tariffs to protect manufacturers from foreign competition, and advocated for the establishment of a Department of Commerce. In addition, NAM promoted vocational training, conducted public relations campaigns in support of American business, lobbied for legislation to combat the growing influence of organized labor, supported political candidates favorable to its aims, and conducted training sessions for its members. Member companies and associations paid dues to the organization to fund these activities.

Recently, NAM has become increasingly active in supporting the movement toward globalization and economic interdependence. It lobbied on behalf of NAFTA and other efforts to reduce barriers to trade with other nations, which has been an emphasis throughout the organization's long history. Since the 1990s, NAM has also stepped up its lobbying efforts in support of tax policies, such as credits that promote technogical development.

There are many other business organizations or associations similar to NAM. They engage in many of the same kinds of activities, which are designed to promote their particular industry or interest group. Just a few representative examples of hundreds of such organizations are:

- Telecommunications Industry Association (TIA)

- American Pharmacists Association (APhA)

- American Insurance Association (AIA)

- National Association of Home Builders (NAHB)

- National Retail Federation (NRF).

Like labor unions, these organizations impact the economy of the United States through their various activities. They play an important role in helping our nation answer the fundamental economic questions of what goods and services to produce, how to produce them, and who will consume them.

Test Yourself
What is the main goal of a business organization such as NAM?

Farm Organizations

Farmers are important economic players in every nation's economy. Food is a basic human necessity. For more than half of our nation's history, farmers made up a majority of the population. Farming accounts for a huge part of American economic output. Farmers have economic concerns particular to their industry. Just like the workers who formed unions and the business leaders who established associations, farmers have joined together in *farm organizations* to pursue common goals.

The National Grange. The U.S. economy goes through cycles of prosperity, recession, and depression. Farmers, like everyone else, survive by weathering these cycles as best they can. Like U.S. industrial workers and business leaders in the years after the Civil War, farmers decided that their lot could be improved by joining together in organizations to influence the government and thereby, the economy. The first such organization, the National Grange, was established in 1867. Just ten years later, there were some 10,000 chapters nationwide. While the Grange served as a social organization for farmers, it also attempted to address their economic concerns. Grangers maintained that railroads and grain companies charged too much to store and transport farm products to market. Grangers sought legislative redress and also formed *cooperatives* (organizations where they pooled resources and acted together). Buying seeds and tools in large quantities helped lower costs for Grange members.

The Grangers' lobbying efforts had positive results in the 1870s. Several states enacted laws that regulated the rates that railroads could charge farmers to ship their goods. Corporations often challenged these "Granger laws" in court, but in 1877, the U.S. Supreme Court ruled in *Munn* v. *Illinois* that states could regulate businesses of a public nature, such as railroads. Later organizations, such as the Farmers' Alliances, carried on the work of the Grange when its influence declined.

A meeting of the Grangers in the farmers' movement near Winchester, Illinois, in 1873

Government Price Supports. In the 1920s, the focus of farm organizations shifted toward seeking direct government intervention to support farm income. The farm cooperative movement took the lead in lobbying Congress for relief. In 1929, the National Council of Farmers' Cooperatives organized to lobby for price supports. By 1930, there were nearly 12,000 cooperatives across the country, with some 3 million members. It took the Great Depression of the 1930s, however, to get price supports for agricultural products enacted into law. The strategy was to increase prices for agricultural products by reducing the supply. Price supports and control of the supply of agricultural products have been the focus of farm policy pursued by farm organizations since the 1930s. The first Agricultural Adjustment Act of 1933 stated:

> It is hereby declared to be the policy of Congress . . . to establish and maintain such balance between the production and consumption of agricultural commodities . . . as will reestablish prices to farmers at a level that will give agricultural commodities a purchasing power . . . equivalent to the purchasing power of agricultural commodities in . . . the prewar period. . . .

In 1996, Congress responded to globalization in agriculture with the Federal Agriculture Improvement and Reform Act. This act marked a change in the kind of federal assistance sought by farm organizations. The law was based on the premise that farmers would benefit from the freedom to plant all that they wanted as well as the government's efforts to promote American farmers' access to global markets. To buffer the transition from previous policy, the 1996 law provided for fixed income support payments that decreased over time but were not tied to how much the farmer produced.

How these recent changes will affect farmers in the long term remains to be seen. But it is clear that federal farm policy and farm organizations affecting that policy, such as farm bureau federations and cooperatives, have a profound impact on the American economy. This is especially true in regard to those fundamental questions about what and how much of a good, in this case food products, should be produced.

Test Yourself

From the 1920s to the mid-1990s, what was the main goal of farm organizations in terms of federal legislation?

POINTS TO REMEMBER

- The world has become increasingly interdependent largely because of international trade and the resulting exchange of culture, ideas, and knowledge.

- Nations trade because they want to take advantage of opportunity cost, absolute advantage, and comparative advantage.

- Labor, business, and farm organizations attempt to influence government and the economy in order to address the fundamental economic questions of what goods and services to produce, how to produce them, and who will consume them.

- Labor unions try to affect the fundamental economic questions by organizing workers into a kind of labor monopoly.

- Labor union membership has declined in recent years.

- Labor unions, business organizations, farm organizations attempt to influence state and federal legislation to benefit their members.

- The AFL-CIO is an example of a labor union.

- The National Association of Manufacturers (NAM) is an example of a business organization.

- Business organizations usually work to expand markets in which to sell their goods.

- The government's farm policy has recently moved away from price supports and supply control to increased domestic production and increased activity in international markets.

EXERCISES

CHECKING WHAT YOU HAVE READ

1. In economics, what term is used to describe the value of the next best alternative when a choice is made?

   A. absolute advantage
   B. comparative advantage
   C. opportunity cost
   D. specialization

2. What term is used to describe the production of a particular good that will, over time, result in efficiencies and reduce production costs?

   A. absolute advantage
   B. specialization
   C. opportunity cost
   D. comparative advantage

3. When a country can produce more of a good with the same resources as another country, it is said to have

   what advantage in the production of that good?

   A. specialization advantage
   B. opportunity cost advantage
   C. comparative advantage
   D. absolute advantage

4. The existence of GATT, WTO, and NAFTA supports the contention that

   A. economic interdependence has increased in recent years
   B. economic interdependence has decreased in recent years
   C. trade barriers have increased in recent years
   D. free-trade policies do not have much support around the world.

5. What do the AFL-CIO, NAM, and farmers' cooperatives have in common?

   A. They all favor free-trade agreements.

B. They all lobby government to pass legislation favorable to their members.
C. They all oppose free-trade policies.
D. They all oppose the use of government policy to impact economic activity.

USING WHAT YOU HAVE READ

Using a local telephone directory, which can be found in public libraries, identify two large businesses, two small businesses, and two labor unions in your community or state.

Contact each company and ask it to respond to the following questions:

1. Does your company (or in the case of a union, the industry in which your members work) engage in international trade?

2. If the answer is yes to question 1, what product(s) are involved?

3. How has international trade affected your company or union? Has it helped or hurt?

4. Does your company or union support or oppose free-trade agreements, such as NAFTA? Why or why not?

Keep a record of each company and union's responses. Write a brief report about your findings.

THINKING ABOUT WHAT YOU HAVE READ

Free trade and free-trade agreements such as NAFTA are controversial topics. Some people see them as beneficial, while others view them as detrimental. Use the Internet and/or library to read more about NAFTA and its critics. Based upon your research, what position do you predict an environmentalist concerned about air and water pollution would take on NAFTA? Explain your reasons.

SKILLS

Using Data and Evidence to Support a Thesis

Assume the role of one of the following: a member of the AFL-CIO, a member of NAM, or a typical consumer. Use the Internet and/or library to read more about NAFTA and criticisms of NAFTA and free-trade agreements in general. State the position you predict each person would take regarding NAFTA and similar free-trade agreements. Do you support or oppose them? Once you have decided upon your position, list evidence that supports it.

CHAPTER 29

THE U.S. GOVERNMENT AND THE ECONOMY

> **BENCHMARK:**
>
> **Explain how the U.S. government provides public services, redistributes income, regulates economic activity, and promotes economic growth and stability.**

This benchmark requires you to understand the role that the U.S. government plays in economic activity. You should be able to explain how taxes, antitrust legislation, and environmental regulations affect both individuals and businesses. You should also know why the Federal Reserve System was created as well as its importance to the U.S. economy. Finally, you should be able to discuss the ways in which the Great Depression and World War II affected the U.S. economy and caused the federal government to expand its role in economic activities.

★ EFFECT OF GOVERNMENTAL ACTIONS ON INDIVIDUALS AND BUSINESS ★

Since the founding of our nation, the federal government has played an important role in the economy. Although that role may have increased in the 20th century, government action, or lack of action, has always had an important impact on both people and business. Government involvement in economic decision-making exists because of public need and because American citizens have demanded it. The government protects citizens by enforcing contracts and establishing regulations (rules of economic fair play). In 1877, Congress created the Interstate Commerce Commission, for example, in an attempt to regulate trade within the United States and make it fair for all participants. The government also helps to keep people healthy and safe by passing and enforcing laws that are intended to guard against tainted food, impure drugs, air and water pollution, and unsafe automobiles.

The federal government is one of the largest consumers in the American market. It spends billions of dollars every year to equip the armed forces and provide other services to the American people. In short, throughout U.S. history, the federal government has become increasingly involved in economic activity to promote or protect national goals, such as high employment, equity in the workplace and marketplace, public safety, and economic stability.

Taxes

In order to conduct its business and carry out its responsibilities, a government must, among other things, pay its employees, buy equipment, and provide assistance to people in need. These responsibilities require money or revenue. Governments raise money by levying taxes on their citizens. In the United States, Congress enacts tax laws, which go into effect upon the signature of the president. When taxes are increased, businesses have less to spend on expansion or research, and individuals have less to spend on consumer goods. Elected government officials constantly try to find a balance between taxes high enough to raise necessary funds and taxes that are too high and might result in stifling the economy. Politicians and public officials disagree on what is excessive and what is enough. That is why tax policy usually becomes an important issue during election campaigns.

Income Tax. The federal government's major source of income is the income tax. Both individuals and corporations pay taxes on the income they make, but the personal income tax (on individuals) raises about five times more revenue than does the corporate income tax. Payroll taxes paid by employers and employees also provide important revenue for Social Security insurance, Medicare, and unemployment compensation.

The federal income tax is based on the principle that the more a person earns, the more income tax he or she should pay. People with similar incomes, however, may not have the same ability to pay. Interest rates on mortgages, high medical bills, and other expenses can be subtracted as *itemized deductions* to reduce *taxable income*. Exemptions are also permitted for children and other dependents. Deductions such as these lower a person's taxable income and reduce the amount of income tax owed. People with higher taxable incomes pay a larger percentage in taxes. Income taxes are said to be *progressive* because people who have a higher income pay more than those with lower incomes.

Excise Taxes. The federal government also raises revenue through excise taxes on the manufacture or sale of certain items, such as gasoline or airline tickets. Excise taxes are levied on consumers. The gasoline tax, for example, is collected from automobile drivers and is used to pay for highway construction and repair. Those people who use the roads pay for them.

Unlike income taxes, excise (or sales taxes) are *regressive* because goods are taxed at the same percentage regardless of income. Those with lower incomes pay a larger percentage of their income in excise taxes. If a person makes $50,000 a year and pays $5,000 in sales taxes, he or she has been taxed at a 10 percent rate. A person with a yearly income of $100,000 who pays the same $5,000 in sales taxes is taxed at just 5 percent.

Different kinds of taxes have different effects. Some taxes result in reallocation of productive resources. When a business or factory is taxed, the cost of production increases. That cost will be added to the prices of the good or service being produced or offered. If the price increases too much, consumers will purchase less of the good or service. The business will then have to cut back production and perhaps lay off workers. When taxes reach a certain point, workers are less inclined to put in more hours of work. Additional income, they reason, will just be lost to taxes. Businesses also feel less inclined to expand or increase production if taxes rise above a certain point. Investors can also be affected by taxes if economic growth is slowed by high taxation.

Taxes are sometimes aimed at people's behavior. "Sin taxes," as they are called, are levied on such items such cigarettes and alcohol. These taxes not only raise revenue for the government, they also discourage consumption of substances that are generally considered harmful to the user or objectionable to others.

	Federal Government Receipts by Source, 1934–2004 (billions of dollars)					
Year	Individual income taxes	Corporation income taxes	Social insurance and retirement receipts	Excise taxes	Other[1]	Total
1934	$0.4	$0.3	([2])	$1.4	$0.8	$3.0
1940	0.9	1.2	$1.8	2.0	0.7	6.5
1950	15.8	10.4	4.3	7.6	1.4	39.4
1960	40.7	21.5	14.7	11.7	3.9	92.5
1970	90.4	32.8	44.3	15.7	9.5	192.8
1980	244.1	64.6	157.8	24.3	26.3	517.1
1990	466.9	93.5	380.0	35.3	56.2	1,032.0
2000	1,004.5	207.3	652.9	68.9	91.8	2,025.2
2002	858.3	148.0	700.8	67.0	79.1	1,853.2
2003	793.7	131.8	713.0	67.5	76.5	1,872.3
2004	765.4	168.7	732.4	70.8	60.8	1,798.1

1. Includes estate and gift taxes, customs duties and fees, federal reserve deposits.   2. Estimated to be less than $100 million.
Source: Office of Management and Budget of the United States Government, FY 2005.

Test Yourself
Why are income taxes called progressive, while excise taxes are called regressive?

Government Regulation of Business

Taxes are not the only way that government affects individuals and businesses. It can also enact laws that encourage competition in a particular industry, regulate certain monopolies, or even establish government-owned monopolies intended to benefit the public good. A monopoly exists when a single company or person possesses exclusive, or nearly exclusive, control of an industry, commodity, or service. Monopolistic combinations of corporations are called *trusts*. Some of them are legal, while others are not.

Antitrust Legislation. The danger of a monopoly or trust is that it can control supply and demand, and, therefore, set prices at any level because there is no competition. Since the late 1800s, government has attempted to regulate monopolies through the courts and with *antitrust legislation,* or laws that prevent monopolies and the restraint of competition.

Interstate Commerce Act. The U.S. government's first post–Civil War effort to control a monopoly involved railroads, which at that time were the lifeline of trade. In the 1800s, based on the Supreme Court decision in *Munn* v. *Illinois,* individual states passed regulatory legislation, but these laws were largely ineffective. Many reformers began to lobby for federal intervention. Their efforts resulted in the Interstate Commerce Act of 1887, which established, for the first time, a federal commission with authority to regulate interstate trade. The Interstate Commerce Commission (ICC) was given the responsibility of regulating the rates railroads charged businesses to ship goods to ensure that they were reasonable and to prevent monopolistic practices.

Sherman Antitrust Act. In the late 19th century, many trusts had been formed in the steel, oil, sugar, meatpacking, and mining industries. Reformers and consumers clamored for the federal government to rein in these powerful companies. In response, Congress enacted the Sherman Antitrust Act (1890) to combat the formation of monopolies and trusts. It stated that "every contract, combination in the form of trust or otherwise, or conspiracy, in restraint of trade or commerce among the several states, or with foreign nations, is hereby declared illegal."

In the early 1900s, the government used this law to break up the Standard Oil Company monopoly that had been established by John D. Rockefeller. Backed by the Sherman Act, government regulators also broke up several other trusts. Although the law did not completely ban trusts, it did set a precedent for future regulatory legislation. When President Theodore Roosevelt took office in 1901, he enforced the act vigorously and acquired the reputation of being a "trust buster."

Other Business Regulation. Disagreement over the right of the federal government to interfere with business through such laws as the Interstate Commerce Act and the Sherman Antitrust Act continued into the early decades of the 20th century. But the nation was in the mood for further regulation of big business. Based on those earlier laws, Congress passed additional antitrust legislation. The Clayton Antitrust Act (1914) attempted to maintain and protect competition by prohibiting price discrimination (charging different customers different prices for the same product or service) and other business practices that decreased competition or established monopolies. Also in 1914, Congress enacted the Federal Trade Commission Act, which created an enforcement mechanism, the Federal Trade Commission (FTC). The law gave the FTC the power to issue "cease-and-desist orders" that required businesses to abandon unfair practices, such as price-fixing. Other regulatory laws enacted have included the Meat Inspection Act (1906), designed to protect public health; the Securities and Exchange Act (1934), intended to protect stock market investors; the Truth in Packaging Act (1966), passed to provide consumers with truthful information about products; and the Consumer Credit Protection Act (1969), which established protection for people who borrow money and use credit cards.

Court Action Against Trusts. In addition to the legislative action against trusts, reformers sought remedy through the courts. Since the early 1900s, government officials have continued to prosecute antitrust cases. Both the Justice Department and the Federal Trade Commission have the responsibility to combat unfair monopolistic business practices and prevent mergers that adversely affect consumers by decreasing competition. In the late 1990s, for example, a federal court blocked a merger of Home Depot, a large residential supply company, and Staples, a large office supply corporation, because the court believed the merger would inhibit competition.

In all of these efforts, whether successful or not, the federal government played an important economic role by attempting to protect consumers through regulation of business practices. It acted as a referee, attempting to make sure the game was being played fairly.

Test Yourself

Why did some people in the late 1800s and early 1900s want the federal government to break up trusts?

Environmental Regulations

The U.S. government also takes responsibility for public safety. Environmental policies exemplify this kind of government intervention. The modern environmental movement started in the 1960s when many people became increasingly concerned about the impact of air and water pollution on public health. Smog in large cities, particularly Los Angeles, resulted from the increase in automobile travel that accompanied the suburbanization of the United States. In such industrial states as Ohio, factories burned coal and other fossil fuels to produce electricity. These fossil fuels released sulfur dioxide into the atmosphere. The

Smoke from factories causes pollution and other environmental problems such as acid rain.

sulfur dioxide then created acid rain that destroyed trees, lakes, and wildlife as far away as Canada. Many industries also polluted our nation's water supply by dumping toxic wastes into public waterways or by contaminating sources of groundwater.

In the 1960s and 1970s, environmentalists lobbied government officials to address the problem of pollution. Government, they argued, was the only agency far-reaching enough to address the effects of so many different polluters. Many environmentalists believed that federal regulation was critical, even at the cost of economic growth. Several laws resulted from the environmentalists' campaign to raise public awareness and force a legislative response. In 1963, Congress passed the Clean Air Act, followed by the Clean Water Act in 1972 and the Safe Drinking Water Act in 1974.

In late 1970, environmentalists achieved an important milestone with the creation of the Environmental Protection Agency (EPA), which combined several federal environmental agencies under one regulatory agency. The EPA has responsibility for establishing pollution standards and fining or taking legal action against violators who have failed to comply after a reasonable period of time. The EPA also funds research studies that help determine where pollution exists and how it might be eliminated or reduced to acceptable levels. Since the EPA's inception, its efforts have resulted in improved air and water quality.

Test Yourself
What prompted the government to pass environmental regulations in the 1960s and 1970s?

★ THE FEDERAL RESERVE SYSTEM ★

The Federal Reserve System (the Fed) is the central banking system of the United States. It is comprised of 12 regional Federal Reserve Banks, located in major cities throughout the United States and a Board of Governors in Washington, D.C.

In 1913, Congress established the Fed as an independent organization within the U.S. government. The Fed's decisions do not have to be approved by the president or anyone else in the executive branch. Congress, however, can enact legislation to eliminate the Fed or change its duties. The Fed issues currency, makes monetary policy, and oversees the operations of the nation's banking system. The Fed's job is to create policies and banking rules that encourage economic growth and stability while combating inflationary and deflationary trends.

The Federal Reserve's responsibilities are as follows:

- to set the nation's monetary policy by influencing money and credit conditions in the economy in pursuit of full employment and stable prices

- to supervise and regulate banking institutions to ensure the safety and soundness of the nation's banking and financial system and to protect the credit rights of consumers

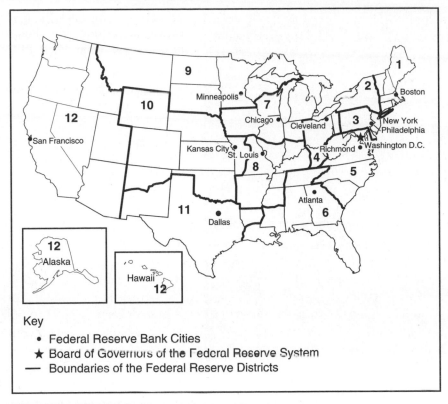

Map of the United States Federal Reserve System

- to maintain the stability of the financial system and contain risk that may arise in financial markets

- to provide certain financial services to the U.S. government, to the public, to financial institutions, and to foreign official institutions, including playing a major role in operating the nation's payments systems

The United States had central banks prior to the Fed—the First Bank of the United States (1791) and the Second Bank of the United States (1816). President Andrew Jackson closed the Second Bank in 1836, and the country went without a central bank until Congress created the Federal Reserve System.

Financial panics, recessions, and depressions periodically plagued the U.S. economy throughout the 19th century. In 1893, the worst depression experienced to that point in U.S. history gripped the country. It became evident to many economists and business leaders that the nation's banking system needed reform. Again in 1907, a banking panic created havoc in the business community. Sentiment for a central banking system grew. Finally, in 1912 and 1913, conservatives and Progressives, who disagreed over who should control the bank, worked out a compromise. In 1913, President Woodrow Wilson signed the Federal Reserve Act into law. All banks with charters from the federal government are required to be members of the system. Banks with charters from the state can choose to become members of the system.

The Federal Reserve Bank of Cleveland headquarters building in Cleveland, Ohio

Open-Market Operations. The Fed uses three basic powers to set monetary policy, which in turn influences interest rates (the amount that borrowers pay to lenders). Interest rates affect nearly all aspects of the economy—growth, prices, and employment. The first (and most powerful) tool, *open-market operations*, changes the amount of excess reserves in the banking system. The Fed can buy or sell Treasury securities in the financial markets. When it buys Treasury securities, the Fed increases reserves in the banking system, which makes money more available, or "loose," and results in lower interest rates. On the other hand, if the Fed sells securities in the open market, it decreases the reserves and makes money less available to banks, or "tight," causing interest rates to rise. The 12-member Federal Open Market Committee (FOMC) of the Federal Reserve System meets every six weeks and decides when to buy and when to sell.

Reserve Requirement. The Fed's second tool is called the *reserve requirement*, which it uses to control the amount of money a bank has to keep in reserve to take care of its customers. By increasing or decreasing the reserve requirement, the Fed can control the amount of money circulating in the economy and thereby either speed up or slow down economic activity.

Discount Rate. The third way that the Fed sets monetary policy is through the *discount rate*—the interest it charges on the loans it makes to the banks in the system. A bank might borrow from the Fed because its excess reserves are too low, and it needs a short-term loan to cover the shortage. By changing the discount rate, the Fed can affect the U.S. money supply. A lower rate creates loose money and more borrowing. Higher rates produce the opposite effect, tight money and less borrowing.

★ IMPACT OF THE GREAT DEPRESSION AND WORLD WAR II ON THE ECONOMY ★

The U.S. government's role in the economy has always been important in American history, but during the Great Depression and World War II, it increased significantly. When Franklin Delano Roosevelt took office as president in 1933, he and Congress acted quickly to combat the deep economic Depression that gripped the nation. Millions were out of work, and people across the United States lacked adequate food or housing. Starting in 1933, Roosevelt pushed a series of laws through Congress that came to be known as the New Deal. Many of the economic laws and regulations that we are familiar today originated in the New Deal.

Effects of New Deal Legislation

New Deal legislation expanded the role of government in the economy to a level never before experienced in the United States. Manufacturing, banking, labor, and agriculture were all affected. The New Deal also instituted a public welfare system to care for those in dire need. New Deal laws set standards for wages and hours and enabled labor unions to establish a firm foothold in many industries, such as rubber and steel. To address problem areas in the economy, Roosevelt's administration established regulatory agencies, such as the Securities and Exchange Commission, which regulates the stock market, and the Federal Deposit Insurance Corporation, which guarantees the safety of bank deposits. Perhaps the most famous and lasting New Deal creation is the Social Security system. This system pays pensions to retired people who contributed to the system through payroll taxes while they were working. Because of the New Deal, a new power relationship developed among business, labor, and government. Both labor and government henceforth played a larger role in making economic decisions.

Effects of World War II

World War II also affected this new power-sharing arrangement among government, business, and labor. Because of the immediate need to manufacture war material, labor and business readily cooperated when the U.S. government took an even more direct role in the economy.

Congress created the War Production Board, which coordinated the nation's industrial output so that the armed forces were adequately supplied. The board basically took control of American industry during the war years. Factories that previously made cars were converted to making tanks, jeeps, and airplanes. Other plants changed over to produce weapons and other necessary war material. To manage things on the home front, the Office of Price Administration (OPA) established rent control on some housing and set up a system to ration consumer goods, such as gasoline, meat, butter, sugar, and other necessities. During World War II, the supply of consumer goods decreased drastically. In a free-market economy, a decreased supply of desirable goods usually results in higher prices. The OPA's goal was to keep that from happening.

After the war, many of the agencies that had been created to address the crisis were abolished. Government, however, continued to play a key role in making economic decisions about public services, redistribution of income, and economic activity to promote growth and stability.

POINTS TO REMEMBER

- Governments raise revenue by levying taxes.
- Personal income taxes provide the largest percentage of revenue to the U.S. government.
- Trusts and monopolies decrease competition and allow price fixing.
- The U.S. government's first post–Civil War effort to control a monopoly involved railroads, which at that time were the lifeline of trade.
- In the late 1800s and early 1900s, the U.S. government passed legislation to combat the formation of trusts.
- The U.S. government also fought the formation of trusts through the courts.
- Environmentalists in the 1960s and 1970s lobbied the federal government to enact laws that would regulate and reduce pollution.
- Congress created the Federal Reserve System to manage the nation's economy by establishing banking rules and setting monetary policies.
- The Federal Reserve System uses the reserve requirement, open-market operations, and the discount rate to set monetary policy.
- As a result of both the Great Depression and World War II, the federal government's role in the economy increased dramatically.

EXERCISES

CHECKING WHAT YOU HAVE READ

1. Which of the following is a "progressive" tax?

   A. excise tax
   B. state income tax
   C. sales tax on an automobile
   D. "sin" tax on tobacco

2. The largest source of revenue for the U.S. government is the

   A. sales tax
   B. excise tax
   C. personal income tax
   D. "sin" tax on tobacco.

3. Why did many people in the late 1800s and early 1900s want the government to break up trusts?

   A. Trusts created excessive competition.
   B. Trusts decreased dividends for their shareholders.
   C. Trusts advocated an increase in labor union membership.
   D. Trusts decreased competition and fixed prices.

4. Which of the following is a federal regulatory agency that focuses on air and water pollution?

   A. EPA
   B. FTC
   C. the Fed
   D. SEC

5. Which of the following would result in a "tight" money policy?

   A. The Fed buys securities on the open market.
   B. The Fed sells securities on the open market.
   C. The Fed raises the discount rate.
   D. The Fed raises the reserve requirement.

USING WHAT YOU HAVE READ

Contact your local government (school district, city, village, or county) to get information about its sources of revenue. Create a bar graph or a pie chart that shows the amount or percentage of each source. Explain whether the major source of revenue is a progressive or regressive tax.

THINKING ABOUT WHAT YOU HAVE READ: CREDIBILITY OF SOURCES

Some people have proposed that the U.S. government replace its current personal income tax with a "flat" income tax, that is, a tax levied at the same rate on all levels of income. A flat tax is designed to charge the same percentage of tax above a certain stipulated income level. The current income tax system charges higher rates as a person's income increases up to a certain point.

Use the library or Internet to read more about flat tax proposals and about criticisms of the flat tax. After reading articles both for and against the flat tax, select the article that you think is the most credible and reliable. Write a short essay in which you explain why you think the article that you selected is the most reliable and credible.

SKILLS

Evaluating a Muckraker's Article

During the early 1900s, a group of journalists called muckrakers wrote books and articles exposing the practices of monopolistic corporations. Ida M. Tarbell, for example, wrote about the Standard Oil Company. These roused such public indignation that the federal government was moved to investigate the company's practices. As a result of the investigation, Standard Oil was dissolved in 1911.

Read the following extract from one of Tarbell's articles. Then evaluate it as an effective exposé of a monopoly. Does Tarbell give a clear idea of what is wrong with the way in which Standard Oil operates? Does she base her objections to the company on facts or opinions? Although this article in its complete form was successful in exposing Standard Oil, the extract given here has a defect. What is it? How might Tarbell have corrected it in a complete version of this article? Is the analogy she makes in the last paragraph effective? Why or why not?

. . . (Standard Oil) controls the great pipeline handling all but perhaps 10 percent of the oil produced in the Eastern fields. This system is fully 35,000 miles long. It goes to the wells for every producer, gathers his oil into its storage tanks, and from there transports it to Philadelphia, Baltimore, New York, Chicago, Buffalo, Cleveland, or any other refining point where it is needed. This pipeline is a common carrier by virtue of its use of the right of eminent domain (the right to take private property for public use), and as a common carrier, is theoretically obliged to carry and deliver the oil of all comers, but in practice, this does not always work. It has happened more than once in the history of the Standard Pipes that they have refused to gather or deliver oil. Pipes have been taken up from wells belonging to individuals running or working with independent refiners. Oil has been refused delivery at points practical for independent refiners. . . .

It is exactly as if one corporation aiming at manufacturing all the flour of the country owned all but 10 percent of the entire railroad system collecting and transporting wheat. They could, of course, in time of shortage, prevent any would-be competitor from getting grain to grind, and they could and would make it difficult and expensive at all times for him to get it.

CHAPTER 30

THE EVOLUTION OF THE CONSTITUTION

> **BENCHMARK:**
>
> Analyze the evolution of the Constitution through post-Reconstruction amendments and Supreme Court decisions.

When the Framers drafted the Constitution, they included the means to change it in order to adapt to new circumstances. The Constitution can be changed by adding amendments, a difficult process that requires the approval of two-thirds of the House and the Senate and three-fourths of the states. When it decides cases, the Supreme Court, depending on the views of its nine justices, can reinterpret the Constitution. This benchmark asks students to analyze the ways the United States Constitution has changed over time as the result of amendments and Supreme Court rulings. Specifically, it refers to three court cases—*Plessy* v. *Ferguson*, *Brown* v. *Board of Education of Topeka*, and *Regents of the University of California* v. *Bakke*—and two amendments—the Nineteenth, which gave women the right to vote, and the Twenty-sixth, which lowered the voting age to 18. Questions on the OGT will refer to these cases and amendments, focusing on how they helped the Constitution evolve and change. Chapter 23 also addresses the *Plessy* case.

★ JUDICIAL REVIEW ★

When the Framers of the Constitution met in Philadelphia during the summer of 1787, they devised a framework for government that included checks and balances. The three branches of government—executive, the legislative, and judicial—possess certain powers that enable them to check and balance one another. By dividing the government into three separate and coequal branches, the Framers ensured that the federal government would not become too powerful.

One of the judicial branch's most important checks on the legislative and executive branches is *judicial* review, the power of the federal courts, especially the Supreme Court, to determine whether laws and actions are constitutional or not. If a majority of the nine justices agree, the Supreme Court has the power to strike down any law passed by Congress and signed by the president. The Constitution does not explicitly list judicial review as a power of the judiciary. The Supreme Court, under Chief Justice John Marshall, established the power in the landmark case of *Marbury* v. *Madison* (1803). Since then, judicial review has become a principle of American government that has been used many times by both the federal and state courts. In most cases, the courts have upheld government actions and laws. There have been, however, about 150

Chief Justice John Marshall
(1801–1835)

cases since 1803 in which the Supreme Court ruled against the government and declared a law passed by Congress to be unconstitutional. Judicial review gives them, in effect, the power to change the Constitution, and help it evolve to address historical change.

Post–Civil War Amendments

In the years following the Civil War, the nation ratified three amendments to the Constitution aimed at correcting wrongs committed against African Americans during the era of slavery. The Thirteenth Amendment (1865) abolished slavery. The Fourteenth Amendment (1868) made anyone born in the United States a citizen and guaranteed due process and equal protection of the laws to all people. In 1870, the Fifteenth Amendment stated that no one could be denied the right to vote because of race, color, or previous enslavement.

Jim Crow Laws

When Reconstruction ended, many Southern states passed laws intended to bypass rights guaranteed in these recent amendments. They passed Jim Crow laws to establish and enforce racial segregation. Aimed primarily at African Americans, Jim Crow laws required segregated facilities for blacks and whites. The laws dictated that schools, restaurants, train and bus stations, hospitals, parks, and drinking fountains should be segregated. Poll taxes and literacy tests were also enacted to keep African Americans from voting. These states were trying to thwart the Constitution by passing laws that violated the rights guaranteed in the Fourteenth and Fifteenth amendments.

Homer Plessy Challenges Jim Crow. Like many states in the 1890s, Louisiana enacted a law that required African Americans and whites to sit in separate railroad cars. In 1892, Homer Plessy, a shoemaker who was seven-eighths white and one-eighth black, sat in a railroad car reserved for whites. When Plessy was ordered to move, he refused and was arrested. Plessy decided to take his case to court, arguing that the Louisiana law requiring blacks and whites to sit in separate cars violated both the Thirteenth and Fourteenth amendments. Judge John H. Ferguson ruled against Plessy and found him guilty. Plessy appealed to the Louisiana Supreme Court, which upheld Ferguson's original ruling. Plessy then appealed to the U.S. Supreme Court. The case raised the question of whether the Louisiana law that mandated racial segregation on trains violated the Fourteenth Amendment's guarantee of privileges and immunities and equal protection under the law.

Plessy v. Ferguson. In 1896, the Supreme Court ruled that the Louisiana law was not a violation of the Fourteenth Amendment. With an eight-to-one vote, the justices upheld Homer Plessy's conviction and, at the same time, state-mandated racial segregation. The decision provided a legal basis for Jim Crow laws by establishing that separate facilities were acceptable if they were of equal quality. The Court ruled that the Louisiana law did not violate the equal-protection clause of the Fourteenth Amendment because separate facilities for whites and blacks—in this case railroad cars—were equal. The phrase "separate-but-equal" did not appear in the *Plessy* decision, but the justices' ruling did, in effect, affirm the principle.

The *Plessy* decision set a legal *precedent* (an example to be followed in future cases). Public officials saw the ruling as the government's approval of Jim Crow laws. Based on the *Plessy* precedent, if racial segregation was legal on railroad cars, it was also legal in other aspects of life such as schools and public facilities. By virtue of the *Plessy* decision, the interpretation of the Constitution changed, violating the spirit and intent of the Fourteenth Amendment and diminishing the civil rights of African Americans and other minority groups. Racial segregation became legally entrenched in American society for the next six decades.

***Justice Harlan's Dissent in* Plessy.** A single Supreme Court justice, John Marshall Harlan, dissented (disagreed with the majority) in the *Plessy* decision. He wrote:

Justice John Marshall Harlan
(1877–1911)

Our Constitution is color-blind, and neither knows nor tolerates classes among citizens. In respect of civil rights, all citizens are equal before the law. . . . In my opinion, the judgment this day rendered will, in time, prove to be quite as pernicious [damaging] as the decision made by this tribunal in the Dred Scott case. . . . The present decision . . . will not only stimulate aggressions, more or less brutal and irritating, upon the admitted rights of colored citizens, but will encourage the belief that it is possible, by means of state enactments, to defeat the beneficent [good] purposes which the people of the United States had in view when they adopted the recent amendments of the Constitution.

Test Yourself
How did the *Plessy* decision affect African Americans?

Brown Case

Not until 1954, in the famous *Brown* v. *Board of Education of Topeka* decision, did the court overturn the "separate-but-equal" doctrine established in the *Plessy* case. Because the *Plessy* decision legalized racial segregation in the United States, most schools in the 1950s were segregated. On the basis of the separate-but-equal doctrine, schools within a district should be equal even if they were segregated. This was seldom the case, however. Most African American schools were inferior, usually understaffed and underfunded.

Linda Brown: Challenge to School Segregation. In 1950, Linda Brown attended a black elementary school in Topeka, Kansas. Even though there was a white school just a few blocks from her home, Linda had to walk over a mile to the black school and pass through a dangerous railroad yard. Linda's father, Oliver, tried to convince the school system to admit his daughter to the white school near their home, but the district refused. In 1951, with the help of the local chapter of the National Association for the Advancement of Colored

Linda Brown

People (NAACP), Oliver Brown sued the Topeka school system. The suit asked the Kansas court to end school segregation in Topeka. The NAACP's lawyers argued that segregated schools made black children feel inferior to whites and were, by their very nature, unequal. Dr. Hugh W. Speer, an expert witness who testified at the trial, said:

> . . . if the colored children are denied the experience in school of associating with white children, who represent 90 percent of our national society in which these colored children must live, then the colored child's curriculum is being greatly curtailed. The Topeka curriculum or any school curriculum cannot be equal under segregation.

The attorneys for the Topeka Board of Education contended that segregation was a common condition in the United States and that segregated schools actually prepared black children to deal with segregation when they became adults. They also argued that segregated schools did not harm African American children, citing great black leaders and scientists such as Frederick Douglass, Booker T. Washington, and George Washington Carver.

The judges hearing the case admitted that segregation harmed black children. In their decision, they recognized that "segregation of white and colored children in public schools has a detrimental effect upon the colored children. . . . A sense of inferiority affects the motivation of a child to learn." Despite this admission, they ruled against Brown, citing the precedent from the *Plessy* case as justification. (Since the Supreme Court had not overturned *Plessy*, the Kansas court could cite it as a precedent.)

Court Overturns Separate-But-Equal. In 1951, Oliver Brown and the NAACP appealed the decision to the Supreme Court. The Court heard the case a year later, but could not reach agreement on a decision. The justices reheard the case in December 1953. In May 1954, Chief Justice Earl Warren announced the court's unanimous decision:

Chief Justice Earl Warren
(1953–1969)

We come then to the question presented: Does segregation of children in public schools solely on the basis of race, even though the physical facilities and other "tangible" factors may be equal, deprive the children of the minority group of equal educational opportunities? We believe that it does. . . . We conclude that in the field of public education the doctrine of "separate but equal" has no place. Separate educational facilities are inherently unequal. Therefore, we hold that the plaintiffs and others similarly situated for whom the actions have been brought are, by reason of the segregation complained of, deprived of equal protection of the laws guaranteed by the Fourteenth Amendment.

Thus the Supreme Court overturned the "separate-but-equal" doctrine established in *Plessy* and ordered the desegregation of all schools in the United States. But the ruling did not address other kinds of segregation, such as in public facilities or restaurants. Nor did the Court set a timetable to accomplish school desegregation. By using its power of judicial review, the Supreme Court changed the understanding of the Constitution. The decision expanded protections guaranteed in the Fourteenth Amendment to African Americans and other racial minorities who had long been denied their civil rights and discriminated against.

Test Yourself

What effect did the *Brown* decision have on the ruling in the *Plessy* case?

Schools were not immediately desegregated across the nation following the *Brown* decision. About a year after the Court's ruling, Chief Justice Warren issued the unanimous decision known as *Brown II*. It established some expectations about how soon school districts should desegregate. The Court ordered states to begin desegregating "with all deliberate speed." It took nearly two decades and several court cases ordering school districts to desegregate before the intent of *Brown I* was finally realized.

Bakke Case

In 1978, the Supreme Court demonstrated again how the power of the judicial review can be used to change previous interpretations of the Constitution and influence its evolution to meet the changing needs and conditions of society. In the early 1970s, a white man named Allan Bakke applied twice to the University of California Medical School at Davis. The school rejected his application both times. As part of its affirmative action program, the school instituted a quota system that reserved 16 slots in each class for minority applicants. For a college or university, an affirmative action program awards admission to minorities in order to make up for past injustices. Most universities in the 1970s had similar programs. It was difficult to gain admission to medical school because of its rigorous standards and the high number of applicants. Bakke's qualifications for admission—based on factors including grades, test scores, and interviews—were higher than those of all the minority students admitted under the affirmative action program when he was rejected. Bakke sued the University of California, arguing that he was denied admission on the basis of his race in violation of the Fourteenth Amendment. Bakke claimed he was a victim of reverse discrimination.

The *Bakke* decision was not as clear as *Brown*. Four justices agreed that any quota system based solely on race violated the Civil Rights Act of 1964. A fifth justice, Lewis F. Powell, Jr., joined those four to order the school to admit Bakke. Justice Powell wrote in his opinion that rigid adherence to quotas based on race, such as the one at the university, violated the equal-protection clause of the Fourteenth Amendment. The decision also held, however, that it was constitutional to use race as a criterion for admission decisions, just as long as it was one of several criteria, and there was no strict quota system. Thus the Court ruled in favor of Bakke and ordered his admission, but it also allowed affirmative action programs to continue.

Test Yourself
What was the Supreme Court's decision in the *Bakke* case?

★ CONSTITUTIONAL AMENDMENTS ★

The Constitution changes through the amendment process, which was written into the document by the Framers. In 1819, Chief Justice John Marshall wrote, "We must never forget that it is . . . a Constitution intended to endure for ages to come and, consequently, to be adapted to the various crises of human affairs." Article V of the Constitution states that amendments can be proposed in two ways. The first method is by a two-thirds vote of both houses of Congress. The second is by a national convention called by Congress at the request of two-thirds of the states. This method has never been used. Although hundreds of amendments have been introduced in Congress, few have received the necessary votes to advance to the ratification procedure. There are also two ways to ratify an amendment. The first way is for the legislatures in three-fourths of the states to ratify it. The other is for each state to hold a ratifying convention. When three-fourths of those conventions vote in favor of the amendment, it is ratified. This method has been used only once, in 1933, to ratify the Twenty-first Amendment, which repealed Prohibition.

Women Seek the Right to Vote

Since the end of the Civil War, suffragists had campaigned and lobbied for voting rights for women but with little success. By 1911, only six states, all in the Western half of the nation, allowed women to vote. The state-by-state approach to voting rights was clearly not working. Some reformers began to look at another strategy, a constitutional amendment. Women's rights advocates such as Susan B. Anthony had suggested that approach as early as the 1860s, but the movement did not gain any ground until the 1900s.

Suffragette Movement. In the early 1900s, Alice Paul, a suffragette, helped build support for a constitutional amendment that would give women the right to vote. Her militancy and tactics alienated some suffragists and briefly split the movement. Some activists wanted a constitutional amendment, but others wanted to stick with the state-by-state approach. At about the same time, another fiery leader, Carrie Chapman Catt, appeared on the scene. Beginning in 1915, her leadership helped revive the National American Woman Suffrage Association (NAWSA) and the movement to amend the Constitution to guarantee women the right to vote. Catt developed a plan to campaign at both the state and federal levels.

Nineteenth Amendment. Although they encountered many obstacles, suffragists made gains at the state level. The outbreak of World War I helped their cause. Throughout the war, suffragists vigorously supported the military effort, while still advocating their cause. Their strategy was to demonstrate that they were responsible and worthy citizens who deserved to vote in national elections. When the United States entered the war and many women assumed jobs previously held by men, they gradually gained support for their cause. In 1918, President Woodrow Wilson endorsed voting rights for women, and Congress narrowly voted to submit the amendment to the states for ratification. After two more years of vigorous campaigning throughout the country, the Nineteenth Amendment won approval in the required three-fourths of the states and was ratified in 1920. It states: "The right of citizens of the United States to vote shall not be denied or abridged by the United States or by any state on account of sex." The amendment changed the Constitution and met the people's demand to expand American democracy and guarantee a basic right of citizenship to women.

Suffragettes march for the right to vote in New York City in 1915.

Test Yourself
What effect did the Nineteenth Amendment have on the United States?

Calls to Lower the Voting Age to 18

The Twenty-sixth Amendment extended voting rights to citizens who were at least 18 years old. Until its ratification in 1971, Americans had to be at least 21 to vote. In 1941, Congressman Jennings Randolph of West Virginia first introduced an amendment to lower the voting age. He argued that if people were old enough to be drafted for wartime service, they were old enough to vote. Since the nation was focused on World War II, the amendment did not have enough support at the time. After Randolph was elected to the U.S. Senate in 1958, he introduced the bill once again and in subsequent sessions of Congress.

Support for the amendment increased over time. Both Presidents Eisenhower and Johnson supported the amendment. Several states, including Oregon, also passed laws lowering the voting age. Opponents challenged the Oregon law in court, and the Supreme Court eventually overturned it. This spurred many advocates to increase their efforts for a constitutional amendment.

Twenty-sixth Amendment. Just as World War I increased support for the Nineteenth Amendment, the Vietnam War played an important role in the passage of the Twenty-sixth Amendment. As more young people under the age of 21 fought and died in Vietnam or became politically active in the antiwar movement during the late 1960s and early 1970s, support for the amendment increased. In 1971, Randolph reintroduced the bill in Congress, where it quickly won approval. Within months of its passage, the legislatures in the necessary 38 states approved the amendment. Ohio was the final state required for ratification.

Jennings Randolph, U.S. Representative and Senator from West Virginia

Both the Nineteenth and Twenty-sixth amendments expanded a basic right of citizenship—voting—to more people. They expanded democratic government in the United States, and they are prime examples of how the Constitution evolves to meet the needs of new generations of citizens.

Test Yourself
In what way was the Twenty-sixth Amendment similar to the Nineteenth?

> ► **POINTS TO REMEMBER**

- The Constitution can be changed through amendments.
- The Supreme Court uses the power of judicial review to interpret the Constitution so that it can meet new situations and challenges.
- Despite protections guaranteed in the Fourteenth Amendment, after Reconstruction many Southern states enacted Jim Crow laws that established a system of segregation based on race.
- The *Plessy* decision legalized the separate-but-equal doctrine and Jim Crow laws.
- The *Brown* decision overturned *Plessy* and found the separate-but-equal doctrine unconstitutional.
- The *Bakke* decision limited affirmative action programs, but it did not eliminate race entirely as a criterion for admission to school.
- The Nineteenth Amendment gave women the right to vote in all states.
- The Twenty-sixth Amendment gave 18-year-olds the right to vote.
- Both the Nineteenth and Twenty-sixth amendments expanded the nation's electorate.

EXERCISES

CHECKING WHAT YOU HAVE READ

Use information from the chapter to answer the following questions.

1. In which case did the Supreme Court establish its power of judicial review?

2. How did the *Plessy* case affect the Fourteenth Amendment?

3. What was the separate-but-equal doctrine, and how did the *Brown* case relate to it?

4. What happened as a result of the ruling in *Brown* v. *Board of Education of Topeka*?

5. How did the Nineteenth and Twenty-sixth amendments change the Constitution?

USING WHAT YOU HAVE READ: CHARTING INFORMATION

Sometimes it is helpful to create graphic organizers to help you understand a particular concept or idea. Draw a table with headings like the one below and fill it in.

Court Case or Amendment	Effect on the United States

THINKING ABOUT WHAT YOU HAVE READ

1. Which of the three court cases covered in this chapter do you think has been the most important or significant for the United States? Support your opinion with evidence from the chapter or from additional research. Be sure to give reasons for your opinion.

2. Of the two amendments addressed in the chapter, which do you think has had the most important or significant effect on the United States? State your opinion and then support it with evidence from the chapter or from additional research. Be sure to give reasons for your opinion.

SKILLS

Evaluating Choices

Assume you are a judge hearing the *Bakke* case. There are four possible decisions you can reach:

1. admit Bakke to medical school and declare affirmative action programs unconstitutional;

2. support the medical school's decision not to admit Bakke and support the constitutionality of affirmative-action programs;

3. admit Bakke to medical school, but allow certain types of affirmative action programs;

4. admit Bakke but make no decision regarding affirmative action programs.

Can you think of any more possibilities? If so, add them to the list. Now, rank the options by listing them from best to worst. Explain why you selected this order. In other words, why do you think the first option you listed was the best and why each of the others were not as good? What criteria did you use for evaluating each choice?

CHAPTER 31

GOVERNMENTAL CHANGE

BENCHMARK:

Analyze ways in which people achieve governmental change including political action, social protest, and revolution.

This benchmark requires you to know the ways in which people achieve governmental change—whether through political action, social protest, or revolution. Political parties, interest groups, lobbyists, the media, and public opinion have all helped to shape government policy. You should be able to analyze how change occurred in the following topics: extension of suffrage, labor legislation, civil rights legislation, military policy, environmental legislation, business regulation, and educational policy. You should also be able to discuss civil disobedience and how it differs from other forms of dissent. You should be able to describe examples of the various means of bringing about governmental change when discussing the women's suffrage movement of the late 1800s, the civil rights movement of the 1960s, and student protests during the Vietnam War.

Some of these topics have been addressed in other chapters. Some aspects of women's suffrage are covered in Chapter 21 (women's right to vote, women's liberation movement), Chapter 22 (National Organization for Women), and Chapter 23 (struggle for gender equality), while extension of suffrage is examined in Chapter 21 (women's right to vote) and Chapter 30 (Nineteenth Amendment). Labor issues and legislation appear in Chapter 17 (rise and growth of labor organizations; regulation of child labor), Chapter 21 (New Deal), and Chapter 28 (impact on the economy). The civil rights movement of the 1960s received attention in Chapter 21 (changes in goals and tactics; linkages to other movements) and Chapter 22 (NAACP). The environmental movement was considered in Chapter 29 (environmental regulations), and the topic of protests against the Vietnam War was discussed in Chapter 21. Finally, educational policy was included in Chapter 17 (movement for public schooling). Review these chapters for help with this benchmark.

★ METHODS OF EFFECTING GOVERNMENTAL CHANGE ★

People attempt to change government in a number of ways. Revolution is the most extreme way to bring about governmental change. Sometimes it is the only effective way for people to achieve their goals. The United States, for example, grew out of a colonial revolution against Great Britain. In democracies there are a number of options besides violent revolution for achieving governmental change, such as using the political process to enact laws. Somewhere between revolution and ordinary political action is social protest. Protest goes beyond normal political action, but not as far as revolution. In this chapter, we will discuss political activity and social protest as methods of achieving governmental change.

Revolution ———	*Social Protest* ———	*Political Action*
This is the overthrow of a government, usually by violent means.	This form of dissent can be legal, but it may take the form of civil disobedience, in which case it is illegal. Protest can be either violent or nonviolent.	This method of changing government policy works within the system. It is nonviolent and usually socially acceptable.

Political Action

This method uses the institutions within a government to effect governmental change. You will recall that before their revolt against King George III, the American colonists used political action when they petitioned Parliament to repeal the tax laws that they considered unfair. In Chapter 30, you learned that when the Founders of the United States framed the Constitution, they made sure that it could be changed to meet new circumstances. In other words, they built into the very foundation of the U.S. government a political process for changing it when necessary.

Political Parties

In the United States, political parties and their elected officials are the vehicles through which changes in government policies and practices are achieved. A *political party* is an organization whose chief purpose is to elect its members to office. Most party members have similar ideas about government policy. If the party's candidates succeed in winning election, they have an opportunity to run the government according to their ideas of what is best for the nation. Elected officials are not the only people, however, who influence or have access to the political process. Interest groups, lobbyists, the media, and public opinion also play important roles.

Interest Groups

Interest groups are organizations whose members share similar views and attempt to influence public policy. The National Organization for Women (NOW) and the National Association for the Advancement of Colored People (NAACP) are interest groups. They are examples of private organizations whose members work toward the same end—to change government policy of some kind.

The change that interest groups seek is often achieved through political action. Therefore, interest groups are sometimes referred to as *political action groups*. In order to persuade politicians and government officials to support them, interest groups often create *political action committees* (PACs). PACs and interest groups are separate organizations, but they work for the same goals. PACs raise money and contribute to the political campaigns of candidates who support the groups' agendas. Interest groups have to form PACs because federal election laws do not allow most interest groups to directly contribute money to political candidates.

Interest groups also attempt to influence public opinion by mounting public information campaigns. Their purpose is to inform people about the group's views and persuade the public to support their positions. In recent years, NOW, the NAACP, the United Farm Workers (UFW), the American Indian Movement (AIM), and other interest groups have organized successful public awareness campaigns that helped to influence political parties and government officials to bring about some kind of change.

Lobbyists. Interest groups often employ lobbyists. Lobbyists bring a group, an organization, or a point of view to the attention of a legislature or government agency. Their job is to persuade government officials to vote for or against a particular law, regulation, or policy. These people are called lobbyists because, in the past, they gathered in the lobbies of legislative chambers in order to approach and persuade lawmakers to agree with their point of view and sway legislation.

Lobbyists may work for organizations, labor unions, large corporations, or interest groups. They may work for free or receive payment for their services. Their primary task, however, is to convince government officials to enact laws or make changes that will benefit their clients. They sometimes even write the bills that legislators then submit as their own. Lobbyists, by their very definition, are not objective. They represent a point of view and try to persuade government officials to agree with them.

The table below, Interest Groups and Their Accomplishments, will give you an idea of how interest groups operate and what some of them have achieved.

Interest Groups and Their Accomplishments

Issue	Interest or Political Action Group	Activities Used to Achieve Goals	Result or Change
Extension of suffrage	National Woman Suffrage Association (NWSA); National Organization for Women (NOW)	public awareness campaigns; lobbying Congress; dissent; civil disobedience	Nineteenth Amendment; Equal Pay Act (1963); Title VII of the Civil Rights Act (1964); ERA passed in Congress (not ratified by states)
Labor legislation	Unions: Knights of Labor; AFL-CIO	lobbying Congress; strikes (sometimes violent); public awareness campaigns; dissent; civil disobedience	National Labor Relations Act (1935), Fair Labor Standards Act (1938), established collective bargaining rights, gave unions more power

Civil rights legislation	National Association for the Advancement of Colored People (NAACP); National Urban League; Congress of Racial Equality (CORE)	lobbying Congress; public awareness campaigns; court suits; dissent; civil disobedience	Civil Rights Act of 1964; Civil Rights Act of 1991; Voting Rights Act of 1965; *Brown* decision (1954); end of segregated schools
Military policy	Vietnam Veterans Against the War (VVAW); antiwar activists	lobbying Congress; protests; dissent; civil disobedience	Eventual withdrawal of troops from Vietnam; abolition of military draft
Environmental legislation	Greenpeace; Sierra Club; Environmental Defense Fund; environmental activists	public awareness campaigns; lobbying Congress; dissent, civil disobedience	Clean Air Act (1963); Clean Water Act (1972); Safe Drinking Water Act (1974); creation of Environmental Protection Agency (EPA, 1970); Occupational Safety and Health Act (OSHA, 1974)
Business regulation	Business associations; Progressive reformers	lobbying; PACs to influence congressional legislation	Sherman Antitrust Act (1890); Clayton Antitrust Act (1914); ICC, FTC
Educational policy	NAACP; National Education Association (NEA); American Federation of Teachers (AFT)	actions in federal court, dissent	*Brown* decision, end to segregated schools; federal legislation; Department of Education created by Congress (1979)

Test Yourself

What are the main goals of interest groups, and what activities do they engage in to achieve their goals?

★ DISSENT AND CIVIL DISOBEDIENCE ★

There are times when people disagree intensely with a U.S. government action or policy and try through political means to stop the action or change the policy. In some cases, however, lobbying, public awareness campaigns, and political action do not achieve the desired result. Sometimes, people turn to dissent and civil disobedience to produce change. Civil disobedience usually involves more extreme forms of protest than dissent.

Dissent

Dissent refers to intense disagreement with authority, usually the government, and often involves some kind of protest action or organized movement. For example, when anti-Vietnam war protesters staged marches in the 1960s or civil rights activists demonstrated against segregation, they were dissenting against government laws or policies. Occasionally, those events involved clashes between the police and the protesters that resulted in violence and arrests. Dissent can take many forms, such as marches, staged protest events with speakers, publications, picketing, boycotts, and public awareness campaigns.

Women's Suffrage. The women's suffrage movement shows how frustrated political action can develop into dissent. The movement began in the United States in the mid-1800s as an offshoot of the abolitionist movement, which involved such methods of civil disobedience as the establishment of the Underground Railroad. As many women worked hard to ban slavery, they began to make comparisons between their own positions and those of slaves. At that time, women were not only denied the right to vote, they were also denied the right to an education equal to that of their male peers. Married women could not manage their own property; often they were forced to put it into their husbands' names. Working wives could be compelled to give their wages to their husbands. In case of divorce, women were not permitted to keep their children if their husbands claimed custody of them.

Lucretia Mott, who had been one of the founders of the American Antislavery Society, Elizabeth Cady Stanton, and other early feminists joined together in a campaign to increase public awareness of how unfairly women were treated. This campaign was launched in July 1848 by a conference at Seneca Falls, New York. Over 240 people attended the meeting and listened as Stanton read a document called "The Declaration of Rights and Sentiments." Stanton demanded that women be given the right to vote so they could help make the laws that controlled their lives.

In 1851, Stanton gained a strong partner in her fight for women's rights, Susan B. Anthony. Under the leadership of these two women, suffragists primarily used political action to attain their goals. One of their early achievements was the Married Women's Property Law (1860). It was passed after a speech that Stanton delivered to the New York State legislature. The law gave the women of New York State many new rights, including the right to own property, conduct their own businesses, manage their own incomes, and be joint guardians of their own children. They still, however, lacked the right to vote.

Many female abolitionists, who otherwise supported women's suffrage, felt that it should be put on hold until African American males were assured of the right to vote. Stanton and Anthony did not agree. In 1869, they formed the National Woman Suffrage Association (NWSA), the goal of which was to gain passage of a constitutional amendment that gave all female citizens of the United States the right to vote. Some of the women who had formerly worked with them on feminist issues formed the American Woman Suffrage Association (AWSA), which chose a more gradual process of obtaining the vote for women.

The members of NWSA felt that stronger measures should be used to gain the vote, and they began to engage in civil disobedience. Susan B. Anthony and other suffragettes defied the ban against female enfranchisement by casting ballots in the presidential election of 1872. This act was to test the way in which the Fourteenth Amendment was interpreted at that time. In Section 1, the amendment states: "All persons born or naturalized in the United States, and subject to the jurisdiction thereof, are citizens of the United States and of the state wherein they reside. No state shall make or enforce any law which shall abridge the privileges or immunities of citizens of the United States." Section 2, however, stipulates that *male* citizens cannot be denied the right to vote. Since this was the first time that the writers of the Constitution used the word *male* to describe U.S. citizens, the suffragists decided to challenge it. All the women who voted in this election were arrested, found guilty of breaking the law, and sentenced to pay a fine and the court costs. Susan B. Anthony refused to pay the fine, saying that the penalty was unjust and that "resistance to tyranny is obedience to God." The judge did not, however, order her to prison but indicated that he expected her eventually to pay the fine.

Susan B. Anthony

In 1890, NWSA and AWSA joined forces under a new name—the National American Woman Suffrage Association (NAWSA). During the 1890s, new Western states such as Wyoming entered the union with constitutions that gave women the vote. Encouraged by support from these new states and by the examples of New Zealand and Australia, which also gave women the same voting rights as men enjoyed (New Zealand in 1893, Australia in 1902), the suffragists stepped up their campaign.

NAWSA and other suffragist groups began to use a more sophisticated political strategy. They enlisted the help of the leaders of the Progressive and Socialist parties, who were then gaining power in state legislatures and exploited differences of opinion among the leaders of the Republican and Democratic parties. They also began to use more militant tactics when necessary.

In 1913, after Congress narrowly defeated a proposed constitutional amendment to extend the vote to women, the members of NAWSA organized a huge march down Pennsylvania Avenue in Washington, D.C. It was held on the day before President Woodrow Wilson's inauguration. The intent of the marchers was to hold a peaceful demonstration that would persuade the new president to support their amendment. But a large group of male opponents attempted to block the marchers. Violence ensued, and hundreds of people were injured. In the end, federal troops had to be brought in to quell the disturbance. In this case, a legal demonstration of dissent degenerated into a violent melee. In general, however, the suffragists used peaceful means of dissent, such as picketing, boycotting, petitioning, and pamphleteering.

Civil Rights Movement. More recent examples of dissent occurred during the civil rights movement of the 1960s. Civil rights advocates successfully used several nonviolent tactics to further their cause. In the mid-1950s, for example, they protested the arrest of Rosa Parks, who had refused to give up her seat to a white man, by boycotting the bus company in Montgomery, Alabama. African Americans in Montgomery refused to ride the buses until the company agreed to change its policies in regard to black passengers. The capstone event of this movement was the 1963 March on Washington. On a hot August day, over 200,000 demonstrators arrived in the nation's capital to join in the March on Washington for Jobs and Freedom. It turned out to be the largest protest demonstration for civil rights in U.S. history. Civil rights groups such as the NAACP, the National Urban League, the Congress of Racial Equality (CORE), the Southern Christian Leadership Conference (SCLC), and the Student Nonviolent Coordinating Committee (SNCC) cooperated to organize the event and make it a success. It was a peaceful expression of dissent against racism, discrimination, and segregation.

Martin Luther King, Jr. at the March on Washington in 1963

Starting at the Washington Monument, the marchers walked one mile down the National Mall to the Lincoln Memorial, where the speakers talked for about three hours. It was here that Martin Luther King, Jr., gave his famous "I Have a Dream" speech. After the speeches, President John F. Kennedy met with the organizers at the White House to discuss civil rights issues and prospects for future government action.

This is how Martin Luther King, Jr. described his dream to the assembled marchers:

> . . . I still have a dream. It is a dream deeply rooted in the American dream. I have a dream that one day this nation will rise up and live out the true meaning of its creed: "We hold these truths to be self-evident: that all men are created equal." . . . I have a dream that my four little children will one day live in a nation where they will not be judged by the color of their skin but by the content of their character.

Anti–Vietnam War Movement. In the 1960s and 1970s, Vietnam War protesters dissented against America's military intervention in Vietnam. When the first U.S. troops went to Vietnam, few Americans knew exactly where that country was located. Opponents of the war staged a few demonstrations when the United States first began military intervention there, but the extent of protest was insignificant until the late 1960s.

To raise public awareness of their objections to the war, antiwar protesters conducted *teach-ins* all over the country and staged hundreds of protest marches and rallies. Sometimes these events escalated into violence, but many of them were peaceful expressions of dissent. Increasingly, protesters engaged in civil disobedience during their demonstrations. You will read more about this movement below, in the section dealing with civil disobedience.

Civil Disobedience

Civil disobedience is willful, active refusal to obey a law that the dissenters believe to be immoral. Acts of civil disobedience are usually planned in advance. Getting arrested is, in fact, sometimes the goal of people engaged in civil disobedience. They may want to be taken into custody in order to draw attention to their views and thereby influence public opinion. Nonviolent civil disobedience includes such tactics as organizing a blockade or illegally occupying a facility and refusing to leave. Protesters expect to be arrested, perhaps even beaten, by the authorities, and they often undergo training on how to behave nonviolently during a protest. In the 1930s and 1940s, Mahatma Gandhi employed civil disobedience in the Indian struggle against British colonization. Gandhi said, "Noncooperation with evil is a sacred duty." In other words, he believed that Indians were spiritually and morally obligated to oppose British rule of India, which he considered illegal occupation. He nonviolently disobeyed British laws in India to gain sympathy and support for his movement.

There are many examples of nonviolent civil disobedience in U.S. history. In the 1930s and 1940s, labor unions used nonviolent protest effectively. Between 1935 and 1937, for example, the Congress of Industrial Organizations (CIO) conducted sit-down strikes in auto plants to force management to bargain with union representatives. Employees stopped working, literally sat down, and occupied the factories until the owners agreed to bargain.

Civil Disobedience in the Civil Rights Movement. Organizations in the civil rights movement of the 1960s also engaged in nonviolent civil disobedience. The Congress of Racial Equality (CORE) used sit-ins as early as the 1940s. To publicize their cause, members entered white-only facilities and refused to leave, knowing that they would be arrested and/or beaten.

In the early 1960s, civil rights leaders stepped up these acts of civil disobedience. Activists conducted sit-ins at segregated lunch counters and other public facilities across the South. Civil rights groups such as the Southern Christian Leadership Conference (SCLC), the Student Nonviolent Coordinating Committee (SNCC), CORE, and the NAACP used these nonviolent strategies to increase public awareness and support for their cause.

Freedom Rides. In 1947, CORE organized a Journey of Reconciliation, in which buses carrying both black and white passengers toured the South on what became known as *freedom rides*. CORE's goal was to test Southern reaction to a Supreme Court decision that found segregated seating of interstate transportation unconstitutional. As soon as these buses entered states in the South that had laws requiring segregated public transportation, they met opposition. Several freedom riders were arrested in North Carolina. Some even ended up serving on chain gangs there.

Fourteen years later, CORE put together another freedom ride to challenge segregated public transportation. Just as in the Journey of Reconciliation, a racially mixed group boarded buses to travel through Southern states in May 1961. African Americans sat in the front, while whites sat in the back, violating Jim Crow laws that forced African Americans to sit at the back of the bus. When the buses arrived at stations or rest stops, black passengers entered white-only waiting areas or restrooms, and whites entered black-only facilities. James Farmer, director of CORE, said:

> We felt we could count on the racists of the South to create a crisis so that the federal government would be compelled to enforce the law [that found segregated public transportation and facilities to be unconstitutional]. . . . When we began the ride, I think all of us were prepared for as much violence as could be thrown at us. We were prepared for the possibility of death.

By carrying out this act of civil disobedience, CORE wanted to force the federal government to step in and compel Southern states to abolish segregation.

Freedom riders expected to find resistance, and they did. When one of the two buses they occupied reached Anniston, Alabama, a mob that had been waiting for it threw stones and slashed its tires. Later the bus was firebombed when it stopped outside the town to fix the tires. A mob also greeted the other bus in Birmingham, beating some of the riders. After a few weeks' pause, the civil rights workers resumed the freedom rides. Although promised protection by the police, when the bus reached Montgomery, it was attacked by a mob. Several freedom riders were beaten before state troopers arrived to stop the violence.

Despite threats of more violence, the freedom riders continued into Mississippi, where they were arrested and tried for breaking state law. The local judge sentenced some riders to 60-day terms in the state penitentiary. As news of the arrests spread, more freedom riders went to Mississippi to replace those who had been jailed. Before it was over, Mississippi officials arrested more than 300 civil rights workers. Despite the beatings and arrests, the freedom riders achieved their goal—governmental change. Their efforts publicized the problem of segregation and forced the Kennedy administration to take action. Attorney General Robert Kennedy convinced the Interstate Commerce

A police dog attacks a civil rights marcher in Montgomery, Alabama, in 1965.

Commission (ICC) to issue a ruling that made segregation in interstate bus travel unlawful. The ICC ruling added teeth to the original Supreme Court decision. At great personal cost, freedom riders made an important contribution to achieving goals of the civil rights movement, and their actions vividly exemplify nonviolent civil disobedience.

Some Events of the Civil Rights Movement

1964	CORE and SNCC launched a massive drive to get African Americans registered to vote; known as the Freedom Summer.
	Civil Rights Act of 1964 made segregation in public facilities and discrimination in employment illegal.
1964	Three civil-rights workers in Mississippi killed by racists.
1965	Black nationalist leader Malcolm X assassinated in Harlem, New York City, by Black Muslims.
	African Americans led by Martin Luther King, Jr., marched to Montgomery, Alabama, in support of voting rights; stopped by police blockade; several marchers injured after police used tear gas, whips, and clubs; known as "Bloody Sunday."
	Congress passed Voting Rights Act of 1965, making it easier for Southern blacks to register; literacy tests became illegal.
1965–1968	Urban riots in Los Angeles, Newark, Cleveland, Detroit, and Chicago

1968	Martin Luther King, Jr., assassinated in Memphis, Tennessee.
	Civil Rights Act of 1968 prohibited discrimination in the sale, rental, and financing of housing.
1971	In *Swann* v. *Charlotte-Mecklenburg Board of Education,* Supreme Court ruled that busing is a legitimate means for achieving integration of public schools.

Vietnam War Protesters Engage in Civil Disobedience. In 1967, antiwar activists organized resistance to the draft and held nationwide protests. In violation of the law, young men of draft age turned in their cards to the draft boards. In October 1967, over 50,000 protesters surrounded the Pentagon, resulting in about 700 arrests. Increasing antiwar protests and growing public sentiment against U.S. involvement in Vietnam forced the Johnson Administration to change its military policy and halt the bombing of North Vietnam in 1968. The antiwar movement reached its peak after Richard Nixon became president in 1969. In November of that year, more than half a million opponents of the war marched in Washington, D.C., and protest demonstrations spread across the nation.

Anti–Vietnam War protesters in Washington, D.C., in 1967

Nixon took several actions in an effort to quell the growing antiwar movement, including an end to the draft. But in the spring of 1970, President Nixon ordered the invasion of Cambodia, igniting the biggest round of college protests in U.S. history. Over 500 colleges and universities had to shut down because of a nationwide student strike. National Guard troops shot protesting students at Kent State University in Ohio and at Jackson State in Mississippi. Antiwar protests exploded in cities throughout the country, including Washington, D.C. A year later, demonstrators again descended on Washington. Vietnam Veterans Against the War (VVAW) and other protesters employed mass civil disobedience events that ended in thousands of arrests.

Between 1971 and 1975, the American government started to bring troops home and reduce U.S. involvement in Vietnam. In this respect, the anti-Vietnam War movement proved to be successful. It played a large role in forcing the Johnson Administration's 1968 reversal of policy on bombing North

Vietnam and in Nixon's decision to withdraw troops and wind down U.S. involvement in Vietnam. Anti-Vietnam War demonstrators, like suffragists and civil rights workers, had used social protest to bring about governmental change.

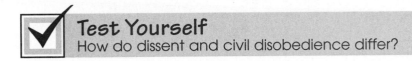

Test Yourself
How do dissent and civil disobedience differ?

POINTS TO REMEMBER

- Revolution is the most extreme attempt to bring about governmental change.

- Americans have used social protest—dissent and civil disobedience—throughout their history.

- Lobbying, public awareness campaigns, and working to get one's chosen political candidates elected are attempts to achieve governmental change through political action.

- Dissent and civil disobedience can bring about governmental change.

- Civil disobedience is a form of dissent that involves willfully disobeying a law that the protester believes is unfair, immoral, or unconstitutional.

- The women's suffrage movement, the civil rights movement, and the anti-Vietnam War movement all used civil disobedience as a tactic.

EXERCISES

CHECKING WHAT YOU HAVE READ

For each of the issues below, name at least one group that protested or engaged in civil disobedience and describe the outcome or result of the group's actions.

women's suffrage
labor legislation
civil rights
  legislation
military policy

environmental
  legislation
business regulation
educational policy
anti-Vietnam protests

USING WHAT YOU HAVE READ

Imagine that Congress passed a law that reinstated the military draft for people 18 years of age and older. You are opposed to the law. Make a list of various means of legal dissent that you could use to reverse the law and stop the draft. Identify the one that you think would be most effective and explain why.

THINKING ABOUT WHAT YOU HAVE READ

If you were against the Vietnam War or in favor of the civil rights movement in the 1960s, what actions do you think you would have taken to support your position? Write a letter to the editor of a local newspaper in which you state your position—either against the war or for civil rights—and explain why. If you choose the war, discuss what you think about people who burned their draft cards. If you choose the civil rights movement, explain your opinion about freedom riders.

SKILLS

Interpreting a Photograph

Use the photograph on page 438 to answer the following questions.

1. What do you believe the people in the photograph are doing?

2. Judging from the photograph, who was president at the time?

3. Why would the protesters accuse the president of being a "war criminal"?

4. Judging by other evidence in the photograph, what type of people most likely participated in this protest?

CHAPTER 32

INDIVIDUAL RIGHTS

To meet the requirements of this benchmark, you should be able to explain why constitutional rights are not absolute. You should know the considerations and criteria used to determine when and how limits might be placed on individual rights. These include: clear and present danger, compelling government interest, libel or slander, national security, public safety, and equal opportunity. You will be expected to be familiar with examples of groups whose individual rights were restricted: conscientious objectors in World War I, immigrants during the Red Scare of the 1920s, intellectuals and artists during the McCarthy era, and African Americans throughout U.S. history. OGT questions may use any of these historical examples and ask you to relate them to the six criteria listed above.

Information about the Red Scare and McCarthyism can be found in Chapter 21, and the civil rights movement is addressed in Chapters 22 and 31. Review those sections before reading this chapter.

★ THE RIGHTS OF U.S. CITIZENS ★

The Bill of Rights (the first ten amendments to the U.S. Constitution), guarantees Americans certain rights, freedoms, and protections. Among them are:

Amendment	Guarantees
First	Freedom of religion, speech, and the press
	Right of people peaceably to assemble and to petition the government
Second	Right of people to keep and bear arms
Fourth	Protection against unreasonable searches and seizures
Fifth	Protection against double jeopardy (being tried twice for the same crime)
	Right to refuse to testify against oneself
	Protection against being deprived of life, liberty, or property without due process of law

Sixth	Right to speedy, public trial by an impartial jury
	Right to confront witnesses against oneself
	Right to subpoena witnesses (summon witnesses to appear in court under a penalty for failing to do so)
	Right to have an attorney
Seventh	Right to a jury trial in a civil suit
Eighth	Protection against excessive bail or fines
	Protection against cruel and unusual punishment

In earlier chapters, you learned that the Fourteenth Amendment extends due process of law and equal protection of the law to all citizens; the Fifteenth Amendment guarantees the right to vote to all citizens regardless of race, color, or previous condition of servitude (slavery); the Nineteenth Amendment extends the vote to women; and the Twenty-sixth Amendment guarantees the vote to citizens 18 years and older.

Restrictions on Rights of U.S. Citizens

The rights of U.S. citizens, however, are not absolute. Freedom of religion, for example, does not include the right to perform human sacrifice as a religious observance. Nor does freedom of speech mean that one person can threaten another person with physical harm or make false statements that create panic. Rights are relative, not absolute. In a democracy there must be a balance among individual rights, the rights of others, and the common good. Disputes do, of course, arise over the nature of that balance, which is why the Framers of the Constitution created the federal judiciary. At times, the courts have found that government restrictions on individual rights were excessive. At other times, the courts have upheld government restrictions on individual rights. Many cases were finally decided by the Supreme Court.

What criteria (guidelines or standards) are used to determine when limits can or should be placed on individual rights? The criteria that are commonly accepted fall into these categories:

- clear and present danger
- compelling government interest
- libel
- national security
- public safety
- equal opportunity

Some of these criteria are easy to understand. Public safety is a good example. After all, no one objects to laws that restrict the freedom to drive recklessly or too fast. Nor does anyone consider laws that restrict the right to pollute sources of drinking water unfair. These are common sense restrictions that exist to protect everyone's safety.

Test Yourself
Give two examples of cases when it is constitutional for the U.S. government to restrict the rights of its citizens.

★ TIMES WHEN INDIVIDUAL RIGHTS HAVE BEEN RESTRICTED ★

There have been many times in the history of the United States when individual rights have, for one reason or another, been restricted or denied. African Americans and women have only recently attained their full rights as citizens. In times of national danger, all citizens have lost some of the freedoms promised in the Bill of Rights. This chapter discusses several cases that occurred during the 20th century.

World War I and the Standard of Clear and Present Danger

During times of war, the government has found it necessary to place some restrictions on individual rights. Government leaders claim that since the nation is threatened by an enemy, *clear and present danger* can be used as a criterion to restrict certain basic rights. The Supreme Court first expressed the doctrine of clear and present danger in a case that involved violations of the Espionage Act. Congress passed this act in 1917, shortly after the United States entered World War I. It outlawed interference with troop recruitment or the draft, encouraging disloyalty, inciting insubordination in the military, obstructing the sale of government bonds, and disclosure of information that might jeopardize national defense. The law provided up to 20 years' imprisonment and a $10,000 fine for anyone convicted. It also included penalties for anyone who refused military duty. Within a few months, about 900 people were imprisoned under the Espionage Act. Eventually, over 2,000 were convicted.

Several Supreme Court cases challenged the constitutionality of the Espionage Act: *Schenck* v. *United States* (1919), *Debs* v. *United States* (1919), *Abrams* v. *United States* (1919), *Gitlow* v. *People of New York* (1925). Nonetheless, the Court consistently upheld the act.

Schenck v. United States. The most important of these cases was the *Schenck* case. Charles Schenck, a member of the Socialist Party, sent some 15,000 flyers to recent draftees urging them to refuse to serve. He was arrested and convicted under the Espionage Act. In 1919, Justice Oliver Wendell Holmes, Jr., wrote the Court's opinion, establishing the clear-and-present danger rule.

We admit that in many places and in ordinary times, the defendants in saying all that was said in the circular would have been within their constitutional rights. But the character of every act depends upon the circumstances in which it is done. The most stringent protection of free speech would not protect a man in falsely shouting fire in a theatre and causing a panic. . . . The question in every case is whether the words used are used in such circumstances and are of such a nature as to create *clear and present danger* that they will bring about the substantive evils that Congress has a right to prevent. . . . When a nation is at war many things that might be said in time of peace are such a hindrance to its effort . . . that no Court could regard them as protected by any constitutional right.

Speech, in other words, is not absolutely free. Speech (in this case, written material) can be restricted if there is a clear and present danger of its producing harm to others.

Debs v. the United States. In 1918, Eugene V. Debs, a Socialist labor leader, gave a speech in Canton, Ohio, entitled "Socialism Is the Answer." In the speech, Debs said, "I might not be able to say all that I think, but you need to know that you are fit for something better than slavery and cannon fodder." For this relatively mild statement, he was arrested, convicted, and sentenced to ten years in prison. He appealed to the Supreme Court, which again upheld the conviction, using the clear-and-present-danger standard.

Abrams v. the United States. The Espionage Act was challenged six times in the Supreme Court, and it was upheld in every one. In *Abrams* v. *United States* (also in 1919), however, the court began to alter its standard of what constituted clear and present danger. Under the Sedition Act an amendment to the Espionage Act, Jacob Abrams was sentenced for distributing leaflets that criticized the U.S. government for sending troops to Russia to assist the czarist forces against the Bolsheviks.

Justice Oliver Wendell Holmes, who drafted the majority opinion in the *Schenck* case, and Justice Louis D. Brandeis, wrote the dissenting opinion in the *Abrams* case. They contended that the leaflets distributed by Abrams were

Justice Oliver Wendell Holmes, Jr. (1902–1932)

no threat to U.S. war effort, and that they posed no clear and present danger to the government. "I regret," wrote Holmes, "that I cannot put into more impressive words my belief that the defendant has been deprived of rights under the Constitution of the United States."

Clearly, in times of national security threats, individual rights have been restricted. The test established in *Schenck* v. *United States* is "clear and present danger." But what exactly does this phrase mean? Its definition changes with time and issues. The USA Patriot Act, enacted after the terrorist attacks of September 11, 2001, restricted some rights regarding privacy. Some people felt that these restrictions were unconstitutional. Others felt that they were necessary to protect Americans from terrorists. The question of what constitutes clear and present danger remains for courts to interpret, and it changes with circumstances.

Test Yourself
On what basis, or using what rule, did the Supreme Court limit freedom of speech and expression during World War I?

Conscientious Objectors

The Military Service Act of 1917 established a draft for men ages 21 to 31 (later expanded to 18 to 45). The law stated that it did *not* "require any person to be subject to combat training and service in the armed forces of the United States who, by reason of religious training and belief, is conscientiously opposed to participation in war in any form." Religious training and belief, the law said, "does not include essentially political, sociological, or philosophical views, or a merely personal moral code." It included provisions for any person whose status as an objector was approved by the local draft board to be assigned to noncombatant service, or if opposed to noncombatant service, to civilian work that contributed to maintenance of the "national health, safety, or interest."

Treatment of Conscientious Objectors. Objectors who refused any kind of alternative service under this law, or who violated the Espionage Act and/or the 1918 Sedition Act, were treated harshly. (The Sedition Act reinforced the Espionage Act and gave the government virtually unlimited power of censorship.) About 500 conscientious objectors were convicted under the Espionage Act during World War I. Many conscientious objectors (COs) refused to serve for moral, political, or religious reasons. Some COs refused to register for the draft or to serve when drafted. Others demonstrated their objection to the war by refusing to pay war taxes. Some men were allowed to avoid military service if they worked in essential jobs, such as farming, or if they agreed to perform noncombat duties in the army, such as medical service. But those who refused to serve in any capacity were usually sentenced to prison and subjected to public humiliation.

Only members of churches that could demonstrate a long history of pacifism were given the option of performing noncombat service. Conscientious objectors who belonged to churches without historical pacifist traditions or those who objected for political or philosophical reasons were usually drafted against their will and then court-martialed. Of the nearly 500 objectors court-martialed, 17 received death sentences, and 142 were sentenced to life imprisonment. The government did not execute any of the 17 objectors who had been sentenced to death, and it eventually reduced prison terms for many of those given long sentences. The objectors did, however, suffer mistreatment in military camps, such as beatings, solitary confinement, and inadequate food, clothing, and shelter.

Most conscientious objectors were Jehovah's Witnesses, Mennonites, Quakers, Seventh-Day Adventists, and members of other churches whose beliefs included pacifism. A few objected for political reasons. This group included, among others, members of radical labor unions, anarchists, and others who held radical political views. Well-known conscientious objectors who fit in this nonreligious category included Socialist Party leader Eugene V. Debs (see below) and social worker Jane Addams, who worked with immigrants in settlement houses. Emma Goldman, a Russian immigrant anarchist arrested in 1917, was charged with conspiring to obstruct the draft. The court sentenced her to two years. Later she was stripped of her citizenship and deported to Russia.

The general public in the United States viewed conscientious objectors as subversives and favored the government's actions taken against them. Debs was sentenced to ten years in prison for giving an antiwar speech. Many other objectors suffered similar punishments. Thus, the government, using clear and present danger and national security as justifications, severely restricted conscientious objectors' constitutional rights. Later these restrictions became somewhat less severe. During the Vietnam War era, for example, Supreme Court decisions in 1965 and 1970 ordered that "religious training and belief" must be interpreted more broadly to include moral, ethical, or philosophical beliefs that have the same force as traditional religious beliefs.

Eugene V. Debs

Test Yourself

During World War I, what was likely to happen to a conscientious objector who did not belong to a traditionally pacifist church or who refused to perform alternative, noncombatant service?

Compelling Government Interest

As noted above, provisions in the Bill of Rights protecting free speech, which includes freedom of the press, are not absolute. They can be restricted, for example, when there is a *compelling government interest* involved. Protecting children from "indecent" content on television or the Internet is widely recognized as one of those compelling interests.

Communications Decency Act. In 1996, Congress used the idea of compelling government interest to pass the Communications Decency Act, which set up restrictions on what can appear on the Internet. In 1997, the Supreme Court found that this act violated the First Amendment and struck it down. The justices pointed out that the Communications Decency Act did not address child pornography, obscenity, or stalking children via the Internet—other laws already prohibited these dangers to children. Moreover, under the terms of the Communications Decency Act, important literary works that include "dirty words" could be excluded from the Internet.

As with the idea of clear and present danger, there can be disagreements over what constitutes a compelling government interest. Some examples are clear. There is obviously a compelling government interest in restricting private citizens from experimenting with or manufacturing chemical or biological weapons in their homes. But what is the line over which the government should not step? When does government regulation exceed a compelling interest? That is not always clear.

Equal Opportunity and Compelling Government Interest

Affirmative action is the principle of giving preference to African Americans and other minorities in school admissions and job opportunities to make up for past unfair treatment of those groups. Some people feel that it violates the Fourteenth Amendment by discriminating against white Americans.

In the case of *Grutter* v. *Bollinger* (2003), however, the Supreme Court ruled that the use of race as a criterion in law school admissions did not violate the Fourteenth Amendment's equal protection clause. The law school in question argued that using racial diversity as a guiding principle in its admissions policy constituted a compelling interest because it fostered equal opportunity. The two concepts, it maintained, are complementary.

In 1997, Barbara Grutter, a white woman, applied to the University of Michigan Law School. Although she had good qualifications, the school denied Grutter's application. The law school used race as one factor in making admissions decisions because it served a "compelling interest in achieving diversity among its student body." The district court, where the case originated, disagreed and ruled that achieving diversity at the school was not a compelling interest. The case then went to the court of appeals, which reversed the lower court's decision. The court of appeals ruled that the *Bakke* decision in 1978 established diversity as a compelling government interest that could justify the use of racial preferences in admissions under certain conditions.

When the case reached the Supreme Court, the justices voted 5–4 to uphold the law school's consideration of race as one of its admissions criteria. They ruled that the equal protection clause did not prohibit the law school from pursuing student body diversity as a compelling interest.

Grutter v. *Bollinger* demonstrates that reasonable people can disagree over the definition of compelling government interest and equal opportunity as a justification for limiting rights (in this case, rights guaranteed in the Fourteenth Amendment's equal protection clause and in the Civil Rights Act of 1964). Two different courts disagreed with one another and, as demonstrated by their 5-to-4 vote, the Supreme Court justices disagreed among themselves.

 Test Yourself
How did the Supreme Court apply the compelling government interest standard to *Grutter* v. *Bollinger*?

Libel

Although the First Amendment protects freedom of speech and freedom of the press, it does not give anyone the right to defame someone's reputation with *libel*, spoken or written statements that are knowingly false. A person who is the victim of libel can sue the offending party for damages in civil court. According to the present law, only living persons who are victims of libel can sue for damages. The dead cannot be legally defamed. True statements, however, are never considered libel by the courts. For example, a neighborhood supermarket cannot win a libel suit against a local newspaper that truthfully and accurately exposed its health code violations despite the fact that the disclosure damaged its reputation in the community.

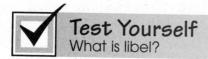 **Test Yourself**
What is libel?

National Security and the Red Scares

No one would deny that since national security affects the common good, it is more important than some individual rights. But as a criterion for limiting individual rights, it can be misused. Most historians agree that during the two so-called Red Scares that took place during the 20th century, government officials as well as the general public applied this standard to rights that did not actually threaten national security. Both these periods were characterized by an exaggerated fear of Communists and their influence on the U.S. government. On the basis of this fear, the government restricted individual rights and harassed groups suspected of being Communist and of wanting to infiltrate the government.

Red Scare of 1917 to 1920. During and after World War I and the Bolshevik (Communist) Revolution in Russia, many people in the United States became caught up in the Red Scare, or an irrational fear of Communists. The war made people suspicious of all things German, including German Americans. Once the war had ended and the Bolshevik Revolution took place, many Americans turned this suspicion on Eastern Europeans. Many political radicals and anarchists came to the United States from Southern and Eastern European nations, as did most immigrants at that time. Many people feared that radicals would stage a Communist revolt in the United States, as they had in Russia. That fear heightened already existing anti-immigrant sentiment and led to restrictions on constitutional rights by the U.S. government.

Bombing of the J. P. Morgan Company. A great deal of labor unrest occurred during this period. In 1919, strikes occurred in many cities across the nation. Many Americans believed the strikes were the work of Communists and anarchists who had infiltrated the labor movement. That feeling was confirmed by a series of bombings in the summer of 1919. Then, in September 1920, a bomb composed of dynamite and steel fragments exploded near the Wall Street offices of the J. P. Morgan Company, killing 40 people and injuring hundreds more. Most people blamed radical elements in the labor movement for the attack.

One senator suggested that all radicals be sent to a penal colony in Guam. In Centralia, Washington, a mob dragged a radical from the town jail and lynched him. The strongest government action was the Palmer Raids—named after Attorney General A. Mitchell Palmer—against "red" groups of all sorts. In his 1920 essay entitled "The Case Against the Reds," Palmer claimed that "tongues of revolutionary heat were licking the altars of the churches, leaping into the belfry of the school bell, crawling into the sacred corners of American homes, seeking to replace marriage vows with libertine laws, burning up the foundations of society."

Palmer Raids. Palmer's rhetoric played on current fears and established a justification for a series of raids in which he had several radical leaders arrested. He used the Espionage Act of 1917 and the Sedition Act of 1918 to apprehend such dissenters as Eugene V. Debs and Emma Goldman for criticizing the U.S.

Attorney General
A. Mitchell Palmer

entry into World War I. Palmer organized mass arrests and deportations of immigrants, and he expelled elected officials from office for dissenting against the government. Overreaction based on fear became commonplace. A Connecticut man, for instance, was sentenced to six months for simply saying that Lenin, leader of the Bolshevik revolution in Russia, was intelligent. And in Chicago, a sailor shot a man merely for failing to stand during the national anthem. Political dissenters became criminals subject to imprisonment and deportation or victims of mob violence.

Sacco and Vanzetti. Perhaps the most sensational event of the Red Scare of the 1920s was the arrest and trial of Sacco and Vanzetti, Italian immigrants charged with robbery and murder. Chapter 21 discusses their case in some detail. As you read in that chapter, they were eventually executed. Many people in the United States and around the world believed the two immigrants had been convicted, not because of the evidence against them but because of the fear and hysteria that gripped the nation. Much like suppression of dissent during the war, the postwar Red Scare grew out of fear of radical political ideas and uneasiness about freedom to express those views. It demonstrated how constitutional rights can easily fall victim to mass hysteria and public anxiety.

Test Yourself
In what way did A. Mitchell Palmer restrict the rights of individuals?

McCarthy Era

The second Red Scare, which took place from 1948 to about 1956, is generally referred to as the McCarthy era. As you learned in Chapter 21, it was named after Senator Joseph McCarthy of Wisconsin. Just as a period of national hysteria centering on communism followed World War I, the years after World War II also witnessed a similar outbreak of intolerance.

Several events following the defeat of Germany and Japan helped raise the level of fear in the United States. In 1948, Whittaker Chambers, an admitted former spy for the Soviet Union, charged that Alger Hiss, a former State Department official, had passed government secrets to him. In a well-publicized trial, Hiss was convicted of perjury and sentenced to prison. When it became clear in 1949 that the Soviet Union had developed an atomic bomb, the fear of Communist espionage intensified. Then in 1951, Julius and Ethel Rosenberg, members of the Communist Party, were convicted of passing atomic secrets to the Soviet Union and sentenced to death. They were executed in 1953. In 1950, when American troops began fighting Soviet-backed North Korea in the Korean War, fear and hatred of Communists increased.

House Un-American Activities Committee and the "Hollywood Ten." In 1947, the House Un-American Activities Committee (HUAC) added to the atmosphere of fear by investigating the Hollywood motion picture industry. HUAC investigators interviewed 41 people who worked in the film industry. These so-called friendly witnesses accused 19 others of being Communists or Communist sympathizers. Claiming freedom of speech under the First Amendment, ten of the accused refused to answer questions when they were called to testify; they came to be known as the "Hollywood Ten." HUAC charged the Hollywood Ten with contempt of Congress. They were found guilty and sentenced to between six and twelve months in prison.

Joseph McCarthy. From 1950 to about 1954, the focal point of anti-Communist hysteria in the United States was Joseph McCarthy, a heretofore obscure senator from Wisconsin. In February 1950, McCarthy gave a speech in which he held up a sheet of paper that he said contained the names of 205 State Department employees who were members of the Communist Party. They had, he further charged, committed traitorous acts. Most Americans believed McCarthy, who then began a crusade to ferret out Communists in the government. He chaired a congressional committee that threatened and bullied many witnesses over the next four years. Several government officials were fired or resigned under the pressure of McCarthy's attacks.

Between 1950 and 1954, McCarthy's mostly groundless charges met with little opposition, mainly because politicians were afraid of being accused of softness toward Communists and leftists. One opponent did, however, speak up. On June 1, 1950, Senator Margaret Chase Smith of Maine stood up to McCarthy's heavy-handed tactics on the floor of the Senate when she gave a speech entitled "Declaration of Conscience." The following is an excerpt from that speech.

> . . . Those of us who shout the loudest about Americanism in making character assassinations are all too frequently those who, by our own words and acts, ignore some of the basic principles of Americanism—the right to criticize; the right to hold unpopular beliefs; the right to protest; the right of independent thought.
>
> The exercise of these rights should not cost one single American citizen his reputation or his right to a livelihood, nor should he be in danger of losing his reputation or livelihood merely because he happens to know someone who holds unpopular beliefs. Who of us doesn't? Otherwise none of us could call our souls our own. Otherwise thought control would have set in.
>
> The American people are sick and tired of being afraid to speak their minds lest they be politically smeared as "Communists" or "Fascists" by their opponents. Freedom of speech is not what it used to be in America. It has been so abused by some that it is not exercised by others. The American people are sick and tired of seeing innocent people smeared and guilty people whitewashed. But there have been enough proved cases . . . to cause nationwide distrust and strong suspicion that there may be something to the unproved, sensational accusations.

McCarthy's downfall came in 1954 when, during televised hearings, he claimed that the U.S. Army was being infiltrated by Communists. For weeks, the American public watched transfixed as McCarthy used unproven, reckless, and cruel attacks to smear his opponents. Joseph Welch, the army's counsel, summed up what the public, after watching McCarthy's wild accusations and relentless badgering of witnesses, finally realized. "Until this moment, Senator,

Army counsel Joseph Welch (sitting) listens in disbelief as Senator Joseph McCarthy (pointing to map) outlines Communist subversion at a Senate hearing in 1954.

I think I never really gauged your cruelty or your recklessness. . . . Have you no sense of decency, sir, at long last?"

Since the time of Joseph McCarthy's ascendancy, the term *McCarthyism* has come to be generally recognized as a term referring to the use of harassment, groundless accusations, appeals to fear, and blacklisting to force conformity with an official position. McCarthyism is a reminder of the way skillful politicians or government officials, in the name of national security, can manipulate public sentiment and fear to restrict constitutional rights.

Test Yourself

How did Senator Joseph McCarthy manipulate public opinion to restrict individual rights?

Civil Rights Workers. Civil rights activists in the 1960s also experienced instances in which their rights of speech and expression were limited. Freedom riders, marchers, picketers, and participants in sit-ins faced arrest and violence when they tried to exercise their constitutional rights in many Southern states. Review Chapter 31 for more information about the struggle of African Americans to claim their rights as citizens.

POINTS TO REMEMBER

- In the United States, individual rights are relative, not absolute.

- In a democracy, there must be a balance among individual rights, the rights of others, and the common good.

- The following criteria have been used to place limits or restrictions on rights: clear and present danger, compelling government interest, national security, libel, public safety, and equal opportunity.

- The Supreme Court established the clear-and-present-danger rule in *Schenck* v. *United States*, during World War I.

- During World War I, conscientious objectors were required to perform alternative service or risk being jailed.

- In *Grutter* v. *Bollinger*, the Supreme Court ruled that pursuing diversity in school admissions is a compelling interest and therefore constitutional, if certain guidelines established in the *Bakke* case are followed.

- The treatment of conscientious objectors during World War I, immigrants during the Red Scare, suspected Communists during the McCarthy era, and African Americans before and during the civil rights movement of the 1960s are examples of instances in which individual rights have been restricted.

EXERCISES

CHECKING WHAT YOU HAVE READ

1. To silence critics during World War I, the government used which of the following criteria for limiting individual rights?

   A. compelling government interest
   B. clear and present danger
   C. libel
   D. equal opportunity

2. Which Supreme Court case used the compelling-government-interest criterion?

   A. *Schenck* v. *United States*
   B. *Debs* v. *United States*
   C. *Grutter* v. *Bollinger*
   D. *Abrams* v. *United States*

3. Laws that restrict toxic emissions from factory smokestacks are an example of which of the following criteria for limiting rights?

   A. national security
   B. libel
   C. public safety
   D. equal opportunity

4. What tactic did both A. Mitchell Palmer and Joseph McCarthy use to gain support for their actions?

   A. They sponsored public forums to debate communism.
   B. They encouraged free expression of communistic ideas.
   C. They organized protest rallies to raise public awareness.
   D. They manipulated public fear of communism.

5. In a letter to the editor of a local paper, a citizen made knowingly false statements about a neighbor in order to cause the neighbor public embarrassment. This is an example of

   A. clear and present danager
   B. libel
   C. due process
   D. compelling interest.

USING WHAT YOU HAVE READ

Using the Internet or library, research one of the Supreme Court cases mentioned in this chapter. Complete a chart like the one below with the information that you find and answer the question that follows it.

Supreme Court Case:
Facts of the Case/Background:
Issues for the Court to Decide:
Court's Decision:

What was the impact of the Supreme Court's decision in the case that you selected? In other words, what effect did it have on American society at the time?

THINKING ABOUT WHAT YOU HAVE READ

Debs v. *United States* (1919)

In 1918, Eugene V. Debs, a leader of the American Socialist Party, gave an antiwar speech in Canton, Ohio. In the speech, Debs supported other Socialist leaders who had already been arrested for their opposition to the draft. Debs said, "You have your lives to lose. . . . You need to know that you are fit for something better than slavery and cannon fodder." Because of this speech, Debs was arrested, tried, and convicted for violating the Sedition Act (1918), which was an amendment to the Espionage Act. The Sedition Act prohibited any speech that interfered with the military draft.

Do you think Debs' speech constituted a clear and present danger to the laws of the United States? Why or why not? Do you agree with the Court's decision in this case? Why or why not?

Gitlow v. *New York* (1925)

Benjamin Gitlow was a member of the American Communist Party. After World War I, Gitlow distributed several thousand copies of a pamphlet entitled "Left Wing Manifesto," in which he called for a Communist revolution in the United States. It also encouraged workers to go on strike. Authorities arrested Gitlow for violating New York State's law against anarchy, which made it a felony to advocate the overthrow of the government by force. The Supreme Court upheld the New York law.

Do you think Benjamin Gitlow's "Left Wing Manifesto" constituted a clear and present danger to the United States? Why or why not? Do you agree with the Supreme Court's decision in this case? Why or why not?

SKILLS

Interpreting a Political Cartoon

Herblock: A Cartoonist's Life (Times Books, 1998)

Study the political cartoon above by the famous cartoonist Herbert Block, who was known as "Herblock." Interpret the cartoon by answering the following questions.

1. What objects and/or person do you see?

2. What is the caption or title?

3. What does the hand with the torch represent?

4. What does the man carrying the bucket of water represent?

5. What action is taking place in the cartoon?

6. What is the message of the cartoon?

CHAPTER 33

SOCIAL STUDIES SKILLS AND METHODS

BENCHMARK:

(A) Evaluate the reliability and credibility of sources.
(B) Use data and evidence to support or refute a thesis.

Like Chapter 16, this chapter combines the two benchmarks that comprise the social studies skills and methods standard. This standard differs from the others in that it focuses on skills rather than particular content. Questions on the OGT may use content from other standards to assess the skills addressed in these two benchmarks.

To meet the requirements of these benchmarks, you should be able to evaluate sources of information for reliability and credibility. In particular, you should be able to determine whether sources are credible based on the following criteria: the qualifications and reputation of the writer, agreement with other credible sources, recognition of stereotypes, accuracy and consistency of sources, and the circumstances in which the author prepared the source.

This chapter will teach you to critique—that is, to evaluate—evidence used to support a thesis. After reading it, you should be able to analyze one or more issues and present a persuasive argument to support a position related to that issue. You should also be able to identify, among several arguments, the one that supports, or refutes, a particular position.

★ CREDIBILITY OF SOURCES ★

There are many things to consider when you choose a source of information. The most important factor is whether the source is credible—that is, trustworthy. Ohio standards recommend five characteristics that a person should consider in determining whether or not a source is credible. These are the questions one should ask to determine credibility:

● What are the qualifications and reputation of the source's writer?

● Does the source agree with other credible sources? Disagreement with other credible sources does not necessarily mean that the source in question is not credible. It means only that the source should be examined and researched further.

● Does the source use stereotypes as evidence?

- Is the source accurate and consistent?

- What were the circumstances under which the author prepared the source?

By answering these questions, a reader should be able to evaluate the credibility of a source with confidence.

What We Should Know About the Author of a Source

Whether you are using printed or online sources, it is extremely important to check the author's reputation. First of all, look for the writer's name. A source without an identified author cannot be considered credible. The source may not be written by a single person but by representatives of an organization. You will need to ask the same questions about an organization as you would a person. You also need to be able to determine if the author or the organization is a recognized authority on the subject that has been covered by the source.

One way to evaluate the reputation of the author is to determine if other writers in the same field refer to him or her as an authority. To find other experts who use the author as a source, read through a bibliography or browse through Web sites. Check to see if the author is associated with a college, university, or professional organization that has a good reputation.

Agreement With Other Credible Sources

Credibility can also be evaluated in terms of whether or not the information in a source agrees with other trustworthy sources. If it disagrees with other sources, ask yourself if the disagreement is important or trivial. If it is important, you must check more sources to see if other reputable writers disagree with the same points.

Stereotypes

The use of stereotypes should raise questions about a source's credibility. A *stereotype* is a generalization that indicates bias or prejudice. For example, the statement "Redheads have quick tempers" is not only too general to have real meaning, it also expresses a bias against redheaded people. Sometimes stereotypes dismiss the ideas and feelings of certain groups as valueless. Suppose you express your indignation about an injustice reported in the news, and an adult labels your reaction as "adolescent idealism." That grown-up is not only stereotyping teenagers, he or she is trivializing their opinions.

Another form of stereotyping treats all members of a group as being the same. Those who are thus stereotyped are made to feel inferior, and in some cases become victims of discrimination or hate. Immigrants to the United States in the years after the Civil War and Reconstruction experienced this kind of stereotyping. Resentment (feeling of ill-will regarding an assumed wrong or insult) against the many waves of immigrants was widespread in the late 19th century. Some Americans worried that we would never unite as one people because of the constant influx of foreigners. There was resentment against

Poles, for example, because most Polish immigrants did not speak English when they first arrived in this country. Many Americans, most of whom were Protestant, resented immigrants from Italy and Russia because they were either Roman Catholic or Jewish.

Another source of stereotyping of immigrants had to do with economics. New immigrants were often poor. They would take any job that they could find in the United States. Employers liked to hire immigrants who would work for low wages. As a result, American workers disliked these immigrants. They feared that the new workers would take away their jobs by offering to work for less money. U.S. workers feared that immigrants would prevent wages from rising. These prejudices led many Americans to stereotype immigrants as being all the same and helped to perpetuate the bias against them.*

Sources that use stereotyping should not be considered credible. Painting an ethnic group, or any other group, with broad brushstrokes hides details and differences. The writer of a credible source will see things with a fresh eye and give details and differences their proper weight.

Accuracy and Consistency

To be credible, sources obviously need to be accurate and consistent. You must check the accuracy of such data as names and dates to make sure that the author has researched his or her material properly. Another important way to determine accuracy is to ascertain if the author has based his or her argument on fact or opinion. Read the following statements. Which one is based on data that can be checked for accuracy and which includes an opinion that is based on feelings and beliefs and, therefore, cannot be checked?

> *Statement 1*: More people in the United States are killed each year by guns than by all other weapons put together.

> *Statement 2*: Banning the sale of guns in the United States would result in more crime, not less.

One of these statements is a fact. The other is an opinion. How can you tell the difference? A fact is something that is true or that really happened. A fact can be proven to be true. An opinion is a belief or a particular point of view held by a person. An opinion cannot be proved to be true. If an opinion could be proved true, it would become a fact. So which of the above statements is a fact and which is an opinion?

Government and private studies show that more people in the United States are killed each year by guns than by all other weapons put together. This information proves that Statement 1 is a fact. The statement can be verified by looking at statistics collected by the government or other agencies about deaths caused by weapons.

---

*Adapted from Gerson Antell and Walter Harris, *Current Issues in American Democracy* (New York: Amsco School Publications, 2001), pp. 198–199.

Some people believe that banning the sale of guns in the United States would result in more crime, not less. But other people believe the opposite. Even if the crime rate increases after guns are banned, the increase might be due to reasons other than the gun ban. It would be difficult to prove Statement 2. Therefore, you should view it as an opinion. Writers and speakers sometimes state opinions as if they were facts. Statements in books, newspapers, and magazines, or on Web pages are not necessarily facts. Neither is everything broadcast on the radio or television. It is critical for the reader, viewer, or listener to be able to distinguish between facts and opinions in order to determine the accuracy of a statement.

Judging the accuracy and consistency of a source depends largely upon whether the information can be verified. This can be accomplished by looking at other sources considered to be reliable. Are the sources consistent, or are there discrepancies? If there are discrepancies, are they important or minor? If you are reading a study of some issue or problem, does the author explain the methodology he or she used? It is very important for a source to include a bibliography and/or footnotes that lead the reader to other sources for verifying the information. The level of writing and the presentation of information are also clues to accuracy. If an author uses awkward constructions, makes numerous grammatical or spelling errors, or has not organized the material well, the reader should wonder if he or she was equally careless in researching the topic.*

Motivation of the Author

The circumstances in which a source was written often reveal the author's motivation. Think of the circumstances under which you might write a paper for a history class. Because your purpose is to inform, you will be as logical and factual as possible. But suppose you are writing a story for a language arts class. In that case, you would probably write an imaginative, playful piece rather than a sober, accurate one. To find out the circumstances in which a source was written, consider the author's purpose in writing it and the audience to whom he or she has addressed it. A scholarly study, for example, has a different purpose and is intended for a different audience than a pamphlet extolling the virtues of a political candidate written by the candidate's campaign staff. Did the source result from extensive, verifiable research, or did it come from someone with a particular agenda to pursue?

Asking the Right Questions

A scoring sheet like the one that follows is sometimes useful in comparing several sources:

---

*Adapted from Gerard J. Pelisson, *Mastering United States History Skills* (New York: Amsco School Publications, 2003), p. 44.

Scoring Sheet

Source Title:

Publisher/Organization:

Copyright/Publication Date:

Rating		1 = Poor			5 = Excellent
Qualifications and reputation of source's author	1	2	3	4	5
Agreement with other credible sources	1	2	3	4	5
Absence of stereotypes in source	1	2	3	4	5
Accuracy and consistency of source	1	2	3	4	5

A list of questions like the ones below is also useful when looking at sources of information:

1. Who is the author (person or organization)?

2. Is the author trustworthy? Does she or he have professional or academic standing? What are the author's credentials or qualifications?

3. What is the purpose or goal of the information? Will the author benefit financially or professionally by promoting a particular point of view? In other words, what is the author's motivation?

4. Does the author acknowledge other points of view in presenting the information?

5. Who is the intended audience?

6. When was the source published? Does it include current information?

7. What is the ratio of facts to opinions?

8. Does the source include a bibliography and footnotes or other citations that help you verify the information presented?

Test Yourself

If you are trying to determine who to vote for in a U.S. Senate election, would you look at a campaign brochure from each candidate or a verbatim (word-for-word) transcript of a debate between the candidates? Explain your choice.

★ USING EVIDENCE TO SUPPORT A THESIS ★

To make a point or support a thesis, a writer must provide convincing evidence. Evidence is made up of examples, statistical data, and statements from experts. Evidence can come from primary or secondary sources. The kind of evidence you use will depend on the subject matter. Evidence may consist of quotations from experts, excerpts from primary sources, or hard data (statistics) gathered from a variety of credible sources.

Without the evidence to back it up, a thesis is simply an opinion. A good argument will not only include evidence that supports your thesis but also evidence that contradicts it. It is important to include contradictory evidence so that you can refute it (argue against it). Like a lawyer in a trial, you must present credible evidence and explain clearly why it supports your thesis. A list of facts unconnected to the argument will not support your case. The sources of the evidence should be given either in the text or in bibliographical form.

Test Yourself

If you planned to write a paper arguing that an important cause of the American Revolution was Great Britain's economic policy toward its American colonies, which would you prefer to use as evidence, contemporary history books or primary sources written by Patriot leaders who were angry about the taxes that Great Britain imposed on Americans?

★ ANALYZING ISSUES ★

Most issues in society involve some sort of problem. To analyze a problem, you must figure out how its different parts are connected to one another and how they make up the whole. The first step in analyzing an issue is to identify the problem that needs to be solved.*

Analyzing a Sample Problem

Suppose a bill is introduced into your state legislature to raise the minimum age for getting a driver's license from 16 to 18. What position should you take on the issue? In order to decide, you must first determine what problem the bill is intended to solve.

Identify the Problem. In this case, the bill's sponsors believe that they have identified a problem. They define the problem as one of public safety. They believe that until people are 18, they are too immature to be trusted to drive carefully and safely. They claim that young drivers are a threat to the safety of the community. You know that there are many accidents in your state. You think that it is likely that many of them involve drivers under the age of 18. But you are not sure of the facts of the matter. You must investigate to see if the problem, as stated by the supporters of the bill, really exists.

---

*Adapted from Gerson Antell and Walter Harris, *Current Issues in American Democracy*, pp. 483–485.

Provide Evidence That the Problem Exists. The next step is to provide evidence that the problem exists. You may think that a problem exists, and you may be convinced that something needs to be done about it. But you cannot *know* these things without gathering evidence. This usually means investigation and research. Depending upon what kind of problem you are dealing with, it might involve examining published sources (books, magazines, newspapers, government reports, Web pages), interviewing people who know about the situation or even collecting facts from your own observation.

Whether you suspect that young people are or are not safe drivers, you need to find evidence to back up or refute your suspicions. You will want to look for statistics that show whether 16- or 17-year-old drivers are actually involved in more accidents than are drivers in other age groups, and whether they are more or less likely to be arrested for driving under the influence of alcohol or other drugs. You could look for articles in medical and psychological journals that explain how age relates to the physical, mental, and emotional factors involved in driving. Are young people less able to concentrate than older people, or more able? Are they more observant of the conditions around them, or less? Are they better coordinated, or worse? Are they more likely to lose their tempers and become reckless, or less?

Identify Contributing Factors. Next you need to identify factors that contribute to the problem. Few problems are as simple as they seem at first. In order to come up with an effective solution to any problem, it is vital to understand all the elements that contribute to it. These may include economic and political considerations, as well as geographic, emotional, and sociological factors.

If you find that young people do, in fact, have more accidents, is their age the main reason? Are there other circumstances that might help to explain the higher accident rate? You might ask questions like these: Do young drivers tend to drive older cars? (Such cars might be less safe than newer models.) Do young people have their cars serviced as often as older drivers? (Less servicing can also result in more risk of accidents.) If factors like these turn out to be major problems, then perhaps a policy that focuses on the condition of automobiles, rather than the age of the drivers, might make more sense.

Describe Current Solutions. The next step is to describe the current policies or solutions, if there are any. Before stating a thesis that formulates a solution for the problem, it is necessary to find out what efforts are already being made to solve it. Consider all levels and branches of government (local, state, federal) or private-sector activity that relate to the problem at hand. In the case of setting a minimum age for driver's licenses, the problem is essentially a state matter. Driver's licenses are issued by the state. The federal government may have studied the problem, however, and issued a report. In the hypothetical state we are dealing with, the minimum age for such licenses is currently 16. Now you should find out what other steps are being taken to ascertain the ability of new drivers. Is driver training required? Is there a driving test? Is it a written test, a behind-the-wheel test, or both? Is there a different form of examination for applicants under 18?

Choose the Best Solution. Finally, you need to choose the best solution or policy alternative to address the issue. What are the possible alternative policies or solutions that might deal with the problem (issue) more effectively? In the

A driver's education class

question we have been examining, there are more alternatives than simply passing or rejecting the bill to raise the age for drivers' licenses to 18. The minimum age might be raised even higher—to 21, for example. The licenses of younger drivers could be restricted in various ways. Their driving skills could be frequently tested. Young drivers could be forbidden to drive without an adult in the car, or forbidden to drive at night. Penalties for traffic violations may be increased for young drivers. New and higher license standards could be set for all drivers, whatever their age. Many other alternative policies might be suggested as well.

Each of the alternatives could be considered in light of the following factors:

- *Effectiveness.* How effective will each proposed policy be? Will it eliminate the problem completely? Or will it make the situation only slightly better, or slightly worse? Will it have any effect at all?

- *Feasibility.* Is each policy or solution practicable? Can it actually be put into effect? Are there political, social, or other factors that make it unworkable? Existing court rulings may forbid certain kinds of license restrictions—those based on age, for example.

- *Expense.* Are the economic costs of each solution or policy reasonable when weighed against the benefits to be gained from it? Regular testing of young drivers, for example, could mean that the state would have to hire more driving examiners. Would this expense be justified?

- *Side Effects.* What unintended results might each proposed policy have? Is it likely to create other problems that would be as bad as, or worse than, the one the policy is designed to solve?

Depriving 16- and 17-year-olds of their right to drive would deprive them of the chance to function in society in the way that they function today. There are many social, psychological, and economic reasons why a driver's license may be important to a young person. Forbidding all young people to drive could prevent many of them from finding jobs that are not located close to their homes. It could prevent them from attending important social functions, including school activities that take place after regular school hours. Most important of all, for many young people, it could rob them of their sense of independence.

Once each of the alternatives has been evaluated, it must be compared with each of the others. You can then choose the best among them. Let us assume that you choose to support a public policy alternative that calls for higher standards for all drivers, whatever their age. Not just drivers under 18, but all licensed drivers would be required to pass a driver's test each year. Any traffic violation, for drivers of any age, would be cause for taking their licenses away. This strict policy would address the problem of traffic safety without discriminating against young drivers because of their age.*

Analyzing a Problem by Stating It as a Question

Another way to look at issue analysis is to state the problem as a question. For example: Is an unbalanced federal budget detrimental to the national economy? Once you have stated the issue as a question, you need to take several more steps:

1. *Explain or define the problem.* First of all, prove there is a problem. Present your factual evidence in a logical, coherent format that will show the problem does in fact exist.

2. *Explain the causes of the problem.* What has caused this problem to become an issue worth addressing?

3. *Describe multiple perspectives on the issue.* Most issues can be approached from more than two perspectives or points of view. How do different people and interest groups view the problem?

4. *Describe existing strategies to address the issue.* How has the issue been dealt with in the past? What other solutions have been offered? Have they been successful or not?

5. *Select the best strategy (solution) for dealing with the issue.* What solution to the problem do you think is the most likely to result in success? Why do you think so? What evidence can you use to support your choice?

 Test Yourself
In the example of the proposal to raise driver's license age to 18, which step of the analysis process do you think is the most important and why?

★ PRESENTING A PERSUASIVE ARGUMENT ★

Once you have analyzed an issue, you must then persuade other people to agree with you on a solution. In order to do that, you need to show that your idea is better than all others. Therefore, you need to anticipate ideas that challenge yours so that you can argue against them. You need to conduct research that

---

*Adapted from Antell and Harris, *Current Issues in American Democracy*, Ibid., pp. 483–485.

provides evidence in support of your arguments and refutes your opposition. A persuasive argument can be written or spoken, and it can be organized in different ways. One strategy employs four basic steps:

1. *State the issue.* Introduce the reader or listener to the problem and provide evidence to show that the problem is real.

2. *State your position.* Explain your idea(s) for addressing the issue. Present various kinds of evidence to support your thesis or solution. Explain how the evidence is connected to your thesis. Explain why your approach is the most likely to succeed.

3. *Describe other approaches or ideas and show why they would not be effective.* Make sure your audience knows that you have considered all the alternatives and that your approach is the best. Point out why these other approaches will not work. What are their flaws? What are they missing? Why do they fail to address the problem adequately?

4. *Restate your position.* Remind the audience of the main points of your argument and some of the supporting evidence. Briefly recap why opposing solutions fall short and why yours stands the best chance of success.

Test Yourself

What do you think is the most important factor or strategy in persuading someone to agree with your solution to a problem or issue?

POINTS TO REMEMBER

- Sources should be evaluated for credibility using five considerations: qualifications and reputation of the writer or author, agreement with other credible sources, recognition of stereotypes, accuracy and consistency of sources, and the circumstances under which the author prepared the source.

- Evidence used to support a thesis or an argument must be credible and directly related to the thesis.

- In order to analyze an issue you first must state the issue, preferably as a question, and then do the following: explain the causes of the problem, describe multiple perspectives on the issue or problem, describe existing strategies to address the issue, select the best strategy (solution) for dealing with the issue, and explain why it is the best.

EXERCISES

CHECKING WHAT YOU HAVE READ

1. Which of the following would be the most credible source for evidence about air pollution?

   A. a television ad for a political candidate on the issue of pollution
   B. a report from the Environmental Protection Agency (EPA) on toxic emissions
   C. a report on toxic emissions published by an association of electricity producers
   D. a letter to the editor from a private citizen who claims that toxic emissions have decreased

2. Describing all politicians as crooks is an example of

   A. credibility
   B. verifying
   C. stereotyping
   D. feasibility.

3. If you wanted to find out how many accidents a year were caused by drivers under the age of 18, which author of a national highway safety report would you find most credible?

   A. the National Highway Traffic Safety Administration
   B. a reporter for the local paper
   C. a major automobile manufacturer
   D. a person seriously injured in an automobile accident

4. In analyzing the issue of whether or not immigration to the United States should be severely restricted, what would be the most credible evidence?

   A. interviewing a senator who is sponsoring a bill to restrict immigration
   B. interviewing a senator who is sponsoring a bill to increase immigration
   C. interviewing several immigrants
   D. interviewing both advocates and opponents of immigration restriction

USING WHAT YOU HAVE READ

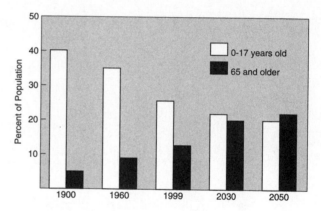

Distribution of young people to older people in the United States, 1900–2050

Using the bar graph above as evidence, either support or refute the thesis (argument) that municipal governments should convert space in public schools for use by the elderly. Explain your position using data from the graph.

THINKING ABOUT WHAT YOU HAVE READ

Choose a social issue or a policy issue in which you are interested and analyze it by developing a concept map (web) similar to the one at the right. The number of blank ovals radiating from each labeled oval can vary.

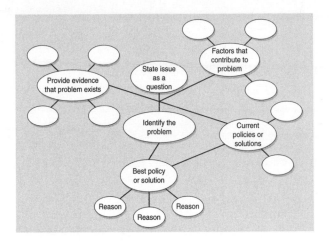

SKILLS

Writing a Persuasive Argument

When you develop a persuasive argument, you need to use evidence that will convince your readers:

1. Clearly state your argument. It can be in the form of a question. For example, should the United States restrict immigration? Or it can be presented as a statement of belief. For example, the United States should (or should not) restrict immigration.

2. Support your argument with credible and appropriate evidence. It is important to show readers how your evidence is connected to the argument.

3. Explain to readers why your argument deserves their support.

4. Anticipate counterarguments and answer their objections.

5. Organize your points in a logical sequence.

6. Write in clear, direct language. Make your points and support them with evidence in a straightforward way with simple, forceful language.

7. Summarize by restating the argument and listing your main points.

Select an issue in which you are interested. Do the necessary research. Using the steps outlined above, write a persuasive essay.

INDEX

A

Abdullah, King, of Saudi Arabia, 190
Abolitionist movement, 209, 432
Abortion, 330–331, 342
Abrams v. *United States*, 444–445
Absolute monarchies, 5, 189–191; advantages and disadvantages of, 193; citizen participation in, 212; Enlightenment and, 7–8
Acid rain, 410
Addams, Jane, 247–248, 248, 446
Affirmative action, 422–423, 447–448
AFL-CIO, 398. *See* American Federation of Labor, Congress of Industrial Organizations
Africa: Bantu speakers in, 160–161; ethnic strife in, 81; imperialism in, 31, 33–34, 39; independence movements in, 73–74
African Americans: education of, 332, 340, 420–422; great migration of, 306–308, 319–320; Harlem Renaissance and, 303, 306, 309, 339, 346; Jim Crow laws and, 350–352, 418–420; Ku Klux Klan and, 307–308; labor relations and, 240, 321; lynchings and, 307, 339; NAACP and, 338–340; post-Civil War amendments and, 418; race riots and, 307, 333, 338, 437; in South, 320; in Spanish-American War, 259; voting rights of, 340, 351, 418; in World War I, 274; in World War II, 320. *See also* Civil rights movement
African National Congress (ANC), 99–100
African Union (AU), 130
Age of Reason, 4
Agricultural Adjustment Act (1933), 315, 402
Agricultural Workers Association (AWA), 345
Agricultural Workers Organizing Committee (AWOC), 344, 345
Agriculture: decline in farmland and, 366; Dust Bowl and, 312–313; Farmers' Alliances in, 244, 401; farmers in, 147; farm organizations in, 401–402; government price supports in, 402; immigrants in, 356; Populism and, 243–245; sharecroppers in, 306; technological advances in, 232–233, 373–376; United Farm Workers and, 344–345; victory gardens in, 319
Agriculture Improvement and Reform Act (1996), 402
Aguinaldo, Emilio, 260

Akihito, Emperor of Japan, 192
Alaska Native Claims Settlement Act (1971), 343
Albania, 69
Aldrin, Edwin "Buzz," 326, 375
Alexandra, Czarina, 50
Allen, Frederick Lewis, 310
Alliances (World War I), 44–45, 270
Allies (World War II), 58
Altgeld, John, 241, 248
Amalgamated Clothing Workers, 242
Amazon.com, 377
America: Spanish and English colonization of, 161–164
American Antislavery Society, 432
American Expeditionary Force (AEF), 275
American Federation of Labor (AF of L), 241–242, 305, 317. *See also* AFL-CIO.
American Federation of Teachers (AFT), 431
American Indian Movement (AIM), 337, 342–344, 430
American Insurance Association (AIA), 400
American Liberty League, 316
American Pharmacists Association (APhA), 400
American Protective Association, 358
American Revolution (1775-1783), 9–10, 190
American Woman Suffrage Association (AWSA), 432, 433
Amnesty International, 132
Amritsar Massacre (1919), 93
Annan, Kofi, 65
Anthony, Susan B., 423, 432–433
Anti-Semitism, 87
Antitrust legislation, 239, 246, 408, 431
Anti-Vietnam War Movement, 328, 334, 435, 438–439
Apartheid, 98–100; domestic opposition to, 99–100; end of, 100, 211
Apollo 8, 326
Appeasement, 281–282; events leading to, 56–58
Apple Computer Company, 368, 375, 384
Arab-Israel conflict, 79–80
Arafat, Yasir, 90
Arbitration, 240
Architecture: neoclassical style of, 7
Argentina, 131
Aristocracy, 8
Arkwright, Richard, 19

Armenia, genocide in, 109–111
Arms race: effect of, 63, 67, 74–75; national security and, 295
Armstrong, Neil, 375
Arts: in Enlightenment, 7; minority groups in, 346
Asia: ethnic strife in, 81; Japanese imperialism in, 58, 279–280, 282
Assembly line, 17
Association of Southeast Asian Nations (ASEAN), 130
Atlantic Charter, 64
Attlee, Clement, 291
Austria, 130; under Joseph II, 8; Soviet control over, 291; World War II and, 56
Austria-Hungary: post-World War I, 277; in World War I, 45, 269, 270
Automobiles, 376
Axis powers (World War II), 58
Azerbaijan, 127

B

Baby boom, 387
Babylon, 149
Bacon, Francis, 4
Bakke, Allan, 422–423, 447
Bakke decision, 422–423, 447
Baldwin, James, 346
Baldwin, Stanley, 281
Balfour, Arthur James, 88
Baltimore, 154
Banking Act (1933), 316
Banking panic (1907), 411
Bank of North America, 411
Banks: Great Depression and, 311–312; national, 411; regulations of, 411
Banks, Dennis, 342
Bantu speakers in Africa, 160–161
Bantustan, 99
Barnard, Henry, 248
Bastille, 207
Batista, Fulgencio, 296–297
Battle of Britain, 284
Bay of Pigs, 297
Begin, Menachem, 90
Belarus, 127
Belgium, 69, 130, 270
Bell, Alexander Graham, 26, 374
Bell, Daniel, 383
Ben-Gurion, David, 89
Bering Strait, 159
Berlin: airlift to, 96, 293–295; blockade of, 96, 295; division of, 68–69, 97

Berlin Wall: fall of, 78–79, 97, 211
Bethlehem Steel Company, 386
Big Stick diplomacy, 262–263
Bill of Rights, 441–442, 443, 447. *See also specific amendments*
Birth control, 138–139
Birth of a Nation, The (film), 339
Birthrate, 138–139
Bitter Cry of the Children, The, (Spargo), 248
Black Hawk, 342
Black Muslims, 333
Black nationalism, 437
Blue-collar workers, 235
Boers, 97
Boer War, 98
Bolívar, Simon, 13
Bolivia, 131
Bolkiah, Hassanal, 191
Bolshevik Revolution, 49–52, 206, 208–209, 304, 449, 450
Bosnia, 113–116, 126; ethnic conflict in, 82
Boutros-Ghali, Boutros, 65
Boxer Rebellion, 37, 38, 262
Brandeis, Louis D., 444
Brazil, 13, 131
Brest-Litovsk, Treaty of (1918), 51, 275
Briand, Aristide, 52–53
British East India Company, 92
Brotherhood of Sleeping Car Porters, 321
Brown, Linda and Oliver, 420–421
Brown v. *Board of Education of Topeka,* 332, 340, 420–422, 431
Broz, Josip (Tito), 114
Brunei, 130, 190–191
Bryan, William Jennings, 244–245, 284
Bulgaria, 68–69, 291
Bush, George H. W., 396
Business: downsizing in, 385, 399, 405–410
Business organizations, 399–400

C

Cambodia, 70, 72–73, 130; U.S. invasion of, 438
Camp David Accords, 90
Canada, 69, 198–199
Candide (Voltaire), 6
Cape of Good Hope, 97
Capitalism, 174; democratic, 289
Capra, Frank, 319
CARE, 132
Carpetbaggers, 351
Carter, James Earl, Jr., 90
Carver, George Washington, 421
Castro, Fidel, 185, 194, 296–297

Catherine the Great, 8

Catt, Carrie Chapman, 424

Ceausescu, Nicolae, 78

Central American Free Trade Agreement (CAFTA), 131

Central Intelligence Agency (CIA), 297

Central Pacific Railroad, 232

Central Powers (World War I), 270, 271, 276

Chamberlain, Neville, 56, 281, 282, 283

Chambers, Whittaker, 324, 450

Chaplin, Charlie, 309

Chase, Andrew, 232

Chavez, Cesar, 344, 345

Chechnya: ethnic conflict in, 82

Checks and balances, 6, 10

Chiang Kai-shek, 283

Chicago, 151, 240–241, 307, 333, 357

Child labor, 23–24, 231, 232; legislation on, 248–249

Children's Bureau, 248

Chile, 131

China: Boxer Rebellion in, 38, 262; communism in, 38, 69, 323–324; Japanese aggression toward and, 58; Nationalist, 69; Open Door Policy in, 37, 261–262; Opium War in, 37; population of, 138; reforms in, 37–38

Chinese Exclusion Act (1882), 240, 358

Cholera, 21, 235

Churchill, Winston, 283; iron curtain speech of, 291; signing of Atlantic Charter by, 64; at Yalta Conference, 96, 290–291

Cincinnati, Ohio, 152

Cities: characteristics of, 148–149; communication and travel between, 152; in developing countries, 152–153; development of, 148; ghettos in, 306; growth of, and industrialization, 21; immigrants in, 357–358; living conditions in, 21, 231–232; middle class in, 235–236; poverty in, 234–235; primate, 153; reforms in, 247–248; revival of, 150; slums in, 21

Citizen action: influence of, on public policy, 205–211

Citizen participation: in absolute monarchy, 212; in constitutional monarchies, 212; in democracy, 212; in dictatorship, 212; in theocracy, 213

City-states, 149

Civil disobedience, 206, 431, 435–439

Civilian Conservation Corps Reforestation Relief Act (1933), 315

Civilizations, 147, 148

Civil Rights Acts (1957), 340; (1964), 333, 340, 423, 431; (1968), 334, 340, 438; (1991), 431

Civil rights movement, 332–334, 434–435, 452; civil disobedience in, 435–436; Eisenhower and, 332; events of, 437–438; in Little Rock, 332; Montgomery bus boycott and, 332–333; Truman and, 332

Civil wars: migration and, 166; in Russia, 51, 52

Clayton Antitrust Act (1914), 408, 431

Clean Air Act (1972), 410, 431

Clean Water Act (1972), 410, 431

Clear-and-present-danger standard, 443–445

Clemenceau, Georges, 48, 276

Cleveland, Grover: Hawaii and, 261; Spanish-American War and, 258

Cleveland, Ohio, 151; race riots in, 333; reforms in, 247

Clinton, William Jefferson "Bill": NAFTA and, 396; State of the Union Address (1998), 188

Cockerill, John, 25

Cohan, George M., 275

Cold War, 66–69; Berlin Crisis and, 293–295; conflicting goals of superpowers and division of Europe, 68–69; containment and, 292; Cuban Missile Crisis and, 296–298; domino theory and, 299; end of, 126; Korean War and, 296; Marshall Plan and, 293; national security and the arms race and, 295; origins of, 288–300; regional and ethnic conflicts after, 79–82; space race and, 325–326

Collective security, 126–127

Collectivization, 52

Collins, Michael, 326

Colombia: Panama Canal and, 263, 264

Columbian Exchange, 127–128

Combination Acts, 25

Coming of Post-Industrial Society, The (Bell), 383

Command economy, 175

Commerce, U.S. Department of: establishment of, 246, 400

Committee for Industrial Organization (CIO): formation of, 242

Committee for Union and Progress, 110

Commonwealth of Independent States (CIS), 127

Communication: advances in, 26; between cities, 152

Communications Decency Act (1996), 447

Communism, 175; in China, 38, 69, 323–324; comparison of fascism and, 55; fall of, in Europe, 210–211; Red Scares and, 304–306, 323–325, 448–450; in U.S.S.R., 51–52; in Vietnam, 298–300; in Yugoslavia, 114

Comparative advantage: trade and, 395

Compelling government interest, 447

Computers, 377–378, 385

Concentration camps, 109
Conditions of the Working Class in England, The (Engels), 29
Conflicts, 142; cultural, 143–144
Congress of Industrial Organizations (CIO), 317, 435
Congress of Racial Equality (CORE), 333, 431, 434, 435, 436, 437
Conscientious objectors, 445–446
Constantinople, 87, 113
Constitution, U.S., 10; evolution of, 417–425; judicial review and, 417–423
Constitutional amendments, 423–425. *See also by number*
Constitutional Convention (1787), 10
Constitutional monarchies, 191–193; citizen participation in, 212
Consumer Credit Protection Act (1969), 408
Containment policy, 292
Cooperatives, 401
Copernican heliocentric universe, 4
Copernicus, Nicholas, 3
Corporations: development of, 236–238; multinational, 26
Costa Rica, 131
Counterculture, 329–330
Crisis, The (NAACP journal), 339
Croatia: independence of, 114
Crompton, Samuel, 19
Crusades, 150
Cuba: Bay of Pigs in, 297; Castro's takeover of, 296–297; in Philippines, 257–258, 259
Cuban missile crisis, 296–298
Cuéllar, Javier Pérez de, 65
Cullen, Countee, 309, 339, 346
Cultural diffusion, 121
Cultural exchanges, 124–134
Czars, 49
Czechoslovakia, 68, 69, 78, 291; post-World War I, 277; in World War II, 56, 281–282

D

Daladier, Édouard, 281, 282
Dardanelles, 292
Darwin, Charles, 23, 32, 255
Darwinism, 23
Data: using to make comparisons, 137–140
Davis, Elmer, 319
Dayton Accords, 116
Death camps, 63, 109
Death rate, 139

Debs, Eugene V., 444, 446, 449–450
Debs v. *United States*, 444
Declaration of Independence (1776), 9, 207–208
Declaration of Rights and Sentiments, 432
Declaration of the Rights of Man and of the Citizen, 12, 207–208
Deism, 6
De Klerk, F. W., 100, 211
Demand, 174
Democracy, 196–200; in Africa, 74; citizen participation in, 212; direct, 196; parliamentary, 197–199; presidential, 199–200; representative, 196–197
Democratization, 75
Demographics of regions, 138
Denmark, 69, 130
Depression: post-World War I, 54; worldwide, 280. *See also* Great Depression
Descartes, René, 4
Developing countries, 152–153
Dewey, George, 259
Dewey, John, 248
Dewey, Thomas, 323
Diaspora, 87
Dictatorships, 194–195; advantages of, 195; citizen participation in, 212
Diderot, Denis, 6
Direct democracy, 196
Direct rule, 35
Discrimination, 104
Disinvestment, 100
Displaced persons, 166
Displaced Persons Act (1948), 327
Dissent, 431, 432–435
Division of labor, 148
Dole, Sanford, 261
Dollar diplomacy, 264
Dome of the Rock, 87
Domestication, 147
Dominican Republic, 131; U.S. intervention in, 264, 296
Domino theory, 299
Douglass, Frederick, 209–210
Downsizing, 385, 399
Dred Scott case, 420
Dubinsky, David, 242
Du Bois, W. E. B., 338–339
Dust Bowl, 312–313
Dutch, 97–98
Dutch East India Company, 97
Dyer Bill (1918), 339
Dylan, Bob, 329
Dysentery, 259

E

Earth Simulator, 375

Eastern Europe: collapse of Communist countries in, 77–79; Soviet control over, 291

East Germany, 69, 78–79, 97, 295

East Timor, 81

Economic growth: imperialism and, 254–255

Economic independence, 395–397

Economic systems: benefits and costs of trade, 170–171; colonization and, 34; comparison of, 394–402; traditional economy as, 173; use of productive resources and, 172–173

Economic theory, 6–7

Economy: command, 175; effects of New Deal on, 413; effects of World War II on, 413–414; free-market, 7, 174; growth of U.S., 229–232; laissez-faire, 7, 238–239; mixed, 176; as motivation for imperialism, 32; of the 1920s, 308–309; postindustrial, 383–384; stereotyping and, 458; United States government in, 180–182, 405–414

Edison, Thomas Alva, 26, 374

Education: affirmative action and, 422–423; of African Americans, 332, 340, 420–422; civil rights movement and, 332; G.I. Bill of Rights and, 322–323, 365; of immigrants, 360; of Native Americans, 343; reforms in, 248; technology and, 376

Egypt, 89

Eighteenth Amendment, 248, 310

Eighth Amendment, 442

Eisenhower, Dwight D.: Bonus Army and, 314; civil rights movement and, 332; Cuba and, 296; space exploration and, 325; Vietnam and, 299, 300; voting rights and, 425

Elections: of 1896, 244–245; of 1916, 272; of 1948, 323; of 1968, 328

Elizabeth II, Queen, of England, 191–192

Ellison, Ralph, 346

El Salvador, 131

Emergency Banking Relief Act (1933), 315

Emergency Railroad Transportation Act (1933), 316

Emergency Relief and Construction Act (1932), 313

Emergency Wetlands Resources Act (1986), 367

Emigration, 159; effect of industrialization on, 23; reasons for, 390–392. See also Immigration

Enclosure movement, 18, 150

Encyclopedia (Diderot), 6

Engels, Friedrich, 29

England: American Revolution and, 9–10; colonies of, 161–162; enclosure movement in, 18; industrialization in, 18–21; signing of Magna Carta, 8. See also Great Britain

ENIAC computer, 375

Enlightened despots, 8

Enlightenment, 3–13, 207–208; absolute monarchy and, 7–8; arts in, 7; influence of thinking in, 6–7; political revolutions and, 8–13; political thinkers in, 4–6; scientific method and, 3–4

Entrepreneurs, 21

Environment, 124–127; invasive species, 124–126

Environmental Defense Fund, 431

Environmental Protection Act (EPA), 410, 431

Environment regulations, 409–410

Equal opportunity, 447–448

Equal Pay Act (1963), 331, 340, 430

Equal Rights Amendment (ERA), 330, 331, 341–342, 430

Eritrea, 81

Espionage Act (1917), 443, 444, 445, 449

Estonia, 127; formation of, 49; independence of, 77; post-World War I, 277

Ethiopia, 31, 81; Italian invasion of, 58, 281

Ethnic cleansing, 82, 114–115

Europe. *See individual countries*

European Union (EU), 130, 143

Everglades, 367

Evers, Medgar, 333

Evolution, 255–256

Excise taxes, 406–407

Exploration: migration and, 161–163

Explorer 1, 325

Exports, 171

F

Factories, 19, 23

Factory Aid Act, 24

Fair Credit Act (1933), 316

Fair Deal, 323

Fair Employment Practices Committee (FEPC), 321; establishment of, 339–340

Fair Labor Standards Act (1938), 249, 430

Famine, 163

Farmer, James, 436

Farmers' Alliances, 244, 401

Fascism, 279, 280; comparison of communism and, 55; in Italy, 54–55

Faubus, Orval, 332

Federal Deposit Insurance Corporation (FDIC), 413

Federal Emergency Relief Act (1933), 315

Federal Employee Loyalty Program, 324

Federal Home Loan Board, 331

Federal Housing Administration (FHA), 386–387

Federal Open Market Committee (FOMC), 412

Federal Reserve Act (1913), 411

Federal Reserve System, 181–182, 410–412; discount rate and, 412; open market operations, 412; reserve requirements of, 412

Federal Securities Act (1933), 315

Federal Trade Commission (FTC), 408, 409, 431

Federation of Organized Trades and Labor Unions, 241

Feminine Mystique, The (Friedan), 330

Feminist movement, 340–341

Ferguson, John H., 352

Fertility rate, 138

Feudalism, 149–150

Fifteenth Amendment, 418, 419, 442

Fifth Amendment, 441

Final Solution, 109

Finland: formation of, 49, 130, 277

First Amendment, 441, 447, 448, 451

First Bank of the United States, 411

Fitzgerald, F. Scott, 308

Forced migrations, 162–163

Ford, Henry, 374

Fourteen Points, 275–276

Fourteenth Amendment, 352, 418, 419, 422, 423, 433, 447

Fourth Amendment, 441, 442

France, 69, 130; fall of, in World War II, 282; imperialism of, 34, 35; Indochina and, 70–71; under Louis XVI, 10, 11; under Napoleon, 12–13, 208, 289; social structure of 18th-century, 10–11; Vietnam and, 298–299; in World War I, 270; in World War II, 56, 58

Franco, Francisco, 281

Franz Ferdinand, Archduke, 269, 270

Frederick the Great, 8

Freedom rides, 333, 436–437

Freedom Summer, 333, 437

Free enterprise, 174

Free-market economy, 7, 174

Free Soil Party, 210

Free trade, 182

Free Trade Agreement (FTA), 184

French and Indian War (1754–1763), 9

French Revolution, 10–13, 206–208, 212

Friedan, Betty, 330, 341

G

Gagarin, Yuri, 326

Galilei, Galileo, 3, 4

Gallipoli, Battle of, 46

Gandhi, Mohandas K., 70, 93–94, 216, 435

Garrison, William Lloyd, 209–210

Gaza Strip, 89

General Agreement on Tariffs and Trade (GATT), 184, 396

General Electric, 237, 399

General Motors, 385, 399

Genocide, 104

Georgia, 127

Germany, 130; division of, 68–69; nazism in, 55–56; post-World War I, 277; post-World War II division of, 291; reunification of, 96–97; in World War I, 45, 270, 276; in World War II, 56

Ghana, 73–74

Ghettos, 108–109

G.I. Bill of Rights, 322–323, 365

Gilded Age, 365

Glasnost, 75

Glenn, John, 326

Globalization: growth of political integration and, 129; as negative force, 123; as positive force, 123–124

Global Positioning System (GPS) satellite, 375

Goebbels, Joseph, 107

Gold Coast, 73

Goldman, Emma, 446, 449–450

Gompers, Samuel, 241–242

Gorbachev, Mikhail, 75–77, 210

Government: effect of actions of, on individuals and business, 405–410; methods of effective change in, 428–431; price supports in agriculture, 402; theories on, 189

Government of India Act (1935), 94

Grandfather clauses, 351

Granger laws, 243–245

Granger movement, 243

Great Britain: abolitionists in, 209; China and, 37–38; colonialism of, in India, 92; constitutional monarchies in, 191–192; creation of Israel and, 66; division of Germany and, 96–97; enclosure movement in, 150; imperialism of, 35; independence of India and, 94–95; industrialization in, 150–151; Palestine Mandate and, 88–89; struggle over South Africa, 97–98; trade unions in, 25; in World War I, 270; in World War II, 56, 58, 284. *See also* England

Great Depression (1929-1940), 54, 311–314, 386; attempts to alleviate, 313–314; Dust Bowl and, 312–313; effects of, 311–312; New Deal and, 314–318

Great Gatsby, The (Fitzgerald), 308

Great Trek, 97

Greece, 69, 130; Truman Doctrine and, 292

Greenpeace, 132, 431

Griffith, D. W., 339

Gross domestic product (GDP), 138, 140; per capita, 140

Group of Seven/Eight (G7/8), 132

Grutter, Barbara, 447

Grutter v. *Bollinger*, 447, 448

Guam: U.S. annexation of, 260

Guatemala, 131

Guinn v. *United States*, 339

Gulf of Tonkin Resolution, 299

H

Haiti: revolution in, 13; U.S. intervention into, 264

Hargreaves, James, 19

Harlan, John Marshall, 419–420

Harlem Renaissance, 303, 306, 309, 339, 346

Havel, Vaclav, 78

Hawaii, 260–261. *See also* Pearl Harbor

Hawley-Smoot Tariff, 313

Hay, John, 37; Open Door Policy in China and, 261, 262; Spanish-American War and, 260

Hay–Bunau-Varilla Treaty (1903), 263

Hayes, Rutherford B., 240

Haymarket riot, 240–241

Hearst, William Randolph, 256

Hendrix, Jimi, 329, 330

Henry, Patrick, 9

Hepburn Act (1906), 246

Hidalgo, Father, 14

Hillman, Sidney, 242

Hinduism, 91

Hindus: India-Pakistan conflict and, 141–142

Hine, Lewis, 231, 248

Hip-hop, 346

Hippies, 329

Hirohito, 54

Hiroshima, 62

Hispanic Americans: growth in numbers of, 389; as migrant workers, 344–345

Hispaniola, 13

Hiss, Alger, 324, 450

Hitler, Adolf, 55–56, 58, 107, 279, 280, 289

Hobbes, Thomas, 4, 5, 13, 189

Ho Chi Minh, 70, 71, 298

Hoefler, Don C., 368

Hollerith, Herman, 374

Hollywood Ten, 324, 450–451

Holmes, Oliver Wendell, Jr., 443, 444–445

Holocaust, 107–109; Jewish immigration to Palestine and, 63

Home Owners Refinancing Act (1933), 316

Honduras, 131, 264

Hong Kong, 37

Hoover, Herbert, 311, 313–314

Hoovervilles, 311, 312

Hopkins, Harry, 317

House Un-American Activities Committee (HUAC), 324, 450–451

Housing: G.I. Bill of Rights and, 365; Levittown and, 387

Huerta, Dolores, 344, 345

Hughes, Charles Evans, 272

Hughes, Langston, 309, 339, 346

Hundred Days, 314–318

Hungary, 49, 68, 69, 78, 291

Hurston, Zora Neale, 309, 346

Hussein, Saddam, 117

Hussein ibn Ali, 87

I

Iceland, 69

Immigrants, 159; assimilation of, 360–361; backlash against, 358; in cities, 357–358; difficulties encountered by new, 356–358; education of, 360; settlement houses for, 247–248

Immigration: after the Civil War, 356–361; changes in patterns of, 389–390; effect of, on politics, 358–359; labor unions and, 240; in the late 20th century, 359–360; nativism and, 304–306; restrictions on, 240, 305–306, 327–328, 358, 359, 390; shift in patterns of, 326–327

Immigration laws, 327, 328, 359, 390

Imperialism, 30–39, 254–265; in Africa, 31, 33–34, 39; annexation of Hawaii and, 260–261; big-stick diplomacy and, 262–263; as cause of World War I, 44; colonization and, 33–35; development of, 30–33; economic growth and, 171, 254–255; global impact of, 35–39; ideological beliefs and, 255–256; influence of the press on, 256–257; Japanese, in Asia, 58, 279–280; motivations for, 32–33; new, 31; Open Door policy in China and, 261–262; Panama Canal and, 263–264; psychological issues in, 255; reasons for, 254–257; religion and, 256; Roosevelt Corollary to the Monroe Doctrine and, 264–265; roots of, 31; Spanish-American War and, 257–260

Imports, 171

Income: redistribution of, 180–181; tangible gains by African Americans and women in, 353

Independence movements: in Africa, 73–74; in Cambodia, 72–73; in India, 70, 93–95, 210; in Laos, 72

India: British colonialism in, 92; conflict between Pakistan over Kashmir, 141; Hinduism in, 91; independence movement in, 70, 93–95; Islam in, 92; partitioning of, 95–96, 166

Indian Education Act (1972), 343

Indian National Congress, 93

Indian Self-Determination and Education Assistance Act (1975), 343

Indigenous (native) peoples, 32

Individual rights, 441–452; restrictions on, 443–452

Indochina, 70–73, 282, 283

Indonesia, 130

Industrialization, 17–26; balance of international power and, 26; change and, 21; development of corporations and, 236–238; effect of, during the 19th century, 229–232; effect of, on emigration, 23; labor unions and, 239–242; laissez-faire policies and, 238–239; progress of, 25–26; rise of unions and, 24–25; standard of living and, 239; in 21st century, 26

Industrial Revolution, 17, 163, 229, 391; conditions that aided, 18–20; effects of, 26; nationalism and, 44; second, 25–26; spread to United States, 151; urbanization and, 150–152

Infant mortality rates, 139–140

Inflation: labor relations and, 323; post-World War I, 53

Influence of Sea Power Upon History, The (Mahan), 255

Initiative, 247

Intel, 368, 384

Interest groups, 429–431

Internal Revenue Service (IRS), 181

International Committee for the Red Cross, 132

International Ladies Garment Workers Union, 242

International Monetary Fund (IMF), 131

International Workers of the World, 304

Internet, 377

Interstate Commerce Act (1887), 408

Interstate Commerce Commission (ICC), 246, 405, 408, 431, 436–437

Interstate Highway Act (1956), 388

Intifada, 90

Invasive species, 124–126

Iran, 196

Iraq, 49, 89, 117, 142

Ireland, 130

Irish Republic, 142

Iron curtain, 291

Islam, 91–92; Five Pillars of, 91–92; in India, 92

Isolationism, 49, 284

Israel: creation of, 66, 144; historical background of, 86–89; recent events, 89–90

Issues: analysis of, 461–464

Italians of New York, The, 317

Italy, 69, 130; fascism in, 54–55; invasion of Ethiopia by, 281; under Mussolini, 280; in World War II, 58

J

Jackson, Andrew: national banks and, 411

Jackson State University: antiwar protests at, 328, 438

Japan: attack on Pearl Harbor, 283–284, 318; constitutional monarchies in, 192–193; end of World War II, 62–63; feudal society in, 36; imperialism of, in Asia, 58, 279–280, 282; Meiji Restoration of, 36; militarist state in, 54; modernization of, 35–37; Westernization of, 36–37

Japanese Americans: internment of, 321–322

Jazz, 346

Jefferson, Mark, 153

Jefferson, Thomas, 9, 13

Jerusalem, 66, 80, 89

Jews: Holocaust and, 107–109; as immigrants, 356; immigration of, to Palestine and Holocaust, 63; pogroms against, 391; in World War II, 56

Jiang Jieshi (Chiang Kai-shek), 69

Jim Crow laws, 234, 350–352, 353, 418–420, 436; challenges to, 352

Jingoism, 256

Johnson, Henry, 274

Johnson, Lyndon B.: antiwar protests and, 438, 439; Vietnam War and, 299–300; voting rights and, 425

Johnson, Tom, 247

Joplin, Janis, 329

Jordan, 49, 89

Joseph II, 8

Judicial review, 417–423

Jungle, The (Sinclair), 169, 246

K

Kampuchea, 72. *See also* Cambodia

Kashmir: conflict between India and Pakistan over, 141–142

Kay, John, 19

Kazakhstan, 127

Keating-Owen Act (1916), 248

Kellogg, Frank, 53

Kellogg-Briand Pact (1928), 52–53

Kennan, George F., 292

Kennedy, John F.: assassination of, 299; civil rights and, 434; Cuban missile crisis and, 296–298; space exploration and, 326; Vietnam and, 299, 300

Kennedy, Robert, 436–437; assassination of, 328

Kent State University, 328, 438

Kerensky, Alexander, 50

Khrushchev, Nikita, 297–298

Kigali, 111

Kim Jong Il, 194–195

King, Martin Luther, Jr., 206, 332–333, 340, 434–435, 437; assassination of, 328, 333, 334, 438

Knights of Labor, 240–241, 430

Korea, 37, 68

Korean War, 296

Kosovo, 82, 114

Kristallnacht, 107–108

Ku Klux Klan, 307–308, 332

Kurds, 117

Kuwait, 117, 142

Kyrgyzstan, 127

L

Labor, U.S. Department of, 246

Labor unions: African Americans in, 240, 321; American Federation of Labor in, 241–242, 305, 317; Congress of Industrial Organizations and, 317, 435; declining membership of, 399; development of, 239–242; impact of, 398–399; International Workers of the World and, 304; Knights of Labor and, 240–241; membership in, 242; under the New Deal, 317–318; rise of, 24–25; strikes and, 304, 323; United Farm Workers and, 344–345; unrest and, 323

La Follette, Robert, 247, 284

Laissez-faire policies, 7, 238–239

Laos, 70, 72, 130

Latin America: revolution in, 13; Roosevelt Corollary to the Monroe Doctrine and, 264–265

Latvia, 49, 77, 127, 277

League of Nations, 49, 52, 58, 64, 275, 277, 278; Italian invasion of Ethiopia and, 281; Japanese aggression and, 280

Lebanon, 49, 89

Leisure activities: in nineteenth century, 235–236

Lemkin, Raphael, 104

Lenin, Vladimir I. (Ulyanov), 50, 51, 208–209, 275, 450

Leviathan (Hobbes), 5

Levitt, William, 387

Levittown, 387

Lewis, John L., 242, 317

Libel, 448

Liberia, 31

Life in America, 317

Liliuokalani, Queen, 261

Lin Tse-hsu, 42

Literacy rate, 139

Literacy tests, 351, 418

Literature: in the Enlightenment, 7; minority groups in, 346

Lithuania, 49, 77, 127, 277

Lloyd George, David, 48, 88, 276

Lobbyists, 430

Locke, John, 4, 5, 9, 13, 189

Lodge, Henry Cabot, 255, 278

London, 152

Long, Huey, 316

Louis XVI, King of France, 10–11, 11, 207

Lowell, mills in, 25

Lowila, Lewis F., Jr., 423

Luddites, 24–25

Luxembourg, 69, 130

Lynchings, 307, 339

M

MacArthur, Douglas, 314

Madison, James, 10

Magna Carta, 8

Mahan, Alfred T., 255

Majlis, 196

Malaria, 259

Malaysia, 130

Malcolm X, 333, 437

Manchukuo, 280

Manchuria: Japanese invasion of, 37, 280, 282

Mandates, 49

Mandela, Nelson, 99, 100

Manhattan Project, 374

Manifest destiny, 256

Mao Zedong, 69

March on Washington (1963), 333, 434. *See also* Civil rights movement

Marconi, Guglielmo, 374

Market economy, 174

Married Women's Property Law (1860), 432

Marshall, George, 293, 319

Marshall, John, 417, 418, 423

Marshall, Thurgood, 332, 340

Marshall Plan, 293

Marx, Karl, 50, 209

McCarran Internal Security Act (1950), 324

McCarran-Walter Immigration and Nationality Act (1952), 327
McCarthy, Joseph, 325, 450–452
McCarthyism, 325, 452
McCormick Company, 237, 240
McCormick reaper, 233
McDonald's, 128
McKay, Claude, 309, 346
McKinley, William: assassination of, 246, 262; in election of 1896, 245; Hawaii and, 261; labor relations and, 400; Spanish-American War and, 258
McMahon Pledge, 87
McNamara, Robert, 297
Meat Inspection Act (1906), 408
Medicare, 181
Mein Kampf (Hitler), 55, 107
Mercantilism, 9
Mercosur, 131
Mercury 6, 326
Mesopotamia, 148
Mestizos, 161–162
Metropolitan Statistical Areas (MSAs), 364
Mexican Americans: discrimination against, 321. *See also* Hispanic Americans
Mexico, 13
Microsoft Corporation, 375, 384, 399
Middle Ages, 149–150
Middle class: growth of, 22–23; urban, 235–236
Middle East, 79–80; Arab-Israeli conflict in, 66, 79–80; cultural conflicts in, 143–144; peace negotiations in, 90
Migrant workers: unionization and, 344–345
Migration: after World War II, 166; defined, 158; exploration and, 161–163; great, of African Americans, 306–308, 319–320; internal, 159; involuntary, 158; in nineteenth century, 163; reasons for, 158–159; rural-to-urban, 18, 234–235; voluntary, 158
Milosevic, Slobodan, 114, 115–116
Missionaries, 35
Mississippi River dam system, 366
Mixed economy, 176
Monarchies, 189; absolute, 189–191, 212; constitutional, 191–193, 212
Monopolies, 180, 237–238, 407, 408; laissez-faire policies and, 239
Monroe Doctrine, Roosevelt Corollary to, 264–265
Montesquieu, Baron de (Charles-Louis de Secondat), 6, 10, 13
Montgomery bus boycott, 332–333, 434
Moon landing, 326
Moral diplomacy, 264
Morgan, J. P., Company: bombing of, 449

Morrison, Jim, 329
Moscowitz, Henry, 338
Moses, 86
Mott, Lucretia, 432
Mountbatten, Louis, 95
Muckrakers, 246, 416
Mughals, 92
Muhammad (Prophet), 91
Muhammad Ali Jinnah, 95
Multinational corporations, 26
Munich Pact, 56, 281–282
Munn v. *Illinois*, 401, 408
Muslim League, 93, 94
Muslims: India-Pakistan conflict and, 141–142
Mussolini, Benito, 54–55, 58, 195, 279, 280
Myanmar, 130

N

Naidu, Sarojini, 93
Nanking Treaty, 37
Napoleon, 12–13, 208, 289
National Aeronautics and Space Act (1958), 325
National Aeronautics and Space Administration (NASA), 325
National American Woman Suffrage Association (NAWSA), 424, 430, 433
National Association for the Advancement of Colored People (NAACP), 332; civil rights movement and, 337, 338–340, 420–421, 429, 430, 431, 434, 436
National Association of Home Builders (NAHB), 400
National Association of Manufacturers (NAM), 399–400
National Child Labor Committee, 248
National Conference of State Commissions on the Status of Women, 340
National Council of Farmers' Cooperatives, 402
National Education Association, 431
National Employment System Act (1933), 315
National Farm Workers Association (NFWA), 344–345
National Industrial Recovery Act (1933), 316
Nationalism: Armenian, 109; as cause of World War I, 43–44, 269–270; decline of Ottoman Empire and, 113; as motivation for imperialism, 32
Nationalist China, 69
National Labor Relations Act (1935), 317, 430
National Labor Relations Board, 317
National Liberation Front (NLF), 299
National Organization for Women (NOW), 330, 331, 337, 340–342, 429, 430

National Origins Act (1924), 166, 306

National Retail Federation (NRF), 400

National Socialist German Workers' (Nazi) Party, 55–56, 107, 279, 280

National Urban League, 431, 434

National Wildlife Refuges, 367

National Woman Suffrage Association (NWSA), 432–433

National Women's Political Caucus (NWPC), 341

Native Americans: American Indian Movement and, 342–344; education of, 343; words taken from language of, 360–361

Nativism, 304–306, 358

Natural resources, 18, 34, 171

Navy: in Spanish-American War, 259; strengthening of, 255; in World War I, 271, 275

Nazism, 107, 279, 280

Negro in Virginia, The, 317

Netherlands, 69, 130

New Deal, 314–318; critics of, 316; effects of legislation, 413; labor movement under, 317–318; second, 317

Newton, Isaac, 4

New York *Journal*, 256

New York Stock Exchange, 236

New York *World*, 256

Nicaragua, 131; U.S. intervention into, 264

Nicholas II, Czar of Russia, 50

Nigeria, 81

Nineteenth Amendment, 308, 340, 424, 425, 430, 442

Nixon, Richard: in 1968 election, 328; Vietnam War and, 328, 438

Nkrumah, Kwame, 73–74

Nonaligned countries: in Cold War, 67–68

Nongovernmental organizations, 132–133

North American Free Trade Agreement (NAFTA), 130–131, 184, 396–397

North Atlantic Treaty Organization (NATO), 69, 126, 295

Northern Ireland, 142

Norway, 69

NSC-68, 295

Nuclear weapons: in World War II, 62–63

Nuremberg Laws, 107

O

Occupational Safety and Health Act (OSHA), 431

O'Connor, Sandra Day, 331

Office of Price Administration (OPA), 318, 413

Office of War Information (OWI), 319

Only Yesterday: An Informal History of the 1920s (Allen), 310

Open Door Policy (China), 37, 261–262

Operation Provide Comfort, 117

Opium War in China, 37

Organization for Economic Cooperation and Development (OECD), 384

Organization of African Unity, 130

Organization of Petroleum Exporting Countries (OPEC), 143

Orlando, Vittorio, 276

O'Sullivan, John, 256

Oswald, Lee Harvey, 299

Otis, James, 9

Ottoman Empire: Armenia and, 109–111; decline of, 113–114; rule of Palestine by, 87; in World War I, 270

Outsourcing, 123

Ovington, Mary White, 338

P

Pacifists: in World War I, 272

Pakistan: conflict with India over Kashmir, 141; creation of, 95–96; partition of, 166

Palestine, 86; formation of, as mandate, 49, 88; Holocaust and Jewish immigration to, 63; partitioning of, 66

Palestine Liberation Organization (PLO), 90

Palmer, A. Mitchell, 304, 449–450

Pan-African Congress (PAC), 99

Panama Canal, 263–264

Panic of 1873, 243; of 1893, 244

Paraguay, 131

Paris, Treaty of (1898), 260

Paris Peace Conference (1918), 48–49, 113

Parks, Rosa, 332–333, 434

Parliamentary democracy, 197–199

Patton, George, 314

Paul, Alice, 424

Pearl Harbor, 261; Japanese attack on, 58, 283–284, 318

Perestroika, 75

Perry, Matthew, 36

Pershing, John J., 275

Persian Gulf War (1991), 117

Philippines, 130; Spanish-American War in, 259–260

Philosophes, 5

Physiocrats, 6–7

Pierce, Franklin, 36

Pinchot, Gifford, 246–247

Plessy, Homer, 352, 418–420

Plessy v. *Ferguson*, 332, 339, 352, 419, 420

Plunkitt, George Washington, 252, 358–359

Pogroms, 87, 163, 391

Poland, 49, 69, 77–78; post-World War I, 277; Soviet control over, 68, 291; in World War II, 58, 282

Political action, 205, 429

Political action committees (PACs), 430

Political action groups, 337–345, 430

Political machines, 358–359

Political parties, 429

Political systems, 129–132

Poll taxes, 351, 418

Pollution, 409–410

Pol Pot, 72

Popular culture, 127–129

Population: growth of, as factor in Industrial Revolution, 18; growth of urban, 231; shifts in, 378

Populism, 243–245

Populist Party, 244–245

Portugal, 13, 69, 130

Postindustrial United States, 383–385; downsizing in, 385, 399

Potsdam Conference, 291

Poverty: in cities, 21, 234–235

Powderly, Terence V., 240, 241

Pregnancy Discrimination Act (1978), 331

Presidential democracy, 199–200

Productive capacity, 172

Productive resources: use of, 172–173

Profits, 174

Progressive Movement, 245–249

Prohibition, 310, 423

Propaganda, 213, 219; identifying, 219–220; in World War I, 271; in World War II, 319

Protectionism, 182

Puerto Rico: U.S. annexation of, 260

Pulitzer, Joseph, 256

Pull factors, 158–159; English colonists and, 162; in immigration, 163, 391–392

Pure Food and Drug Act, 246

Purges, 52

Push factors, 158–159; English colonists and, 162; in immigration, 163, 391

Putting-out system, 19

Q

Quota Act (1921), 305–306

Quotas, 183, 390; costs of, 183

R

Rabin, Yitzhak, 90

Race riots, 307, 333, 338, 437

Railroads: corporations formed by, 237; farmers' alliances and, 244; improvements in, 232–233; refrigerated cars on, 232; steam-powered, 20; technology and, 376; transcontinental, 232, 233

Randolph, A. Philip, 321

Randolph, Jennings, 425

Reagan, Ronald, 75–76, 324

Reconstruction Finance Corporation (RFC), 313

Red Scares, 304–306, 323–325, 448–450

Referendum, 247

Refugee Act (1980), 327

Refugee Relief Act (1953), 327

Refugees, 166; as a result of World War II, 63

Regions: study of, 137–140

Religion: colonization and, 35; imperialism and, 256; spread of, through international trade, 133

Reparations, 53; in Treaty of Versailles, 276, 277

Representative democracy, 197–198

Republic, 208

Republican Party, 210

Revenue Act (1935), 317; (1942), 318

Revolutionary action, 206

Rhineland, 56; remilitarizing, 281

Rhythm and blues, 346

Right-to-life movement, 330–331

Riis, Jacob, 234

Roaring Twenties, 303–311

Rock and roll, 346

Rockefeller, John D., 407, 408

Rockwell, Norman, 319

Roe v. *Wade*, 330–331, 342

Roman Catholic Church: French Revolution and, 10–11; immigration and, 356; Inquisition and, 3–4; Joseph II and, 8

Roman Empire, 86–87

Romania, 68, 69, 78, 291

Roosevelt, Franklin Delano: establishment of Fair Employment Practices Committee by, 339–340; Japanese aggression and, 283–284; Japanese American internment and, 322; New Deal and, 314–318, 413; signing of Atlantic Charter by, 64; World War II and, 318; at Yalta Conference, 96, 290–291

Roosevelt, Theodore: antitrust legislation and, 408; as Assistant Secretary of the Navy, 259; big-stick diplomacy of, 262–263; building of Panama Canal and, 263–264; diplomacy and, 255; as Rough Rider, 259; Square Deal of, 246–247; trusts and, 249

Roosevelt Corollary to the Monroe Doctrine, 264–265

Rosenberg, Ethel and Julius, 325, 450

Rothschild, Edmond de, 88

Rough Riders, 259

Russia, 127; Bolshevik Revolution in, 49–52, 206, 208–209, 273, 275, 304, 449, 450; under Catherine the Great, 8; civil war in, 51, 52; Czarist government in, 49; post–World War I, 277; reforms in, 49–50; signing of Brest-Litovsky Treaty by, 275; in World War I, 50, 270, 273, 275. *See also* Soviet Union

Russian Republic, 76

Rust Belt, 368–369

Rwanda, 111–113

Rwandan Patriotic Front, 111

S

Sacco, Nicola, 304, 305, 450

Sadat, Anwar, 90

Safe Drinking Water Act (1974), 410, 431

San Juan Hill, Battle of, 259, 262

San Martín, José de, 13

Sarajevo, 114, 126; assassination of Franz Ferdinand in, 269, 270

Saudi Arabia, 89, 190

Schenck, Charles, 443

Schenck v. *United States*, 443–444, 445

Scientific method, 3–4

Scientific revolution, 3

Second Amendment, 441

Second Bank of the United States, 411

Second Continental Congress, 9

Second Industrial Revolution, 25–26

Second Treatise of Government (Locke), 5

Securities and Exchange Act (1934), 408

Securities and Exchange Commission (SEC), 413

Sedition Act (1918), 444, 445, 449

Selassie, Haile, Emperor of Ethiopia, 58

Selective Service Act (1917), 274

Seneca Falls conference, 432

Separate-but-equal doctrine, 352, 419, 420–422; challenges to, 339–340, 352; judicial overturn of, 421–422

Separate Car Act, 352

Separation of powers, 6, 10

Sepoy Mutiny (1857), 92

September 11, 2001, terrorist attacks, 445

Serbia, 45, 270

Servicemen's Readjustment Act (1944), 322–323

Seventh Amendment, 442

Shame of Cities, The (Steffens), 246

Shantytowns, 153

Sharecroppers, 306

Share-the-Wealth plan, 316

Sharpeville Massacre (1960), 99–100

Shepard, Alan, 326

Sherman Antitrust Act (1890), 239, 246, 408, 431

Shogun, 36

Sierra Club, 431

Sierra Leone, 81

Silicon Valley, 367–368

Silk Road, 133

Silver: as Populist issue, 244

Sinclair, Upton, 169, 246

Singapore, 130

Sit-down strikes, 435

Sit-ins, 333, 436

Six-Day War (1967), 89

Sixth Amendment, 442

Slavery: movement to abolish, 209–210

Slave trade, 162

Slovenia, 114

Slums, 21, 234

Smith, Adam, 7

Smith, Margaret Chase, 451

Social contract, 5

Social Darwinism, 23, 32, 255

Social hierarchies, 148

Socialism, 175; democratic, 176; undemocratic, 289

Social protest, 205, 206, 429

Social Security, 413

Social Security Act (1935), 317

Social Security Administration, 317

Solidarity, 77–78

Solidarity Party, 210–211

Solomon, King of Israel, 86

South Africa: apartheid in, 98–100; British and Dutch struggle over, 97–98; end of apartheid in, 211; independence of, 98–100

Southeast Asia Treaty Organization (SEATO), 296

Southern Christian Leadership Conference (SCLC), 333, 434, 436

Soviet Union: in Cold War, 67–69; control over Eastern Europe, 291; disintegration of, 211; fall of, 74–77; under Khrushchev, 297–298; satellite nations of, 68; space exploration and, 325–326; in World War II, 58, 282, 288–289. *See also* Russia

Soweto Uprising (1976), 100, 102–103

Space exploration, 325–326, 375

SpaceShipOne, 375

Spain, 13, 130, 161–162

Spanish-American War, 245, 257–260; in Cuba, 257–258, 259; in Philippines, 259–260

Spanish Civil War, 281

Spanish colonists, 161–162

Spargo, John, 248

Speer, Hugh W., 421

Spencer, Herbert, 32

Spirit of Laws, The (Montesquieu), 6

Sputnik I and II, 325

Square Deal, 246–247

Srebrenica, 116

Stalin, Joseph, 51–52, 68, 96, 282; Berlin blockade and, 295; Marshall Plan and, 293; at Potsdam Conference, 291; at Yalta Conference, 290–291

Stamp Act (1765), 9

Standard of living, 170–171, 176; in nineteenth century, 239

Standard Oil Company, 237, 238, 246, 408, 416

Stanton, Elizabeth Cady, 432

Steel manufacturing, 25, 238

Steffens, Lincoln, 246

Stereotypes, 457–458

Stock market: speculation in and crash of 1929, 54, 310–311

Stowe, Harriet Beecher, 209

Strategic Defense Initiative (SDI), 75

Strikes, 304, 323

Strong, Josiah, 256

Student Nonviolent Coordinating Committee (SNCC), 333, 434, 436

Suburbs, 152; growth of, 365–367, 385–389

Sudan, 81

Sudetenland: in World War II, 56, 281

Suez Crisis (1956), 89

Suffragist movement, 424

Sun Belt, 368–369

Sun Yixian, 38

Superpowers, 66–67

Supreme Court, U.S.: affirmative action and, 422–423, 447–448; child labor and, 248; clear-and-present-danger doctrine, 443; compelling government interest and, 447–448; judicial review and, 417–423; under Marshall, 417, 418, 423; New Deal and, 317; under Warren, 421–422. *See also individual decisions.*

Sussex Pledge, 271

Swann v. *Charlotte-Mecklenburg Board of Education*, 334, 438

Sweden, 130, 176

Swift, Gustavus, 232–233

Sykes, Mark, 88

Sykes-Picot Agreement (1916), 88

Syria, 69, 89

T

Taft, William Howard, 248, 264

Taft-Hartley Act (1947), 323

Taiwan, 37, 69

Tajikistan, 127

Tarbell, Ida M., 246, 416

Tariffs, 184; effect on international trade, 184; Hawley-Smoot, 313; political consequences of, 184

Taxes, 406–407; excise, 406–407; income, 406; payroll, 406; poll, 418; progressive, 406; regressive, 406

Teach-ins, 435

Technology: advances in, 25–26, 233, 373–378

Telecommunications Industry Association (TIA), 400

Telephones, 26; technology and, 376–377

Teller Amendment (1898), 258

Temple Mount, 87

Tenements, 152

Tennessee Valley Authority, 315

Terrell, Mary Church, 338

Terrorism, 142; *intifada* as form of, 90; September 11, 2001, and, 445

Textile industry, 19–20

Textile workers, 242

Thailand, 130

Theocracy, 196; citizen participation in, 213

Third World, 68

Thirteenth Amendment, 352, 418, 419

Time Warner, 384

Toomer, Jean, 309

Totalitarianism, 52

Toussaint-L'Ouverture, 13, 14

Town meetings, 197

Townsend, Francis, 316

Trade: benefits and costs of, 170–171; blockades and, 184–185; defined, 170; economic principles and, 395; effect of tariffs on, 184; embargoes on, 185; globalization of, 396–397; protectionism and, 182; quotas and, 183; reasons for, 394; slave, 162; spread of religion through, 133; tariffs and, 184; triangular, 163; World War I and, 271

Trade associations, 237

Trade Expansion Act (1962), 396

Trade organizations: in Western Hemisphere, 130–131

Trade Union Act (1871), 25

Trade unions, 25

Traditional economy, 173

Trail of Broken Treaties, 342–343

Transcontinental railroad, 232, 233

Transportation: advances in, 26, 376, 388–389. *See also specific modes*

Triangular trade, 163

Triple Alliance, 44, 270

Triple Entente, 44, 49, 270

Truman, Harry S, 62, 291; administration of, 323; Berlin airlift and, 293–295; civil rights movement and, 332, 340; foreign policy of, 68; Korean War and, 296
Truman Doctrine, 292
Trusts, 237–238, 407
Truth in Packaging Act (1966), 408
Turkey, 49, 69, 292
Turkmenistan, 127
Turks: strife between Armenians and, 109–111
Tuskegee Airmen, 321
Tutu, Desmond, 100
Twenty-first Amendment, 423
Twenty-sixth Amendment, 425, 442
Typhoid fever, 235, 259

U

Ukraine, 127
Uncle Tom's Cabin (Stowe), 209
Underground Railroad, 209, 432
Union of Soviet Socialist Republics, 51–52. *See also* Soviet Union
Union Pacific Railroad, 232
United Farm Workers (UFW), 337, 344–345, 430
United Farm Workers Organizing Committee (UFWOC), 345
United Kingdom, 69, 130
United Mine Workers, 242, 323
United Nations (UN), 64, 129, 324; Bosnia and, 116; collective security and, 127; Economic and Social Council (ECOSOC), 65; General Assembly, 64; human rights and, 105–106; International Court of Justice, 65–66; Korean War and, 296; Palestinian refugees and, 80; Rwanda and, 112–113; Secretariat, 65; Security Council, 64; Trusteeship Council, 66
United States: abolitionists in, 209; boom and bust in, 53–54; division of Germany and, 96–97; involvement of, in World War I, 46; mixed economies in, 176; role in economy, 180–182
Universal Declaration of Human Rights, 105–106
Urbanization, 365–367, 385–389; in ancient times, 147–149; defined, 147; Industrial Revolution and, 150–152; Middle Ages and, 149–150; problems of, 152; today, 152
Uruguay, 131
U.S. Steel, 238, 386
USA Patriot Act, 445
U.S.S. Maine, 258
Uzbekistan, 127

V

Vanzetti, Bartolomeo, 304, 305
Vaudeville shows, 235
Venezuela, 264
Versailles, Treaty of (1919), 48, 52, 55–56, 56, 277–279; resentment of, 279; terms of, 53, 279; war-guilt clause of, 48
Veterans Administration (VA), 386–387
Victoria, Queen of England, 42
Vietnam, 68, 71–72
Vietnam Veterans Against the War (VVAW), 328, 429, 438–439
Vietnam War (1965–1975), 71–72, 298–300; antiwar protests of, 328, 334, 438–439
Villard, Oswald Garrison, 338
Voltaire (François-Marie Arouet), 5–6, 8, 13
Voting rights: for African Americans, 340, 351, 418; for eighteen-year-olds, 425; for women, 308, 423–425, 432–433
Voting Rights Act (1965), 333, 340, 431, 437

W

Wagner Act, 317
Walesa, Lech, 77–78
Walling, William English, 338
Wal-Mart, 399
War bonds, 318
War Production Board, 318, 413
Warren, Earl, 421–422
Warsaw Pact (1955), 69, 126
Washington, Booker T., 321, 421
Washington, D.C., 154; race riots in, 307
Watt, James, 20
Wealth of Nations, The (Smith), 7
Weizmann, Chaim, 88
Welch, Joseph, 451
Wells-Barnett, Ida B., 338
West Bank, 89, 90
West Germany, 69, 97, 295
Wetlands, 366–367
White, Walter F., 339
White Citizens Council, 332
Why We Fight (film series), 319
Wilderness areas, 366–367
Wilson, Woodrow, 48, 52; banking regulations and, 411; collapse of, 278; in election of 1916, 272; Fourteen Points of, 275–276; League of Nations and, 64; moral diplomacy of, 264; Versailles Treaty and, 276–279; women's rights and, 424, 434; World War I and, 270–273
Women: changing roles for, 23; in Knights of Labor, 240; liberation movement for,

Women (*continued*)
330–331; NOW and, 340–342; suffrage movement for, 308, 432–434; tangible gains by, 352–353; voting rights for, 308, 423–425, 432–434; in workplace, 23, 232, 319–321; in World War II, 319–321

Workplace: in the 19th century, 230–232; blue-collar workers in, 235; changes in, 383–384; children in, 23–24, 231, 232, 248–249; commuting to the, 388–389; minorities in, 319–321; women in, 23, 232, 319–321

Works Progress Administration (WPA), 317

World Trade Organization (WTO), 131, 184, 396

World War I: alliances in, 58; causes of, 43–45, 269–270; connections to World War II, 279–284; postwar problems, 53–54; short-term results of, 48–52; treaty negotiations following, 275–279; United States involvement in, 46, 270–275

World War II, 56–58; alliances during, 58; appeasement and, 281–282; connections between World War I and, 279–284; consequences of, 62–66; costs of, 63; effects on economy, 413–414; end of, 62–63, 89; home front in, 318; Israel and, 87; Japanese attack on Pearl Harbor in, 283–284, 318; minorities in, 319–321; prelude to, 281–282; prosperity following, 322–325; women in, 319–321

Wounded Knee, South Dakota, 343

Wright, Orville and Wilbur, 374

Y

Yalta Conference, 96, 290–291, 324

Yellow journalism, 257–258

Yeltsin, Boris, 76, 82

Yom Kippur War (1973), 89

Young Turks, 110

Yugoslavia: communism in, 114; creation of, 113; ethnic conflicts in, 81–82; formation of, 49; post-World War I, 277; in World War II, 114

Z

Zimmermann, Arthur, 273

Zionism, 63, 87

Zulus, 97

CREDITS

Pre-6 National Archives **4** The Granger Collection **5** (left) John Locke; (center) Voltaire; (right) Denis Diderot **11** Corbis **12** The Granger Collection **14** (left) Corbis; (right) Schalkwijjk/Art Resource **19** North Wind Picture Archives **21** Mansell/Time Life Pictures/Getty Images **22** (top) Hulton Archive/Getty Images; (bottom) North Wind Picture Archives **24** The Granger Collection **33** North Wind Picture Archives **39** Corbis **47** (top) Corbis; (bottom) Brown Brothers **51** Corbis (Novosti) **53** Corbis **57** National Archives **67** James Arthur Wood/Corbis **70** Roger Viollet/Gamma Liaison **73** Corbis **76** UPI/Corbis **77** Corbis **78** D. Aubert/Sygma **82** Pascal Guyot/Getty Images **88** Bettmann/Corbis **93** Hulton Archive/Getty Images **95** Margaret Bourke-White/Time Life Pictures/Getty Images **98** © Alain Ngue/ Corbis Sygma **100** P. Durand/Sygma **108** Corbis **112** Jean Michel Turgin/ Gamma Liaison **115** Corbis **122** (top) © Karen Preuss/The Image Works; (bottom) Liu Jin/AFP/Getty Images **124** Indranil Mukherjee/AFP/Getty Images **125** Reprinted, with permission, from the *Columbus Dispatch* **128** Reprinted, with permission, from YaleGlobal Online, Yale Center for the Study of Globalization (www.yaleglobal.yale.edu) **129** Zheng Xianchang/Panorama/The Image Works **132** Peter Andrew/Reuters **136** Reprinted, with permission, from the *Columbus Dispatch* **138** © Sean Sprague/The Image Works **143** © Jacques Langevin/Corbis Sygma **148** Ann Ronan Picture Library/HIP/The Image Works **149** © Historical Picture Archive/Corbis **150** (both) Cincinnati Historical Society Library **154** (top) © Zoriah/The Image Works; (bottom) DPA/The Image Works **172** © Buddy Mays/Corbis **175** © Jeff Greenberg/The Image Works **181** © Lester Lefkowitz/Corbis **182** © Jim Sulley/Wire Pix/The Image Works **185** © Patrick J. Forden/Corbis Sygma **190** © Thomas Hartwell/Corbis **191** Roslan Pahman/AFP/Getty Images **192** © Tim Graham/Corbis **193** Toru Yananaka/AFP/Getty Images **195** Getty Images **197** Atta Kenare/AFP/ Getty Images **198** Peter Chen/The Image Works **199** © Jim Young/ Reuters/Corbis **204** Cox & Forkum Editorial Cartoons **205** © Jeff Greenberg/The Image Works **207** Gleb Schelkunov/Isvestia/AP **208** © Roger Viollet/Tophan/The Image Works **209** (left) Hulton Archive/Getty Images; (center, both) The Granger Collection; (right) Getty Images **210** Library of Congress **219** The Granger Collection August 8, 2005 **230** Bettmann/Corbis **231** Library of Congress **234** Bettmann/Corbis **235** The Granger Collection **236** Bettmann/Corbis **237** Culver Pictures **238** New-York Historical Society **239** (left) Corbis/Bettmann; (right) Corbis/Bettmann/UPI **241** Library of Congress **243** Bettmann/Corbis **245** Library of Congress **247** Library of Congress **257** Amsco School Publications **258** Naval Historical Foundation **259** Library of Congress **262** Stock Montage **263** Library of Congress **264** Museum of the City of New York/Getty Images **268** Louis Dalrymple, *Judge*, 1895 **272** Library of Congress **273** Bettmann/ Corbis **274** (top) Corbis/Bettmann; (bottom) Bettmann-Corbis **277** Corbis **280** The Granger Collection **281** The Granger Collection **283** Bettmann/ Corbis **290** Library of Congress **292** The Granger Collection **294** Corbis-Bettmann **297** Bettmann-Corbis **298** *Straight Herblock* (Simon & Schuster, 1964) **305** (top) Topham/The Image Works; (bottom) Library of Congress **307** Corbis/UPI **309** Library of Congress **310** Library of Congress/Getty Images **312** (left) Corbis/Bettmann; (right) Corbis/Bettmann **320** Franklin

D. Roosevelt Library   **321** Corbis   **326** NASA   **329** Bettmann/Corbis   **330** Platt Collection/Getty Images   **338** Hulton Archives/Getty Images   **339** Corbis/Bettmann   **341** Library of Congress   **343** Ernst Haas/Getty Images   **345** (top) Arthur Schatz/Time-Life Pictures/Getty Images; (bottom) Jason Laure/The Image Works   **351** Corbis   **374** (left) Corbis; (right) Corbis   **375** Corbis   **384** Dan Loftin/*The New York Times*   **387** Bettmann/Corbis   **396** Jeffrey Markowitz/Corbis/Sygma   **401** Corbis   **409** Corbis   **412** Hedrich Blessing   **418** Corbis-Bettmann   **419** Library of Congress   **420** Carl Iwasaki/Time-Life Pictures/Getty Images   **421** U.S. Department of Justice   **424** Paul Thompson/Topical Press Agency/Getty Images   **425** Library of Congress   **433** National Portrait Gallery, Smithsonian Institution   **434** Bettmann-Corbis   **437** Stock Photo   **438** Bettmann-Corbis   **444** Bettmann-Corbis   **446** Library of Congress   **449** Library of Congress   **452** Corbis/UPI   **455** *Herblock: A Cartoonist's Life* (Times Books, 1998)   **463** Dan Lamont/ Corbis

POSTTEST

1. Enlightenment thought and ideas can be most clearly seen in which of the following?

   A. 19th-century British colonialism
   B. 19th-century slave trade
   C. belief in the divine right of kings
   D. Latin American wars for independence

2. Citizens in an Ohio town want to ban smoking in all public facilities, including restaurants. What statement could help support the position that a ban on smoking is needed?

   A. Many citizens have signed a petition to ban smoking in public facilities.
   B. The town has no way to enforce a ban on smoking in public facilities.
   C. Smoking is already banned in schools, libraries, and other publicly funded facilities.
   D. Smoking has never been proved to be a health hazard in public facilities.

3. Compare Populism with Progressivism. Demonstrate how they are similar and how they are different by discussing at least two similarities and two differences. Write your answer in the **Answer Document**.   (4 points)

4. The cartoon in the next column could be described as

   A. an objective criticism of the flu shot shortage
   B. a biased criticism of the flu shot shortage
   C. an objective criticism of using lotteries to dispense flu shots
   D. a biased criticism of gambling in the United States.

Cartoon by Mike Luckovich in the *Atlanta Journal-Constitution*. Reprinted by permission of Creators Syndicate.

5. By acquiring the Philippines and Puerto Rico following the Spanish-American War, the United States was trying to

   A. preserve indigenous languages in those two cultures
   B. protect the natural resources of those two nations
   C. encourage religious tolerance throughout the world
   D. demonstrate its presence as a world power.

6. One reason Native Americans founded the American Indian Movement (AIM) was that they wanted to

   A. reestablish reservations that had been closed down
   B. repudiate all treaties with the federal government
   C. reawaken pride in their culture and heritage
   D. create a separate and independent Native American state.

7. Which of the following demonstrates a pattern of discrimination during times of war against people feared to be disloyal to the United States?

   A. antiwar protests during the Vietnam conflict
   B. violence against civil rights activists in the 1960s
   C. the Red Scare of the 1920s
   D. Japanese internment during World War II

8. Scientific and technological advances promoted industrialization of the textile industry in England in the 19th century. This partly enabled the spread of the Industrial Revolution to other industries in England, continental Europe, and the United States. What other 19th-century change resulted from the spread of industrialization?

   A. improved working conditions for women and children
   B. increased safety regulations in factories
   C. reversal of the process of urbanization
   D. rise of corporations and trusts

9. During the 20th century, there were instances when people holding left-wing or Socialist views were repressed and treated with intolerance. Identify and explain two such instances. Write your answer in the **Answer Document**.
   (2 points)

10. One effect of interdependence and trade in the decade of 1995–2005 has been

    A. the movement of jobs from the United States to nations with lower wage scales
    B. higher tariffs on virtually all imported goods
    C. higher prices in the United States for most goods and services
    D. increased cultural isolation in the United States.

11. The differences between the cultural perspectives of Jewish people and Palestinian people is most clearly evident in their views about the

    A. reunification of Germany
    B. partition of India and Pakistan
    C. disintegration of the Soviet Union
    D. creation of the state of Israel.

12. A factor that contributed to the rise to power of Hitler and the Nazi Party in Germany following World War I was

    A. the lenient terms for Germany outlined in the Treaty of Versailles
    B. economic hardships in Germany caused by heavy war reparations called for in the Treaty of Versailles
    C. the Nazis' tolerant view of race and ethnicity, which increased party membership
    D. postwar prosperity in Germany that helped the Nazis appeal to a wide range of people.

13. Which of the following would indicate that gender equality in the United States has improved since the late 19th century?

    A. a narrowing of the gap between what men and women earn for the same work
    B. an increase in the numbers of marriages and births
    C. an increase in the number of women dropping out of the workforce to raise children
    D. a decrease in the number of women running for political office

14. The Cold War influenced U.S. foreign policy after World War II. Which of the following demonstrates that influence?

    A. Korean War
    B. Persian Gulf War
    C. internment of Japanese Americans
    D. growth of suburbs in the 1950s

15. In what way were the 19th and 26th constitutional amendments similar in how they affected individuals and groups?

    A. They both restricted due process of law for minority groups.
    B. They both limited freedom of the press in times of national emergency.
    C. They both increased the government's power to conduct searches without a warrant.
    D. They both extended the right of suffrage to groups who previously could not vote.

16. Advances in global communications and transportation have resulted in

    A. more international cooperation and less conflict
    B. the spread of popular culture, such as music, around the world
    C. more tolerance of different religions
    D. fewer international concerns about collective security.

Urban and Rural United States Population, 1900–2000

	Urban	Rural	Percent Urban	Percent Urban Increase Over Previous Decade
1900	30,215,000	45,997,000	39.6	---
1910	42,064,000	50,164,000	45.6	6
1920	54,253,000	51,768,000	51.1	5.5
1930	69,161,000	54,042,000	56.1	5
1940	74,705,000	57,459,000	56.5	0.4
1950	96,847,000	54,479,000	63.9	7.4
1960	125,269,000	54,054,000	69.8	5.9
1970	149,647,000	53,565,000	73.6	3.8
1980	167,051,000	59,495,000	73.7	0.1
1990	187,053,000	61,656,000	75.2	1.5
2000	222,361,000	59,061,000	79.0	3.8

17. Based on the table above, what can you say about changes in urban areas or regions in the United States?

    A. A minority of the population in the 20th century lived in urban areas.
    B. The automobile enabled more people to live in urban areas during the 20th century.

C. The greatest increases in urban population came in the 1950s and 1960s.
D. Urban population decreased between 1930 and 1940 because of the Great Depression.

18. In the 1920s, Attorney General A. Mitchell Palmer arrested and deported hundreds of aliens. In the 1950s, Senator Joseph McCarthy investigated and harassed suspected Communists, ruining the careers of many. In both cases rights of individuals were restricted because

    A. they committed libel
    B. they were threats to public safety
    C. the American public feared communism and radical political ideas
    D. they violated constitutional rights.

19. "Internet sales in the key November and December shopping period are expected to come in at $16.7 billion this year, up 29 percent from $12.9 billion for the same period a year earlier." This report reflects

    A. decreased mall construction
    B. increased computer sales and use
    C. higher shipping costs
    D. decreased consumer spending.

20. Which criteria used to evaluate credibility of a source would you apply to an article that referred to all elderly people as stingy and grumpy?

    A. agreement with other reliable sources
    B. accuracy and consistency of sources
    C. qualifications and reputation of the writer
    D. recognition of stereotypes

21. What factor contributed to the migration of large numbers of Muslims and Hindus in the 1940s?

    A. pilgrimages to holy sites on the Indian subcontinent

B. partition of the Indian subcontinent into the nations of India and Pakistan

C. job opportunities due to industrialization in China

D. British colonial policies that forced relocation

22. You are assigned to write a report about tactics used during the civil rights movement of the 1950s and 1960s. Identify a primary source and a secondary source that would be credible and reliable to use for your report. Explain why each source would be considered credible. Write your answer in the **Answer Document**.   (2 points)

23. One cause of widespread suburbanization in the United States during the 1950s was

A. decrease in the cost of air travel
B. decreased emigration from Asia
C. development of an interstate highway system
D. increased costs of automobiles and gasoline.

24. One result of Jim Crow laws was

A. an end to segregated schools in the United States
B. an increased number of African Americans running for political office
C. legalized discrimination based on race
D. a decrease in the number of lynchings in the United States.

25. A lasting effect of the Great Depression, Roosevelt's New Deal, and World War II was

A. less federal government involvement in the economy
B. an expanded role for the federal government in the economy
C. decreased power of labor organizations
D. increased use of laissez-faire policies in the federal government.

26. Cite and explain two instances of exploitation, genocide, and violation of human rights that resulted from political, economic, and/or social oppression. Write your answer in the **Answer Document**. (2 points)

27. In addition to cleaner air, another likely effect of a government regulation that forces automobile manufacturers to reduce emissions from cars might be

A. lower gas prices
B. more people driving
C. higher car prices
D. increased traffic accidents.

28. Between 1880 and 1920, immigration to the United States from Southern and Eastern Europe increased sharply. As a result of that process

A. mainstream American vocabulary incorporated many words from other languages
B. the rate of urbanization decreased
C. the number of large corporations declined
D. government support for labor organizations increased.

29. Which of the following is an example of civil disobedience?

A. women suffragists carrying signs in support of the 19th amendment
B. environmentalists petitioning Congress to pass clean-air legislation
C. anti–Vietnam War protesters burning their draft cards
D. African Americans in Birmingham, Alabama, boycotting the bus company

30. The creation of the North American Free Trade Agreement (NAFTA) and the European Union (EU) demonstrate that

A. trade among regions has grown in importance as compared to trade among nations

B. developing nations prefer to trade among themselves

C. changing national boundaries have discouraged trade among world regions

D. global conflicts have reduced international trade in the past few decades.

31. Compare the forms of citizen action employed in the Russian Revolution and the independence movement in India. Write your answer in the **Answer Document**.   (2 points)

32. Which of the following is likely to be found in a parliamentary democracy?

A. three separate branches of government with a system of checks and balances

B. a chief executive who is also a member of the legislative branch

C. an active judiciary that settles disputes

D. a prime minister elected by the people, but no legislative branch

33. Rights are not absolute. Governments sometimes place limits on specific rights. Describe two criteria or considerations commonly used to determine what limits should be placed on specific rights. Then give two examples from United States history since 1877 when that has occurred or two scenarios describing when it might be justified. Write your answer in the **Answer Document**. (4 points)

34. Two candidates for political office disagree over the impact of the most recently published economic indicators from the government. What would be the most credible source to investigate the accuracy of those new numbers?

A. an encyclopedia

B. a business newspaper

C. a government report

D. the candidates' campaign literature

35. In which of the following cases would you most likely encounter the use of propaganda?

A. a newspaper report about a newly released university study on acid rain

B. a historical novel set in the Civil War era

C. a televised political ad for a presidential candidate

D. a Web page designed to provide information about heart disease research

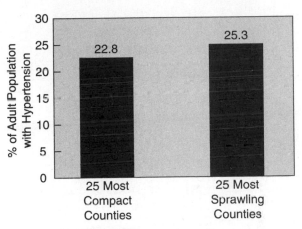

Sprawl and Blood Pressure: A Comparison of Hypertension Rates in Sprawling and Compact Counties

36. Suburban sprawl is the growth of a metropolitan area, particularly its suburbs, over a large area. Which thesis is supported by the graph "Sprawl and Blood Pressure" above?

A. It is healthier to live in more compact counties where people can walk to work and shopping areas.

B. People who live in counties with a high degree of sprawl are healthier because they walk farther.

C. There is no indication that suburban sprawl has any connection to health.

D. People who live in more compact counties suffer health problems due to overcrowded conditions.

37. What belief in the Declaration of Independence demonstrates influence from Enlightenment thinkers?

   A. divine right of kings
   B. government by the consent of the governed
   C. loyalty to the religious authority of the church
   D. absolute monarchy

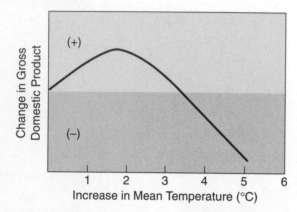

Estimated Economic Effect of Global Warming by the Year 2100

38. Which thesis is supported by the graph above about global climate change?

   A. By 2100, global climate change could have a negative economic effect.
   B. Global climate change will have no effect on the economy in the future.
   C. Global climate change will have an overall positive effect on the economy.
   D. Decreased global mean temperature will have a negative effect on the economy.